This book is the first part of a two-volume investigation into the clothing orders of the British late Georgian army, combined and contrasted with an analysis of fashion in the same army – comparing the regulated dress with the 'modes of the army' as revealed by contemporary writing and illustrations.

The first quarter of the nineteenth century witnessed a refinement of fashionable masculine dress that has not since been surpassed. Military tailoring inspired a parallel flowering of uniform splendour that continued into the 1830s and sparked an enduring fascination with military costume that still rages today.

The army that operated in these cumbersome uniforms managed to achieve fame as one of the most effective British fighting forces ever recognised, and is still remembered and honoured for its achievements.

These three strands: the flowering of late Georgian civilian tailoring; of its martial equivalent; and of military excellence on campaign, have gripped the interest and the imagination of the public, and are endlessly revived and recycled through popular culture, on television, film, through books and all of the other new media.

The reader then might properly ask why another book on uniforms of this period is necessary. Quite simply, it is because the amount of material available to the researcher has increased exponentially since the advent of the internet, especially in regard to the now widely available digital archive files of institutional collections. The huge amount of accessible material makes the task of assembling accurate information much longer and much harder, but the results are consequentially more satisfying and accurate than hitherto.

Ben Townsend, BA History, University of Wales, is a writer and historical consultant for TV, radio, and film, with a particular interest in the Napoleonic and Georgian periods. Previous books on Napoleonic subjects include *Regulations of the Rifle Corps*, and *Serjeant Weddeburne of the 95th Rifle Regiment*.

3/19

www.hants.gov.uk/library

 Hampshire County Council

 Love YOUR LIBRARY

Tel: 0300 555 1387

  35⁰ 140941

Fashioning Regulation, Regulating Fashion

Uniforms and Dress of the British Army 1800-1815
Volume I

An investigation into the connected and conflicting worlds of fashion and regulation in Wellington's Army

Ben Townsend

Helion & Company

Helion & Company Limited
Unit 8 Amherst Business Centre
Budbrooke Road
Warwick
CV34 5WE
England
Tel. 01926 499619
Fax 0121 711 4075
Email: info@helion.co.uk
Website: www.helion.co.uk
Twitter: @helionbooks
Visit our blog at http://blog.helion.co.uk/

Published by Helion & Company 2019
Designed and typeset by Mach 3 Solutions Ltd (www.mach3solutions.co.uk)
Cover designed by Paul Hewitt, Battlefield Design (www.battlefield-design.co.uk)
Printed by Short Run Press, Exeter, Devon

ISBN 978-1-911628-09-5

British Library Cataloguing-in-Publication Data.

A catalogue record for this book is available from the British Library.

For details of other military history titles published by Helion & Company Limited, contact the above
address, or visit our website: http://www.helion.co.uk

We always welcome receiving book proposals from prospective authors.

Contents

List of Illustrations

List of Colour Plates

Notes on the principal artists:

The first ten colour images are by William Loftie (1776–1822). Born in Canterbury, Kent, he joined the 16th Foot as an ensign in 1793, served in the West Indies, and was present at the capture of the South American colony of Suriname from the Batavian Republic in 1804. His subsequent military career was punctuated by watercolours of his fellow officers. The majority of these cover the period 1799-1804, although a few survive from 1815. All of the Loftie images reproduced here are by arrangement with Bibliothèque Nationale de France.

The next set of colour images are by kind permission of Her Majesty the Queen, from the Royal Collection, and are by Robert Dighton Junior (1786–1865). He was commissioned as an ensign 'without purchase from the West Norfolk Militia.' He served in the Peninsula and France from 1810 to 1814, being wounded at Bayonne, and he was reduced with the 2nd Battalion, 71st Light Infantry at Glasgow in 1816.

Robert Dighton (1752–1814) was the father of the notable military artists Robert Dighton Junior and Denis Dighton (among others), and a satirist contemporary to Cruickshank and Gilray. He etched and published under his own name and from his own premises in Charing Cross, London.

Alexander Cavalié Mercer (1783–1868). Studied at the Military Academy at Woolwich and was commissioned as a lieutenant in the Royal Regiment of Artillery in 1799. He served in Ireland in the aftermath of the Irish Rebellion of 1798. He was promoted to second captain in 1806. Mercer was not breveted as a major until 1 March 1824, though this was subsequently backdated to 12 August 1819. Served in Whitelocke's ill-fated Buenos Aires expedition in 1807 and in the Waterloo Campaign. The pictures by Mercer here are from reproductions in *Military reminiscences of latter end of eighteenth and beginning of nineteenth centuries*, in R. McDonald, *The History of the Dress of the Royal Regiment of Artillery*, (London: Sotheran, 1911).

John Augustus Atkinson (1775–1830), was an English artist, engraver and watercolourist, with a pronounced interest in costume. Many of his works, during the Napoleonic Wars, were of naval subjects. He painted many battle scenes and his dispersed water colours are of immense value for the study of uniform in the first seven years of the nineteenth century. Several of the Atkinson images shown here are from his 1807 publication, *Picturesque Representation of the Naval, Military, and Miscellaneous Costumes of Great Britain. By John Augustus Atkinson* (London: Miller and Walker, 1807).

William Henry Pyne (1769–1843), was an English writer, illustrator and painter, He specialized in picturesque settings including groups of people rendered in pen, ink and watercolour. The images of his used here are from his *Microcosm: Or a Picturesque Delineation of the Arts, Agriculture, Manufactures etc. of Great Britain* (London: Pyne and Nattes, 1803).

Thomas Heaphy (1775–1835) was a watercolour painter, and portraitist. In 1812 Heaphy travelled with the British army in Spain and Portugal. Here he painted the portraits of officers, and on his return executed his major work, a representation of the Duke of Wellington giving his orders previous to a general action, which comprised portraits of many of Wellington's staff from life. An engraving from this painting, begun by Anker Smith and finished by Heaphy himself, was published by him in 1822.

Many of the images shown here are the property of the Anne S.K. Brown Military Collection, and are reproduced by courtesy of their unfailing dedicated and generous curator, Peter Harrington.

Preface

This book came about as the result of a conversation with my editor Andrew Bamford. We were discussing the need for a supplement or sequel to Sir Hew Strachan's memorable *British Military Uniforms 1768-96*.[1] I was lamenting the lack of a follow up from Sir Hew covering the later Revolutionary and Napoleonic Wars period, and Andrew said, 'Well, why don't you write it? If not you, then who will? You could wait another forty five years before someone picks up the baton'.

He had a point. From such inconsequential beginnings emerged several years of labour in archives checking that my files were complete, and copious transcribing of illegible or damaged order books. Back in 2008, when I found myself killing time in the then Public Record Office (now The National Archives), I was floundering around in the War Office (WO) papers, looking for information on accoutrements of the 95th Rifles. I found a small quantity of 95th stuff, and many, many, more references to clothing warrants in various departmental letter books. Sat there amongst the usual archive population of the overeducated and underemployed, I decided to photograph as much of the material as I could, in case one of my friends should be likely to find it useful. So when I began this book, thankfully much of the material needed was already to hand. Despite his inflicting me with a case of archival tunnel vision, I am grateful to Andrew for the opportunity he offered to me. My partner, it is fair to relate, much less so. Naturally I had bitten off far more than I could chew, and the process of rendering regulation into a readable and useful form took much longer than anticipated. My blithe avowal that I had already seen all of the useable regulation, and could thus polish it off in a few months was patiently borne by Andrew, who has heard such foolhardy author's overconfidence many times before now. Eventually I was to find out not only that I had grossly underestimated the scope of the project, but also I developed an even greater respect for Strachan's work and perseverance. It has appeared at times that the search for warrant information would become my own nemesis. Nonetheless, after persevering to the limits of my ability, I have called time on the project, knowing well that there will always be more pieces of misplaced paper to find, and more gems to unearth in different archives, several of which will doubtless surface the minute this book goes to press.

Inevitably the final result may suffer in comparison with Sir Hew's original, which is still a benchmark for this sort of study. As these things do, the focus of my work has mutated

---

1   Hew Strachan, *British Military Uniforms 1768-96: The Dress of the British Army from Official Sources*. (London: Arms and Armour Press, 1975).

and shifted in the course of production, and so while in some respects this book strives to emulate Strachan's work, which still occupies an omnipresent position near my desktop, it falls far short of his achievement, which is considerable. Part of the reason for that change of focus was my growing conviction that the study of official regulation is most fruitfully fulfilled with the focus set at battalion level, rather than army level. So why did I persist with a book that primarily focussed on army level regulation? There are two main reasons. Firstly, the overall regulation is the foundation of the more detailed study without which there is no context for the battalion level deviations and adaptations. So it is indispensable in any serious study not to have a thorough grasp of the army level information. Secondly, the paucity of surviving primary material on so many battalions means that the army level regulation is often almost all that remains to detail particular units at any time. Where no specific battalion level material exists, you have necessarily to fall back on the next strata of regulation to achieve any perspective. On these grounds, I came to understand that there was still sufficient reason to present this book, which aims to collect the material available in the National Archives at Kew into two volumes, with the orders arranged chronologically. I have attached some supplementary essays that render the sometimes dense official material into a more pliable and digestible form, while providing context, and which add necessary flesh onto the bare bones of the official orders. These essays inevitably stray across chronological boundaries from time to time, and I have indicated where there are gaps in the ground I have covered that can fruitfully be exploited by subsequent researchers: most especially in the Ordnance papers which require more time than I have been able to devote to them.

It may appear paradoxical that a book that is rooted in the absolute primacy of original documents as a research aid includes my own essays supplying interpretation of the subject material, but this indulgence was driven by a belief that some interpretation is valuable for many readers as a counterbalance to the dry nature of Georgian military documents. In some cases my essays will enable the reader to take a shortcut to some of the conclusions I have drawn. In others the analysis demonstrates the difficulty in drawing conclusions from the material that has survived. Naturally and hopefully there will be other interpretations hidden in the text that I have missed, and that those who follow will discover for themselves.

Prologue

When I was presented to him the Prince Regent was in the uniform of the Hussars, viz. a yellow jacket, pink pantaloons and silver lace morocco boots and a light blue pelisse lined with ermine. The Prince himself was the model of grace and elegance in his time, in a coat of which the waist buttons were placed between his shoulder blades and which if worn now would cause boys to hoot him in Pall Mall.[1]

In autumn of 1811 the smoky rooftops of Regency Brighton were dominated by the towering dome of the Prince of Wales' vast stable complex and the pretty pagoda roofs of his new Royal Pavilion. This cluster of buildings was at the same time both an architectural marvel and a tawdry pastiche of Moghul India's palaces and temples. Whatever the opinion of his future subjects might have been on the Prince's taste in architects, it was known that this man would one day be king, and so where he was, a court in waiting also was. This proto-court formed to caress his ego and indulge him while the courtiers also waited for the riches of preferment that would shower upon them when he came into his birth right. There was very little to curb the Prince's appetites, except the iron will of his father, King George III, and by 1811 his father was so ill that Parliament would impose a Regency upon the country, permitting the Prince to give even freer rein to his fancies. One of these whims was expanding his establishment at Brighton.

The first element of the Brighton pavilions had been the stable complex begun by the Prince of Wales in 1803 and finished five years later. The stables were succinctly described by a member of the Prince's circle, 'They are a superb edifice, indeed, quite unnecessarily so'.[2] At the centre of the stables complex stood the Prince Regent's riding house. By 1811, the Prince was riding less frequently, as his ever increasing bulk deterred him from vigorous exercise. The accounts of his tailors show that they were re-cutting his clothes every six months to accommodate expansion in his girth, and so the riding school had become little used by its royal patron for its original purpose. His daughter was a regular visitor, however, and on 23 October 1811, the Princess Charlotte on her way to drive her ponies came upon her father in the riding house, deep in consultation with two of his younger brothers; the Dukes of York and Cumberland. The object of their contemplation was a group of soldiers cantering around the manege in a variety of bizarre costumes for their royal masters' delectation. These martial mannequins were sporting the borrowed uniforms of various

1   W. Thackeray, *Sketches and Travels in London* (London: Tauchnitz 1856), p.35.
2   A. White, *The Calvert Papers* (London: J. Murphy and Co.), p.221.

'The Royal Stables and Riding House at the Pavilion in Brighton.' Published 1826. Print after John Nash. The gallery at top left is where the Royal Dukes would congregate to admire and comment on uniform innovations displayed by soldiers acting as fashion mannequins below. (Anne S.K. Brown Military Collection, Brown University Library)

foreign and allied powers which had been collected for the Prince Regent by his brothers – especially by the notorious and well-travelled Duke of Kent. Other uniforms were gifts from sovereigns to the Regent. The ruling houses of Europe shared the details of their royal guardsmen's latest uniforms much as children exchange trading cards, and inevitably this cross-fertilisation provoked extremes of taste in an effort to produce the greatest possible sensation.

It was just over five months since the Prince of Wales had become the Prince Regent, and he was intent on re-modelling the dress of the British Army. He was not without experience in the field of uniform design. He had cut his sartorial teeth on designing uniforms for his friends and family: each of his residences had not only a separate livery for the staff, but also a uniform for the guests when resident there. There were also uniforms for the hunts the Prince patronised and even political factions might wear a uniform dress for gathering. The Prince had at one time at least a dozen Fox uniforms to demonstrate his support for Charles Fox, leader of the Whig faction until his death in 1806. As with most of the Prince's enthusiasms, so with the design of uniforms: he craved a broader canvas, and his first chance came with the acquisition of his own regiment. Since receiving the colonelcy of the 10th Light Dragoons (Hussars) in 1783 at the age of 22 the Prince had shown a remarkable interest in clothing and continually re-clothing 'his' regiment to the great benefit of his tailors.[3] His

3   Charles Bazalgette, *Prinny's Taylor* (London: Tara Books, 2015), p.29.

efforts in this direction are a remarkable illustration of the abuses a colonel could inflict upon a regiment when his credit was unlimited and his excesses sanctioned by royal privilege. A description of the regiment at Brighton in November of 1811 states, 'The officers of the Prince's regiment had all dined with him and looked very ornamental monkeys in their red breeches with gold fringe, and yellow boots'.[4]

If the inspection reports for the regiment could speak, they would resound with the groans of inspecting generals as they lowered their heads into their hands in impotence. Every six months without fail the reports note that the regiment is clothed utterly against regulation. One of the pithier reports from November 1812 reads simply, 'The regiment have no standards'.[5] Although almost certainly a reference to the absence of regimental guidons, it nonetheless pungently sums up the general attitude of inspecting officers to the Prince's dolls.

On 5 February 1811, George Prince of Wales took the oath as Prince Regent. A few weeks later his brother, the Duke of York, quietly returned to the Commander-in-Chief's office which he had been forced to vacate in 1809, as a result of the affair of Mrs Clarke and the associated irregularity concerning the sale of Army commissions. During his absence from office, little had been done to improve the clothing and equipment of the British Army, much of which had proved unsuitable under active service conditions. As a result of experience gained in the field, both officers and men had taken to wearing items which were practical but unofficial. Some regiments, notably the 95th Rifle Regiment, had tried unsuccessfully to get their innovations sanctioned by Horse Guards; but it was not until the Duke of York returned that the climate changed and a programme of reforms was inaugurated. How much of this change of heart was owing to the consideration which the duke had always displayed for the welfare of the British soldier, and how much it was owing to the Prince's newly gained power, and consequent ability to impose sartorial innovation, is not clear.

> His morning levees were not attended by men of science and of genius who could have instilled into his mind some wholesome notions of practical economy, but the tailor, the upholsterer, the jeweller and the shoemaker were the regular attendants on a royal Prince's morning recreations. The cut of a coat became of greater consequence than the amelioration of the condition of Ireland; and the tie of a neck cloth, an object of greater importance than parliamentary reform, or the adjustment of our disputes with America. The morning hours which a patriotic prince would have employed in devising measures for the good of the country, were idled away with a favourite tailor, taking measures of his royal person, and receiving his valuable information on the decided superiority of loose trousers to tight pantaloons. The different uniforms of the army became also, at this time, the peculiar objects of the gracious attention of the Prince Regent; and his brothers of York and Cumberland were called in to describe the trappings and fopperies of the German soldiery, the introduction of which into the British army (setting aside the expense to the nation) has rendered some of them the laughing stock of the public.[6]

4   H. Maxwell, *The Creevey Papers 1768-1838* (New York: EP Dutton, 1904), p.148.
5   Percy Reynolds, *Military Costume of the 18th and 19th centuries* (Unpublished manuscript V&A), Vol. IX, p.338.
6   Robert Huish, *Memoirs of George IV* (London: Kelly, 1831), p.118.

'The Dandy Taylor, planning a new Hungry Dress.' Published 1819. Coloured print. Cruickshank. The Prince of Wales is shown right, in the role of a tailor working on his uniform creations. The visitors are bringing new models of uniform for his inspection and inspiration. (Private Collection)

The considerable imagination of the future George IV in matters of dress was fortunately moderated by the advice of his royal brothers and the warrant of 1812 was in many ways an excellent and useful one. The same attention to utility would not be exhibited ten years later when he acceded to the throne in his own right, and embarked on a substantial redesign of the clothing for the army. But for now a useful combination of factors was at play, with the thoughtful considerations of the experienced military dukes counterbalancing the fashionable extravagance of their older brother.

The two volumes of this book will present the actual regulation material arranged chronologically, the first volume concentrating on 1800-1808 and the second 1809-1815. The discursive material and some of the examination in depth will at times necessarily range over the whole period under consideration. So for instance, although the order to curtail the long hair of the men of the army will be found in the regulation for 1808, the accompanying discursive material on that process will extend beyond 1808 the examine the subsequent changes.

Introduction

This book is an investigation into the clothing orders of the British late Georgian army, combined with an analysis of fashion in the same army, comparing the regulated dress with the 'modes of the army' revealed by contemporary writing and illustrations. The ambivalence towards dress regulation existing in some of the regiments of the British army can be encapsulated neatly in two contrasting attitudes.

> His Royal Highness the King, has been Pleased to give His Royal Approbation to the following Orders and Regulations, and His Royal Highness the Commander-in-Chief commands that they shall be forthwith circulated and strictly observed throughout the army.[1]
>
> The fashion of your clothes must depend upon that ordered in the corps; that is to say, must be in direct opposition to it: for it would shew a deplorable poverty of genius, if you had not some ideas of your own in dress.[2]

The period roughly referred to as the Regency saw a refinement of male dress that has not been surpassed since. Although the Regency strictly refers to the period 1811 to 1820, when the future George IV was appointed as Regent to the ailing George III, the term is commonly used to encompass the stylistic period from the beginning of the nineteenth century until the accession of Queen Victoria in 1837, actually covering three separate reigns. Next to the male sartorial pinnacle that developed, there was a parallel flowering of military uniform that lasted until the 1830s and created an enduring fascination with the spectacle of military dress still current today. The army that operated in these uniforms achieved fame as one of the most effective field forces Britain had ever seen, and as such it is rightly still remembered and honoured for its achievements today. These three ingredients: of late Georgian civilian tailoring; of its martial equivalent; and of military excellence, combined to make a potent brew that has established itself in the popular national narrative. The public cannot return to the cup too many times. The stories and style of the age have gripped the interest and the imagination, and are endlessly revived and recycled through popular culture, on television, film, through books and all of the other new media.

---

1   Adjutant-General's Office, *General Regulations and Orders, 1811* (London: Egerton, 1811), p.2.
2   F. Grose, *Advice to the Officers of the British Army* (London: Agathynian Club, 1867), p.74.

The reader then might properly ask why another book on uniforms of this period is necessary. Quite simply, it is because the amount of material available to the researcher has increased exponentially since the advent of the internet and widely available digital files of institutional collections. The huge amount of accessible material makes the task of assembling accurate information much longer and much harder, but the results are consequentially more satisfying and accurate than hitherto.

Like so many others I idled away hours of my childhood looking at beautiful pictures of Napoleonic uniform, recreated by talented artists. These books can be evocative creations, but in this instance what I intend to do is not to show a recreated view of the uniforms, whether that be an idealised view or a re-imagination of the uniforms battered by active service, but instead detail first what the soldiers were required to wear, when and how, and then contrast that with specific images and other information that is dateable and well provenanced to show what the soldiers actually wore, and how and why it was adapted, with a particular emphasis on fashion as much as utility. Period definitions of fashion and regulation are quite clear on the distinction between the two, and at first glance it appears that they are mutually exclusive. *James' Military Companion*, the unofficial handbook in three volumes of the officer class is straightforward on the purpose of royal warrants,

> General Regulations and Orders, a collection of certain general rules which are published by authority. They cannot be altered, or in any sense be deviated from, without the king's or commander in chief's approbation.[3]

Contrast this with the view of fashion espoused by the author of *The Whole art of Dress! Or, the Road to Elegance and Fashion*, a self-proclaimed, if anonymous, cavalry officer,

> In itself, dress, over the habitable globe, has ever been, and is, regulated by *habit* in a great degree more or less, except in civilised Europe, where that staid regulator is fast loosing itself, getting superseded by a *turn-coat whirligig maniac*, yclept Fashion, that is always changing and running into extremes, being scarcely detected in one form before it is out of it.[4]

How can we understand more of the interplay between these factors? Let us look at the available sources. It is absolutely necessary in a study of this kind to begin by looking at the regulated dress. Orders on dress originated from multiple sources. Those most important were issued by the Commander-in-Chief by royal warrant and carried the authority of the King or later the Prince Regent acting with the assumed authority of his father. These warrants were issued periodically and vary in detail from the remarkably precise, to the bewilderingly vague. The latter category can be explained by the practice of issuing sealed pattern items that could accompany the warrant and latterly be distributed to manufacturers and end users as examples of the intended item of kit or uniform. The presence of example items meant that a comprehensive written description was simply not necessary,

---

3   Charles, James, *James's Regimental Companion* (London: Roworth, 1811), p.113.
4   A Cavalry Officer, *The Whole art of Dress! Or, the Road to Elegance and Fashion* (London: Effingham Willingham, 1830), p.115.

the sealed pattern served to illustrate the royal intention. The seal referred to was a wax seal attached to the article by a ribbon to confirm the item's official nature. Sealed pattern items rarely survive, as the items were required to be destroyed on production of subsequent pattern items to avoid confusion. Many 20th century authors described a legendary store of old pattern items at the Tower of London that would have proved a holy grail of sorts to uniform students had it not perished by an inopportune fire. Those items destroyed were not an official record of sealed pattern items as wishful thinking would have it, but part of a private royal collection chiefly assembled by the Prince Regent. The collection included pattern items, but this was not an attempt to systematically maintain a catalogue of old patterns, merely a reflection of the future George IV's interest in costume, and absorption in acquiring collections of virtually anything he came into contact with. Old pattern sealed items were required to be destroyed immediately upon being superseded by new items as otherwise they had a tendency to corrupt and confuse the record, so that any survival of a sealed pattern is owing to an extraordinary circumstance.

Further orders on dress were applied at each level of the command chain below that of the Commander-in-Chief at Horse Guards. So one finds orders from army, station, or garrison commanders, from divisional and brigade generals, from colonels of regiments, colonels commanding regiments, and colonel-commandants of regiments, and then continuing by degree down through the regimental structure with further strictures at battalion and company level. Below this I have not ventured, since the body of information available is correspondingly slimmer at each level below the Commander-in-Chief. At company level pickings are slight indeed, but examples do exist and are reported here. The last official source is the inspection returns of the regiments which occasionally contain useful hints, but can be overwhelmingly disappointing on the actual detail.

After the masses of warrants and orders come other written sources. There is a profusion of letters, memoirs and diaries from the period. This was perhaps the golden age of diarists, and there are thousands to choose from. Those most useful have been those belonging to soldiers or their families. As usual, letters and diaries form the most immediate impression, even when crafted for an audience, whereas memoirs are often edited for much later consumption. This can also be useful though, as with the somewhat long winded memoirs of Captain Gronow, who contrasts the styles of his youth with those of the time at which he was writing. In the natural order of things, he prefers the styles of his youth of course and bemoans the inability of the rest of the world to appreciate his insight into the obvious.

Several contemporary writers made a study of fashion and of military dress, in fact there are even books attributed to George 'Beau' Brummell, sartorial doyen, and sometime officer in the Prince of Wales' 10th Hussars. Brummel's status as a Regency arbiter of taste is well known. He has been recently reinvented as the progenitor of modern style, which is rather over-egging the pudding, but his comments on dress, and especially those parts of dress pertaining to the military, are hugely informative, and have been inexplicably overlooked. Brummel was far from alone in commentating on the dress of the army, and further examples of commentators from all walks of life have been consulted. Of course, some of the most pertinent observers are those who actually wore the uniform, or those who made the uniforms, and neither is lacking in these pages. It may come as a surprise to the reader to see how many soldiers left records of what they wore, and their opinions of it. There are even conscious attempts by soldiers to produce a history of uniform in the various branches of the service, and I make no apology for reproducing at length from these valuable sources.

Besides guides to dress, we find some useful commentary in guides to etiquette, and also in fashion plates. There are a large number of fashion plates from England and France, and it is significant that the plates purport to be taken from life. That is, they are illustrations of actual individuals in the streets of Paris and London, rather than idealised representations, making them a record of fashion as worn, for purposes of emulation, rather than some sort of marketing device to inspire purchases. As such they are a superb primary resource, being a record of fashionable dress taken by an interested observer. They are comparable to the so called 'occupation images' made by artists at Paris in 1815, of which more later, in that they are supposedly taken from everyday life, as compared to say, a portrait, where the sitter may be presenting, and asking the artist to present, an idealised or projected image. The sheer number of these thousands of costume prints allow some generalisations to be drawn, and one could conduct a statistical analysis of all the costume prints available in order to discover valuable clues to the evolution of dress over fifteen years, difference between France and England, and perhaps most usefully, the predominance of particular colours or styles. The resulting data may prove surprising to those reared on a diet of costume drama, or the familiar, but generally later, characterisations of French dress as effete compared to the no-nonsense mode of John Bull.

Portraits were mentioned in the preceding paragraph as a stylised form of portrayal that can easily lead us astray, being especially susceptible to after the fact image-modelling from the sitter and artist owing to their nature as commissioned works. For instance, a general may choose to be portrayed in his full dress uniform in a painting commemorating a battle, although he wore something quite different on the day of the battle represented in his portrait, and may customarily have reserved that full dress uniform solely for meeting his sovereign or for appearances on the very grandest of occasions. The full dress uniform would normally be reserved for extraordinary events and not be in day to day wear. By contrast, another school of portraiture seeks to establish a connection between the sitter and gritty martial reality, by including items of non-regulation dress as used on a daily basis on actual service, albeit absent the mud and so on. This stylised form of anti-glamour can also be prone to distortion, and so can prove equally misleading. An example is the most famous portrait of the French cavalry paragon, Antoine Lasalle. preserved at the French national army museum at *Les Invalides*. Since the establishment of this portrait as the dominant archetype of images of Lasalle, he has always been pictured in subsequent representations wearing a mameluke style of trousers as shown in that portrait. An analysis of the list of his effects, drawn up several days after his death in 1809 for transmission to his widow, reveals that of some twenty four pairs of legwear, only a single example is of the mameluke type that has become so associated with him. The inference is that he was much more likely to be found in cotton nankeen trousers which formed 40 percent of his trouser or pantaloon wardrobe. Nonetheless, portraits do provide a valuable record, and occasionally preserve idiosyncrasies that are otherwise lost. Of especial value in this context are naïve portraits, one sub-genre of which appears to be popular with British soldiers: the embarkation portrait. If the British Army was a projectile launched by the Royal Navy, then the embarkation artist was there to capture the loading process. These naïve paintings, almost exclusively of private soldiers or NCOs, are usually set in maritime settings, and served as keepsakes to be sent to loved ones from the quay of departure. Often containing a few lines of sentimental doggerel, their quality as paintings is low, but their value as reference material is great.

Other images can be gleaned from military manuals, which ran illustrated series on regiments; from pictures of camp or barrack life performed by soldiers themselves; and from illustrated light or satirical works such as *The Adventures of Johnny Newcome*, or Egan's London life series. Each of these resources has its advantages and drawbacks, of which I will treat more thoroughly in the corresponding chapters.

Some of the most charming images of contemporary military life come from uniform plate series, which, like fashion plates, were intended as a collectable guide to uniform. The best known, and perhaps most significant British produced series is that by Charles Hamilton Smith. I am not convinced by claims that this series was produced as an official accompaniment to the 1812 warrant. It was a commercial proposition like any other, but the artist had excellent access to pattern items, and reworked some of his plates to reflect changes in warrants that were preparing. He was not so quick to reflect actual changes in regulation however, re-issuing the same prints under the heading of both the 1812 and 1814 warrants without further alteration to reflect changes, so as always, one has to proceed with caution, and look for corroboration from other sources. Despite this note of trepidation, sometimes the uniform plates comprise the best or only material available, and I have used the 1815 plates produced in Paris by French artists as one of my case studies in Volume II. Although these multiple plate series by many artists display all of the common faults of plate series, the sheer number available, when supplemented by sketch albums and other works, present a substantial enough sample for some conclusions to be drawn.

One of the most exciting sources has been the new availability of tailoring information specific to regimentals. This jigsaw has been assembled from tailoring manuals that treat of uniform, and from specialised tailor's books that were used by tailoring establishments to record details of uniform, or from tailors' account ledgers. These range from the records of the clothier Pearse, who supplied a vast quantity of war material including regimentals to other ranks of many regular regiments, and who was trusted to produce pattern articles; to those of Welch and Stalker, slop sellers and tailors, who meticulously illustrated in colour the coats they made for officers, and included cloth swatches and samples of military lace. I have collated a database of these tailoring drawings and descriptions that includes over eleven hundred entries, covering most regiments of regulars and many auxiliaries.

One could usefully ask whether it is possible to produce a comprehensive study of the uniforms of the army at this period. Certainly it has not been done, or done thoroughly, so far. This book does not attempt that task, which would take many volumes, instead it details the building bricks of such a work without which there is little point in proceeding and it does show what can be achieved, details the sources used to achieve the result, provides some case studies, and illuminates the conflict of dress in the Georgian army. Regulation and fashion were set on opposing courses and their battleground was the dress of the army.

Volume II of this work will contain the extensive quantity of regulation for 1809-1815. Including the important three warrants of 1812, and material on the supply of uniforms to the regiments, and the undress of both men and officers, the different orders of dress, a lengthy dissertation on legwear and officers' greatcoats, and an analysis of the late period dress with reference to the occupation prints, and to Highland dress.

Thanks and Acknowledgements

Some of the illustrations have been reproduced from the magnificent collection of military drawings and paintings in the Royal Collection, by gracious permission of Her Majesty the Queen, and I am grateful for the help given to me by Emma Stuart, senior curator of books and manuscripts, who guided me in all of my subsequent intercourse with the ever helpful staff of the pictures and drawings department. Peter Harrington of the Anne S.K. Brown Collection has been invaluable in sourcing images, as has Sophie Anderton of the National Army Museum. Among other people who have generously helped me with information over the years, I must thank the staff of innumerable local archives and records offices, and national, local, and regimental museums, not forgetting those at The National Archives in London and in the National Library in Edinburgh. Gratitude is due also to the Somerset Records Centre for permission to quote extensively from their papers, to Bankfield Museum in Yorkshire, and to Rotherham Local Archives for a similar courtesy. A last word to all at Meyer and Mortimer at Sackville Street, whose generosity with their treasures threw fresh discoveries into my path.

Many thanks to the friends who have aided me in the hunt, and acted as solid sounding boards especially Paul Durrant and Martin Lancaster. I must also thank Andrew Bamford, Bob Cooper, for additional material, and Iain Wilkinson, who even when I was drowning in the Sisyphean muck of WO papers, was always ready to cheerfully add another bucketful to the mire.

Lastly, and most importantly, thanks to Giulia, who gave purpose and meaning to my pen, and to everything else.

1

Regulation and the Role of the Boards of General Officers

On a cold January morning in 1807, a group of distinguished officers met around a board table in the upper rooms of 19 Great George Street in what is now the West End of London. They intended to fudge out a compromise on cavalry uniform between the practical and the fashionable. The house is no longer there, but in 1807 it was quite new, and typical of the new residential houses that sprang up in late Georgian London. The top floors were dedicated to the needs of the Board of General Officers for clothing, and below, the housekeeper, Mrs Kington, a widow of 54 years, was preparing refreshments in the company of George, the black and white house cat. In a small room next to her a time-served serjeant of the Guards was organising a pile of equipment from the trestle shelves lining a small room. The items of clothing, with their little wax sealed tags hanging from them, were piled so high that further shelves had been erected in the centre of the room, cramping it still further. When the pile of clothing assembled by the serjeant matched the list in his hand, he carried the pieces upstairs to the board room where the officers were assembled. They had convened to discuss how the expensive clothing of the fashionable hussar craze, championed by the Prince of Wales, could be made to match the cost estimates of the usual more frugal light cavalry dress as favoured by the King. In order to reconcile the costs of the frivolous and expensive hussar rig to the rather plain and old-fashioned, but superbly utilitarian, light dragoon dress, and present the two costs as equivalent, which they clearly were not, they would have to jump through some rather convoluted hoops, and stretch logic into an unnatural shape. But that was the business of the day, and logic was a decidedly distant second priority to that of satisfying the interests of each of the two royal personages involved. Looking down the table Lieutenant General Sir Harry Burrard saw that each of the officers present had a few sheets of notes to contribute to assist them all in reaching an elegant, but necessarily nonsensical, solution. With a sigh, he called the meeting to order, and they began.

This imagined scene is based on material contained in the letter books of the Clothing Board. The various boards involved in the clothing of the army change over the period, and the following chapter will detail how they conducted their business concerning army clothing and equipment.

It is sometimes said that no formalised clothing regulations existed for the British Army before 1822. This statement is true in as far as the first book of Clothing Regulations titled as such came in that year (note the capitalisation). The 1822 Clothing Regulation is a regulation solely for officers. The first true one in fact. It regulates things that before were contained in standing orders – for instance the restriction on wearing the sash with the full dress tailcoat and shoes. It also disposes of the full dress tailcoat for hussar regiments and enshrines their dress uniform to serve, with minor elaborations such as the addition of the slung pelisse, as their full dress too.[1]

Naturally before the 1822 publication there existed a great corpus of army clothing regulations, which were issued in various different manners and collected in diverse formats. Changes to dress could happen at army, divisional, brigade, regimental, battalion and company level, but the most authoritative commands came by means of Royal Warrant and were called clothing warrants. The major clothing warrants of the period came in 1801, 1803, and 1812. Minor warrants detailing specific matters were issued in between as they went along. In 1807 a book of regulations was released including accumulated clothing warrants to date, the same happened in 1811 and 1816. In 1802 an attempt was made to collect and clarify all existing regulation on clothing. It was never published, apparently having been abandoned as nigh on impossible to complete. The manuscript version is reproduced here in Appendix I. Various other attempts to complete this project were ordered by Horse Guards over the years, but the wily clerks either dodged the ball, or their efforts have not survived to be transmitted to us.

The most significant changes to dress came in the infantry warrants of 1800 and in the several infantry and cavalry warrants of 1812. In 1800 the army changed from a cocked hat to a cap, heralding the start of the 19th century evolution in army uniform and bidding goodbye to the 18th. The period distinction between a hat and a cap was quite clear. A hat had a brim, cocked or not, and a cap did not, although it could have a peak. In 1812, the army changed its uniforms from a style of predominantly German influence, looking towards the uniforms of Prussia and Austria, to one that regarded Austrian, and to a lesser extent French and Portuguese styles. This was a natural consequence of the Austrian and other continental styles developing in relation to French influence, and of the British exposure to their Portuguese allies in the Peninsula.

A constant throughout the period was the Hungarianisation of the light cavalry through the evolving hussar style, and this is reflected in the important hussar warrant of 1808. The Hungarian influence had been stoutly resisted by King George III, and, until 1800, the British light cavalry uniform had developed in beautiful isolation from those of continental armies, resulting in a fascinatingly novel and idiosyncratic manner of uniform. The Duke of York and the Prince of Wales were not immune to the charm of the rugged hussar look, and they progressed from buying Hungarian masquerade uniforms, through having 'Hungarian hussars' attached to their persons as servant orderlies, to equipping whole regiments by stealth in the modern hussar style. By the time the King was imposed upon to officially sanction the conversion of an extremely limited number of light dragoon regiments to light dragoons (hussars), the royal brothers and their compliant colonels had already

---

1   Adjutant-General's Office, *Regulations for the Dress of General Staff and Regimental Officers* (London: Clowes, 1822).

achieved a fait accompli in the matter. Further conversions followed at regular intervals, until the new fad for lancers overtook, or at least matched, the fascination of hussars in 1816. The reticence of the military royal establishment regarding hussar dress is clearly expressed in the titling of the new regiments, the word 'hussar' being bracketed, as if it were a contagion to be quarantined from the true and honest title of 'light dragoon'. It is not necessary to say a great deal here about the hussar dress that had flourished amongst all major armies (and not a few minor ones, too) in the latter half of the eighteen century. Chapter 18 will cover the matter of hussar dress in more depth. The origin legends found in any book on the subject of hussars are well rehearsed and rest on rather flimsy speculative foundations. What is certain, and worth establishing, is that the mode had developed into certain recognised conventions, and the British adoption of hussar dress, coming very late to the hairy Hungarian party, is notable for the varying degrees to which they complied with, or flouted, the established continental conventions.

The questionable benefits of hussar dress were, of course, extended to other elements of the light cavalry with or without official sanction. The light infantry regiments, in particular the specialist rifle corps, also modelled their dress on this style, and the fever also infiltrated the light company officers, and eventually the line. Images and tailoring records detail the unofficial adoption of the short pelisse by several infantry regiments. The Royal Artillery battalions proved immune, but their reticence was more than compensated for by the burgeoning number of new Royal Horse Artillery troops, who considered themselves not so distant cousins of the light cavalry, and so entered into the spirit of hussar dress with gleeful abandon, as the reminiscences of Mercer on fashion demonstrate in Chapter 5.

Remaining within the confines of army level regulation, there are various strata of official edict that carried authority, and I have tried to make sense of their relative degree of importance, and the relationship between them where they clash. Untangling the bureaucratic skein is not straightforward, and the intricacies were appreciated in period although they are obscure today. Regarding the Parliamentary commissions of military enquiry in 1805, the *Morning Herald*'s editor's noted that,

> The commissioners, will have to pass mountains and labyrinths of figures, drawn up for years in great martial array, and to explore defiles of subtleties which nothing but patience and perseverance can possibly pass through.[2]

For a bureaucracy to be self-maintaining, it has to develop defence mechanisms that sustain it, while excluding outsiders from access or understanding of its systems. Transparency is the death of such systems, which is why so much was not written down, or spelt out – this may be a reason why the 1802 collation was never published. It accounts for the sheer complexity of the intertwining levels of army regulation.

The army level regulation was composed of warrants, general orders, approved submissions, letters, and circulars both general and specific. Ultimately these all carried the authority of the King, or later the Prince Regent, or of the Commander-in-Chief of the Army, HRH the Duke of York. As well as taking advice from the officers of the civil army

---

'The Duke of York.' This print shows the Duke in 1791. His horse is held by one of the fashionable hussar attendants who would popularise the hussar style and lead to its adoption into the line cavalry regiments. Color mezzotint by Dickinson after Hoppner. (Anne S.K. Brown Military Collection, Brown University Library)

departments, such as that of the Adjutant General, the Duke of York was advised by the boards of general officers. These comprised a sitting board, as well as specially appointed temporary boards constituted to ponder specific questions and advise the Commander-in-Chief. A glimpse into the process of preparing the warrants comes in December 1802. The new 1803 warrant was being prepared and the Commander-in-Chief sent it to the Adjutant-General to be circulated, along with additional submissions from Pearse, king of the clothiers, and a list of the officers involved in its composition, all of whom were to peruse, append observations, and return it.[3] The inclusion of a clothier in the parties consulted is an interesting piece of cross fertilisation and indicates the importance that prominent clothiers had attained. This is further demonstrated by their role in the preparation of pattern items, and a continual process of consultation between manufacturers of clothing and equipment would inform the deliberations of the Board of General Officers throughout the period.

The first Board of General Officers was raised by warrant on 18 February 1695. William III ordered the chief officers of the army to meet at least twice a week in the Great Chamber of the Horse Guards to hear complaints against officers and soldiers and to inquire into disputes regarding payments. This board met regularly until June 1699, and then less frequently between November 1702 and February 1703 before lapsing. It was revived by a warrant of 1 February 1705 as a council of general officers of the army to inquire into abuses, especially in recruiting, and by a warrant of 9 February 1706 with similar terms of reference; it was concerned with disputes over pay and accounts and questions of precedence. It was not until 1708 that the Board of General Officers acquired responsibility for regulating the clothing of the army. This duty was exercised by a subordinate clothing board, which took over the clothing functions and the office of the comptroller of army accounts. Its responsibilities extended only to the infantry and cavalry.

The main board was reconstituted in 1711 and 1714, and it continued to be appointed, usually by annual warrant, throughout the 18th century. The Judge Advocate General was secretary of the board until 1809. In peacetime it rarely met, and its main preoccupation was with clothing, which continued to be dealt with by clothing boards. It also dealt with pay, precedence, revision of the articles of war, and important special inquiries. In 1799 the clothing board was made independent of the Board of General Officers, and appointed by separate warrant. It shared the office and secretary of the comptrollers of the army accounts, until the move to Great George Street, probably in 1803 and definitely before 1804, where it would meet regularly, sometimes weekly, and never less than monthly. The different boards of general officers associated with matters other than clothing continued to be constituted from time to time on the same premises. Several of its reports are detailed below, whereas the information from the standing board for clothing is revealed through remaining correspondence and letter books. This will be covered chronologically in following chapters.

A second special standing board was set up on 11 April 1809 to investigate claims for losses during the campaign in Portugal and Spain; subsequently its terms of reference were extended to cover claims for losses in other campaigns and theatres. This board of claims had its own office and secretary. Its findings are not detailed here, but led to the board constituted in 1810 which forms the focus of Chapter 13.

---

3   TNA, WO7/54: Various Departmental out-letters. Board of General Officers, Reports on Clothing.

On 25 December 1816 these separate boards were merged into a single consolidated Board of General Officers, served by an office of military boards. After claims from the Napoleonic Wars had been wound up in the 1820s, this board's functions were again largely confined to clothing matters, though it also became concerned with claims for war medals. Its work was performed by an acting committee which approved and sealed clothing patterns. The board was abolished by royal warrant of 21 June 1855 as part of the general reform of Army administration.

The board would sit annually in June to seal patterns of clothing for the ensuing 25 December delivery. It also had regular weekly meets. Until 1803 they met on a Friday, at the Army Comptroller's office building in Whitehall, but after that year there was a change. It coincided with the move to Great George Street, completed in the course of 1803. After that move the usual date was on a Wednesday at 11:00 a.m. When the Duke of York attended, he was usually invited to arrive at 12:00, after the preliminaries.[4]

Information on the premises of the Board of General Officers occasionally appears in correspondence with the Adjutant General's office, and offers sidelight on the system of storage and inspection of pattern items. Various items from their letter book are tabulated below.

- 12 March 1812. The board want to change house to get more space.[5]
- 19 May, 1812. The board are still waiting and remind the Secretary at War to find them something. Their house is a squash and a squeeze.
- 5 June, 1812. The Deputy Adjutant General suggests to the Secretary at War that they take over the Commissary General of Musters' house, and that he removes his papers immediately in preparation for the move. It appears that the move is not completed as correspondence continues to be issued from Great George Street.

During this period the Board of General Officers for clothing dealt with a diverse range of problems. One of these concerned the bankruptcy of Ross and Ogilvie, one of the major firms of agents handling regimental accounts. A string of correspondence from 26 July–28 August 1804 deals with the aftermath of this seismic event After the agents went bankrupt the regiments concerned were left in limbo having paid for their annual clothing, but being without the recompense from government which was held by the agents. After advice from HM's Attorney and Solicitor General, it was decided to certify and pass clothing assignments in lieu of those held by this firm. Thus compensation was achieved for the regiments concerned. Agents and clothiers concerned and waiting for assignments to be delivered from colonels of regiments were advised to stand by for government assistance.[6]

A comprehensive review of the few remaining papers also reveals the opening skirmish in what became a full scale bureaucratic turf war between the Adjutant General's office and that of the Secretary at War. The Secretary at War was to win this struggle over the control of inspection of clothing. In WO7/54 we find a huge collection of entries in a Board of General Officers letter book of 1807 regarding inspections made by the quartermasters of

---

4   TNA, WO7/33/59: Various departmental out-letters, Board of General Officers, clothing.
5   TNA, WO3/158/122: Office of the Commander-in-Chief: Out-letters.
6   TNA, WO7/33/251: Various departmental out-letters, Board of General Officers, clothing.

No	Articles	Tradesmen's name furnished by.	Date of its being furnished as a pattern.	Price of the article.
1	Serjeants coat Corsican Rangers	Pearse.	1812	Price never known.
1	Privates coat West India Rangers	Pearse.	1812	Price never known.
1	Serjeants coat West India Rangers	Pearse.	1812	Price never known.
1	Privates coat York Rangers	Pearse.	1812	Price never known.
1	Serjeants coat York Rangers	Pearse.	1812	Price never known.
1	Privates waistcoat European wear	Pearse.	1812	Price never known.
1	Privates breeches European wear	Pearse.	1812	Price never known.
1	Serjeants waistcoat European wear	Pearse.	1812	Price never known.
1	Serjeants breeches European wear	Pearse.	1812	Price never known.
1	Privates grey trowsers foreign service	Pearse.	1812	Price never known.
1	Privates pantaloons for Royal Staff Corps	Pearse.	1812	Price never known.
1	Serjeants pantaloons for Royal Staff Corps	Pearse.	1812	Price never known.
1	Privates pantaloons 5th battalion 60th regiment	Pearse.	1812	Price never known.
1	Serjeants pantaloons 5th battalion 60th regiment	Pearse.	1812	Price never known.
1	Privates trowsers for 95th regiment	Pearse.	1812	Price never known.
1	Serjeants trowsers for 95th regiment	Pearse.	1812	Price never known.
1	Privates pantaloons Corsican Rangers	Pearse.	1812	Price never known.
1	Serjeants pantaloon Corsican Rangers	Pearse.	1812	Price never known.
1	Privates pantaloons Royal West India Rangers	Pearse.	1812	Price never known.
1	Serjeants pantaloons Royal West India Rangers	Pearse.	1812	Price never known.
1	Privates serge waistcoat West India regiments	Pearse.	1812	Price never known.
1	Privates blue serge trowsers West India regiments	Pearse.	1812	Price never known.
1	Serjeants serge waistcoat West India regiments	Pearse.	1812	Not communicated to this office.

No	Articles	Tradesmen's name furnished by.	Date of its being furnished as a pattern.	Price of the article.
1	Serjeants serge trowsers West India regiments	Pearse.	1812	Not communicated to this office.
1	Privates jacket working dress Royal Staff Corps	Pearse.	1812	Not communicated to this office.
1	Privates pantaloons working dress Royal Staff Corps	Pearse.	1812	Not communicated to this office.
1	Privates jacket Brunswick Infantry	Pearse.	1812	Not communicated to this office.
1	Privates Waistcoat Brunswick Infantry	Pearse.	1812	Not communicated to this office.
1	Privates trowsers Brunswick Infantry	Pearse.	1812	Not communicated to this office.
1	Privates dress jacket Brunswick cavalry	Not known	7 years in the office.	Not communicated to this office.
1	Privates undress jacket Brunswick cavalry	Not known	7 years in the office.	Not communicated to this office.
1	Privates pair pantaloons Brunswick cavalry	Not known	7 years in the office.	Not communicated to this office.
1	Privates valice two caps Brunswick cavalry	Not known	7 years in the office.	Not communicated to this office.
1	Privates dress jacket cavalry staff	Pearse.	1813	Not communicated to this office.
1	Privates undress jacket cavalry staff	Pearse.	1813	Not communicated to this office.
1	Privates overalls cavalry staff	Pearse.	1813	Not communicated to this office.
1	Privates cloak cavalry staff	Pearse.	1813	Not communicated to this office.
1	Privates dress jacket Royal Waggon Train	Pearse.	1813	Not communicated to this office.
1	Privates undress jacket Royal Waggon Train	Pearse.	1813	Not communicated to this office.
1	Privates pair of breeches Royal Waggon Train	Pearse.	1813	Not communicated to this office.
1	Officers great coat of the line	Pearse.	1812	Not communicated to this office.
1	Officers jacket of the line	Pearse.	1812	Not communicated to this office.
1	Serjeants jacket Greek Light Infantry	Oswald	1811	Not communicated to this office.
1	Serjeants waistcoat Greek Light Infantry	Oswald	1811	Not communicated to this office.
1	Serjeants gaiters Greek Light Infantry	Oswald	1811	Not communicated to this office.

No	Articles	Tradesmen's name furnished by.	Date of its being furnished as a pattern.	Price of the article.
1	Privates jacket Greek Light Infantry	Oswald	1811	Not communicated to this office.
1	Privates waistcoat Greek Light Infantry	Oswald	1811	Not communicated to this office.
1	Privates gaiters Greek Light Infantry	Oswald	1811	Not communicated to this office.
1	Drummers jacket Greek Light Infantry	Oswald	1811	Not communicated to this office.
1	Drummers waistcoat Greek Light Infantry	Oswald	1811	Not communicated to this office.
1	Drummers gaiters Greek Light Infantry	Oswald	1811	Not communicated to this office.
1	Privates pouchbelt and waist-belt Greek Light Infantry	Oswald	1811	Not communicated to this office.
1	Privates set accoutrements for the line	Haswell	1808	Not communicated to this office.
1	Privates forgaing cap for the line	Prater	1813	Not communicated to this office.
1	Privates set pioneer accoutre-ments for the line	Not known	Upwards of ten years in the office	Not communicated to this office.
1	Private swords infantry of the line	Not known	Upwards of ten years in the office	Not communicated to this office.
Several	Muskets and ordnance pieces	Not known	Upwards of ten years in the office	Not communicated to this office.
5	Great coats infantry of the line	Pearse.	1812	Not communicated to this office.
1	Knapsack infantry of the line	Bearsely	1812	Not communicated to this office.
1	Trumpet	Ridge	1813	Not communicated to this office.
1	Bugle	Ridge	1813	Not communicated to this office.
3	Officers caps foot guards	Cater	1811	Not communicated to this office.
2	Officers caps of the line	Oliphaunt	1812	Not communicated to this office.
2	Serjeants caps of the line	Oliphaunt	1812	Not communicated to this office.
4	Privates caps of the line	Oliphaunt	1812	Not communicated to this office.

Time has settled a veil over much of the process of preparing or requesting pattern items. The clothing board letters contain a few references that illuminate the process:

> Horse Guards May 15 1806
> Adjutant General to Clothing Board
> Sir, I have the honour to acquaint you that the Commander-in-Chief has called upon the principal hatters to produce patterns of two kinds of caps, one calculated to last a year, and the other for two years. To be sent to the Clothing Board for examination and inspection. They will then recommend one to HM for the use of the infantry.[13]

When the Prince of Wales assumed the Regency in June 1811, approval of pattern items for the Army was transferred to him from the King. He preserved many of these items, and kept examples of both prototypes and actual sealed patterns in his personal armoury at Carlton House. After his death the collection was dispersed. Some items had been sent to Windsor after the demolition of Carlton House in 1826; a portion of these has survived in the Royal Collection. Others found their way to the Royal Armoury Collection in the Tower where much of it perished in a fire at the grand storehouse in 1841. Details of these pattern items can be found in the records of the Carlton House Armoury. The profusion of caps proposed for the cavalry accounts for the constant sitting of the Clothing Board for the examination of cavalry clothing and equipment throughout 1811 and 1812. A careful examination also allows us to discard old canards, such as the non-adoption of the 1812 infantry cap by the light infantry and rifles. The description of the two caps for line and light infantry is identical except for the cap plates.[14]

Pattern items were exhibited for tradesmen to bid on contracts, and also made available to be consulted. A typical response to a request to view pattern items is this letter concerning flank officer swords (in 1803 these items were produced in the form of the famous lion headed flank officers sword). It is a reply to a Mr J. Eginton, sword maker of Birmingham who had been advised by his patron, HRH the Duke of Kent, to view the new pattern sword for flank officers. He requested it be sent to him. The Clothing Board demurred:

> All patterns which are directed to be lodged here, must of course remain in the office for the inspection of colonels of regiments, and others concerned in the clothing or making of accoutrements, and so you are consequently at liberty to have access to such articles as are deposited in this office."[15]

Almost all of the Board of General Officers for Clothing reports are missing. However, there are occasional survivals which can be very revealing. Three of the most useful are included in this book. Reports on the clothing and equipment of the cavalry and infantry are reproduced below. These date from 1811, and summarise the changes suggested to the Board of General Officers after some eighteen years of hard campaigning. They further presage the

---

13   TNA, WO7/33/453: Various Departmental, Out-letters. Board of General Officers, clothing.
14   Carlton House Armoury Inventories, the Royal Collection. Entries 2236-2241 and 2257-2260.
15   TNA, WO7/33/115: Various departmental out-letters, Board of General Officers, clothing.

elements that the Board of General Officers would be able to incorporate into the three important clothing warrants of 1812 which will be reproduced in the second volume of this work. The much longer report contained in Chapter 13 is unusually complete, and, although referring to deliberations of 1810, it is a reprisal of earlier indicated but now missing reports. The reports on the equipment of the cavalry and infantry, and on camp equipment and baggage, give a useful indication of the scale and breadth of enquiry permitted to the extraordinary boards. A comparison of the accepted scale of compensation for uniform lost, with the sums actually expended on uniform (see Chapter 17) reveal the gulf in expenditure between utility and extravagance.

The report on the equipment of the infantry is representative of Board of General Officers reports. It took a mere twelve days of deliberation to reach its conclusions. The suggestions were then forwarded to the Duke of York in his capacity as Commander-in-Chief of the Army, and shared by him as necessary.

> Report of the proceedings of a Board of General Officers, as appointed by His Royal Highness the Commander in Chief, to be assembled for the purpose of reporting upon the Equipment of the Infantry.
>
> Lieutenant General, Sir Harry Burrard, Bart, President.
> Lieutenant General Sir John C Sherbrooke, K.B.
> Lieutenant General Honourable Edw. Paget
> Major General Henry Clinton
> Major General Oswald
> Major General MacKenzie
> Colonel Robinson
> Colonel Bradford
> Colonel Darling
> Colonel Gifford
> Lieutenant Colonel Adam
> Lieutenant Colonel Anderson
> Lieutenant Colonel Nicolls
>
> Major Generals Oswald and MacKenzie having been in Scotland at the time they were named Members of the Board; The Commander in Chief was pleased to direct that their Attendance might be dispensed with. The President with the other Members of the Board, accordingly sat, at No19 Great George Street, Westminster, on Monday the 17 of June 1811, when His Royal Highness's Instructions, as contained in two letters from the Adjutant General dated the 8 and 13 of the same month, were read, and it appeared therefrom, that the Object which His Royal Highness has in view in assembling the Board, is 'to reduce into one established system, the various Orders and Regulations, at present in force, on the subject of Clothing; Equipment, Provision and Necessaries, and Appropriation of Pay, of the Infantry,' for which purpose the Board was desired 'to take these various Documents into Consideration, and to suggest, for the Commander in Chief's consideration, and for the final Approbation of the Prince Regent, any alterations therefrom, which

they may consider themselves founded in recommending, from the experience of some years past, bearing in mind, however, that the essential object is, to simplify every Article of the Soldier's Equipment, and to prepare him for Active Service, but without increasing the Expence to the Colonel, or making a larger deduction from the Soldier's Pay, than is authorised by His Majesty's present Regulation, so that a perfect uniformity in all these particulars may be established in each Regiment of Infantry.

The Board are also called upon 'to consider, whether it is expedient to recommend any, and what, deviations from the General Regulations which may hereafter be established, in the instance of Corps employed on particular Services Abroad, subject, however, to the before mentioned restrictions in point of expence'.

The first Question, which appears to the Board to arise out of their Instructions, was, whether there should be one, or more Equipment for the Infantry Soldier? – and after fully considering and discussing this point, they are unanimously of Opinion that there should be but one Equipment, provided the whole of the Soldier's Necessaries can be reduced to a Weight not exceeding Twelve Pounds and a Half, – the Great Coat included.

With respect to the Articles of which this Equipment should in future consist, the Board, for the reasons hereinafter assigned, have been induced to recommend certain Alterations, either in the construction, or in the number, of the following Articles now in use, Viz.

Articles of Clothing:
Caps, Breeches, Great Coats.
Articles of Necessaries:
Shoes, Gaiters, Shirts, Knapsacks, Foraging Caps, Brushes, Combs.

It appearing to the Board, that the Cap at present worn by the Infantry is objectionable as to its form, which renders it unsteady on the head, and of little use in defending the head from the weather- much less from Sword Wounds; and the Board, conceiving that, without making any material Alteration as to the quality, or any difference whatever in the Expence, a Cap may be constructed, which would not be liable to the above objections, but might combine the advantages of comfort, durability, and utility in point of defence; have directed that a Cap of this description should be made as a pattern, to be submitted for the inspection and consideration of His Royal Highness the Commander in Chief, and which accordingly accompanies this report. It will last two years, and may be packed in nearly the same compass as the present cap. It presents nothing to the Eye which can serve as a Mark, or direct the Enemy's Aim, and there is nothing about it which is liable to be lost on Service. A sufficient distinction may be made, in the fringe on the Crest, to designate the several Ranks of Officers (if judged expedient) without rendering such distinction too conspicuous.

Strong objections have been found, from experience, to the use of the black cap in tropical climates, the Board have caused a pattern cap, of a light colour, to be made, for His Royal Highness's inspection, which also accompanies this Report; and they beg to recommend the same, for general use, in those climates.

It is the Opinion of the Board, that Grey Cloth Trousers, with a Half gaiter of the same, should be substituted for the White Breeches and the Gaiter now in use, except for such part of the Brigade of Guards as may be on Home Service. From the reasons assigned by the different members of the Board in favour of Trousers and half Gaiters, it appears to be the general opinion, that these articles form a more convenient dress than the Breeches and Long gaiters, from having the joint of the knee and the calf of the leg unconfined, and are therefore more suitable for Marching – the long Gaiter, from buttoning tight over the calf of the leg, being found by experience to produce sores. The Grey half Gaiter is also, in the opinion of the Board, preferable to the Black, in other respects; the material is more durable, the dye of the latter being injurious to the cloth, and the Trousers, when worn out as such, may serve to repair the Gaiters. The advantage of this Dress over the Breeches and long gaiters seems indeed to be sufficiently proved, from the almost universal use thereof in regiments upon Service: it is more easily taken off, and put on, it also obviates the use of pipeclay, and in regard to appearance, it is cleanly, useful, and uniform, and consequently cannot fail of being considered Military and handsome.

It appears necessary to the Board to reduce the length of the Soldier's Great Coat, so as to reach an inch only below the knee, in order that it may not impede his Marching, as well as to keep it within a proper weight. They are also of opinion, that the Cape should be fastened at the corners and behind, so as to prevent the Men from wearing it over their Ears when on Sentry, or the Wind from blowing it in their Eyes in tempestuous Weather.

In order to reduce the Necessaries in a Pack to a weight which the Soldier may be able to carry on Service, the Board are of opinion that he should not be in possession of more than two pairs of Shoes.

For the reason assigned in regard to Shoes, as well as to reduce bulk, the Board are of opinion, that two Shirts are sufficient for a Soldier.

The Board have inspected the pattern Knapsack submitted to them by the Adjutant General, and having caused some few improvements to be made therein, they recommend that one uniform Knapsack of the same dimensions and colour, should be established for the whole Army; it being calculated to contain every thing a Soldier ought to carry, and being a convenient, well looking Pack, either with, or without the Great Coats. The number of the Regiment to be marked on the back, without any ornament. The weight of the Pack, when filled with the articles hereinafter specified, will be Twelve Pounds seven ounces.

It is the opinion of the Board, that the foraging Cap should be the same for the whole Army- that it should be made of black Cloth, with an Oil Skin Crown. A pattern of the proposed Cap accompanies this Report.

The Board are of opinion, that half the number of Brushes, at present carried by the Infantry Soldier, is sufficient for every absolutely necessary purpose, and they therefore propose to reduce the same to two, of such size and shape, as to fill the pocket in the Top of the Pack.

From the manner in which the Soldier's Hair is now directed to be worn, the Board conceive that, instead of two Combs (the number stated in the existing Regulations), a single Comb with small teeth on one side, will be sufficient for each man. For the same reason, the Hair Ribbons and Leather, specified in the Book of Regulations[16] are omitted in the following Schedule of the Articles, now recommended by the Board to be considered as constituting the whole Equipment of the Infantry Soldier.

A Schedule of Articles of Clothing and Necessaries for a Soldier of Infantry.
Clothing.
One Cap, One Coat, One Waistcoat – to be found by the Colonel.
Two pairs of Grey Trousers – one pair to be found by the Colonel.
One Great Coat.
Necessaries.
Two pairs of Shoes – one to be found by the Colonel.
Two pairs of half Gaiters.
Two Shirts.
Three pairs of ancle socks.
One Black Stock.
One Knapsack.
One Foraging cap.
Two Brushes.
Blacking Ball.
Sponge.
Comb, with small teeth on one side.
Razor.
Soap and Brush, without a Box.
Straps for carrying Great Coat.
Turnscrew, Brush and Worm.
Haversack with painted Cover – to be found by the Public.
The Men to be stopped the extraordinary Charge of One Shilling and three pence on the Clothing, in consequence of receiving Trousers instead of Breeches.

It appears to the Board, that there is no part of the Equipment of the Soldier more defective than the Haversack now in use, or more unfit for the purposes for which it was intended. The experience of every member of the Board has convinced him of the distress occasioned to an Army, particularly in wet Weather, from the unfitness of the Material, in its present state; the bread on such occasions being always damaged, and generally rendered useless; they are therefore of opinion, that the pattern Haversack which has been made under their direction, and which accompanies this Report, should be substituted in its room. Though smaller than the other, it is sufficiently large to carry three days provisions, and will, it is conceived,

---

16   For which see Secretary at War, *A Collection of Orders, Regulations and Instructions for the Army.* (London: Egerton, 1807), p.457.

be more durable, it being made of the same Material, and has a painted cover to keep out the Wet. The Board presume that, for the attainment of an object so extremely important to the health and comfort of the Soldier, His Majesty's Government will not object to furnish the cover, in addition to the Haversack in the same manner as at present.

The Board are aware, that a Tin Kettle was proposed as a substitute for the Haversack, by the Board of which Lieutenant General Ross was President; but having examined the same, they consider it to be too heavy, consistently with the intended reduction in the weight a Soldier ought to carry.

The Canteen now in use being very objectionable, on many accounts, and the Tin one, which has been recommended by the afore mentioned Board, not appearing to afford a remedy for those inconveniences, the Board have directed a leather Canteen to be constructed, which, from its being lighter by one half, and infinitely more durable, they strongly recommend as a substitute. It appears to the Board, that though the original cost of the leather Canteen now recommended, is greater than that at present in use, yet that, from its lasting so much longer, the Expence to the Public will be lessened.

The Board having taken into consideration the numerous deficiencies which occur in most Regiments, in the equipment of Canteens and Haversacks, the frequent supply of which is attended with so great expence to the Public, taken the liberty of suggesting, that some general Regulation should be made for obviating these inconveniences, by which Soldiers should be required to preserve in a serviceable state their Canteens and Haversacks, as well as every other Article of Equipment; and any deficiencies arising from carelessness or neglect, they should be required immediately to make good. This very desirable object might certainly be attained, by frequent Regimental and Company inspections, when any damages would be noticed, and the necessary repairs ordered; and by Monthly returns from each Regiment of deficiencies, showing by what cause they may have been occasioned; these deficiencies, at the requisition of the General Officer Commanding the Brigade, should forthwith be supplied by the Commissary, who would receive payment from the Regimental Pay Master, for all such Articles as should not be returned deficient by fair wear and tear. The price to be paid for each Article could of course be fixed and made known. Officers Commanding Companies might further be directed to keep an account of the Expenses incurred by the Men for the repair of damages to their Canteens and Haversacks, occasioned by fair use, or by unavoidable accidents; and it seems just, that Expenses so incurred should be reimbursed.

By some such regulation, although Articles costing more, but of a more durable quality than those at present in use, should be issued to the Army, a considerable saving would be made to the Public, and it is presumed that the Troops would be constantly complete in the necessary Articles of Equipment.

In case the Light Camp Kettle for 5 Men, has not been already substituted for the heavy one, the Board unanimously recommend its adoption.

The Board considering themselves called upon to offer any suggestions, the adoption of which may appear to them likely to be beneficial to the Army, although the subject of such suggestions is not immediately pointed out in the Adjutant General's letter; and thinking it of great importance to the Army, that the Soldiers should, under no circumstances, be required, or even permitted to carry any weight, in addition to the Equipment which shall, by General Regulation, be established, excepting in case where the exigency of the Service may render it necessary for them to carry a greater proportion of Bread; are desirous of recommending, that whenever it may be deemed necessary to issue Blankets to the Troops, in whatever proportion, the Soldiers shall not themselves be required to carry them, but that, in all such cases, sufficient means shall be provided by the Commissary for their conveyance, or that of any other extra Articles which it may be found expedient to carry with Troops.

There is another circumstance connected with the subject of the Equipment of the Army, which the Board also feel themselves called upon to notice, for the same reason. Convinced from their own experience, that Clothing is generally sent to Regiments so ill sewed, as to require its being remade; they are of Opinion that positive directions should be given to the Inspectors of Clothing, not to pass any Clothing which is not sufficiently well sewn for immediate and permanent Wear; and that, in the event of any part of the Clothing, requiring still to be altered for the purpose of fitting, the same Allowance which is at present granted to Regiments at home, should, on a Certificate, upon honor, signed by the Commanding Officer and two next senior Officers, of that necessity, be given for such Articles only as have actually required altering, and that a like allowance should be extended to Regiments on Foreign Service, there appearing to be no reason assigned in any existing Regulation, nor are the Board aware that any can be shown, why the Troops abroad should not equally participate in this allowance. The Board have endeavoured, by inquiries in various quarters, to ascertain on what grounds the allowance for altering Clothing was originally confined to regiments on Home Service, but without success, nor can they even guess at any probable cause for making such a distinction in regard to the Allowance in question, unless it be, that Soldiers abroad, heretofore derived certain advantages from receiving their Provisions free of expence, which advantages, however, no longer exists. Should the suggestion of the Board upon this point be adopted, a very small proportion only of the Clothing would require alteration. The Regimental tailors would not be taken, for a considerable length of time, from their duty, the saving at home, would, it is presumed, be more than equal to the Expence incurred Abroad, and a compliance with the King's Regulations would, to a certain degree, be insured.

The Board cannot close this part of their report, without adverting to the Dress of Regimental Officers, which they are of opinion should be so far assimilated to that of the Men, as the necessary distinctions of Rank will allow; particularly that Caps and Jackets should be substituted for Cocked Hats and Coats, and that the Great Coat and Pantaloons should be of the same colour as those worn by the Men; it's being well known that the present conspicuous distinction between the Officers and Soldiers Dress serves not only to expose the Officer unnecessarily, but is frequently the occasion of drawing on a destructive Fire, which might otherwise be avoided.

It is the opinion of the majority of the Board, that the present Colour of the Clothing for the Light Infantry Corps is objectionable, being too conspicuous for the Service required from them, and that the same objection applies to the Belts, which should be black, like those of the Rifle Corps. The colour of the Clothing is proposed to be Green.

The Board are unanimously of opinion, that it is not advisable to make any alteration whatever in the existing Regulations relative to the Soldier's Pay, either by appropriating any part thereof, to the establishment of a Breakfast Mess, or otherwise, but they conceive that the Commanding Officers of Regiments are authorised to appropriate the stoppage for Messing already specified in the Regulations, in such manner as they may think most advantageous to the Soldier.

It does not occur to the Board, that any deviations from the General regulations which are hereby recommended to be stablished, as far as respects the points now submitted to their consideration, 'in the instance of Corps employed on particular Services Abroad'; further than such as have been already suggested in this report. Or which, as forming a part of the existing Regulations, it may be found expedient, by those on whom the duty of preparing the proposed Warrant for the Prince Regent's Approbation and signature will devolve, to retain and to introduce in that Warrant; are necessary.

Great George Street, 29 June 1811[17]

Immediately after the board on infantry equipment began to sit, a second board was assembled of cavalry specialists. It took much longer to reach its conclusions, taking almost four weeks.

Report of the proceedings of a Board of General Officers, assembled by Order of His Royal Highness the Commander in Chief, at no.19 Great George Street for 'the purpose of reporting upon the Equipment of the Cavalry'.

General His Royal Highness the Duke of Cumberland, K.G. President.
Lieutenant General Lord Paget
Major General Henry Fane
Major General J.O. Vandeleur
Major General Robt. Browne
Colonel O. J. Jones 18th Lt. Dragn.
Colonel C. Grant 15th ditto
Lieutenant Colonel G.B. Mundy 8th Dragoons
Lieutenant Colonel G. Quintin 10 Lt. Dragn.

Major General Bolton and Colonel Davis of the 22nd Light Dragoons were also appointed Members of the Board, but their attendance was dispensed with, the former having been employed on another Duty, and the latter confined at home by ill health.

---

17   TNA, WO7/56/93-104: Various Departmental out-letters, Board of General Officers, reports miscellaneous.

The Board met on the 19 June 1811, when the Instructions of the Commander in Chief, with several other papers, received by the President from the Adjutant General were read and it appeared therefrom, that the object of His Royal Highness in convening the Board is 'to reduce into one established System the various Orders and Regulations at present in force, on the subject of the Clothing Equipment, Provision of Necessaries, and Appropriations of Pay, of the Cavalry,' and for this purpose, 'to simplify every Article of the Soldier's Equipment and to prepare him for active service, but without increasing the Expence to the Colonels of Regiments or making a larger deduction from the Soldier's Pay than is allowed by His Majesty's present regulations, so that a perfect uniformity, in all the above particulars, may be stablished in each Regiment of Cavalry, as connected with the branch of the Service to which it belongs'. The Opinion of the Board is also called for, upon the subject of Forge Carts and Shoeing. They are likewise desired to consider, 'whether it is expedient to recommend any, and what, deviations from the General Regulations which may hereafter be established, in the instance of Corps employed on particular Services Abroad' and to, 'suggest, for His Royal Highness's Consideration, and for the final Approbation of the Prince Regent,' such, 'Alterations in the existing regulations, upon any of the points referred to them, as from the experience of some years past, they may consider themselves founded in recommending'. The Board have endeavoured to keep these several objects distinctly in view, throughout the whole of their proceedings, and, as far as possible, to regulate their opinions, in every instance, conformably thereto.

The attention of the Board has been particularly directed to a minute inspection and examination of the sealed Patterns of Clothing, and other Articles of Cavalry Equipment at present in use; and they have caused new Patterns of several Articles, with such Alterations, or Improvements, as they deemed it expedient to suggest, to be made, for the purpose of accompanying this report.

The Board recommend that a Helmet be substituted for the Hat now worn by the Heavy Cavalry; and a pattern helmet marked no.1 made by Mr Cater of Pall Mall, and weighing Pounds Ounces is submitted for the approbation of His Royal Highness the Commander in Chief, accordingly.

The jackets no.2A and no.2B are recommended for the Heavy Cavalry, instead of the coats at present in use, and the leather breeches of pantaloons no.3A and 3B instead of the plush breeches- as also the grey overalls no.3C instead of the extra breeches- both for the heavy and light cavalry.

The boot recommended by the Board for the Heavy Cavalry (pattern no.4A) is that used by the 3rd regiment of Dragoons – it is a strong boot – made to cover up well with the top of the man's knee, when he is mounted, the seam in front. The top of the boot six inches deep, and of stronger leather than the leg. The advantage derived from the seam being in front is, that the boot does not give way to the putting on or off, which is often the case, when the seam is on the back of the boots, on which there is a constant stress. The boot no.4B is recommended for the light cavalry.

One pair of shoes appears to the Board to be a sufficient for a cavalry soldier, and they consider gaiters to be altogether unnecessary.

It appears from documents laid before the Board that the present expense to Colonels of Cavalry regiments, for providing boots and spurs may be calculated at about eight shillings per annum for each man- The Board, having taken into consideration all the circumstances connected with this subject, are of opinion that every regiment should be placed on precisely the same footing, in regard to the provision of the articles in question, and do therefore recommend that boots and spurs should in future, be considered as articles of regimental necessaries, to be furnished by the Dragoon; and that the Colonels should allow to each man two shillings annually, in aid of the expence of keeping up a proper supply thereof- which together with the saving to the Dragoon on certain articles referred to in the annexed schedule, will be fully sufficient for that purpose. The saving to the Colonels, upon these articles, to be applied to the provision of certain new articles of equipment proposed to be furnished by them, as herein after mentioned.

The Board recommend that a cloth valise – the colour of the clothing of the regiment, and of the pattern no.5 calculated to contain the regulated quantity of a soldier's necessaries be substituted for the leather one at present used both by the Heavy and Light cavalry- Its weight, when filled, not to exceed sixteen pounds.

The saddle pattern no.6 made by Mr Gibson of Coventry Street, and weighing 30 pounds with the housing and capes patterns no.16A and 16B (made by Mr Cuff of Curzon Street), and the bridle collar and Bredoon to act as a snaffle, pattern no.7 (made by Mr Mackintosh, of the Haymarket) are recommended by the Board for the Heavy Cavalry)

The sword waist belt and sabre tasche pattern no.15A are recommended for the Heavy and pattern no.15B for the Light cavalry.

The Board recommend that a black cap of the pattern no.8A for privates and no.8B for serjeants of Light Dragoons; and when serving in tropical climates a brown cap of the pattern no.8C for privates and no.8D for serjeants (all made by Messrs Bicknell and Moore of Bond Street.

The jacket no.9 is recommended by the Board for the light cavalry.

The Board recommend that the leather cap, called the watering cap, and heretofore furnished by the Colonels of regiments once in four years, be entirely abolished.

A sash of the pattern no.10A is recommended for the Heavy cavalry, and one of the pattern 10B for the light cavalry.

The re-adoption of the round cloak without sleeves, and of reduced dimensions, is recommended by the Board- the pattern no.11 for heavy and no.11A for light cavalry, as well for Officers as for men. They also recommend that a sabretache be in future considered as part of the necessary equipment, both of Officers and men of all cavalry regiments, and that the pattern no.12A be adopted for the men of the heavy, and no.12B for those of the light cavalry, the heavy dragoons to wear it close to the bely, the light dragoons in the same manner as the Hussars now wear it.

The Breast Plate for the heavy cavalry to remain as at present.

The Board approve of the carbine and pistol at present used by the heavy cavalry- the bayonet, which on regiments going abroad, is invariably ordered by Commanders in Chief on Foreign stations to be deposited in store, on account of its uselessness and weight, being laid aside; but the improved ramrod (attached by a swivel to the muzzle, as in the sealed pattern for the Light dragoons) is recommended for both. The disuse of the bayonet will of course, be attended with a considerable saving to the public.

want of attention on the part of the farriers, and the interest of the farriers to keep the troop well shod.

8th That the two farriers of each troop should be at all times with their troops, mounted upon horses broke to harness.

9th That the second farrier of each troop should be mounted upon a horse provided with traces; in order to be enabled to replace disabled horses, or to be put to, in order to aid the other horses, when required.

10th That eight men per troop to be selected from amongst those whose former occupations shall appear most likely to have qualified them in a certain degree, for such a duty- should be taught to shoe horses; that they should be provided with hammers and pincers, which they should constantly carry, at the expence of the farrier, who will have been relieved from the expence of keeping the forge carts in repair; that they should be employed, at the discretion of the commanding officer, both in aid of the farriers, in case of emergency, and to make up for their neglect should it occur; and that they should be paid for their work, at the usual rate of shoeing.

11th That each dragoon and hussar should carry as part of their baggage, four horse shoes and forty eight nails, the nails to be carried in the pouch, fitted up in the same manner as the pattern no.14. the horse shoes to be carried in leather bags, at each end of the valise within side.

12th That each farrier should at all times have in his possession, a complete set of shoes, and a set and a half of nails, for each horse to be carried in the forage carts; and

13th That a general regulation founded upon this basis (the substance of which is taken from the suggestions contained in the report and paper already referred to) should be established accordingly.

The Board are further of opinion that it cannot be too strongly impressed upon the minds of such commanding officers as have not been upon actual service, how absolutely necessary it is that their forge carts should be kept at all times very well horsed.

The Board do not conceive that it is expedient to recommend any other deviation from the existing regulations, in regard to corps employed on particular service abroad, than those which may have already been suggested in this report, unless it be with respect to the clothing of the light cavalry serving in India; which it is the opinion of the Board, founded upon the experience of some of the members who have served in that country, should be the same as is used at home, namely Blue- which will obviate the disadvantage to which the present clothing being Grey, is subject, from the necessity of washing, which occasions it to shrink. The Board are also of the opinion that that the cap should be covered with light coloured cloth instead of black.

Great George Street, signed Ernest. General, 13 July 1811.

NB The whole of the patterns referred to in this report not having yet been received back from the different persons by whom they were made; the several patterns, together with the schedule, which contains the prices thereof, and various observations respecting the same, will be transmitted to the Commander-in-Chief, as soon as possible.

In order that the wish and intention of the Commander in Chief, with respect to 'reducing into one established system the various orders and regulations at present in force on the subject of clothing, equipment, provision of necessaries, and appropriation of pay, of the cavalry'. May be fully carried into effect, it appears to the Board to be desirable that a Paper, containing the substance of such parts of every existing regulation upon reach of these points, as it may be necessary to retain, together with such alterations, or new rules, as it may be expedient to propose, should be drawn up, and the whole, when regularly arranged under the proper heads, be submitted, in the first instance, to the consideration of this, or of some other Board of officers, and afterwards to that of His Royal Highness the Commander in Chief, and the Secretary at war, as a draught or outline, of a warrant to be finally laid before the Prince Regent, and the same, when sanctioned by His Royal highness's approbation and signature, to be considered as the only standing regulation for the future guidance and government of the cavalry, upon all points embraced in it, and if this suggestion should be approved of, they beg leave to recommend that the secretary to the Board of General Officers may be directed to prepare a draught of such paper, for that purpose accordingly.

Great George Street, signed Ernest General, 13 July 1811.

Schedule of the different articles of clothing, necessaries and appointments at present used by regiments of cavalry, and of those proposed to be substituted in lieu thereof, in cases where alterations are recommended by the Board, with an estimate of the price of each article.

Heavy cavalry

Articles of Clothing at present furnished by the Colonels with an estimate of the annual amount thereof.

Annually.

One hat 10s 6d

One pair of gloves 1s 6d

Once every two years.

One coat 24s 6d or 12s 3d per year

One waistcoat, with sleeves 14s 3d or 7s 1.5d per year

One pair of breeches 17s 6d or 8s 9d per year

Total per annum of £2 0s 1.5d

Article of Clothing proposed to be furnished by the colonels, with an estimate of the annual amount thereof.

Annually.

One helmet (pattern no.1) to last six years 23s Expence of repairing the same during that period – 12s Per year 5s 10d

One pair of gloves 1sd 6

Once every two years.

One jacket (Pattern no.2A and 2B) 26s or 13s per year

One waistcoat with sleeves 14s 3d or 7s 1.5d per year

One pair of leather breeches or pantaloons (patterns 3A and 3B) 28s* or 14s per year

Total per annum of £2 1s 5.5p

It is understood that the breeches may be procured for 26s, pantaloons are 28s.

Although it appears that there is an increase of one shilling and fourpence per annum upon the sum total of the articles specified in the second column, it is to be observed that such increase of expence will not be equal to what might be expected to take place, were the articles at present in use, to be continued; it having been represented to the Board by Messrs Pearce, that a considerable advance has taken place in the price of Plush, and that the breeches made of that article could consequently no longer be furnished for 17s 6p; the proposed alterations may therefore be considered, upon the whole, as not unfavourable to the Colonels.

Light Cavalry.
Articles of Clothing at present furnished by the Colonels with an estimate of the annual amount thereof.
Once every three years.
One helmet 19s or 6s 4d per year.
Annually.
One pair of gloves. 1s 6d
Once in every two years.
One upper jacket 25s 8d or 12s 10d per year
One under jacket 15s 3d or 7s 7.5d per year
One flannel waistcoat 3s 6d
One pair of leather breeches 28s or 14s per year
Once every four years.
One watering cap. 6s or 1s 6d per year
Total per annum of £2 5s 6.5d

Article of Clothing proposed to be furnished by the colonels, with an estimate of the annual amount thereof.
One cap (pattern 8A) to last two years 10s 6d or 5s 3d per year.
Annually.
One pair of gloves. 1s 6d
Once every two years.
One upper jacket (pattern no.9) 24s or 12s per year.
One under jacket 15s 3d or 7s 7.5d per year.
One flannel waistcoat 3s 6d or 1s 9d per year
One pair of leather pantaloons (Pattern 3B) 28s or 14s per year
Total per annum £2 2s 1.5d

NB The difference in favour of the colonels of light cavalry according to this estimate, will be 5s 5d per man, per annum.[18]

---

18 TNA, WO7/56/117: Various Departmental out-letters, Board of General Officers, reports miscellaneous.

2

The Regulation of 1799–1800

It is perhaps not seemly that a book on the regulation of the army between 1800 and 1815 should commence the lists of regulations with a chapter on the regulation of 1799 combined with that of 1800. It will equally be found that the last chapter on regulation covered in the second volume will be that of 1815-1816. The reason behind this aberration is that certain orders both prior to 1800, and post 1815, must necessarily be reproduced, because of their bearing on what happened in the period of study. By including several of these orders we can enhance our understanding of changes in period. For instance, the changes in infantry regulation cap wear between 1800 and 1815 can be represented as follows. In 1800 a cap is first introduced for the universal use of the infantry. In 1806 a second revised model is adopted, and in 1812, a third, final model of cap is issued, before the advent of the first true 'shako' (a leather topped cap) for the infantry in August 1815. The first cap model lasted six years, as did the second, but the third was in service for a mere four years. This has been construed as reflecting badly on the utility or appearance of the third model: the model was swiftly withdrawn, and therefore it must have been unpopular, poorly constructed, or both, runs the reasoning. However, by examining the situation post-1815, we find that the regulated cap of late 1815 was replaced in 1816,[1] and again in 1817.[2] With this perspective added, by comparison the 1812 Waterloo or Belgic cap appears a model of good favour and longevity. Either the caps that succeeded it were very bad models indeed, or the reigning influence of fashion, and love of novelty, as expressed through the Prince Regent's influence over uniform design, was proving superior to the advantages of practicality.

Just two regulations are included for 1799. The first deals with staff dress, and is of especial interest as it forms the basis of the successive changes in staff uniform that would be made every two years throughout the period. The ability to track these changes is really helpful in dating portraits and other iconographic material.

The dress of staff officers was one of the most rigorously controlled areas of dress in the service. The requirement for aides de camp to represent their masters meant that the extent to which they followed or departed from regulation on dress was that of the general officer

---

1   TNA, WO123/131-315: Army Circulars, Memoranda, Orders and Regulations. Adjutant-General's office, Horse Guards, General Orders.
2   TNA, WO123/137: Army Circulars, Memoranda, Orders and Regulations. Adjutant-General's office, Horse Guards, General Orders.

the particular aide represented. Wellington took a famously lax approach to the dress of his immediate staff on service, but the same did not apply at home, or on grand occasions, when a strict adherence to form was *de rigeur*. If the staff officers were sometimes imposed upon to subject their personal taste to the exigencies of high society they were at least recompensed by a uniform that underwent frequent changes and modifications, and which compensated them by reflecting the latest style, according to Horse Guards at least. A French staff officer recalls the very similar requirements in his own service,

> We had all got ourselves up in gala array, so as to be worthy of the grand occasion. Fashion, which controls the costumes of soldiers as rigorously as those of ladies, has changed so much since then that the day will doubtless come when many will be interested in knowing what uniforms were worn by aides de camp on occasions such as this, so I will describe the dress of the little group to which I belonged.[3]

31 January, 1799. Regulation on staff dress

> Adjutant General to Forces,
> His Majesty having, on several occasions, remarked a want of uniformity in the dress of staff-officers, HRH the Commander in Chief is pleased to direct that the following regulations on this head, which have been established by the King's order, shall be strictly complied with:
> The dress of the Adjutant-general, the Quarter-master general, and Barrack-master general, is the same as the frock uniform of lieutenant-generals, in silver.
> The dress of the deputy Adjutant-general, the deputy Quarter-master general, and deputy Barrack-master general, is the same as the frock uniform of major-Generals, in silver.
> Any of the above staff officers, being general officers, are permitted to wear, in silver, the button appropriated to officers of that rank, instead of the raised staff button, which is commonly in use.
> The Adjutant and Quarter-master general of the forces, the Barrack-master general in England, and their respective deputies, as also aides-de-camp of His Majesty, and of HRH the Commander in Chief, are distinguished exclusively, by wearing two epaulettes.
> All other Adjutants-general, Quarter-masters general, and Barrack-masters general, with their deputies, wear one epaulette, on the left shoulder.
> Aides-de-camp to general officers of cavalry wear one epaulette, on the left shoulder; those attached to general officers of infantry, one epaulette, on the right shoulder.
> The uniform to be used in future, by Assistant Adjutants-general, Assistant Quarter-masters general, and by majors of brigade, is to be in silver, the same as the uniform prescribed for aides-de-camp; but the two former officers, viz. the

---

3   L. Lejeune, *Memoirs du General Lejeune* (London: Firmin-Didot, 1895), p.92.

Assistant Adjutants-general and the Assistant Quarter-masters general, are to be distinguished, by wearing two epaulettes.

Majors of brigade, attached to brigades of cavalry wear one epaulette, on the left shoulder; those attached to brigades of infantry, wear one epaulette on the right shoulder. The buttons used by Assistant Adjutants-general, Assistant Quarter-masters general, aides-de-camp (with the exception of His Majesty's) and majors of brigade, are plain. These uniforms and distinctions are, by His Majesty's command, appropriated exclusively to the officers above specified.

His Majesty is graciously pleased to permit generals, and the staff officers above mentioned, to appear in the field in plain uniforms; but they are at all times to wear the distinguishing epaulette or epaulettes, buttons and facings as above prescribed; and their dress is, in every other particular, to be most pointedly exact and uniform.

By order of HRH the Commander in Chief.

Harry Calvert, Colonel, Adjutant-General of the Forces.[4]

12 August, 1799. General Order on serjeant's sashes

Adjutant General to Forces,
The Commander-in-Chief having observed that the serjeants of some regiments of cavalry and infantry having lately appeared in plain crimson sashes, HRH is pleased to direct that in future the most scrupulous attention shall be paid to this part of the serjeants' appointments, and that His Majesty's regulations relating thereto shall be strictly observed, viz, that the serjeant's sashes shall be made of crimson worsted, intermixed with the colour of the facings of the regiment; and in those regiments which have crimson or scarlet facings, white is to be intermixed with the crimson groundwork, instead of the colour of the facings of the regiment.

Harry Calvert Adjutant General.[5]

The second order contains an easily overlooked peculiarity in the dress of serjeants, the facing coloured stripe in their sash. This mark of distinction would endure throughout the period under study. Other than this, the sashes of serjeants were not altered at all. The other changes in serjeant's distinctions were the shoulder knot giving way to the chevrons in 1802, and the institution of the appointment of colour-serjeant, with its colourful badge, in 1813.

Sashes of officers were to make some changes driven by fashion, with some regiments, notably the two rifle corps (5/60th and 95th) adopting the barrel sash that properly belonged to the hussars, and then changing along with much of the rest of the light infantry to the whipcord sash, which differed from the line infantry sash, in that it terminated in long woven tasselled cords, that could be worn looped down from the body of the sash. No official regulation has been found for the introduction or use of this whipcord sash variation. Its use can be inferred solely from images, survivals in museums, and a couple of contemporary

---

4   TNA, WO123/120/12: Army Circulars, Memoranda, Orders and Regulations. Army Regulations, etc from Various Sources.
5   TNA, WO123/128/17: Army Circulars, Memoranda, Orders and Regulations. Adjutant General's Office (Horse Guards).

'British staff officer in undress uniform', 1805. Robert Dighton Junior. (Anne S.K. Brown Military Collection, Brown University Library)

references in memoirs, tailors' books, and letters. Perhaps the earliest mention of this particular style is in the 1813 Standing Orders of the 85th Light Infantry, which detail for officer's full dress, 'The belt to be of buff leather… over which is to be constantly worn what is called, the light infantry sash'.[6]

Occasionally a regiment would have a peculiarity of its own, for instance, an inspection report of the 80th Foot from 1815 states that the officers were, 'wearing cavalry pattern sash'.[7] A Board of General Officers report of 19 June 1811 for the purpose of reporting upon the equipment of the cavalry, lists two cavalry sashes, 'A sash of the pattern no.10A is recommended for the Heavy cavalry, and one of the pattern 10B for the light cavalry'.[8] It is not known which of these two pattern models the officers of the 80th had adopted.

1800 saw the introduction of a new warrant for clothing that was intended to be published on 9 April that year. As the letter below reveals, the draught had to be returned to the Board of General Officers for Clothing to allow some last minute revisions to be made. The revised version was resubmitted on 26 April, which gives some idea of the time scale involved in preparing these publications. The warrant was to remove almost all of what had formerly been paid to the colonel to supply what had constituted the half mounting,[9] and instead credit the soldier with an equivalent sum, that was to be expended on a similar list of items that fell into the category of necessaries. The previous warrant of 1797 had been the last with a full quantity of half mountings – which were now to be phased out as a relic of the 18th Century.

The 1800 warrant also included the order for caps that had been issued in February while the warrant was still in preparation. This was the beginning of the story of the caps that were to define the British Army for the next fifteen years. The British Army issued caps universally to the infantry other ranks from 1800, and revised the pattern three times during that period: in 1806, 1812 and 1815. The first cap replaced the ultimate version of the cocked hat. In period terminology a hat was head-wear with a brim (even if cocked), whereas the term cap described head-wear without a brim, and so cap was also used in the term 'helmet-cap' that was used by Horse Guards to describe what we now call the Tarleton helmet. It was not until 1816 that the British infantry began to term the fourth, latest, model of cap a shako. The British cavalry had adopted a 'chacot' or 'chaco' in 1810, but the infantry continued to refer to their headwear as a cap throughout the period, the term shako can properly only be applied retrospectively. The terms 'stovepipe', used to describe the first two models, and 'belgic', for the third or 1812 model, are also not contemporary but are evocative later constructs. As we shall see Horse Guards termed these items 'a pattern cap' or 'a new pattern cap' and naturally the soldiers developed nicknames for each model.[10] The first 1800 cap was known colloquially at the time as the 'smoke-jack', the second 1806 cap the 'sugar-loaf' and the third 1812 cap as the 'bang-up' or 'Wellington cap'. Bang up is defined

6   Anon. *Standing Orders and Regulations for the 85th Light Infantry* (London: Thomas Egerton, 1813), p.86.
7   The National Archives TNA, WO/27/135 Office of the Commander in Chief and War Office: Adjutant-general and army council: inspection returns.
8   The National Archives TNA, WO7/56/117 Report of the proceedings of a Board of General Officers, assembled by Order of His Royal Highness the Commander in Chief, at no.19 Great George Street for 'the purpose of reporting upon the Equipment of the Cavalry'.
9   Charles James, *A New and Enlarged Military Dictionary* (London, Egerton, 1805).
10   T. Connolly, *History of the Royal Sappers and Miners* (London: Longham, Brown and Green, 1855), Vol.I, p.134.

by period dictionaries as, 'Quite the thing, hellish fine. Well done. Compleat. Dashing'.[11] For convenience, I have appended a date to each mention of 'pattern cap' in order to distinguish the successive developments.

It is my intention here to list only the caps issued to private soldiers through the regimental purchase system. This 18th century system had survived into the 19th century and required the colonel of a regiment, or colonel commandant for regiments with multiple battalions to purchase clothing, including caps, from a contractor through a regimental agent. The colonel then recouped his outlay from government at an agreed rate. Officers were required by regulation only to equip themselves with a cap, or caps, similar (so not necessarily identical) to those of the men.[12] The choice of cap maker and style of cap was controlled by the colonel of the battalion or regiment, and the degree of control ran the whole gamut from no imposition at all, through a light description of the cap required, to prescribed cap makers and styles, and in some cases, caps being bought by the colonel and supplied through the quartermaster to the officers to ensure uniformity. In practice this meant that officers' headwear was prone to be more fashion-led, tailored to individual taste or colonel's vagaries, depending on the regiment, and also naturally of a higher quality. Crucially, although each colonel-commandant of battalion suggested a cap maker to his officers, they were not always absolutely required to follow his recommendation, so officer's caps cannot be considered strictly regulated in the way that the men's were. However, even if constructed of infinitely better materials, they generally seem to have followed the style of regimental caps closely, as we shall see when images of officers in caps are examined. These images are necessary to our study owing to the relative paucity of images of other ranks or surviving other ranks caps.

Our inquiry is focussed on the first three caps which were distinguished as follows.

- In 1800 the first infantry cap of felt with a plume centre front was issued. It was lacquered or shellac'd.[13]
- In 1806 a similar pattern of felt cap without the lacquer was substituted.[14]
- In 1812, a third pattern with a raised front and a side plume was introduced perhaps as a result of Wellington's desire to create a distinctive silhouette for his forces in Spain.[15]

In addition to this regular issue of new sealed patterns for the army, some orders related to minor changes in the cap are pertinent, and others are unique to either light Infantry, rifle corps, or both.

The first model of cap was trialled by the 5/60th as early as 1797, and by the 16th, 22nd, 34th, and 65th Foot in 1798.[16] This accorded with the standard method of trialling kit used by the Georgian army. This form of experimentation involved small quantities of proposed new equipment, say 10 or 20 units, being issued to several battalions whose colonel then

11   Grose, F. *Dictionary of the Vulgar Tongue* (London: Egan, 1811), p.11.
12   Adjutant General's Office, *General Regulations and Orders for the Army 1811* (London: Clowes,1811), p.376.
13   TNA, WO26/39 Warrant for compensation, dated 1803, for lacquered felt caps.
14   TNA, WO7/56/95 Various Departmental out-letters. Board of General Officers, reports, miscellaneous.
15   Adjutant-General's office, *General Regulations and Orders for the Army 1811* (London: Clowes,1811), p.376
16   B. Fosten, and G. Gibbs, *The British Infantry Shako 1800-1897* (London: Military Historical Society, 2008), p.4.

reported back to the Adjutant General on the utility of the new item. Sometimes several different versions were sent out to different regiments.[17] It appears these at least some of these early models of proto-cap may have been of leather since in 1799 a sketch of the cap to be made of felt instead of leather was forwarded to HRH the Commander in Chief.[18] By 11 December 1799 a model of this cap in felt had been approved by the King, and on 24 February 1800 Horse Guards issued the General Order to adopt the new headwear.

The cap was composed of a felt crown, 8 inches high and 7 inches in diameter: it was shaped as a cylinder and flat at the top. The felt was lacquered by an unrecorded process. Some surviving models have an unfolding fall internally or externally to cover the neck. There was a leather sector peak over the eyes extending 2.5 inches at the apex of the curve. A thin brass die struck plate of universal pattern occupied the front. The plates measured 6.25 by 4 inches, but were not used by the rifle regiments: 'The Rifle Corps not to wear the brass fronting on their caps, but in lieu to have a bugle and crown with a green cord round the cap'.[19]

A black Hanoverian cockade of tooled leather was at centre top, held by a button of regimental pattern, behind which was a central plume or tuft holder, usually internal. All measurements are by nature approximate, variations being common in surviving examples.

Further details on this first pattern of cap are found in the collection of warrants today known as the 1802 collation, and reproduced here as an appendix.

> Caps made of Felt and Leather with a Brass Plates, Cockade and Tuft (conformable to a Pattern left at the Controller Office for Army Accounts) to be Worn, instead of Hats, by the Non-Commissioned Officers, Drummers, Fifers and Privates of the Guards and be every Description of Corps of Infantry, excepting the Highland Corps, who are, when in Europe, N. America, to continue to wear the Highland Bonnet, but when in the East and West Indies, are to wear the Felt Caps similar to other Regiments. They are to be made of sufficient size to come completely on the head. To be worn straight and even and brought well forward over the eyes. The felt cap and the tuft is to be supplied annually. The leather part, brass plate and leather cockade once in every two years. It is permitted to engrave the number of the Regiment on each side of the Lion, on the lower part of the brass fronting (plate) and those regiments that are entitled to badges are permitted to bear them in the centre of the Garter. The Grenadiers who are allowed to wear these caps occasionally may also bear the Grenade in the same manner as other regiments wear their badges. The tufts worn by the Battalion Company to be white with a red bottom, by the grenadier company to be all white and by the Light Infantry to be dark green. The whole to wear the button of their respective Regiments in the centre of the cockade, excepting the Grenadiers who are to have a grenade. The Rifle Corps not to wear the brass fronting on their caps, but in lieu to have a bugle and crown with a green cord round the cap. The serjeants, buglers and rank and file to wear green feathers.[20]

---

17   TNA, WO3/367/429: Office of the Commander-in-Chief: Out-letters, letters to regimental officers.
18   Fosten and Gibbs, *The British Infantry Shako 1800-1897*, p.4.
19   See Appendix 1, 1802 collation, para 37a.
20   See Appendix 1, 1802 collation, para 37a.

That the cap was intended to be lacquered and continued to be so is demonstrated in numerous references. For instance in 1805 a letter regarding compensation details them as such.[21] The author has found one anomalous letter from the 96th Foot dated 1804 in which the regiment details why they are not using lacquered caps. Their excuse? That they had caps to use up before adopting the lacquered cap. Since the lacquered cap was the first model adopted, presumably the 96th had acquired non-regulation caps and were being taken to task by the Commander in Chief, through the Army Inspectors.[22]

The last order of 1800 is a request to army clothiers to forward information on lace and loopings to the Adjutant General's office. This information is contained in the 1802 collation reproduced in chapter seven and it is tempting to consider this as evidence that the 1802 collation was being assembled at this time.

24 February, 1800. General Orders for infantry

> Adjutant General to infantry,
> It is His Majesty's pleasure, that in the future the use of hats is to be entirely abolished throughout the whole of the infantry of the army; and that instead thereof, caps are to be worn, of which a sealed pattern has, by order of HRH the Commander-in-Chief, been deposited in the office of the comptrollers of army accounts, there to be had recourse to, as occasion may require.
>
> His Majesty is pleased to permit the colonels to engrave the number of their respective regiments on each side of the lion, on the lower part of the brass fronting; and likewise to the regiments, which are entitled to that distinction, His Majesty grants permission to bear their badges in the centre of the garter. The grenadiers, who are allowed to wear these caps occasionally when they do not use their proper grenadier caps, may, if their colonels choose it, bear the grenade in the same manner as regiments entitled to them, wear their badges. It is His Majesty's pleasure, that the tufts, used by the grenadiers, shall be white; those of the light infantry (who are likewise included in this order) dark green.
>
> All soldiers shall wear the button of their respective regiment in the centre of the cockade, except the grenadiers, who will use the grenade.
>
> The caps are to be made of a sufficient size, to come completely on the soldiers' heads: they are to be worn straight and even, and brought forward well over the eyes.
>
> The field and staff officers, as also the officers of battalion companies, are to continue to wear hats as usual. The grenadier officers are permitted to wear hats when their men do not parade in dress caps. The officers of the light companies are to wear caps similar to those ordered for the light infantry.
>
> Harry Calvert Adjutant General.[23]

21 TNA, WO26/39/220: Entry Books of Warrants.
22 TNA, WO3/152/420: Office of the Commander-in-Chief, general letters.
23 TNA, WO123/128/23: Army Circulars, Memoranda, Orders and Regulations. Adjutant-General's Office, (Horse Guards) General Orders.

An interesting correction to bring a troop within the same regulation as the rest of the regiment. The original reason for the waistcoats being non-uniform in this troop is not clear.

1 March, 1800. Letter regarding waistcoats of 5th Dragoon Guards

> Adjutant General to clothing board,
> I have the honour to acquaint you for the information of the clothing board, that HRH the Commander-in-Chief has been pleased to approve of the waistcoats of the clothing for the ninth troop of the 5th dragoon guards being made of white, instead of red cloth, that it may be in uniform with the present clothing of the regiment.
> Harry Calvert Adjutant General.[24]

This letter refers to the drafting of the 1800 warrant, and the process of revision and proposal. Giving an idea of the process by which such warrants were approved.

7 March 1800. Letter,

> Adjutant General to Comptroller's Office, Whitehall,
> Sir, The general officers appointed by His Majesty's warrant to transact all matters relative to the clothing of the army having revised the draught of a new regulation and paid due attention to the subject of the highland dress, as likewise to the clothing of the 5th battalion of the 60th and the black regiments, have directed me to return the draught to you in the amended state, together with a list approved by them of articles of clothing for the corps above named as distinct from other regiments of the line. And I am to request that you will transmit the same to the Secretary at war, in order that a warrant may be proposed and laid before the King for His Majesty's approbation.
> On behalf of the Adjutant general.[25]

30 September, 1800. Circular to clothiers

> Adjutant General to all army clothiers,
> The Adjutant General's compliments to 'blank', and request he will transmit as soon as possible to the officer in Crown Street, Westminster, patterns of the facings, with the lace and the methods of looping the button holes of all the regiments, cavalry and infantry, to which he is a clothier, made exactly to the size of the enclosed card.
> Adjutant General's office.[26]

This is an interesting survival, which shows that the Adjutant General's office was requesting information on specifics of uniform from the clothiers who had developed peculiarities in conjunction with the regiments. It is conceivable that the information so requested and

---

24   TNA, WO7/32/45: Various Departmental out-letters. Board of General Officers.
25   TNA, WO7/32/45: Various Departmental out-letters. Board of General Officers, clothing.
26   TNA, WO123/134/58: Army Circulars, Memoranda, Orders and Regulations. Adjutant-General's Office, (Horse Guards).

gathered was used to compile the 1802 collation, reproduced here as an appendix and discussed in a later chapter.

The full text of the 1800 warrant

1800 Warrant, 9 April,
Regulation relative to the clothing and half mounting of the infantry; and of the clothing of the army in general.

Whereas the Commander-in-Chief of our forces, and the general officers comprising with him Our permanent Clothing Board, have submitted to us their opinion upon the several particulars referred to their consideration, touching the clothing of Our army, and the expediency of making some change in the articles supplied to our soldiers under the name of half mounting, which opinion hath been entirely approved by Us; we are therefore pleased to authorise and direct that such of Our former regulations respecting clothing, as are not in conformity to these orders hereinafter given, be, and they are, hereby annulled; and that, in future, the following regulations be duly observed in the several points to which they apply.

In a regiment of infantry of the line, or fencible infantry serving in Europe, in North America, or at the Cape of Good Hope (Highland Corps excepted), each serjeant, corporal, drummer and private man shall have annually,
For clothing,
A coat
A waistcoat, or waistcoat front.
A pair of breeches; unlined, except the waistband, and with one pocket only.
A cap made of felt and leather, with brass plate, cockade and tuft, conformable to a pattern approved by us, and lodged at the office of the comptrollers of the accounts of Our army; the felt crown of the cap, cockade and tuft to be supplied annually; the leather part and brass plate, every two years.
And in lieu of the former small articles of clothing, called half mounting, and of the breeches lining,
Two pair of good shoes of the value of five shillings and sixpence each pair.
Each serjeant shall also be credited with the sum of three shillings, being the difference between the value of the former articles of half mounting for a serjeant and private man.

In the Highland corps on the above stations, each serjeant, corporal, drummer and private man shall have annually,
For Clothing,
A coat;
A waistcoat;
A bonnet;
And a pair of hose;
Six yards of plaid once in every two years; and a purse every seven years:
And in lieu of the former small articles of clothing called half mounting,

Two pair of shoes of the value above mentioned. Each serjeant shall also be credited with the sum of three shillings; being the difference of the value of his half mounting as above stated.

In a regiment of infantry serving in the West Indies (except the 5th battalion of Our 60th regiment and the regiments of people of colour) each serjeant, corporal, drummer and private man shall have annually
  For Clothing,
  A coat, unlined, except the breast facing and turn-up at the skirts;
  A waistcoat complete, of milled serge, with sleeves of the same; with regimental buttons, collar and cuff (agreeable, as to size and quality to as pattern lodged at the office of Our said comptrollers: the saving of one shilling for the lining of the coat to be applied in the purchase of the waistcoat; and the men paying for the sleeves as a part of their regimental necessaries;
  A pair of linen Trowsers;
  A cap, cockade and tuft as above specified and in lieu of the former small articles of clothing called half mounting,
  Two pair of good shoes: of the value of five shillings and sixpence each pair.
  Each serjeant is also to be credited with the sum of three shillings fro the difference of the value of his half mounting, as above stated.

In the 5th battalion of Our 60th regiment, each serjeant shall have annually,
  For Clothing,
  A green coat
  A white serge waistcoat,
  A hat;
  A pair of blue pantaloons; and for half mounting,
  Two pair of shoes of the quality and value abovementioned: but he is not to be credited, as in other corps, with the sum of three shillings for the difference of half mounting, as he receives an equivalent in the difference between the value of the pantaloons and of breeches.
  Each corporal, drummer and private man shall have annually,
  For Clothing,
  A green coat;
  A white serge waistcoat,
  A hat;
  A pair of blue pantaloons, and for half mounting,
  Two pair of shoes, of the quality and value aforementioned; but towards the price of which the colonels shall only pay 4s 6d a pair, the men paying the difference in consideration of their being furnished with pantaloons instead of breeches.

In a regiment composed of people of colour, each serjeant, corporal, drummer and private man shall have annually,
  For Clothing
  A red cloth jacket

A round hat and cockade

Two pair of Russia duck Trowsers;

Together with a grey kersey greatcoat, to last two years, and for half mounting,

One pair of shoes, of the quality and value abovementioned, and one pair of shoe soles.

Each serjeant shall also be credited with the sum of three shillings being the difference in value of his half mounting, as above stated.

In a regiment of infantry serving in the East Indies, each serjeant shall have annually,

For Clothing,

A coat, unlined, except the breast facing, and turn-up at the skirts;

A cap, cockade and tuft, as before specified; and a compensation in value,

For the waistcoat front and buttons, 4s and 11d

For a pair of breeches 10s 9d

Lining for the coat, 1s 2d

Total 16s 10d

And in lieu of the former small articles of clothing called half mounting,

Two pair of good shoes, of the value of five shillings and sixpence each pair; and further the sum of three shillings for the difference of the value of his half mounting as above stated. Each corporal, drummer and private man shall have annually,

For clothing

A coat, unlined, except the breast facing and turn-up of the skirts;

A cap, cockade and tuft, as above specified and a compensation in value,

For the waistcoat front and buttons, 1s 9d

For a pair of breeches, 4s 6d

Lining for the coat, 1s

Total 7s 3d

And in lieu of the small articles of clothing called half mounting,

Two pair of good shoes, of the value of five shillings and sixpence each pair.

The clothing of regiments on foreign stations is not to be furnished in materials, but is to be sent out made up, except in instances where We shall be pleased to grant a special dispensation through Our Commander-in-Chief, or Secretary at War.

The shoes ordered to be substituted for the former articles of half mounting, are to be provided in conformity to a pattern lodged at the office of the comptrollers of the accompts of Our army, and patterns of the shoes are to be approved and sealed by the general officers of our Clothing Board, at the same time and in like manner, as for the clothing: one pair is to be delivered out of the annual period of clothing, and the other pair at the end of six months from that time, and in order to prevent the injury that the shoes might sustain from remaining a long time in store in the East and West Indies, they shall be forwarded to corps on those stations at two different periods, instead of sending the whole quantity with the clothing.

Should the price of good shoes at any time exceed five shillings and sixpence a pair, the difference, which shall be declared by Our Clothing Board at their first meeting on or after the 25 of April in each year is to be charged to the respective accounts of the non-commissioned officers and soldiers receiving them; but with respect to the 5th battalion of Our 60th regiment, the difference is to be taken between four shillings and sixpence paid by the colonel, and the actual price declared as abovementioned.

Highland corps in the East and West Indies, are to conform to the species of clothing and half mounting used by other corps of infantry on the same station.

The allowances directed to be given by the colonels as above stated in lieu of parts of the clothing, and of the former small articles of clothing known as half mounting, are to be regularly credited to the men, and to be expended for their use in such articles as are suitable to the respective climates in which they shall be serving.

Certificates of the credits having been properly given, and of the money having been actually expended for the use of the men are to be signed by the respective commanding officers, and to be transmitted half yearly through the adjutant general, to Our Clothing Board, care being taken to provide against accidents by sending a duplicate of each certificate by a subsequent opportunity.

Sealed patterns of the clothing and shoes furnished in lieu of the smaller articles, shall in future be sent to, and remain deposited at, the headquarters of every corps of infantry as well as at home, in order that the new clothing and shoes may be compared therewith at any convenient time by the general officers commanding on the respective stations abroad and in the several districts at home, or by the officers who may be appointed to inspect the said clothing and shoes: and certificates of the conformity thereof to the sealed patterns and of the same having been delivered in due time to the men, shall be in future transmitted by such general or other officers as aforesaid through the Adjutant General to Our Clothing Board. And to obviate any inconvenience that might otherwise arise from the want of such view of the clothing being taken at an early period, it is hereby directed that in each regiment abroad or at home, the commanding officer present with the corps when the clothing is received together with the two officers next in seniority, not under the rank of captain, do, immediately on its arrival, make a strict inspection into the same, and do cause to be drawn out an accurate state of the quality, quantity and condition thereof; which state he shall transmit, through the Adjutant general of Our forces, to Our Clothing Board: and it is our pleasure that such state shall be entered in the regimental books, for the future inspection of such superior officer as may be ordered from time to time to inspect or review the regiment.

And whereas it appears highly expedient, that a uniform rule should be laid down in regard to the claims of soldiers of infantry to clothing, and to the shoes substituted in lieu of half mounting, at stated times, or broken periods; and to the rates at which compensation shall be made, in such cases as shall admit of a payment in money in lieu of the articles in kind, under the restrictions thereafter mentioned; We do hereby declare, and make known, that non-commissioned officers and soldiers of infantry, dying or discharged before the completion of a full year from the usual day of delivering the annual clothing of their regiment have no demand whatever on account thereof.

If a serjeant is reduced to the ranks, his clothing is to be given in for the use of his successor, and he himself will receive private's clothing equally worn (or as nearly as may be) with the clothing he has given in.

A recruit who comes into the regiment after the proper time of the delivery of the clothing shall be immediately entitled to clothing of that year, as good as that in wear by the next of the regiment; and to a pair of shoes at the next delivery of that article: and he shall be entitled to new clothing (shoes included) at the next period of general delivery to the regiment.

It is the duty of the colonels, and of those employed by them, to take especial care that the annual clothing be forwarded and delivered to their respective corps, as near the stated periods as possible; and few cases ought to arrive in which it should become a question whether an allowance in money might not be substituted by the colonels in lieu of delivering in kind the articles which by Our regulations they are required to furnish, but if, from any extraordinary circumstances of the service, such an instance should be supposed to have occurred in any of our regiments serving abroad, the grounds on which a commutation in money is proposed, should be fully stated to the Commander-in-Chief, or when there is no Commander-in-Chief, to Our Secretary at war, in order that Our pleasure may be previously taken thereupon.

If he should think proper to signify Our approbation of the measure, the following sums being the estimated amount of what the colonels would have paid to their clothiers after a reasonable deduction for incidental charges to which they are liable, shall be given to the men:

To each serjeant,
Clothing £2 18s
Half mounting 14s
Total £3 12s
To each corporal, drummer and private,
Clothing £1 5s 6d
Half mounting 11s
£1 16s 6d

And whereas in consequence of the orders herein given for substituting a new species of half mounting in lieu of the former articles of which it was composed, it is necessary to revise and amend the list of necessaries annexed to our warrant of the 25 May 1797 and therein directed to be provided by stoppages from the pay of the non-commissioned officers and men, so far as regards Our corps of infantry of the line and fencible infantry serving at home; Our will and pleasure is that from and after the 25th day of December next, the same stoppage of one shilling and sixpence per week shall continue to be made from the pay of the said corps; but that the same shall be expended (in the manner directed by Our said warrant) for the use of the men in the articles specified in the schedule annexed to this Our warrant, instead of those contained in the list above referred to: and it is Our further will and pleasure that no further stoppage be made at home from their pay without the sanction of a regimental court martial or court of enquiry, except for the extra price of shoes beyond five shillings and sixpence a pair, and for the straps for carrying their greatcoats.

Finally, We declare it to be Our intention, that all colonels, commanding officers, or other officers who shall direct or permit any alteration whatever to be made in any part of the clothing or appointments so that the same shall differ in the smallest degree from the patterns of the several articles sealed by Our Clothing Board, and sent to the respective regiments or shall allow any deviation from Our existing regulations for the clothing and appointments of our forces, shall be considered as guilty of disobedience of orders, and be liable to such punishment for the same as by general court martial shall be awarded.

And to prevent ignorance of these regulations being pleaded in excuse of not having conformed thereto, it is Our pleasure that a copy of the same be inserted in the orderly book of every regiment of cavalry and infantry in our service,

Given this 9th day of April 1800 in the fortieth year of Our reign

By His Majesty's command,

W. Windham.[27]

---

27   TNA, WO26/38: Entry Books of Warrants, Regulations and Precedents.

3

The Influence of Volunteer Style and Rifle Fashion

Contemporary assessment of the military value of the volunteers was often less than a complete endorsement. On a particularly fussy volunteer statement of embodiment that insisted, 'The association will never be required to serve outside the country', Prime Minister Pitt pithily scrawled in the margin, 'except in case of actual invasion'.[1] His cynicism did not prevent him from raising his own volunteer force, and serving with it. Anecdote suggests that when Pitt asked Sir John Moore where his battalions of volunteers would be deployed in the event of invasion, Moore replied that they would be drawn up on the hills to present a formidable appearance to the enemy, while the real soldiers would be fighting on the beach.[2]

Rowlandson's *Loyal Volunteers of London and the Environs* was first published as a complete text in late August 1799.[3] The book is of particular interest because it is a pictorial record of the London Volunteer Associations, with the text accompanying the plates written by the artist's collaborator and publisher, Rudolf Ackermann, and therefore internally consistent. Unlike those of the Militia, who hardly differed from the regulars, especially after 1809 when they came under the same uniform inspection process, Volunteer uniforms were sourced by each unit and also chosen by the colonel, or committee. They therefore reflect fashionable variants to a greater extent than the uniform of the regulars, sometimes verging on the whimsical. The cross fertilisation of inspiration between these 'fantasy' uniforms and regulated military fashion is profound. The same tailoring houses made uniforms for auxiliary units and for regulars, and this may have proved part of the process for transmission of styles. The cavalry chaco is described in pattern descriptions as a 'Yeoman's cap,' or as 'a cap with a Yeomanry crown'. We have also seen how clothiers for other ranks clothing were involved in the preparation of pattern items and prototypes for consideration as patterns, so dismissing the uniforms of auxiliaries as a source of inspiration for official models should not be done lightly.

An examination of the depiction of breeches and gaiters in Rowlandson reveals that some 82 unmounted units are represented, and nine of cavalry. All cavalry not in boots are in breeches and full gaiters. Some of the notable features are detailed below to give a snapshot

1   George Pellew, *The Life and correspondence of Henry Addington, Viscount Sidmouth* in, The Quarterly Review, (London: John Murray, 1843), No. CLVIII, March, 1843, p.513.
2   I.F.W. Beckett, *The Amateur Military Tradition* (Manchester: Manchester University Press, 199), p.105.
3   Thomas Rowlandson, *Loyal Volunteers of London and Environs* (London: Ackermann, 1799).

of fashionable military modes among the Volunteers of the capital at the commencement of the period under study.

- All gaiters are represented outside the pantaloons, even half gaiters and short gaiters which are distinguished in the text but rendered in the same way. Whole gaiters and long gaiters are terms used indistinguishably with 'gaiters' for under-the-knee length gaiters in black or white. Several units have a full gaiter in black or white with a garter of the opposite colour.
- Three units have full or half gaiters in dress and undress respectively.
- All units wear some form of gaiter except the Honourable Artillery Company who wear them only in full dress, and shoes with breeches otherwise. Two further units wear 'mosquito pantaloons', the fashionable term for a combined gaiter-trouser.
- There are three units where light infantry are shown with half gaiters and the rest wear full gaiters.
- Pantaloons are worn by 31 units. Breeches by 41. In six cases it is not possible to tell.
- Half gaiters are worn by thirty five, short gaiters by thirteen and full gaiters by twenty one. Thirteen units wear a buskin type boot. There may be a few more, but it is not always easy to tell whether a boot or a half gaiter is indicated.

The use of various terms for gaiters does seem to settle down later, with a short gaiter meaning something around the ankle by the time of the various 1812 warrants, and a half gaiter referring to a mid-calf gaiter to be worn outside pantaloons, often with a picqued rear point. Brigadier General William Stewart's brigade orders of 1805, issued at Messina during the British occupation of Sicily state that,

> Officers' summer dress to be white or nankeen pantaloons with the boot or black half gaiter to be worn over them. On marches, but not parades or quarters, an overall pantaloon is permissible.[4]

What else does this tell us about military fashion in 1799 and 1800? The Volunteers occupy a unique position to cast perspective on this form of fashion. They were to be equipped militarily, were usually led by colonels with some military experience, and yet were unfettered by regulation so could indulge in unorthodox variety. Considering this, Rowlandson's crew are remarkable heterogeneous, which gives the impression that there was a defined style which the Volunteers aspired to. In this respect, the Volunteers are a useful prism for examining aspirations in military style. The London Volunteers were the apotheosis of military style, having access to the shops, tailors, and materials to reflect fashionable styles, the British and foreign troops to influence that taste, and most importantly, being at the epicentre of the fashionable world. They therefore had the means, the opportunity, and the motive to create and reflect fashionable changes. An unkind observer might also suggest that the role of most Volunteer units was to create an image or gloss of martial style and effect without the necessary military efficiency or effectiveness.

---

4   NLS, ACC.9074.38.90, Brigade Orders, Messina, 14 June 1805.

The London-based Loyal North Briton Association of Volunteer Rifleman Corps combined rifleman and Highlander styles in one of the most glorious sartorial dead ends of the period. The uniform comprised long pantaloons buttoned seven times below the knee to the ankle, with black gaiters picqued at the rear, and a rifle officer's dolman jacket with a tartan checked fabric in blue and green substituted for the usual green broadcloth, with green collar and cuffs, and a Highland plaid in tartan pinned to the shoulder. The cap was similar to that of the rifles, but with golden cords instead of green. This smorgasbord of styles represented by F.C. Lewis in an aquatinted print of April 1804. Fortunately for the British Army, this was a combination that failed to make an impactful influence on the dress of the regulars. Or indeed on anyone.

One of the most popular vogues in 1800 military fashion was that of riflemen. Derived from the *jäger* tradition of German and other north European states, it was in some ways a further corruption of a national dress, or a form of national dress unique to the forester tradition. There was a general belief that certain martial traits were more naturally present in some cultures than others, but this was no barrier to adopting the particular dress that distinguished the *jäger*, regardless of the presence of the *jäger* characteristics or not. The *jäger* tradition was supposed to exemplify the skills of the forester and marksman. These were particularly embodied in the idea of the rifleman, who was considered to be adept in light infantry micro-tactics, and uniquely capable of using the technical and delicate rifled arms to full effect. This faith in particular national characteristics or proclivities led the British to repeatedly raise formations of ethnic Germans to equip with rifles in an attempt to form natural light infantryman. There were some successful experiences with Hessians in America, and with the 60th, or Royal American, Regiment. The 5/60th was a notable success in this role, and would become the first full battalion of a regular regiment to be equipped in 'rifle uniform'. The 5/60th was supposed to be largely constituted of German recruits at this point in 1798, but their success meant that it was soon being considered whether it was possible to cultivate these desirable Germanic qualities in Englishmen, given they were provided with the right training, uniform, and esprit de corps. The ideal called for recruitment from gamekeepers and professional huntsmen, who would have presumably imbued the essence of the requirements with their mothers' milk, and then refined them through their professional occupation. However the net was later to be cast wider as the 95th rifles demonstrated that the English possessed the qualities needed for this work in ample proportion, and the prejudice in favour of Germans was ameliorated. The 95th focussed on recruiting small, intelligent, and active men. Whether this was because the supply of ethnic Germans was not considered sufficient to raise further battalions, or because of a natural faith in British light infantrymen, is a moot point. Both the 60th's rifle battalions and the 95th would be equipped in 'rifle costume' and that particular vogue was already defined as a British variant on the German style. The elements that forged the rifle costume, were composed as follows.

The light infantry uniform had developed during the eighteenth century American wars (Seven Years War and War of the American Revolution), the notable features being the conversion of the long tailed coat into a coat with truncated tails, then into a jacket with minimal tail, and then into a sleeved waistcoat. The development of the distinctive rifle style with three rows of buttons in green is not reflected in the Loyal Volunteers plates. The inference is that in 1798 there were no riflemen Volunteer units, but by the time the reasonably

'The Honourable Edward Harbord, Lieutenant Colonel. 1st East Norfolk, Local Militia, Rifle Corps', 1806. Engraved by S.W. Reynolds, engraver to the King from a drawing by T. Edridge. The hussar style pelisse was unofficially adopted at regimental or battalion level by officers of rifle corps. Some evidence suggests light infantry officers also followed this trend. (Anne S.K. Brown Military Collection, Brown University Library)

comprehensive list of 1806 was published, the situation had changed. At least 81 rifle or sharpshooter Volunteer Associations existed clothed in the green 'rifle uniform'. From a total of 1,321 units listed in England, Scotland and Wales, more than six percent were now clothed in green.[5]

The rise in popularity of the rifle costume can be ascribed to its adoption by Coote Manningham's Experimental Corps of Riflemen in 1800, and their subsequent substantiation as the Rifle Corps, and then entry into the line as the 95th. It is not possible to be certain however, and a number of other influences have to be taken into account. The 5/60th has been mentioned above, as the first regular battalion to be entirely clothed in green, and they were themselves part of a previous tradition. John Graves Simcoe, speaking of his Queen's Rangers after the War of the American Revolution, 1787 said,

> Green is without comparison the best colour for light troops with dark accoutrements; and if put on in the spring, by autumn it nearly fades with the leaves, preserving its characteristic of being scarcely discernible at a distance.[6]

Simcoe had been commanding officer from 15 October 1777, but the Queen's Rangers were raised as provincials in New York by Robert Rogers in 1775 and dressed in green.[7] 1777 also saw the formation of Ferguson's Rifle Corps in green.[8] Closer to the 5/60th's adoption of green was a request for the formation of a rifle corps to serve in the West Indies in 1795.[9] Cavalry precedents also existed, with Tarleton's Legion and the 22nd and Burgoyne's 23rd Light Dragoons in green until 1784 when all light dragoons changed to blue.[10]

There were elements of all of these precursors in the 95th's regimentals, and so the strands can be defined as: the German *jäger* costume; the British light dragoon uniform, especially in regards to the 'Tarleton' helmet cap as worn by the officers of the 95th; the hussar tradition. The epitome of this relationship between light cavalry and light infantry is the jackets worn by the officers of the rifle battalions. The final element to be considered is the British archer or forester tradition, as exemplified by the Sherwood Rangers Volunteers uniform of 1797-1802. This comprised an elegant confection of green broadcloth accented with white cassimere and with silver lace and silver horn badges to turn backs. The regiment also wore full length gaiter pantaloons in white.[11] This is of course, an infantry kit, although the title Sherwood Rangers would be adopted by the notable Nottinghamshire Yeomanry regiment in the 1830s. The identification of green with *jäger* or chasseur troops in the German and British tradition was so strong that even temporarily raised 'rifle corps' could be induced to shed their red coats on such service. John Shipp of the 22nd Foot recalled growing out

---

5   A. Sapherson (ed.), *Figures from Volunteer Regiments of Scotland, England and Wales, 1806* (Leeds: Raider Books, 1989).

6   J.G. Simcoe, *Simcoe's Military Journal* (New York: Bartlett and Welford, 1844), p.38

7   TNA, WO3/10/.81: Office of the Commander-in-Chief: Out-letters.

8   TNA, WO30/55/433: Miscellaneous Papers. Defences of Great Britain. Military Description of parts of England and Ireland, by General Roy.

9   TNA, WO6/25/251: Secretary of State for war and Secretary of State for War and the Colonies, Out-letters.

10   Strachan, *British Military Uniforms*, p.98.

11   Victoria and Albert Museum, National Art Library, MSL/1933/2993. Pattern Book of military, naval, militia, yeomanry and volunteer uniforms, 1795-1809.

of his clothes and being made part of an ad hoc rifle company at the Cape, and receiving 'a Green Coat'. He is imprecise regarding the date, but this was almost certainly at some point during 1800 or 1801. He wrote: 'A rifle company was formed from men of the 8th dragoons, the 22nd, 34th, 65th, 81st and 91st Regiments... We were dressed in green and our pieces browned to prevent them being seen in the woods'.[12]

The use of green for the uniforms of these specialist formations is usually presented as a utilitarian decision, and is presented as such by Simcoe above, but there are grounds for considering the use of green to be a sartorial as much as a utilitarian choice.

The 5/60th were formed from Lowenstein's Chasseurs, who wore grey, and the Hompesch Chasseurs. They inherited the uniform of Hompesch's unit, that is, a green coat with red facings, and blue pantaloons, and this was adopted in March 1798.[13] It was a matter of discussion as to which of the two colours, green or grey, was most effective in terms of concealment. Though it might appear to be slow at times, the British Army did not stand still regarding the experimentation or introduction of acceptable new ideas during the Napoleonic Wars. This included questioning the suitability of red as the uniform colour for the Army particularly for its light troops. One such experiment occurred in 1800 being a controlled test on the effect aimed rifle fire had on coloured targets, these targets being either of a red, green, or grey colour. The resulting tests showed that grey was the most suitable colour for a uniform and a recommendation was made for its adoption by riflemen and light infantry. The tests were carried out by the rifle company of the 6/60th under the supervision of Charles Hamilton Smith.[14] The rifle company of the 6/60th had just returned from the 1799 Helder campaign in which they had worn a light iron-grey uniform. Two years later the uniform had changed, the regulations describing it as:

> The rifle companies of the 1st/2nd/3rd/4th and 6th battalions of the 60th Regiment. The Jackets for the rifle corps of the above battns, are of green cloth without lapels or lining except the sleeves. The inside of the breast fronts (faced) with red cloth, and made to button over the body down to the waist with 10 buttons. Short skirts not turned back, but cut to slope off behind, with the pocket flaps sloping like light infantry and the pocket in the plait. Round cuffs with 4 buttons on each and without slits. The cuffs, Shoulder straps and a standing collar of green cloth. No wings or lace, but the edges of the whole jacket feathered with red cloth. The back skirts to fold well over between the hip buttons, and all the buttons on the Jacket small. A white milled serge waistcoat with sleeves. Green cloth breeches, and black cloth woollen gaiters'[15]

Details of the experiment were preserved by Charles Hamilton Smith in his papers[16] and he later detailed the experiment in an article for the Royal Engineers.[17]

---

12   John Shipp, *Memoirs of the extraordinary career of John Shipp* (London: Hurst, Chance and Company, 1829), p.189.
13   Lewis Butler, *The Annals of the King's Royal Rifle Corps* (London: Cooper, 1913), Vol.II, p.17.
14   Charles Hamilton Smith, *Aide-Memoire to the Military Sciences* (London: John Weale, 1852), Vol.I, p.257.
15   S. Milne and T. Atley, *The Annals of the King's Royal Rifle Corps* (London: Cooper, 1913), Vol.VI, Appendix II.
16   NAM, 1968-07-126: Smith, Charles Hamilton, Military Manuscripts.
17   Smith, *Aide-Memoire*, Vol .I, p.257.

Under general circumstances; and in battles, when the distance, the smoke of cannon and musketry, partially, at least, concealed contending armies from each other, glaring uniforms may not have caused serious bloodshed; but in the later wars, and the mode of engaging introduced during the French Revolution, where the rifle service is greatly increased, and clouds of skirmishing light Infantry cover the front of their forces so far in advance as to be checked only by similar combatants pushed forward by the opposing army, the fire of both parties is commonly guided by individual aim, and good marksmen make considerable havoc. The colour of the uniform becomes therefore a question of importance, particularly where it is of so distinct a nature as to offer a clear object to the marksman.

Observation teaches military uniforms to fade from the eye, in proportion as they are neutralized; from red, the most conspicuous, to earthen brown and neutral greys. To the marksmen, white enlarges the object, and is so far deceptive; blue reduces the real magnitude; black and dark green assimilate with blue, and light green has a tendency to appear neutral.

The relative distinctiveness of these colours was readily ascertained by the normal rifle company of the 6th battalion 60th Regiment, which, after rather severe service in the Helder expedition, returned to the Isle of Wight, and there had, with the sanction of its Colonel, permission to undertake a series of experiments on the comparative effect of rifle fire upon different colours.

After some preliminary observations on plain white and on black targets without ring or bull's-eye, and where the first mentioned was evidently more maltreated by rifle shot than the second, it was resolved to confine the trials to plain red, green, and grey, that is, a light iron-grey made with distemper being then the uniform of a Highland regiment, of a Dutch rifle battalion, both in the same garrison, and the normal company in question, which then still had the same Austrian Tyrolean costume which it had worn in the last Helder expedition. From this Company were selected the best six marksmen, all educated Jager, and each was supplied with six bullets. The red target, placed on the open heath, was distant 125 yards from the stand; the time selected was seven in the morning, with weather sufficiently moderate not to have perceptible influence on the direction of the shot; the men were to load as to them seemed best, and to fire at leisure. After each had fired six shots, the party returned home. On the next day, when the weather was equally favourable, and the sun at the same angle of elevation, the same number of shots, were delivered by the same men, and under the same conditions, at the green target; and on the third, at the grey.

On the third day of the second series of trials, the men immediately observed that they were now so familiar with the distance, that their fire would be more effective than in the first. But it was this time the grey target that was to be aimed at, and the result turned out by no means commensurate with the expectation of the marksmen. In this manner the second series of experiments was conducted, even with more care, if possible, to maintain the conditions perfectly similar: each day the targets had the shot-holes stopped, and the surface repainted; but now the red target was already so much damaged, that fearing it would not hold together for the day's trial, the distance for the third and last series of rounds was increased to 150 yards, and notwithstanding the changes resulting therefrom, it fell to pieces before the last shot was delivered, and, being bound together by withies, was brought home in a bundle. The green also was so much battered in the fiery ordeal as to be unfit for repairing; but the grey remained sound, and was afterwards used again.

There had been fired 108 shots at each, 72 of which at 125, and the last 36 at 150 yards. It is to be regretted that the exact number of shot-holes which had been each day carefully noted down is not now in the possession of the writer; the copy of the report which was sent up to Sir Robert Brownrigg, the Quarter Master General of the forces and Colonel of the battalion, having been lent to a Military acquaintance who never returned it. But so far as recollection can be depended on, there were, it is believed, more than double the number in the red than in the grey target, and the state of the green was intermediate.

It was observed also that the grey was comparatively unhurt when the distance was increased, and to ascertain the fact more fully, that target was afterwards painted vertically one half red and the other left grey, and the same result was obtained. It was then suggested to set up the triangle stand, upon which the rifle can be laid, in order to level it at the centre, and screw it fast. The most experienced Tyrolean in the company took pains to effect the object, and still the red bore the great majority of hits, upon which last occasion only it is proper to observe that both ring and bull's eye were painted black, none having been used during the three first series of experiments.

The general result is, however, of so important a nature, that it appears exceedingly desirable they should be repeated, and if possible, with still greater precautions, because, in case of further confirmation, the question arises whether all riflemen and light infantry should not take the field in some grey unostentatious uniform, leaving the parade dress for peace and garrison duty.[18]

Charles Hamilton Smith (1776-1859) was a soldier, artist and author. His military career began in 1787 when he served as a volunteer in the 8th Light Dragoons, subsequently he was a cornet in Hompesch's Hussars. In December 1797 he joined the 60th Regiment in the West Indies. He went on half-pay in 1820 and was never again actively employed, but he was awarded brevet rank of Lieutenant Colonel in 1830.[19] Hamilton Smith's service in the 60th is the key element and his memory of the trials is a unique piece of contemporary evidence. However, Hamilton Smith's recommendation for the use of grey uniforms by light infantry was not heeded by Horse Guards. Instead green was to become the colour associated with the rifle-armed battalions. Indeed, in 1811 it was recommended that all light infantry be clothed in green, though nothing came of that proposition either.[20] The matter was proposed again by Major General William Stewart, on the raising of the third battalion of the 95th. In Stewart's papers is a copy of a letter in his handwriting, written on 19 September 1809, when Stewart was preparing to render effective the 3/95th:

18 Smith, *Aide-Memoire*, Volume. I, pp.257-259.
19 Christine E. Jackson, 'Smith, Charles Hamilton', *Oxford Dictionary of National Biography*, https://doi.org/10.1093/ref:odnb/25786 (acessed 24 September 2018).
20 TNA, WO123/135: Army Circulars, Memoranda, Orders and Regulations. Adjutant-General's office (Horse Guards).

'His Royal Highness Edward Duke of Kent and Stratheam', 1808. Engraved by Skelton after Beechey. The Duke of Kent gave his name to various articles of apparel. Among these were the Duke of Kent pantaloons, and the Duke of Kent boots. (Private Collection)

the colonel's taste in fashion was only partially restricted. Records of exceptions granted are fairly extensive and will be detailed in more depth in the second volume. A large part of the correspondence on the subject concerns battle-honours or distinctions like the alterations to cap plates above. The second most common condition under which exceptions were made was in cases of utility. This is illustrated by a notable and possibly unique example where the 1812 cap was not issued owing to practical expediency. This involved the 28th Foot which was notoriously rumoured to have persisted in the 1806 cap with a bizarre combination of brass ornaments. The visual evidence for this comes from the painter George Jones who rushed a set of pencil sketches into print in 1817 to exploit public interest in Waterloo.

The artist George Jones' military career belies his habit of calling himself 'Captain' George Jones. He appears to have been commissioned into the South Devon Militia 1808, and subsequently, as captain, into the Royal Montgomeryshire Militia on 17 February 1812. There is no evidence that he served abroad. His output as an artist 1812-16 suggests he was fully employed in Great Britain. Post-Waterloo he sketched the battlefield and some of his drawings were published 1817. These drawings are often presented as eyewitness drawings, which obviously they are not, but they may be as early as late 1815 or from 1816. It must be borne in mind that by 1816 some uniform and cap changes had taken place, so he was probably already relying on actual eyewitnesses to tell him *what was worn* rather than drawing from life. Jones must have seen, or had described to him the anomalous arrangement of the 28th's regimental cap, and since he was demonstrably in Paris in 1816 where the 28th formed part of the occupation forces it is possible that he was an eye witness to its use at that point.[3] In fact the exception is corroborated by details in War Office papers, and was granted owing to a loss of uniform stores suffered by the 28th Foot on account of a supply shipwreck.[4] As with all other cases of exemption from regulation granted by the Commander-in-Chief, this exception was made for one year only. It may have applied only to the service battalion, as model 1812 cap plates for the 28th are extent in at least three examples. All three are 1812 model plates with regimental distinctions, so were presumably the property of the depot battalion.[5] The occasion of the 28th's exception was unusual enough to be the subject of Board of General Officers discussion in May 1816.[6]

The full text of the 1801 Warrant, 20 May 1801

Regulation relative to the clothing and half mounting of the infantry; and to the inspection of the clothing of the army in general.

Whereas the Commander-in-Chief of our forces, and the general officers composing with him Our permanent Clothing Board, have submitted to us their opinion upon the several particulars referred to their consideration, touching the clothing of Our army, and the expediency of making some change in the articles supplied to our soldiers under the name of half mounting. We were pleased, by

3   J. Booth *The Battle of Waterloo also of Ligny and Quatre Bras, by a near observer, Illustrations to the Battles of Quatre-Bras, Ligny, and Waterloo, with circumstantial details* (London: Booth, 1817), Volume III.
4   TNA, WO7/56/539-541: Various Departmental out-letters. Board of General Officers, reports, miscellaneous.
5   Cap plates exist in the Bristol Social Museum, The Glosters Regimental Museum, and as an example dug at Berry Head.
6   TNA, WO7/56/539-541: Various Departmental out-letters. Board of General Officers, reports, miscellaneous.

our warrant bearing date the 9 of April 1800 to establish certain regulations in conformity to the opinion of the Board. And whereas our said Board have suggested some Alterations and Additions, with a view of rendering those regulations more accurate and comprehensive: and have humbly advised, that the same, where so amended, may be again published in Our army; which We, thinking for the benefit of our service are pleased entirely to approve. We do accordingly declare it to be Our will and pleasure, that instead of the orders contained in our said warrant, the following regulations be duly observed in future, in the several points to which they apply.

I Clothing of regiments in Europe, in North America, and at the Cape of Good Hope, except Highland corps
    In a regiment of infantry of the line, or fencible infantry serving in Europe, in North America, or at the Cape of Good Hope (Highland Corps excepted), each serjeant, corporal, drummer and private man shall have annually,
    For clothing,
    A coat
    A waistcoat, or waistcoat front.
    A pair of breeches; unlined, except the waistband, and with one pocket only.
    A cap made of felt and leather, with brass plate, cockade and tuft, conformable to a pattern approved by us, and lodged at the office of the comptrollers of the accounts of Our army; the felt crown of the cap, cockade and tuft to be supplied annually; the leather part and brass plate, every two years.
    And in lieu of the former small articles of clothing, called half mounting, and of the breeches lining,
    Two pair of good shoes of the value of five shillings and sixpence each pair.
    Each serjeant shall also be credited with the sum of three shillings, being the difference between the value of the former articles of half mounting for a serjeant and private man.

II In the Highland corps on the above stations, each serjeant, corporal, drummer and private man shall have annually,
    For Clothing,
    A coat;
    A waistcoat or waistcoat front:
    A bonnet and four pair of hose;
    Six yards of plaid once in every two years; and a purse every seven years:
    And in lieu of the former small articles of clothing called half mounting,
    Two pair of shoes of the value above mentioned. Each serjeant shall also be credited with the sum of three shillings; being the difference of the value of his half mounting as above stated.

III In a regiment of infantry serving in the West Indies (except the 5th battalion of Our 60th regiment and the regiments composed of people of colour) each serjeant, corporal, drummer and private man shall have annually

For Clothing,

A coat, unlined, except the breast facing and turn-up at the skirts;

A waistcoat complete, of milled serge, with sleeves of the same; with regimental buttons, collar and cuff (agreeable, as to size and quality to as pattern lodged at the office of Our said comptrollers: the saving of one shilling for the lining of the coat to be applied in the purchase of the waistcoat; and the men paying one shilling and ten pence each for the sleeves as a part of their regimental necessaries;

A pair of linen Trowsers;

A cap, cockade and tuft as above specified and in lieu of the former small articles of clothing called half mounting,

Two pair of good shoes: of the value of five shillings and sixpence each pair.

Each serjeant is also to be credited with the sum of three shillings for the difference of the value of his half mounting, as before stated.

IV In the 5th battalion of Our 60th regiment, each serjeant shall have annually,

For Clothing,

A green coat, unlined, except the breast facing and turn-up at the skirts;

A white serge waistcoat; with sleeves etc. as specified in the preceding article;

A cap, cockade and tuft as above specified;

A pair of blue pantaloons; and for half mounting,

Two pair of shoes of the quality and value abovementioned: but he is not to be credited, as in other corps, with the sum of three shillings for the difference of half mounting, as he receives an equivalent in the difference between the value of the pantaloons and of breeches.

Each corporal, drummer and private man shall have annually,

For Clothing,

A green coat; unlined, except the breast facing and turn-up at the skirts;

A white serge waistcoat etc. as before specified,

A cap, cockade and tuft, as above specified;

A pair of blue pantaloons, and for half mounting,

Two pair of shoes, of the quality and value aforementioned; but towards the price of which the colonels shall only pay 4s 6d a pair, the men paying the difference in consideration of their being furnished with pantaloons instead of breeches.

V In a regiment composed of people of colour, each serjeant, corporal, drummer and private man shall have annually,

For Clothing

A red cloth round jacket; part lined;

A cap, cockade and tuft, as above specified;

Two pair of Russia duck Trowsers;

Together with a grey kersey greatcoat, to last two years, and for half mounting,

One pair of shoes, of the quality and value abovementioned, and one pair of shoe soles.

Each serjeant shall also be credited with the sum of three shillings being the difference in value of his half mounting, as above stated.

VI In a regiment of infantry serving in the East Indies, each serjeant shall have annually,
    For Clothing,
    A coat, unlined, except the breast facing, and turn-up at the skirts;
    A cap, cockade and tuft, as before specified; and a compensation in value,
    For the waistcoat front and buttons, 4s and 11d
    For a pair of breeches 10s 9d
    Lining for the coat, 1s 2d
    Total 16s 10d
    And in lieu of the former small articles of clothing called half mounting,
    Two pair of good shoes, of the value of five shillings and sixpence each pair; and further the sum of three shillings for the difference of the value of his half mounting as above stated. Each corporal, drummer and private man shall have annually,
    For clothing
    A coat, unlined, except the breast facing and turn-up of the skirts;
    A cap, cockade and tuft, as above specified and a compensation in value,
    For the waistcoat front and buttons, 1s 9d
    For a pair of breeches, 4s 6d
    Lining for the coat, 1s
    Total 7s 3d
    And in lieu of the small articles of clothing called half mounting,
    Two pair of good shoes, of the value of five shillings and sixpence each pair.

VII In a corps of rifle men serving in Europe, in North America, or at the Cape of Good Hope, each serjeant shall have annually
    For clothing,
    A green coat, without lace;
    A kersey waistcoat;
    A cap, cockade and tuft, as before specified,
    A pair of green pantaloons,
    In lieu of the former small articles of clothing called half mountings,
    Two pair of shoes of the quality and value abovementioned: but he is not to be credited, as in other corps, with the sum of three shillings for the difference of half mounting, as he receives an equivalent in the difference between the value of the pantaloons and of breeches.
    Each corporal, drummer and private man, shall have annually,
    For clothing,
    A green coat, without lace;
    A kersey waistcoat;
    A cap, cockade and tuft, as before specified,
    A pair of green pantaloons,
    In lieu of the former small articles of clothing called half mountings,
    Two pair of shoes of the quality and value abovementioned: but towards the price of which the colonels shall only pay four shillings and nine-pence a pair, the men

paying the difference in consideration of their being furnished with pantaloons instead of breeches.

When the corps shall be stationed in the East or West Indies, they are to conform to the rules prescribed in the 3rd and 8th articles of the warrant.

VIII In our staff corps each serjeant, corporal, drummer and private man shall have annually
    For clothing,
    A coat;
    A waistcoat or waistcoat front;
    A pair of blue pantaloons;
    A cap, cockade and tuft, as before specified;
    And in lieu of the former small articles of clothing called half mounting,
    A pair of half boots;
    And further in consideration of the laborious nature of their service, each serjeant, corporal, drummer, and private man shall have annually,
    A Russia duck waistcoat, with sleeves, and
    A pair of Russia duck pantaloons.

IX The clothing of regiments on foreign stations is not to be furnished in materials, but is to be sent out made up, except in instances where We shall be pleased to grant a special dispensation through Our Commander-in-Chief, or Secretary at War.

X The shoes ordered to be substituted for the former articles of half mounting, are to be provided in conformity to a pattern lodged at the office of the comptrollers of the accompts of Our army, and patterns of the shoes are to be approved and sealed by the general officers of our Clothing Board, at the same time and in like manner, as for the clothing: one pair is to be delivered out of the annual period of clothing, and the other pair at the end of six months from that time, and in order to prevent the injury that the shoes might sustain from remaining a long time in store in the East and West Indies, they shall be forwarded to corps on those stations at two different periods, instead of sending the whole quantity with the clothing.

Should the price of good shoes at any time exceed five shillings and sixpence a pair, the difference, which shall be declared by Our Clothing Board at their first meeting on or after the 25 of April in each year is to be charged to the respective accounts of the non-commissioned officers and soldiers receiving them; but with respect to the 5th battalion of Our 60th regiment, and to our corps of riflemen, the difference is to be taken between the prices paid by the colonels of the said corps respectively as before specified, and the actual price declared as abovementioned.

XI Highland corps in the East and West Indies, are to discontinue, while serving there, the Highland appointments.

XII The allowances directed to be given by the colonels as above stated in lieu of parts of the clothing, and of the former small articles of clothing known as half mounting, are to be regularly credited to the men, and to be expended for their use in such articles as are suitable to the respective climates in which they shall be serving.

Certificates of the credits having been properly given, and of the money having been actually expended for the use of the men are to be signed by the respective commanding officers, and to be transmitted half yearly through the Adjutant General, to Our Clothing Board, care being taken to provide against accidents by sending a duplicate of each certificate by a subsequent opportunity.

XIII Sealed patterns of the clothing and shoes furnished in lieu of the smaller articles, shall in future be sent to, and remain deposited at, the headquarters of every corps of infantry as well as at home, in order that the new clothing and shoes may be compared therewith at any convenient time by the general officers commanding on the respective stations abroad and in the several districts at home, or by the officers who may be appointed to inspect the said clothing and shoes: and certificates of the conformity thereof to the sealed patterns and of the same having been delivered in due time to the men, shall be in future transmitted by such general or other officers as aforesaid through the Adjutant General to Our Clothing Board. And to obviate any inconvenience that might otherwise arise from the want of such view of the clothing being taken at an early period, it is hereby directed that in each regiment abroad or at home, the commanding officer present with the corps when the clothing is received together with the two officers next in seniority, not under the rank of captain, do, immediately on its arrival, make a strict inspection into the same, and do cause to be drawn out an accurate state of the quality, quantity and condition thereof; which state he shall transmit, through the Adjutant general of Our forces, to Our Clothing Board: and it is our pleasure that such state shall be entered in the regimental books, for the future inspection of such superior officer as may be ordered from time to time to inspect or review the regiment.

XIV And whereas it appears highly expedient, that an uniform rule should be laid down in regard to the claims of soldiers of infantry to clothing, and to the shoes substituted in lieu of half mounting, at stated times, or broken periods; and to the rates at which compensation shall be made, in such cases as shall admit of a payment in money in lieu of the articles in kind, under the restrictions thereafter mentioned; We do hereby declare, and make known, that non-commissioned officers and soldiers of infantry, dying or discharged before the completion of a full year from the usual day of delivering the annual clothing of their regiment have no demand whatever on account thereof.

If a serjeant is reduced to the ranks, his clothing is to be given in for the use of his successor, and he himself will receive private's clothing equally worn (or as nearly as may be) with the clothing he has given in.

A recruit who comes into the regiment after the proper time of the delivery of the clothing, if not raised for an augmentation, shall be immediately entitled to clothing of that year, as good as that in wear by the rest of the regiment; and to a pair of shoes at the next delivery of that article: and he shall be entitled to new clothing (shoes included) at the next period of general delivery to the regiment.

XV It is the duty of the colonels, and of those employed by them, to take especial care that the annual clothing be forwarded and delivered to their respective corps, as near the stated periods as possible; and few cases ought to arrive in which it should become a question whether an allowance in money might not be substituted by the colonels in lieu of delivering in kind the articles which by Our regulations they are required to furnish, but if, from any extraordinary circumstances of the service, such an instance should be supposed to have occurred in any of our regiments serving abroad, the grounds on which a commutation in money is proposed, should be fully stated to the Commander-in-Chief of Our forces, or when there is no Commander-in-Chief to Our Secretary at war, in order that Our pleasure may be previously taken thereupon.

   If he should think proper to signify Our approbation of the measure, the following sums being the estimated amount of what the colonels would have paid to their clothiers after a reasonable deduction for incidental charges to which they are liable, shall be given to the men:

   To each serjeant,
   Clothing £2 18s
   Half mounting 14s
   Total £3 12s
   To each corporal, drummer and private,
   Clothing £1 5s 6d
   Half mounting 11s
   £1 16s 6d

XVI And whereas in consequence of the orders given for substituting a new species of half mounting in lieu of the former articles of which it was composed, it became expedient to revise and amend the list of necessaries annexed to our warrant of the 25 May 1797 and therein directed to be provided by stoppages from the pay of the non-commissioned officers and men, so far as regarded Our corps of infantry of the line and fencible infantry serving at home; and whereas the list annexed to Our subsequent warrant of the 9 April 1800 is found to require further alteration; Our will and pleasure is that the same stoppage of one shilling and sixpence per week shall continue to be made from the pay of Our said corps; but that the same shall be expended (in the manner directed by the former of Our said warrants) for the use of the men in the articles specified in the schedule annexed to this Our warrant, and it is Our further will and pleasure that no further stoppage be made at home from their pay without the sanction of a regimental court martial or court of enquiry, except for the extra price of shoes beyond five shillings and sixpence a pair, and for the straps for carrying their greatcoats.

XVII And whereas We have been pleased to order that the clothing of Our army should be viewed by two permanent Inspectors of clothing, instead of being viewed, as heretofore, by a general officer of the clothing board, and have appointed Lieutenant Colonel W Wynyard and Lieutenant Colonel Robert Anstruther to be Inspectors of clothing accordingly; We do hereby authorise and direct the said Inspectors, or the inspectors for the time being, to view and compare with the sealed patterns the clothing of Our several regiments of cavalry and infantry, as soon as the same shall have been prepared by the respective clothiers; and if the said clothing appear conformable to the sealed patterns, to grant two certificates of their view and approval thereof; one of which certificates is to be delivered to the clothiers, to be sent with the clothing to the headquarters of the corps, and the other to be lodged with Our Clothing Board, as the necessary voucher for paying the assignment of the allowance for the said clothing.

It is Our further will and pleasure that the clothing be viewed, and certificates be signed, by both the Inspectors; except in cases where the absence of one of them shall be unavoidable: in all which cases, the cause of such absence is to be stated by the other Inspector in his certificate of the view of the clothing.

The Inspectors shall follow such further instructions as they may from time to time receive from the Commander-in-Chief of Our forces, Our Secretary at war, or Our Clothing Board.

XVIII Finally, We declare it to be Our intention, that all colonels, commanding officers, or other officers who shall direct or knowingly permit any alteration whatever to be made in any part of the clothing or appointments so that the same shall differ in the smallest degree from the patterns of the several articles sealed by Our Clothing Board, and sent to the respective regiments or shall allow any deviation from Our existing regulations for the clothing and appointments of our forces, shall be considered as guilty of disobedience of orders, and be liable to such punishment for the same as by general court martial shall be awarded.

And to prevent ignorance of these regulations being pleaded in excuse of not having conformed thereto, it is Our pleasure that a copy of the same be inserted in the orderly book of every regiment of cavalry and infantry in our service,

Given this 20th day of May 1801 in the forty-first year of Our reign
By His Majesty's command,
C Yorke

List of necessaries to be provided by stoppage from the pay of the soldiers of regiments of infantry of the line and fencible infantry serving at home, referred to in the preceding warrant.

Cost per annum
*For two pair of black cloth gaiters @4s per pair 8s
*For a second pair of breeches 6s 6d
One hair leather 2 and 1/2d
One pair shoes 6s
Mending ditto and shoe soles 6s
Three pair of socks @8d per pair 2s
Three shirts @ 5s and 6d per shirt 16s 6d

A foraging cap 1s 3d
A knapsack at 6s once in 6 years 1s
Pipe clay and whiting 4s 4d
A clothes brush at 1s once in two years, 6d
Three shoe brushes @ 5d each 1s 3d
Black ball 2s
Worsted mitts 9d
Black stock 9d
Hair ribbon 9d
Two combs @ 6d each, 1s
Washing, at 4d per week, 17s 4d
Total £3 16s 1 and 1/2 d

See asterisk above. In such corps as are authorised by the foregoing warrant, or as may hereafter be directed by His Majesty's orders to wear cloth pantaloons, the following articles are to be substituted in lieu of the two pair of black cloth (long) gaiters and the second pair of breeches abovementioned, viz:

Two pair of short black gaiters at 22s 9d a pair, 5s 6d
A second pair of cloth pantaloons 8s
Total 13s 6d

NB In Highland corps, instead of the two pairs of black cloth gaiters, and the second pair of breeches above specified, the following articles are to be substituted:

Kilt 5s 6d
Feather 6s
Additional hose 3s

The soldiers are also liable to stoppage for straps to carry their greatcoats, and for the extra price of their shoes in lieu of half mounting beyond five shillings and sixpence per pair (and in the 5th battalion of the 60th regiment, and corps of riflemen, beyond four shillings and nine pence per pair, respectively). In corps serving at home, the actual expenditure for altering clothing, not exceeding two shillings and sixpence per annum, per man, and for articles to clean the arms not exceeding two shillings and nine pence per annum, each man, will be defrayed by the public, as expressed in former warrants.[7]

7   TNA, WO26/38/312: Entry Books of Warrants, Regulations and Precedents.

5

Fashion in the Artillery

> Many are the insignificant trifles which, associated as they are with times gone by,
> I would not wish to let slip, and therefore throw them together while still living in
> my mind's eye.[1]

External to regulation, both the officers and the men of the Peninsular army were subject
to sometimes absurd fads in both their clothing and their personal appearance. Sources for
these fashions and trends that swept the army are naturally few. Sometimes images show
unusual details that cannot be explained by regulation or necessity, for example, the stripe
on the pantaloons of infantry officers so often seen in the 1815-17 occupation prints. These
are usually documented as mere personal idiosyncrasies, but are perhaps better suited to
the category of fashion, whether that be an individual's expression or a collective one by
a regiment, ordered or sanctioned by the colonel. Sometimes memoirs record these deviations from the norm, for instance the wearing of light cavalry overalls with overlong chain
attachments by the officers of both the light infantry and of the line, as well as by Mercer's
artillery as he records below. A third line of enquiry is through the examination of regulation, or rather, the genesis of regulation. Although fashion is by nature external or opposed
to regulation, its general adoption sometimes leads to alteration in regulation at which point
the contrary becomes the new norm.

Besides the occasional passing mentions of modes and fads in general memoirs, I have
isolated five authors who devoted much of their time to detailing these modes. The first is a
history of military costume of a very narrative and delightfully rambling nature. The second
a set of reminiscences written for the writer's family, the third a precise set of instructions
on fashion that allude often to the military mode, and the fourth a bloated set of general
social memoirs. The last is a set of notes in a narrative poem, with illustrations the details of
which appear to have been dictated by the author to the artist (Rowlandson), so well do they
interlock. All of these works suffer from being written sometime after the fact. However,
since this is a usual and inevitable failing of memoirs we shall not labour the point of the
fallibility of memory but proceed with them as one of the few possible windows onto this

---

1   C. Mercer, *Military reminiscences of latter end of eighteenth and beginning of nineteenth centuries*, in R. McDonald, *The History of the Dress of the Royal Regiment of Artillery* (London: Sotheran, 1911).

ephemeral world of military fashion, and look wherever possible for corroboration from our other sources. In fact, Luard is ahead of us in this respect for he illustrates his work with reproduction versions of the occupation prints, and not only attests to their accuracy as a record and not a caricature of the mode of the moment, but also identifies and supplies anecdotes on some of those soldiers illustrated. These five principle sources on fashion are:

1. Luard.[2]
2. Mercer[3]
3. 'A cavalry officer'.[4]
4. Gronow[5]
5. Roberts[6]

Luard will be dealt with in the second volume. He presents a rather useful commentary on the 'occupation prints' of 1815. By his own account his service commenced in 1809 and encompassed both heavy and light dragoons, in the Peninsula and at Waterloo respectively, and subsequently lancers and then staff appointments.[7]

Recently a case has been proposed for Beau Brummell as the author of 'The Whole Art of Dress' by an anonymous cavalry officer.[8] Brummel's writing on military matters are limited to a few observations in his work on historical dress, and it seems that if he was the author, more would have been made of his celebrity. Whether this case for attribution has been settled or not, and it does not seem likely, the work is of extraordinary value and will be referred to again

Gronow's reminiscences were protracted through multiple money-spinning volumes and editions. They are better presented piecemeal in the appropriate sections, and stronger on the late period where the memoirs run parallel to his military service. On 24 December 1812 he was commissioned into the 1st Foot Guards and, after a few months duty in London, he was despatched to Spain with a detachment of his regiment. The following year found him taking part in the campaign under Wellington in that country and in France, and in 1814 he returned with his battalion to London. He stablished himself among the beaus of Bond Street and mingled in fashionable society. Finding himself likely to be left in London during the events of 1815, he pulled strings to enable Sir Thomas Picton to employ him in Flanders as an 'honorary aide de camp' – essentially a volunteer carried off the books with no official allowance or employment. Once he had arrived Picton claimed he was excess to requirements on his personal staff, and he was advised instead to join the 3rd Battalion of the

---

2   J. Luard, *A History of the Dress of the British Soldier* (London: Clowes, 1852).

3   Mercer, *Military reminiscences of latter end of eighteenth and beginning of nineteenth centuries*, in McDonald, *The History of the Dress of the Royal Regiment of Artillery*. This is General A.C. Mercer, colonel-commandant of the 9th Brigade, the Captain Mercer of Waterloo fame.

4   Anon., *A Cavalry Officer, The Whole art of Dress! Or, the road to elegance and fashion* (London: Effingham Willingham, 1830).

5   R. Gronow, *The reminiscences and recollections of Captain Gronow* (London: Nimmo, 1900).

6   D. Roberts, *The Military Adventures of Johnny Newcome, with an account of his campaign on the Peninsula and in Pall Mall* (London: Methuen, 1904).

7   Luard, *Dress of the British Soldier*, p.v.

8   I. Kelly, *Beau Brummell: The Ultimate Man of Style* (London: Freepress, 2005).

1st Foot Guards and was subsequently present at the battles of Quatre Bras and Waterloo. He entered Paris with them on 25 June 1815, and on 28 June was promoted lieutenant by vacancy. He was later a captain in the same regiment until going onto half pay on 24 October 1821.[9]

Roberts is the author identified as having composed *The Military Adventures of Johnny Newcome*. Colonel David Roberts (1757-1819) served in the 22nd Light Dragoons and 1st Life Guards, served in Portugal and on the retreat to Coruna with the 51st Foot: in temporary command at Vittoria, he was wounded on the Bidassoa in the combat of Vera, retired from the Army in 1815 and died in 1819.[10] This poem of nearly 3,000 lines was first published in 1815, and much of the value lies in the author's notes, and in the illustrations by Rowlandson. Again, Roberts is most useful for the late period and features in the second volume of this work.

Mercer's military reminiscences on dress are reproduced in full here, as they form the most valuable work dealing with the dress of the Royal Artillery, which is otherwise rather under- represented in sources. They are especially worthwhile on the early period, and also benefit from Mercer's sketches to illustrate his text, which are reproduced here. The first edition of these memoirs was reproduced by Captain R.J. MacDonald in *The History of the Dress of the Royal Regiment of Artillery*, and the 1911 edition has been followed here.

1789. Dress. Hair clubs.
My first and earliest recollections on this subject present to me the soldiers of the 8th and 12th regiments (successively quartered in the island of Guernsey in the year in or about 1789 or '90), dressing each other's heads under a lamp in one of the bastions of Fort George. The operation was to plaster well with grease, whiten with flour, and to roll the hair behind in a club, which was effected by means of an iron something of the sort as here shown.

The hair was rolled up on no.1 and when the club was made the instrument was removed by drawing it out sideways, the branches a, a, of no.3 fitting into the pipes b. b. of no.2. The club when completed, was nearly of the annexed form. It was fastened by a black leather band, a, ornamented with a rosette. The whole was made as white as a cauliflower.

1794: Queues.
My next recollection on this subject was at Plymouth in 1794, when the officers wore small queues tied with a few turns of riband, and ornamented with a rather large silk rosette. What the men wore, I now forget, but all were still powdered. My own experience gave me the next chance to notice military friseurship when, in the beginning of 1798, I went to the Royal Academy at Woolwich, and the doctoring my head underwent at that time will give the fashion of the day. On the top the hair was cut close, and the stumps rubbed well back with hard or stick pomatum, a kind

9   Christopher Hibbert, 'Gronow, Rees Howell', *Oxford Dictionary of National Biography*, Vol.23, 270. https://doi. org/10.1093/ref:odnb/11654 (accessed 24 September 2018).

10 Roy Palmer, 'Roberts, David', *Oxford Dictionary of National Biography*, Vol. 16, 162.https://doi.org/10.1093/ ref:odnb/23745 accessed (24 September 2018).

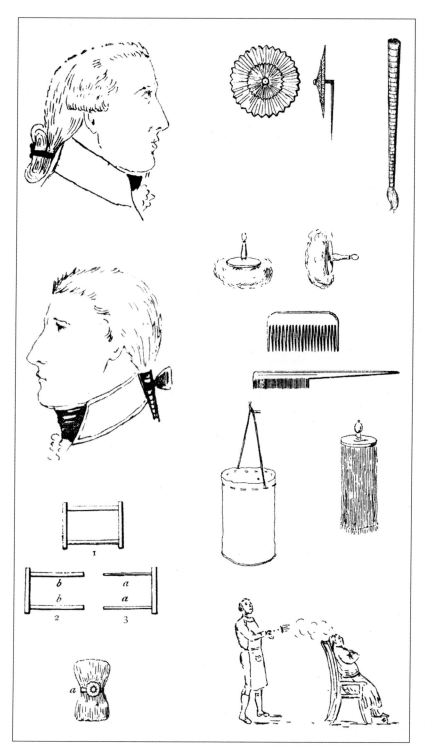

Hair and hair implements. (C. Mercer, in MacDonald, *The History of the Dress of the Royal Regiment of Artillery*).

Queues, round-hats and cocked hats. (C. Mercer, in MacDonald, *The History of the Dress of the Royal Regiment of Artillery*).

of sixteen, whose hair was as haggy as that of a wild colt. He was going then to join the Duke's regiment, whence he had been sent, with six months' leave of absence and positive orders not to cut his hair, which on his first joining had been found too short to admit of being properly put into shape. The 1st Royals long retained their queues after every other regiment had discarded them, and, after all, may be said to have been taken from them by force, the general officer commanding (at Wheely Malder or Danbury Borray, I forget which) having threatened to have them cut off on parade unless removed by a specific day. Meanwhile courier upon courier was said to have passed between the Commanding Officer of the regiment and Kensington Palalce where His Royal Highness then lived. Alas, poor queues!

The exact year when powder and queues expired, I don't exactly remember. It appears to me that the death bow was given by the earlier peninsular campaigns, but there are other things that stagger me in this belief. I remember, for instance, powdering the side locks after putting on my helmet in 1808, and wearing queues in 1809-10 etc. Yet do I also remember, in 1802-03, at Cork, on some occasion of rejoicing, that our colonel (Howarth) ordered the party which paraded to fire a salute on the quay at George Island, to powder, and I also remember the impression on my mind made by their appearance with white heads, which I thought ridiculous, which would not have been the case had my eye been accustomed to it. Further, I remember how conceited I was about my own brown hair (which was certainly luxuriant and beautifully curling), and how certain ladies, whose pet I was, taught me to brush and anoint it with Huile Antique, then the fashionable application; and it was this conceit and preference to a brown head that made me, as I have stated above, powder my sidelocks after putting my helmet on, so keeping the rest clean, which shows it was still necessary to appear powdered at parade in 1808. And I remember, also, that it was as necessary in going to mess, there being a fine for any one going to dinner without- a most cogent reason for my dining so often in my room, as I did whilst at Woolwich that year.

All this induces me to believe that powder was left off by the men much earlier than by the officers, and that queues were worn by both long after powder had ceased among the men. In Kane's book I find the order for discontinuing queues is dated August 1st, 1808, for the Ordnance Corps, but Sir Augustus (then Captain) Frazer made us leave queues and feathers behind in 1807, when we went to the Rio de la Plata. Still, the Master-General's order for providing the men with spunges to wash their heads etc looks as if they had been powdered up to that time. In civil life, every one must remember Lord Matthew, afterwards Lord Llandaff, remarkable at once for his large and commanding figure, and retaining his queue and powder long after it had disappeared everywhere else.

Coiffure.

The first head-dress I remember as worn by the Royal Artillery was at Plymouth, 1794 or 1795. That of the non-commissioned officers and gunners was what would now be considered very ridiculous. How others might have considered it at that epoch I cannot decide, but that in my eyes it was exceeding smart is undeniable. It was a round hat of the true Mother Shipton breed. Narrow (very narrow) brim, very

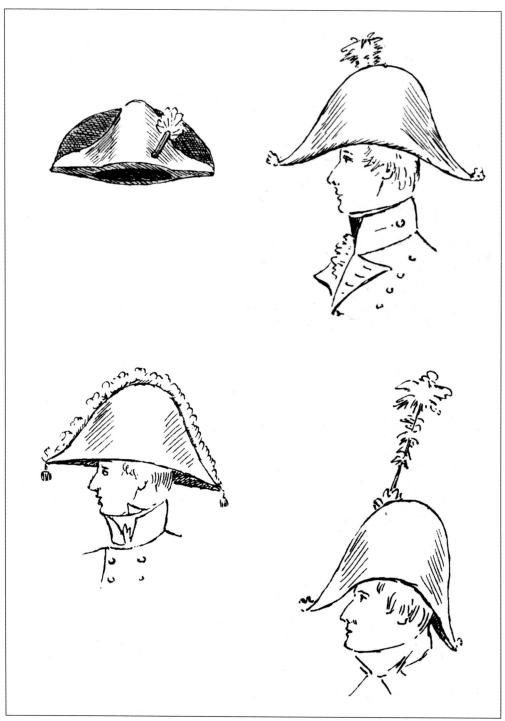

Cocked hats. (C. Mercer, in MacDonald, *The History of the Dress of the Royal Regiment of Artillery*)

high crown, going smaller upwards, so that it formed a frustrum of an acute cone. This elegant coiffure was ornamented with a broad yellow band, and a cockade in front of the roof, surmounted by a scarlet tuft. The hat worn by the officers at the same period would not even now be considered ungraceful- round, with a brim somewhat broad, and curling up at the sides; low, rounded crown, over all a bear-skin in the helmet fashion, cockade, and I think a a white feather in the left side-of this last not quite sure. When this was changed for the cocked hat I am also uncertain, but think it must have been about 1797, or perhaps earlier, for in Kane's book there is an order of 12 October 1796, that the Artillery shall conform to the regulation hat and sword etc and when I first went to Woolwich, latter end of 1797, I remember seeing all the men in cocked hats.

Horrid ugly things they were too, especially the men's, made of very coarse felt, and heavy as lead; they turned upwards, instead of drooping, as was afterwards considered the criterion of beauty. Just fitting on the crown of the head, the slightest breeze sufficed to uncover a whole regiment, had it not been for weight and a small string made into a loop, both ends of which being attached to the hat, the bend was passed under the hair behind; so that, on going to church, the men had rather an awkward operation to perform ere they could uncover. When I got my first commission, not having the slightest idea of the points constituting beauty in a cocked hat, I went to Wagner, in pall mall, simply ordered a hat and feather according to the regulations; and until I found myself the laughing stock of all my companions at the first guard-mounting parade, had no suspicion that such a respectable house would have taken in a boy, by palming on him that which no one else would have ever taken off their hands. In a word, it was large, ungainly, and- horror of horrors!- the sides curled upward, like the gunners', whereas the droop had just begun to be all the go. Moreover, the conical feather, though strictly of the regimental length, etc, was like nobody else's, and hideous. I shall never forget my first hat and feather.

The infantry hat was decorated by a crimson-and-gold rosette in each lock. The cavalry by a pendant tassel of the same material. This of course we aped whenever we dared.

The regulation mode of wearing this hat was with the loop, etc, perpendicularly over the left eye, and the right corner, or wing, thrown a little forward. What might be termed right shoulders forward. Some of the old men still adhered as nearly as the regulations would permit to the form of their antique Dettingen hats- triangular. The Navy, instead of wearing their cocked hats square over the brow, like the soldiers, slewed them round, bringing the ends off, as they called it, 'fore-and-aft'. This the Army soon began to imitate, when off parade, and many a youngster got took for being caught with his beaver in this unlawful fix.

I think it must have been about 1810, 1811, or 1812, that general Officers wore feathered hats in imitation of the French. The fashion did not last many years.

The relaxation admitted on actual service, however, was always taken advantage of to get rid of the feather and the square position of the hat, so that, from seeing people returning from expeditions with their hats fore-and-aft, an idea of service got to be associated with this form of wearing it, wonderfully taking, particularly with the young aspirants for glory, and by them communicated to the

Cocked hats. (C. Mercer, in MacDonald, *The History of the Dress of the Royal Regiment of Artillery*)

women, who soon learned to look upon a man as a spiritless quiz, who stuck to regulation in wearing his uniform. Somehow or another, this fashion in the end has completely gained the ascendency, and the present wearers of hats (Staff and Engineers) never dream of bringing the loop perpendicularly over the left eye. Like every other article of clothing, the hat has continually varied its shape within my day. The original cocked hat was triangular as may be seen in old portraits of the Duke of Cumberland, General Elliot, General Wolfe, and a host of others; then came the broader brim, which made the cocks longer and fan higher, but with the base line straight, or even inclining upwards. An improvement on this was the droop as exhibited in the last sketch. But dandies, as I said, are dandies by running everything into extremes- in extremum are. The droop, once suggested, was gradu-ally increased until, when square, the rosettes interfered with a man's shoulders; when fore and aft, the foremost part hid the face, and the hinder served instead of a hand to scratch between the shoulders behind. Still, the fan was high, By-and-by, id est, about 1805 I think, low fans (or lower) became the fashion, which recalls to me what a conceited little puppy I was, when the Cavalry and Horse Artillery adopted the cocked hat as an undress, which was worn with the pelisse. Mine, I remember, was one of the low fans, with the spunge head feather. What a jackanapes I must have been, caracoling about Stephen's Green and Merrion Square, in the little, ugly, poor pelisse of yon day with this selfsame hideous hat!

After the peace of 1815, the high acute fan obtained generally, and still holds its ground. Thenceforward I think the fan, and, indeed, the general bulk of the hat, gradually diminished until 1815, when imitation of the French had begun to make it look up again. The acme of petitesse was, I believe, attained by the immortal Wellington, whose funny little hat is now familiar to all the world.

Feathers naturally follow hats; their fashion has been as variable, and may be briefly stated. I have already said that I forget whether ant feather was worn in the bearskin hat- the earliest of recollections. When I joined the Royal Artillery, the ugliest thing ever devised by tasteless adjutants was stuck up in our hats, a conical white feather, about six inches high and stiff as could be. How long this lasted I know not, but its successor was an incumbrance- ten inches long, the top spreading out in long hackles, stiff stem; this was improved after a time by having the whalebone weaker, so that instead of standing bolt upright, the feather (still of the same make and dimensions) drooped gracefully as it was thought) over the fan of the hat. How such hideous incumbrances could ever have been devised I cannot imagine, and thought the ridiculous had reached the extreme until the absurd, horrid, preposterous, tasteless mountain of feathers worn by our Hussars and Staff of enlightened aujourd'hui met my astonished gaze. Then, indeed, I did wonder!

After the hats became established for and aft, it became very fashionable to sport a handsome silk pocket-handkerchief stuck in the cock, fault of pockets, etc.

Helmets, etc.

The first head-dress of the Horse Artillery was a helmet- the old English light dragoon helmet (helmets with green turbans were always worn by Light Infantry companies), the favourite of George III; the handsomest, most military, and most serviceable of all military coiffures; the admiration of all foreigners, and the only article truly national ever worn in the British Army. Vain were the attempts of His Royal Highness the Prince of Wales, of Lord Paget, of the Duke of Cumberland, and of Sir Charles Stuart, to get rid of the helmet, and denationalising the 10th, 7th, 15th, and 18th Light dragoons to make Hussars of them; so long as old George lived, or at least retained his reason, the helmet he would never allow to be changed. The good old man was aware of all its excellences, and he loved it as a truly national costume. With our venerable Sovereign disappeared the helmet from every corps in the army. Light Dragoons as well as Hussars, excepting the Horse Artillery, who in spite of modern dandyism, retained it until very recently- I believe 1835, or thereabouts- when, under the reign of a Hussar Master-General, Whinyates, Dunn, Michell, cum multis aliis, who, instead of feeling pride at being distinguished as Horse Artillery sui gencris, longed to become Hussars themselves, at last succeeded in banishing the helmet, and with it every particle of dress, and perhaps feeling, that once distinguished the corps from, and elevated above, every other in the Army. Like the cocked hat the helmet in the course of years varied

A YOUNGSTER OF
1800.

HELMET OF 1799.

Helmet-caps. (C. Mercer, in MacDonald, *The History of the Dress of the Royal Regiment of Artillery*)

in ornament and form, and although essentially the same, yet latterly was a very different, and far more elegant article of dress than when I first saw it in 1797. Here I must confess in one point to be uncertain- I mean as to the nature of the turban or ornamental fillet, surrounding the lower part; but I think it was of leopard-skin similar to the helmets of the Light Dragoons. This, however, could not have lasted long, for my first distinct recollection is of a crimson silk turban. On or about 1805, we succeeded, through the medium of Lady Chatham (his Lordship was Master-General), in getting turbans of black velvet; for all the Light Dragoons wore black silk turbans, and alas! Even in those days the mania for imitating the cavalry existed. The drivers (or Wee Gee corps) had dark-blue turbans, which was a sad nuisance to us, so nearly resembling our own, that another change was obtained in a few months, to black silk, which delighted us all, for the Cavalry wore black silk. This might have been about the latter part of 1805, or beginning of 1806, and afterwards no alteration took place until their abolition. The form of the helmet formerly was very ugly, straight line at bottom, with the shade or peak sticking straight out, and very large. The bearskin low and poor.

By degrees this all changed, until, from an ugly, it became really an elegant article of dress. Like the cocked hat, one of its principal improvements consisted in an alteration of the base line from straight to curved, which, with the shade, made it droop over the face in front, and into the neck behind, thus at once improving its appearance and its qualities as a defence for the knowledge-box. At the same time, the bearskins were raised and made fuller.

The first time this was done for the non-commissioned officers and men, I remember, we made the alteration ourselves (ie-our collar maker did it) by uniting the bearskin of the old helmet to the new one just served out, and a monstrous improvement it made in the appearance of para. There is nothing like a lofty head-dress to make soldiers look imposing, particularly so when drawn up in a body. The feathers worn in the helmets of officers differed like those for the cocked hats; those of the men, I believe, were always the same, for the feathercase was always of the same form and dimensions. The helmet was latterly decorated, and perhaps rendered more perfect, by gilt scales attached to the sides. When not worn down, these were turned to and tied in rear of the bearskin.

Forage caps
The most ungraceful head-dress that could well be devised, I think, was the fatigue-cap worn by the Foot Artillery when first I entered the regiment, and only required the combination with the loose canvas frock and waistcoat to make it hideously unmilitary. It was of black leather, with a brass ornament in front (G.R. and crown, etc), the leather not stiff, full of cracks, and looking rusty, for they were never cleaned or expected to be. The Horse Artillery and drivers had a similar mitre-shaped cap, but better, inasmuch as, being made of thick stiff leather, it was kept polished, and looked smart. This was used for undress parades, watering order, etc. But for common stable parades, fatigues etc, the Horse Artillery had a blue cloth cap edged with red, and tied behind with red ferreting. This was also worn at night by stable sentries and others.

Forage caps. (C. Mercer, in MacDonald, *The History of the Dress of the Royal Regiment of Artillery*)

The captains of troops must have been greater men, and enjoyed much more latitude formerly, than in the present day. Many circumstances which I call to mind make me think this, but among other, the circumstance that Duncan, in 1804, took it into his head to give his troop a new and frenchified forage-cap, such an one as until then was only known to us through the medium of costumes, etc., although familiar to him, a service officer. Numerous were the fancies he and I tried, some in sketches, some he actually had made up, until at last we pitched upon the annexed as the most elegant; and the tailors were forthwith set to work making them up.

In a short time they were finished, Duncan delighted; inspected the watering order parade himself, and contemplated the beautiful effect of his frenchified troop with rapture. It was marched off, and again he took his stand at the end of the lane by which (en route for the Phoenix Park) they must gain the street of Island Bridge. The last of them had scarcely passed the bridge when, issuing from the barracks appeared the drivers, also in watering order. But, oh horror! Carefully as the intended change had been concealed, and carefully as had the intended pattern been guarded, old Colonel Schalch had managed to ferret it out, and there went the Wee Gees bridling in their finery, to the disgust of Duncan, whose rage I shall long remember. These caps, or something similar, were afterwards adopted generally, and here let me confess my uncertainty whether the 16th Light Dragoons, or the 12th or both, had not these caps before us.

(In those days there was no undress cap for officers, ergo when off parade they were usually lounging around in round hats, and in some small or slack garrisons I have seen them walking about the streets in them. In the Foot Artillery, at some of our outquarters, we always wore them, with a cockade and button, as substitutes for cocked hats. In the West Indies, I think, they were worn by authority.)

Coats, Jackets etc.
From the chief, descending to the middle man and taxing my memory as to its earliest impressions in or about 1795, I remember the gay young officers of Artillery sporting about the streets or dock at Plymouth in blue coats with red facings buttoned back, hooked at the collar, and falling off as they descended, so as to show the white kerseymere waistcoat. Whether the skirts were sewn or hooked back, I cannot remember, but believe the former. A single epaulet decorated the shoulder of this coat, on the right shoulder of captains and lieutenants; field officers alone wearing two. To these coats succeeded the double breasted one, equally plain with the other, which was sometimes worn closely buttoned up; but more generally (and I think such was the order) the three upper buttons undone and the lappels turned back with the cambric shirt-frill pulled out in the form of a cock's comb. Still no lace, no ornament, save for the epaulet. I remember at Clonmel, in 1802, venturing (out of the world, as we then considered ourselves) to stick grenades in our skirts, and thus decorated fancying ourselves uncommon fine fellows, as we figured away at the balls in the Court-house. After this, I know nothing further of the Foot Artillery, except that their uniform underwent several changes, from coat to jacket etc. The first lace (beside the epaulet) was an embroidered true lover's knot upon red cloth, as a skirt ornament; then they got cord lace and embroidery- always

1795.   1797.

1806.   1804.

Jackets. (C. Mercer, in MacDonald, *The History of the Dress of the Royal Regiment of Artillery*)

something very tasteless and ugly. At one time they had no less than five different coats or jackets. The Horse Artillery, which I joined in 1804, wore flat lace on their jackets, although the Light Dragoons had been wearing the cord lace for some years. The regulation jacket was to have on the breast equal blue and lace, that is, the space between the lace was to be of the same breadth as the lace itself. This, however, was too poor to satisfy us; and as regulations in those days were little adhered to away from headquarters, every one put on as much more lace as his fancy dictated or his purse permitted. For my part, my first jacket resembled a furze bush in full blossom, for it was one mass of gold from the collar to the sash. No great space, after all, for the waists were then worn so exceedingly short that my sash was nearly under my arms; and other jackets which I had afterwards of more modest description, had only six loops of lace on the breast. It was the fashion of the day for boys to imitate or try to resemble women, wearing as they did such short waists, and filling out the jacket with handkerchiefs to resemble the female figure. Yet, with all this, it strikes me that the youngsters then, in spite of their feminine appearance, were in reality much more manly and less effeminate than those of aujourd hui. As all fashions are very variable, so was this of short waists, as I experienced to my cost; for when, in 1807, we went out to Buenos Ayres, supposing our absence from home would be a long one, I took a full and complete outfit of everything, and among the rest three new jackets. These the nature of our service hardly ever allowed me to wear half a dozen times, so that they were quite fresh when we returned to Woolwich, and to my horror, useless,- the mode being so completely changed that the jacket reached below the hips, and was made with something like the old fashioned skirt. Long before this we had got rid of our flat lace- once thought so fine, now so mean- and our jackets were laced with the cord as at present. I think the change took place in 1806. But I have altogether omitted the 1 st Horse Artillery jacket, or at least the first I recollect. I never remember seeing any other English troops wear such a one, but think it was the Chasseur jacket in the French army.

Hooked at the collar, it sloped away toward the little skirt which terminated it behind, and had half facings. On the shoulders a sort of wing, made of interwoven rings; with leather breeches, long boots, and the helmet; this was rather a soldier-like service dress.

Chassure, etc.
Continuing my downward course to the nether man, we come next to his inde-scribables or About 1805 we first began to wear pelisses, and poor shabby concerns they would be thought in the present day, although we then looked upon them as marvellously fine. They were trimmed with some brown fur, such as was then in common use for ladies' tippets etc, perhaps sable- I don't know; the braiding on the breast also was sparse and of very small cord. Altogether it was a shabby thing. Somewhere about 1808 the pelisse, only tolerated before, became a regular and authorised part of our uniform. The sable fur gave place to the grey astrakhan, the braiding became richer with barrel buttons, and the whole affair more Hussarish.

Inexpressibles- words which I must throw away for the present, since, although not of any very great importance, yet there are a few reminiscences connected with

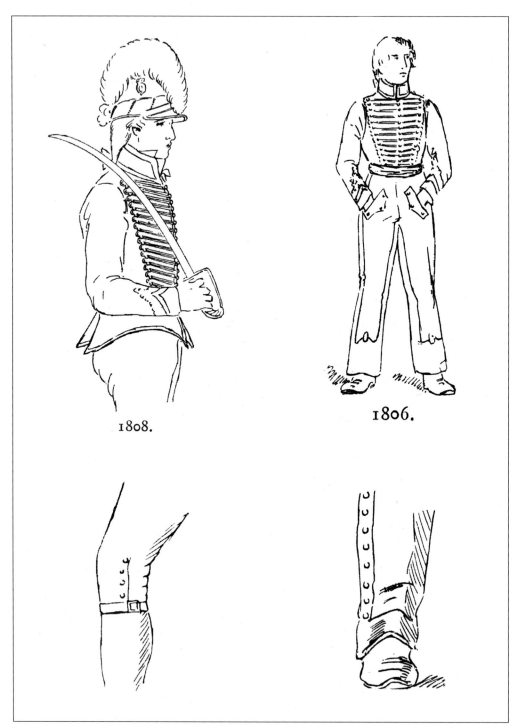

1808.

1806.

Breeches and Overalls. (C. Mercer, in MacDonald, *The History of the Dress of the Royal Regiment of Artillery*)

these articles not altogether uninteresting, which I must both express and describe. When I got my first commission, the Horse Artillery Officer clad his thighs in well-pipeclayed doe or buckskins; the Padnagge in well-whitened kerseymere, fastened at the knee with four small buttons and a buckle. These, for aught I can remember, constituted the one only pair of thigh-cases for each service. Morning parade, evening parade, wet weather or fine, breakfast, dinner, tea-party, ball or court- always white breeches. It was a sort of innovation when, after a time, the Foot Artillery assumed to themselves the skins, which eventually became also their uniform.

Dark blue pantaloons (cloth) began to creep ion about 1802 (though they had always been worn by Officers on expeditions etc.) and we were very proud of ourselves when at outquarters we could dress thus, as it looked so like service. So far is all I know of the Foot Artillery. (Blue pantaloons permitted by a general order in 1803; see Kane.) In the Horse Artillery, besides our leather breeches, we wore the blue cloth pantaloons for common undress parades, and the same with gold lace for full dress etc. The fronts of these were profusely decorated nearly halfway down the thigh, in the same style as worn by drum-majors of aujourd hui. (1840)

For marching order, we had blue cloth overalls, having leather down the inside of the thighs, and about the whole of the leg, in the shape of hessian boots. These articles were then what the name implied, really overalls, being worn over pantaloons and buttoning from top to bottom outside; the pockets were in front of the groin, set slopingly. To keep the overall down, instead of straps, we used chains, about the size and made like curb-chains, which, when walking about, instead of being under the foot, were suspended across the back of the leg by one of the buttons near the knee, as in the annexed. These chains, being kept highly polished, really looked very well, at least to eyes of those days.

The dandyism of the day consisted in having them very long, half a yard, par exemple (for undress parades and common wear).

For dress, foot parades etc, we had white stocking-net fitting quite as tight as the blue mentioned below. One of the Buenos Ayres Hussars fell desperately in love with a pair I wore at a ball, and teased me the whole night to sell them to him.

About the same period, I think, that we exchanged our flat lace for cord, we also got rid of our breeches and long boots in exchange for leather pantaloons and Hessian or Hussar boots. These, as well as the blue stocking net, which came in about the same time, were worn as tight as possible. (And about the same period the overall became simply trousers or pantaloons, merely retaining the fly as an ornament.)

At a subsequent period pepper-and-salt coloured overalls were worn, and the shades or tints of grey were altered more than once; but when this took place I know not now, nor can I call to mind when the red stripe down the side was introduced- I think somewhere about 1810 or 1811. At the same time the black leather inside the thighs, and boot below, gave place to brown leather, and instead of finishing in a boot, there was only a band of 3 or 4 inches round the bottes to save the cloth from the stirrup. The present purply half-tint was introduced in 1815. I remember Frazer showing me some of it one day at Paris, as a new thing.

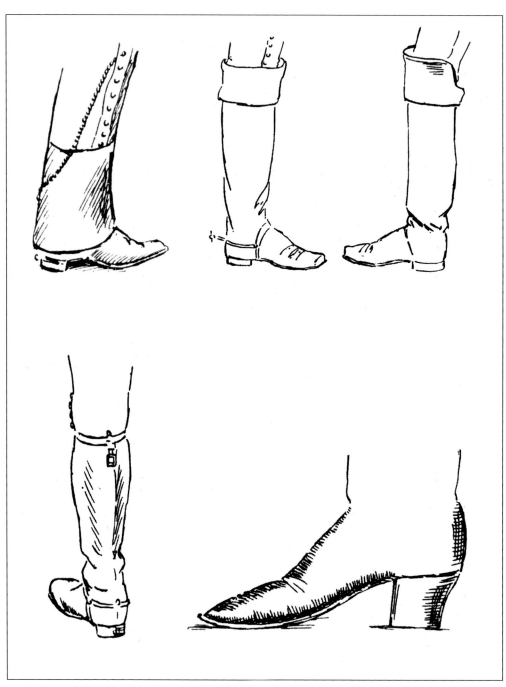

Boots and shoes. (C. Mercer, in MacDonald, *The History of the Dress of the Royal Regiment of Artillery*)

From breeches we slip down naturally to boots. The first time I saw a Hussar boot, it was worn by a very handsome well-made man, and I though it grand. Captain Foy had just arrived from Vienna, and I saw him at practice in the Warren, somewhere in 1798, for I was a cadet. But the first boot I wore myself was the regimental one when I got my commission, up to the knee, with a stiff top, but not cut out behind, which was then a piece of dandyism, and only became regimental afterwards. These boots were made large, and did not fit the leg; but when a cadet, I remember the Officers wore a more flexible boot, fitting closely the shape of the leg. This was kept up by a tongue attached to the kneeband of the breeches, and a buckle on the calf of the boot. The late father of the Regiment, General Sir John Smyth, when a lieut-colonel, was an amazing beau, and flattered himself he had a good leg. Of course, his boots used to fit like gloves. The half-boots then worn were the very reverse of what afterwards came into fashion, for instead of being higher in front, they were cut down and rose to a point behind. I remember Dr Hutton sporting a pair. These were made with a single seam down the back, but subsequently it became quizzical not to have a double one, with a broad band between them. (The heels worn in 1804 by exquisites were very high and very small, tapering too; just such as women used to wear some forty or fifty years before, per exemple.) The Hussar boot is well known at the present day, rising in front, decorated with a silk tassel, and having a seam down each side. A sort of half-boot, rising in front like this, but having the double seam behind, became fashionable about the beginning of the century, and I shall not in a hurry forget the sensation cause at Plymouth dock, by lieutenant Anderson (afterwards Colonel Morehead) making his appearance at the promenade in front of Government House one Sunday Evening in a pair of these. 'Oh, the puppy!' was heard on all sides. 'If he has not silk tassels to his boots!' Only think! Silk tassels on boots!

The greatest of all comforts and improvements, in my opinion, was when (after the general adoption of the trousers in imitation of overalls) we ceased casing our poor legs in leather, and substituted the short or ankle boot for the high Hussar.

Spurs.
As a matter of course, follow boots, and there is little to be said on the subject. Like all other articles of dress, they went through a great variety of vagaries in the course of forty years. The first I remember worn by my father and by general or Field Officers was silver, with a short bent neck, flat short branches, the deficiency iun length made up by small chains, of silver also; this was the field officer's spur par excellence. The Horse Artillery (and I believe the Cavalry) used to wear a plated spur (the men's steel), with a long straight neck. It was not until 1805 or 1806 that we first began to wear spurs screwed on the heel of the boot. The form I do not remember, but think they had crooked necks. In 1807, I took out several pairs of spurs in the most exquisite style of the day. These were very small, beautifully made and finished, of blue steel, and with straight, cocked up necks. At Monte Video nothing could exceed the admiration of the Gauchos at the sight of these elegant little spurs;- a striking contrast there was, to be sure, between them and their own huge misshapen silver ones. This is all that can be said about spurs, as far as I recollect; but before dismissing the boot and its appendages I must say a

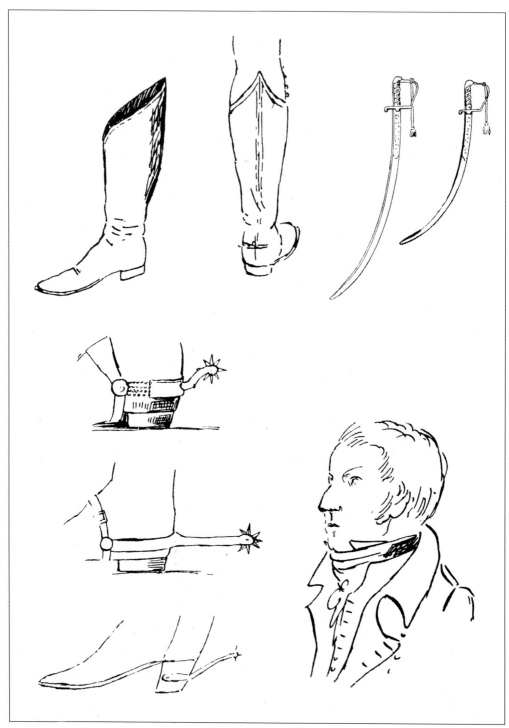

Spurs and swords. (C. Mercer, in MacDonald, *The History of the Dress of the Royal Regiment of Artillery*)

word about the iron heels, which, like many other parts of our military costume, have been borrowed from the Germans. In 1802 the Hompesch chasseurs a cheval were quartered at Cork, and long shall I remember the impression produced whenever I met a party of these (dismounted) marching through the streets, the heavy tread of so many iron heels on the pavement, accompanied by regular clang of their steel scabbards and jingling of their carbine slings, the solemn unvarying features of their bronzed and moustachioed faces. To me there was something exquisitely picturesque and imposing in all this. We did not begin to wear iron heels for a year or two after this, my first recollection of them being in 1804.

Stocks, etc- In the beginning of my career, the neck was enveloped in a balck velvet stock, into which a padded stuffing was introduced to keep it up; or it was worn over a sufficient accumulation of white muslin, of which one-eighth of an inch in breadth was to border the upper edge of the stock as a finish. In plain clothes, white muslin cravats were then invariably worn, and none but masters or mates of merchantmen and such-like craft ever dreamed of wearing black. Captain, (now Colonel) Birch of the Engineers, was an exception, and it is curious to recall in the present day, when all wear black, the vulgarity imparted to his appearance by this departure from the established mode. At one period it was fashionable to wear cravats of immense size, or rather an immense number, one put on over the other, so as to form a mass of considerable thickness, in which the chin was buried almost up to the under lip. Whilst I wore this accumulation of cotton I was always subject to violent sore throat and stiff neck; in 1820 I left off every species of wrap that the usages of society would permit, and now for twenty years I have neither known one nor the other of these maladies.

The eighth of an inch of white shown above the stock was intended for the men, and in their kits were included six false collars. These were narrow strips of linen, which were doubled over the leather stock and confined there by a hook at each end. The exact period when the shirt-collar began to be substituted in the shape of 'dogs ears' I cannot precisely say, but think it must have been about 1810. In the Horse Artillery these became almost regulation, but I took it into my head that all black was more soldier-like, consequently would not wear them. One day when our two splendid troops were drawn up on Rushmere Heath, by Ipswich, ranks open, and every moment expecting the arrival of His Royal Highness George Prince Regent, by whom we were to be reviewed, Sir Augustus Frazer (then only Captain), who was one of the most precise little men in the world, happening to turn his head towards the lines to see that all was right, perceived me in front of G troop, all black, no dog's ears! Hastening to me, he begged that I would make myself like the rest by pulling up my collar, as the Royal family were noted for their quick perceptions in all matters of military uniform. I told him my collar was too low. Dilemna! Frazer was not to be refused, and it ended by his tearing off the blank leaf of a letter he luckily had in his sabretache, with which we fitted up a pair of dog's ears which answered perfectly to receive and march past His Royal highness, and were thrown away as soon as we began to manoeuvre.

Sashes.

I remember, when a boy, the old ones had a large boss or rose, whence the fringes depended; this was worn in front of left side, and was tied behind, under the coat

armourer; his pay, clothing, and all other appointments will be the same as those of other serjeants, in addition to which he will be entitled to a moderate compensation for the repair of arms, for which the captains of troops and companies, will, as usual, remain responsible.

Harry Calvert Adjutant General.[2]

Serjeant armourers had existed in certain regiments prior to this order. A warrant for passing and allowing an assignment for the clothing of a Regiment of Rifle Men under the command of Colonel Coote Manningham from 25 August, 1800 to 24 December, 1801 inclusive allows for this post, although it is termed armourer-major until the 1802 change to armourer-serjeant was universally established.

For the Clothing of the several numbers above mentioned amounting to 53 Sergeants, 50 Corporals, 1 Bugle-Major, 20 Bugles, 1 Armourer-Major, 10 Armourers, and 770 Private men.[3]

The term serjeant-armourer may have been an honourific, with the position being held by a private, corporal, or serjeant. A letter of 1806 indicates that armourers will wear the uniform of their rank, whatever that might be.[4] There was a window between the institution of the post, which, as we can see from the Rifle Corps, clearly existed from at least 1800, and the corrective order of 1802 when armourers appear to have been equipped in peculiar regimental uniforms.

Armourers Jackets for the Rifle Corps.
The Jackets for the Armourers of the Rifle Corps to be of dark Grey Cloth, and in the Formation, number of Buttons etc. and setting them on to be similar to the Rank and File. The Cuffs and Collar to be of Dark Green Cloth and the Seams throughout feathered with Green.[5]

A manuscript pencil amendment to the above crosses it out, perhaps indicating that this uniform did not survive past 1802.

The order of 6 July 1802 establishing a badge to recognise the Egyptian campaign, has several interesting elements that merit its inclusion, even though strictly speaking it refers to a badge to be borne on the colours, rather than a uniform element. Firstly, the order illustrates the process by which regiments were considered to merit inclusion in the award with the attached memoranda listing extracts from returns at Alexandria, and notes on various small detachments and late arrivals. Secondly, the colour badge honours were later extended to be worn on cap plates, and though this volume does not list the numerous granting of battle or campaign honours, this campaign award occupies a peculiar place, since another

2   TNA, WO123/118/37: Army Circulars, Memoranda, Orders and Regulations. Army Regulations, etc from Various Sources.
3   W. Verner, 'The First Clothing Warrant of the Rifle Corps' *The Rifle Brigade Chronicle* (1900), p.241
4   TNA, WO26/40/86: War Office: Entry Books of Warrants, Regulations and Precedents.
5   See Appendix 1, 1802 collation, Para 52.

campaign award was not made until 'Peninsula' and it is also useful as an example of how the awards were made. Thirdly, the order notes that the flank companies of the 40th were already wearing 'Egypt' on their cap plates in 1802, an extraordinary circumstance that is not further commented on here, and is apparently not recorded elsewhere.

The staff corps and rifle corps are both struck out, presumably as neither unit carried colours. The fencible cavalry is an interesting inclusion, as the fencibles were supposedly disembodied in 1800 in an attempt to persuade their men to enlist into the regular cavalry, which subsequently many of them did.

6 July, 1802, Circular to Regiments

> Adjutant General to regiments which have served in Egypt, viz, 12th Light Dragoons, 26th (now 23rd) Light Dragoons, Coldstream Guards (1st battalion), 3rd Foot Guards (1st battalion), Royals, (2nd battalion), Queens, 8th Foot (or Kings), 10th, 13th, 18th (or Royal Irish), 20th, 23rd (or Royal Welsh Fusiliers), 24th, 25th, 26th, 27th, 28th, 30th, Flank companies of the 40th regiment wear the badge on their caps, 42nd (or Royal Highland), 44th, 50th, 54th, 58th, 61st, 79th, 80th, 86th, 88th, 89th, 90th, 92nd, and Irish Fencibles, Queens German regiment, De Rolles, Dillons,
>
> I have the honour to inform you, that His Majesty has graciously been pleased to grant permission to the several regiments of his army which served during the late campaign in Egypt, to assume and wear on their colours, a badge, as a distinguished mark of His Majesty's royal approbation, and as a lasting memorial of the glory acquired to His Majesty's arms by the zeal, discipline and intrepidity of his troops on that arduous and important campaign.
>
> HRH the Commander-in-Chief has directed me to make this communication to you, and order that the regiment under your command may avail itself of the honour hereby conferred by His Majesty, and I am commanded at the same time to apprize you, that a pattern of badge approved by His Majesty is lodged at the office of the comptroller of army accounts, to be had recourse to as circumstances may require.
>
> Harry Calvert Adjutant General.

Attached handwritten note:

> Mem.
> Are the undermentioned detachments of regiments which served in Egypt entitled to wear the badge?
> 80th, 503 rank and file effective.
> 86th, 277 in Egypt.
> 88th, 456 in Egypt.
> De Rolles, Dillon, Ancient Irish, These regiments were all in [illeg.] for Egypt and therefore [illeg.] are entitled to the Egyptian Badge.

Further handwritten note: Extract from Alexandria Return dated 1 March, 1802 written on back.

> List of regiments serving in Egypt extracted from return dated 1 July 1801
> Cavalry,
> 11th Light Dragoons (cross next to entry)
> 12th ditto
> 26th ditto
> Detachment Hompesch's mounted riflemen.
> Foot Guards,
> 2nd, 1st battalion
> 3rd (1st battalion)
> Infantry,
> 1st, 2nd battalion
> 2nd
> 8th
> 13th
> 18th
> 20th 2 battalions
> 23rd
> 24th
> 25th
> 26th
> 27th
> 28th
> 30th
> 40th, 2 battalions, flank companies.
> 42nd
> 44th
> 50th
> 54th
> 58th
> 79th
> 89th
> 90th
> 92nd
> Rifle Corps (struck out)
> Staff Corps (struck out)
> Queens German regiment,
> Corsican Rangers.[6]

---

6   TNA, WO123/134/170: Army Circulars, Memoranda, Orders and Regulations. Adujutant-General's office (Horse Guards).

14 July, 1802. General order on chevrons

> Adjutant General to Forces,
> It is His Majesty's pleasure, that in future the use of epaulettes and shoulder knots is to be discontinued by the non-commissioned officers of the foot guards and regiments of infantry, and they shall hereafter be distinguished by chevrons made of the lace at present used in their regimentals, viz.
>   Serjeant majors and quarter master serjeants, four bars to be placed on the right arm.
>   All other serjeants, three bars to be placed on the right arm.
>   Corporals two bars to be placed on the right arm.
>   Harry Calvert Adjutant General.[7]

30 December, 1802, General Order on chevrons

> Adjutant General to Forces,
> The sleeve of a Sergeants coat with chevrons and a Privates coat with Corporals chevrons according to the regulations which directs that they shall be worn on the right sleeve at right angles and extend to within half an inch of the seams, half an inch of the cloth appearing between the bars of the chevrons.
>   Harry Calvert, Adjutant General.[8]

There exist an interesting set of garrison orders for Gibraltar in 1802. After being appointed Governor of Gibraltar on 23 March 1802, the Duke of Kent arrived to take up his post on 24 May 1802. His mandate was to restore order to the notoriously ill-disciplined garrison after a recent mutiny. Unfortunately the Duke's reception was not universally popular, and his martinet approach was to provoke a second mutiny precipitated a mutiny by soldiers under his command on Christmas Eve 1802. After an immediate inquiry, the Duke of York, acting in his capacity as Commander in Chief, recalled his brother to England in May 1803. Despite this direct order he protested that it would be inappropriate to return to England before his successor arrived. The orders imposed by the Duke on the garrison were a favorite subject for memorialists and journal writers, and yet they were not excessive by home service standards. The Duke applied them successfully in the regiments of which he was colonel. The problem seems to have been in the perception, popular among officers and soldiers alike, that different standards applied on foreign service to those on home service. The root of the Duke's unpopularity may have lain in his application of home standards to a foreign based garrison. Be that as it may, the orders are worth reproducing at length, as an example of regulation in theatre, below army level, but above regimental level, and also an ephemeral set, as they would be applied to regiments posted to Gibraltar on garrison, and even to officers visiting ashore when their transports were anchored in the Gibraltar roads.

---

7   TNA, WO123/118/37: Army Circulars, Memoranda, Orders and Regulations. Army Regulations, etc from Various Sources.
8   TNA, WO7/33/53: Various Departmental, Out-letters. Board of General Officers, clothing.

'His Royal Highness William Frederick Duke of Gloucester and Edinburgh', 1807. Engraved by William Say after Beechey. The duke is here wearing the hussars' hessian boots that were worn with pantaloons in many fashionable regiments in certain orders of dress. (Private collection)

A useful extract from the orders was discovered among the loose manuscripts in Somerset Local Archives and are reproduced here by kind permission.

Officers:

Regimental coats. The lapels to be worn buttoned across from top to bottom, and to come down sufficiently low to cover every button of the waistcoat, the skirt to reach one inch below the ham, and to be, at the bottom, of the width of four inches; the collar of the coat to range exactly with the top of the stock, two holes to be worked in each side of the collar, and two waistcoat side buttons fixed at the back of each hole.

Waistcoats of white kerseymere (no other stuff being allowed for that part of the dress.) These are to be round at the bottom, single-breasted without flaps, and with regimental buttons. No part of the waistcoat to appear either above, or in front of the collar of the coat.

Established regulation swords with the appropriate sword knot. These are to be worn in a shoulder belt made of buff, or buckskin, coloured perfectly white, of the width of two inches and a half, to hang perfectly perpendicular, not obliquely, the hilt close down to the frog, which is to be fitted to the scabbard, so as to receive it, exactly, leaving no room for it to play, the button to be on the inside of the top chape, with a corresponding hole in the inside of the frog, the guard ranging just above the hipbone, the breastplate precisely in the centre of the body.

The established regulation sash. This is to be worn over the coat around the waist, and to go twice around the body, confining the sword belt just above the frog; the bottom of the sash top come half an inch below the waistcoat, (of which therefore, when the sash is on, no part is to be seen) to be kept at an equal width of five inches, perfectly smooth and level all round; for which purpose, that part next the body is to be lined with thin scarlet cloth; the ends of the sash to be tied in a double knot, without a bow, immediately above the third button hole (counting from the fore-part) of the pocket flap, and the ends to hang both correctly level, the one with the other, and not to exceed the bottom of the skirt of the coat.

The established regulation gorget. This is to be worn hung to the lower buttons on the collar of the coat, by loops made of half inch wide ribbon, of the colour of the facings of the regiment. Five inches in length, and the rosette attached to them, not exceeding one inch and a quarter in diameter.

White leather breeches, with regimental buttons, and plain stitched seams, are to be worn by the mounted officers of the regiments, viz., field officers and adjutant, and by the surgeon and assistant surgeon/ three of the buttons at each knee to be kept in sight above the boot top.

Black topped wax leather polished boots, are to be worn by the same class of officers, and by captains, and subalterns of the Royal Artillery and Royal Engineers. They are to be made so as to come up in front to within two inches of the cap of the knee, being hollowed out about one inch in the ham, with a double seam in the back, and to be fixed up to a regimental button sewed on the breeches, just below the ham, so as to draw well. And sit close to the leg without wrinkles.

Horizontal rowelled plain plated spurs, with single studs, the necks two inches in length, to be worn with those boots, by the field officers and adjutants, with oval spur leathers, of the same quality as the boot legs.

White kerseymere breeches with regimental buttons are to be worn by all other officers, viz., captains, subalterns, pay master and quarter master; two of the buttons at each knee to be in sight above the gaiters, the buttons of the breeches to be a size smaller than the waistcoat ones.

Black cloth gaiters with regimental buttons of the same size as ordered for the breeches, are to be worn by these officers; they are to be made so as to come up within two inches of the cap of the knee in front, to be hollowed out one inch in the ham, by a button hole, worked in the back seam of them, within half an inch of the top, so as to sit perfectly close to the leg, and to come down flush with the bottom of the heel, the buttons ranging correctly with those of the breeches serving for the top one of the gaiter, which is therefore to have no button at the top, but a hole worked on both sides; the tongue to come within two inches of the point of the toe, and to be confined quite close to the foot, with a broad strap of strong black calfskin sewed down the inside and fixed to three buttons on the out.

Wax leather polished shoes, rounded moderately at the toe to be worn with the gaiters.

The regulation cocked hat, with a crimson and gold cord passed once round the top, and once round the bottom of the crown. This is to be worn perfectly level over both eyebrows, the cock to be well to the left, and the bottom part of the back of the hat, to be somewhat higher than the front, which will bring the sides within half an inch of the top of the ear, but at no time to be worn with the largest end foremost. The infantry rosettes and feather are always to be used.

Black leather horizontal ribbed polished stocks, edged with black morocco leather. These are to be three and a half inches high in the front and fastened with a stock buckle or clap behind. No turnover, or false collar to be allowed of.

White wash leather gloves, plain stitched, are the only ones to be admitted of, and no officer, at any time, is to appear without them. The tops to come well under the cuff of the coat.

Officers when off duty will lay aside the gorget, but otherwise invariably dress precisely the same as for duty.

As nothing tends more to the good appearance of military dress, than an exact uniformity in the mode of having the hair cut and dressed, and as this is a point, to establish which much attention will be required, the commanding officer of each corps is expected to be most particular in enforcing the following directions on this subject.

The hair of the officers to be at all times cut, in the course of the first week of every month, and no oftener, by one established regimental hairdresser, who is responsible to do it according to this simple rule, viz. The top to be cut as close as possible, being left no longer than is necessary to admit of it being turned with curling irons of the smallest size; the back line of the top is not to exceed a line formed by passing packthread from the back of one ear to that of the other, vertically over the crown of the head; the hind hair to be parted from that of the top in the shape of a horseshoe, which will occasion the sides to extend to half an inch behind the ear, and which, therefore, forms the extreme breadth of the top; the remaining hair so parted off behind the string, is to be combed back, to grow down in one even length, from the crown and the back of the ear, so that the whole of it may tie into the queue; No part of the hind hair, so parted off from the front, or brush top, is to be thinned off, and none of the short hair in the neck to be cut away.

When the hair is cut in this manner, it is then to be dressed as follows: viz., the top and sides to be turned with irons, and combed from the ear upwards to the crown, the hind hair to be tied exactly level with the stock, which, when the officer has his coat on, should bring the queue even with the bottom seam of the collar. The hair above the tie to be moderately filled and mixed with powder, and pomatum, well combed into the roots so as to look white, and prevent the powder from falling out on the clothes, but not so as to appear stiff and constrained. The regulation queue which is made so as to receive the hair, is to be at all times worn, excepting by grenadier, and fusilier officers when they are ordered to appear in their bearskin caps, at which time they are to have plaits, which are to be formed according to the following direction. The hair, in the first place, is to be tied with a string close to the head, and then filled with powder and pomatum well mixed, and next to be divided into three strands which are to be braided as flat as possible, without appearing stiff, the plait to be turned up level with the bottom of the collar, and fixed with a comb two inches in width, which is to be placed at the top of the crown exactly where the hind hair is turned back from the top, and forms the centre of the horseshoe, the plait is to cover the whole of the comb, and at the bottom to be half an inch wider than at the top: the string with which the hair is tied, previous to its being divided for the purpose of its being plaited, is to be covered with a flash of inch wide black ribbon, (as that is found to be sufficient to cover the string with which the hair is tied) and the fall down, consisting of two double and two single parts, to be five inches deep and no more.

Officers whose beards will grow sufficiently high to admit of having side-whiskers, may let them grow, provided they do not come down lower than half an inch below the bottom of the ear, and are not shaved behind, or kept clipped too close, as they are always to be combed up with pomatum and powdered; those that have them not, are to shave as high as the top of the ear, so that, when they take the powder off, the side hair may be perfectly level with the corner of the eye; the ear is to be kept free from powder, and no part of the beard below the whiskers, or in the neck etc., to be suffered to grow.

When officers go to Balls, then and then only, they will be permitted to appear in shoes and stockings; at which time their lapels are to be buttoned back, and hooked from top to bottom, showing eight inches of a frill, not exceeding two inches in depth; for which purpose they must have holes worked in the tape, to which the frill is sewed, so as to pass the four upper hooks through, which are to be fixed opposite to each buttonhole from top to bottom. Sashes are then to be laid aside, the bottom button of the waistcoat only to be in sight, and the sword to be worn in the cross belt over the waistcoat, and not over the coat, but on no account in what is termed the small sword or waist belt. The shoes to be worn with buckles of the same colour metal as the buttons of the coat; and no other waistcoat, or breeches, but kersey-mere (and these with regimental buttons) are to be worn; nor any deviation allowed from the other established rules for dress, such as wearing nankin, or linen, small clothes, neck cloths, stocks or shoes with strings, small swords etc.

Soldiers.
White linen shirts. The frill, which is the only part to be seen when on, is to be nine inches long, and two in depth; including the hem, which is to be the narrowest possible, ironed in as small plaits as can be done; one inch of the frill being confined under the stock, which will ensure its remaining parted, and perfectly smooth, at the length of eight inches.

Directions for cutting the hair. The top or brush to be cut as close as the scissor can catch it, allowing the comb between that and the head: the underpart, viz., that immediately over the ear, to be left somewhat longer, so as, when rubbed up with soap and grease, and combed upwards, to look as if it was frizzed after being turned with a small curling iron. The hind hair is to be parted from the brush with a string passed ear to ear, vertically over the top of the head, the same as for the officers, except that no horseshoe is to be formed, every part of the hair that comes behind the string, being combed back so as to go into the queue, that which comes before it forming the brush. No whiskers to be allowed of but for drum-majors and pioneers; but the beard to be always shaved up to the top of the ear, where the side hair is to be left perfectly square and level with the corner of the eye. No part of the beard below the top of the ear, or in the neck, to be permitted to grow, as that always gives an appearance of uncleanliness. NB The top hair is always to be regularly cut in the first week of every month, by one established hairdresser.

Dressing the hair. In order to prepare the hair to receive the queue, it is first to be moderately thickened with powder, and grease, both well combed into the roots; a small pad or cushion covered with black sheepskin, and stuffed with bran, about two inches and a half in length, and of thickness proportional to the man's hair (known by soldiers under the appellation of a mouse) is next to be placed within-side, above the tie. So as to make it appear full and round, without spreading it too much, and in order to prevent it from splitting; but this is on no account to be placed so high as to touch the head, as that would occasion the queue to stand off from it, or make it bag at the tie, which are the two greatest faults that can be found in any soldier's head-dress. After this, the hair is to be tied exactly level with the bottom of the stock, and particular care must be taken, that the tie sets close to the neck; the top hair is then to be well rubbed up with soap, flour, and grease, and combed from the ear straight upwards, so as to have the appearance as if turned up with curling irons, the back hair is next to be covered with soap lather, well beat up with flour in a box, until it becomes a stiff paste, which is to be laid on with a small brush (commonly called by housepainters a sash tool) and then, regularly and neatly marked with a comb the teeth of which should be about ten to the inch, each mark coming directly down from the crown, where the hind hair is parted off from the top, to the tie, after which the whole hair is to be lightly powdered with a thread or cotton puff, until it is perfectly white; but not so as to fill up the marks of the comb. When this is done, all loose powder, that has not attached itself to the paste, where it is directed to be laid upon the hind hair, is to be blown off, so that none may by chance fall on the clothes. The queue, which is to be made to receive the whole of the man's hair, and to cover the string with which it is tied, is to be fixed on, so that, when the man has his coat on, the queue may be even with the lower row of lace on the collar, and lastly the flash is to be fixed on so as to cover the top of the queue.

For the undress, the hair is to be done according to the foregoing directions, except that the soap lather and powder are to be altogether omitted, and no part to shew at all white; the marks of the comb which is used for combing the hair to be left without being smoothed down, although the marking comb is not to be used.

No.1 Officers to be allowed to wear whiskers, serjeants and soldiers not. The whiskers must be allowed to grow so as to come immediately forward into the face, but not to suffer them to grow more than half an inch below the bottom of the ear, nor to be longer than ¾ of an inch; at the same time they are desired not to shave between the whisker and the ear, nor otherwise to thin or clip them. NCOs and privates (except the drum-major and pioneers, by whom HRH desires them to be invariably worn) are on no account to wear side whiskers, but to have their hair shaved off perfectly square in a line with the top of the ear.

No.2 Officers to appear at all times in white cross belts and regulation swords, with sashes. No dirks to be worn at all. The coat to be buttoned all the way to the neck, and no part of the shirt or waistcoat seen. The stock to be black leather with horizontal ribs, white breeches with regimental buttons and long boots, off duty. No short boots to be worn, or blue pantaloons.

The hair to be cut and dressed according to the following form. The top hair to be cut so close as only to admit of its being turned with turning irons of the smallest size. The hind hair is to be parted from that of the top in the shape of a horse shoe, commencing from half an inch behind the ear, which is to be the extreme breadth of the top. This hair so parted off is to be combed back, and allowed to grow down in one even length, so that the whole of it may be in the queue. No part of the hind hair is to be thinned off and none of the short of the neck to be cut away. The hair being cut in this manner is to be dressed as follows, viz. the top to be turned with irons and combed from the ear upwards, the ear being left perfectly free from all powder. The queue to be tied at the distance of two inches from the head, the hair above the tie being moderately filled with powder and pomatum, but not so as to render it stiff or constrained. The regulation queue of which two are in the possession of the quarter master of the Royals, one for the officers, the other for the NCOs and men, which are so contrived as to enclose the hair to be at all times worn, except by grenadiers and fuziliers, when they are ordered to wear their bearskin caps, at which time they are to have their hair plaited according to the following directions.

The hair in the first place to be tied with a string close to the head, then filled with powder and pomatum well mixed, next to be formed into these strands, which are to be braided as flat as possible, not to appear stiff, the plait to be turned up at the length of three inches from the tie, and fixed with a comb two inches in width which is to be placed at the top of the horse shoe, exactly where the back hair is separated from the front, the plait to cover the whole of the comb, and at the bottom to be half an inch wider than at the top. The string to which the hair is ties previous to its being divided for the purpose of being plaited is to be covered with a flash- particular care is to be taken that the hair is at all times thoroughly mixed with powder and pomatum. Such officers whose hair is too short at present to tie, must wear the regulation queue fixed with a string round the head, but will on no account be permitted to wear a queue, as they do at present, sewed to their neck cloths, or to the collar of their coats.

Shoes never to be worn except at balls. On the 1st day of October, all officers must provide themselves with cocked hats, and further flank officers with regulation caps, patterns of which sealed with HRH seal, are to be procured on application to Mr Hawkes, accoutrement maker Piccadilly, until that period, during which round hats are still permitted to be worn, officers are desired to attend to wear them perfectly level on the head, and close down upon both eyebrows. Upon no account to press them so deep on the back of the head that the edge of the crown passes the top of the ear, by attending to which the hat will be even all round, and not sit lower behind than before, which is particularly disapproved of.

The surgeons are to wear black ribbed leather stocks 2 and a half inches broad, and whole boots that come within an inch of the knee, and to sit without a wrinkle. The artificers parade for work at half past three, remain at work 'til one, except an hour for breakfast, from one till four eat and dress, and from four 'til eight at drill. Every serjeant to show himself sober to the adjutant at 9 O clock, who is then to see every man is sober that mounts guard next morning.[9]

---

9   Somerset Local Archives, (SLA), DD/SLI/2/12: Loose Manuscripts Somerset Archives.

7

Fashion in 1802. The Failure of Army-Level Regulation

A persistent theme of the story of the Army of the early years of the nineteenth century was the need to summarise Army regulation in a fully comprehensive and easily accessible format. This is something that the warrants were in part supposed to accomplish, but they fell a long way short of achieving that aim. The reason for this failure is not apparent: it may be that the idea of making a warrant comprehensive in terms of detail ran counter to the primary function of the warrant as a legal document to regulate financial transactions and obligations between government and regiment. The 1768 warrant had contained substantially more detail than the 1800 edition, so it appears that there was a major revision in the concept of warrants away from specific detail between these two dates. With the removal of specific detail from the new warrants there was little to guide regiments except the process of referring to previous warrants to elucidate specific detail where information was absent in the latest warrant. There was clearly a need for something else that went into more precise detail in the same manner as the 1768 warrant. Horse Guards wanted this, and so did the officers of the Army. The need was neatly summarised by Charles James in his *The Regimental Companion*, which in some ways attempted to supply the missing information in three volumes of miscellaneous Army commentary:

> With regard to the other parts of regimental dress, such as breeches, boots, gaiters etc., it is impossible to specify any direct regulations, since custom, the darling of England, has given to different regiments as many deviations from the strict law of uniformity as convenience or caprice can dictate. A general rule, however seems to prevail relative to the appearance of officers at general parades, on guards and in field exercises, this is, that every officer on duty shall wear kerseymere breeches and waistcoat, with the button of the regiment, and cloth gaiters. The stock, which among the serjeants, corporals and privates, must invariably be leather, differs materially among officers, some preferring black velvet, and others silk, It will be impossible not to allow the necessity of some regulation on this head, when it is know that's officers have been ordered to the rear of a battalion for, inadvertently perhaps, appearing in black silk handkerchiefs, or with the ends of the tie-ribbands, floating upon their frills. A government rule would obviate all disputes, and it is

devoutly to be wished, that, as every component part of the British Army is now under consideration, those minutiae will be attended to in one military code, the strict observance or the neglect of which may more or less affect the general system. Nothing is so easy as correct attention to general rules and nothing so liable to perversion and contradiction as partial regulations. The former have all the advantages resulting from collective instruction: the latter are almost always subject rather to dual whim and misapprehension. During a march, officers are permitted to wear boots or pantaloons. Boots are sanctioned by his Majesty's regulation. Pantaloons have insensibly grown into general use from that manifest convenience.[1]

James' three volumes were reprinted with minor updates and amendments throughout the period under discussion, but the lack of a complete updating meant that many passages were out of date in later editions, and attempts by other authors to fill the gaps with army specific periodicals also foundered.[2] It fell to Horse Guards to consider the requirement for official, and more considered, information, in doing so they went all of the way back to the 1768 warrant to try and track subsequent changes forward from there.

By the beginning of the nineteenth century, the 1768 clothing warrant, the last full clothing warrant issued, was hopelessly out of date, having been modified and updated out of existence. This process has been admirably charted by Sir Hew Strachan in his *British Military Uniforms, 1768-96* which tracks all of the clothing orders over most of that period. Because the mass of orders, exemptions, peculiarities, and cancellations had become so byzantine, there were repeated appeals by beleaguered Horse Guards clerks, and inspecting officers for the Adjutant General, for the production of a new and full warrant and consequently an attempt was made by the authorities to codify the existing clothing regulations. In fact, two new warrants were issued, the first in 1800 and another in 1801, and neither addressed the problem fully. The problem was that clothing warrants were limited to the form we have seen in those reproduced elsewhere in this book. They did not deal with the minutiae of clothing, or the dimensions of particular items. And as soon as a new warrant was issued, it was immediately succeeded by a veritable avalanche of alterations. However, it appears that a very significant attempt was made in 1802, to collect all of the information available on clothing. The nature of the project meant that the consultation must have extended beyond warrants and other regulation produced at Army level. Not only were particular regimental orders relating to clothing and appointments included, and some items that were supplied by the Ordnance were permitted to bleed into the fabric of the manuscript, but one can deduce that the interrogation extended to regimental agents, who of course, dealt with the clothiers on behalf of the colonels, and perhaps even to some of the tailoring houses responsible for clothing the officers.

What remains of this investigation is two manuscript volumes, revising the original 1768 warrant by incorporating the various amendments which had been issued subsequently. No new warrant appears to have been issued as a result of this revision; in fact, the next warrant in 1803 follows the same format as its immediate predecessor. Were these volumes not

1   C. James, *The Regimental Companion* (London: Roworth, 1811), volume I, p.59
2   See for instance, *The Royal Military Chronicle* (London: J Davies, 1810 onwards), *The Royal Military Panorama or Officer's Companion* (London: C. J. Barbington, 1812 onwards)

'Colonel Coote Manningham. The founder of the Rifle Corps', 1806. Mezzotint after Edridge. Coote Manningham chose to have his portrait painted in the service uniform, rather than in the full dress of the regiment. (Private Collection)

'Foot Guards', published 1807. Coloured engraving. John Augustus Atkinson. The seated guardsman is carrying his forage cap rolled above his cartridge pouch and attached by two straps in the approved manner. (Private Collection)

'Highlanders', published
1807. Coloured engraving.
John Augustus Atkinson. The
plaid is shown here passing
to the shoulder. The bottom
edge is on the lower thigh,
substantially above the.
'middle of the knee', that is
mentioned in regulations.
(Private Collection)

'Artillery Men', published 1807.
Coloured engraving. John
Augustus Atkinson. A useful view
of the powdered hair towards
the end of its use in the army.
The figure on the left wears
a half gaiter with pantaloons
and carries a cane, in a form of
'walking out' dress. In contrast,
the central figure is carrying his
cartridge pouch and belt and
wears long gaiters, the usual or
parade dress. (Private Collection)

considered suitable for general consultation or for publication, and consequently shelved? Furthermore, since it appears that they were suppressed, or at least their contents have never been recorded as being actively disseminated, what was the motivation behind obscuring this really rather comprehensive and impressive collection of material? No certain answers are forthcoming, and the 1802 collation of orders stands alone and above the other regulation of the period, as a glorious, perfectly formed, but solitary monolith. By some extraordinary chance the two manuscript volumes in question were preserved in first, the collections of the Royal United Services Institute, and latterly in the War Office Library, and transcribed from there by W.Y. Carman in an article for the *Journal of the Society for Army Historical Research*.[3] On the dispersal of the War Office Library collection, one of the volumes subsequently found its way to the National Army Museum. The present whereabouts of the other is not known. They are here placed in context with the rest of the surviving regulation for the first time, and because the annotation necessary to make sense of the volumes is rather dense and impenetrable, they have been reproduced in full as Appendix 1.

The most important elements of the 1802 collation are information on the infantry and the staff. Regrettably, it fails to engage with either cavalry or artillery. The latter omission is understandable, as the regulation for the technical services was derived from an entirely separate source, the Board of Ordnance having jurisdiction over this area, although in practice they appear to have followed the infantry at every opportunity. The lack of information on cavalry is more worrying as the cavalry was almost all under the aegis of Horse Guards regulation. It raises the possibility that there may survive further books forming a part of the 1802 collation that deal exclusively with the cavalry. Any hope of finding these, or any other versions of those we have, must be diminishing.

A very few notes are appropriate here by way of introduction to show the value as well as the limitations of this source.

Coats

The collation details three styles of coat for generals – a full dress coat, 'or grand dress'; a half dress or embroidered coat; and finally a plain or undress coat. Other members of the staff have an embroidered and a plain coat, but lack the 'Grand Dress' or full dress coat. The rifle corps have a full dress tail coat and both a service and an undress uniform. Line regiments specify just one coat. This is a little disingenuous, as in practice even very humble officers of unfashionable line regiments would not be expected to get by on just one coat in which to perform all of their various duties. A fashionable regiment would lie at the other extreme. George Elers described his purchases on being promoted captain from the 90th to the 12th, which was commanded by one of the great fashionable society lions and beaus, Colonel Aston,

---

3   W.Y. Carman, '1802 Clothing Regulations,' *Journal for the Society of Army Historical Research*, volume 19, (1940) p.66.

My outfit cost me about £300. No officer, with the exception of Colonel Aston, had such a kit. I had six regimental jackets, besides dress coats, great-coat, shirts about twelve dozen, and everything in the same proportion'[4]

Elers here distinguishes the dress coats as a separate style from his regimental jackets, but regrettably does not further subdivide the latter by style. The possibility remains that the six were more or less identical, and existed in such numbers solely to spread the wear and prolong their life. However, as noted in Chapter 5, minute variations in style are recorded by Mercer of the artillery, who remembers that pre 1804 the Royal Artillery officers had no less than five different coats in use at the same time.

Elers' colonel in the 12th, as a recognised beau of the Ton, naturally took the matter of clothing to excess, and on the death of Colonel Aston after a duel in India Elers had this to say concerning his wardrobe,

His stock of clothes etc. that he bought in England was immense; I have heard from fifty to one hundred pairs of boots. I remember on the passage out I had a painful boil on my arm; the scar I have to this day. He lent me a loose jacket to wear. I said I was afraid I should deprive him of it, as there were no laundresses on board ship. He said, 'Never mind; I have two hundred more'. His tailors made for me when I returned home- the Croziers, of Panton Square- and they assured me they used to take him home thirty coats at a time. And if they did not fit exactly he used to kick them out of the room.[5]

The dangers of this sort of frivolous outlay was that the details of the regimentals would be changed by regulation or the cut of the coat would simply fall out of fashion before they could be used, Mercer experienced this difficulty with his RHA dolman jackets, which were cut very short and high in the waist. This was the fashionable extreme for an established or an aspiring beau of the Bon Ton. By way of contrast, the notoriously thrifty Lieutenant George Simmons, of the 95th Rifles had the following advice for his mother. She was outfitting George's younger brother for Spain in 1811.

You must procure a superfine red jacket. I was thinking of letting you get him a regimental 34th coat, but am afraid it would be too expensive, although it would in the end be a great saving; as cloth is very dear in Lisbon; however, do as you can. The collar and cuffs; white kerseymere, a white kerseymere waistcoat, two pairs of strong grey trousers, made wide like sailor's trousers, three pairs of strong shoes (one pair short), strong leather gaiters. I have always found them the most preferable, as they keep your shoes from slipping off, and also prevent sand and gravel getting into your stockings. Three pairs of socks. If you could purchase a sword, (not a sabre) similar to the officer's ones you may have observed on parade, and can get it cheap, buy it; it's being new is of no consequence. An old sash also you might

4   George Elers, *Memoirs of George Elers, Captain in the 12th Regiment of Foot* (New York, Appleton and Co. 1903), p.37.
5   Elers, *Memoirs*, p.88.

procure cheap; it would answer as well as any other. However these things are now and then to be met with here. He must have a haversack made of dark fustian (not too large), a clasp knife, fork and spoon; also a tin mug, which will serve him for tea, wine and soup. You may also buy some pasteboard and make a cocked hat, or at least have it cut out in order that he can put it into his baggage, with some oil silk, some broad black ribbon for a cockade, and some broad stuff for a binding. The tailor of the regiment will form it; a gold bullion for each end. His baggage must be as small as possible, as the convenience of carriage is very scarce- three shirts will be enough. He must also have a black leather stock with a buckle, a common rough greatcoat, let it be big enough (any colour, it is of no consequence). Could you get three or four dozen of buttons like the 34th? They would be very useful afterwards. He must bring two or three tooth-brushes and three little towels.[6]

The reality for most was that their outfitting costs probably fell somewhere in between these two extremes. Although most officers would have several different styles of coats to fulfil their various functions, and various coats of different ages within each of those subsets, the exigencies of service meant that not many of the coats would be with the officer at any time, and those that were, would be disproportionately well worn in. The number of Colonel Aston's several hundred fatigue jackets would have been whittled down substantially once the heavy baggage was left behind, and ultimately when transport was pared back to mules, he may have had to rough it with the rest of the army. Making a virtue out of necessity led to modes among the officers that will be investigated more fully in Volume II; these included the substitution of greatcoats of a more or less military style for the red rag under most circumstances on active service.

According to the 1802 collation the officers of the Guards were to have a full dress coat, and then a frock uniform coat. The only difference in the description is that the frock coat has lapels that can be buttoned over rather than being sewn down, and there is more lace and a better lining in the dress coat. Indeed, the 'Account of the Foot Guards' in *The British Military Library* for 1799 observes that, 'the full dress, which is superb, is only worn on extraordinary occasions,' whereas the undress, 'with narrow lace,' was considered, 'very elegant.'[7] Colonel William Stewart, one of the founding officers of the 95th Rifles, asserted that the full dress of that regiment was not necessary for the officers, and recommended them not to bother acquiring it as it was so seldom used or worn, and on all occasions where it could be required, the light-cavalry-style service dress would serve just as well.[8] Certainly a full dress coat intended largely for court wear would not have been a priority purchase for many officers of regiments outside the Guards. Lapels fastened back were considered smarter, and those that can button over across were required to be buttoned back when appearing at court. Note that officers of the Guards were also permitted here to wear leather breeches with their frock coats, further evidence that this was a dressing down option, as leather breeches were considered as a more casual option than the usual cassimere, although sometimes specified in standing orders specifically for mounted or field officers.

6   G. Simmons, *A British Rifle Man* (London: N&MP, 2007), p.209.
7   Anonymous, 'Account of the Foot Guards', *The British Military Library* (London: J. Carpenter, 1799), p.75.
8   NLS, ACC.9074.16.144, Colonel Stewart to Norcott in bound Rifle Brigade correspondence.

A limited set of tailoring accounts over the year 1809 to 1810 for Francis Holburne of the 3rd Guards at the time of his lieutenancy details rather more styles of coats than the recommended two. They distinguish between, 'a fine scarlet cloth regimental frock', 'a plain regimental surtout', and 'a superfine scarlet undress coat',[9] all of these are presumably in addition to the full dress coat specified. The full dress coat would have been replaced much less frequently than the others, as it was likely to see less use, and when it was used, for levees and the like, the conditions were less rigorous than actual field wear with the consequent wear and tear being minimal.

There is a lot of latitude for line regiments. They may be without embroidery or lace on the lapels, but if the Colonel thinks it proper to have either gold or silver embroidered or laced button holes these are permitted. Loftie's album of sketches records some of the versions that were used in these instances.

There is a further peculiar variant for officers of regiments of people of colour which are to have 'half lapels' 3 inches in breadth at the bottom, rising to 4 inches at the top. A strange stipulation. Line regiments lapels were to be three inches. Rifle corps, 3 inches increasing to 3.5 inches at the top, and Guards and staff 3 inches. The lapels for Rifles officers were only intended to apply to the full dress coat, as the light-cavalry-style service jacket was not lapelled. There are two examples of this coat (dated to 1817 and to the 1820s) in the Royal Green Jackets Museum. Despite the comparative rarity of this coat, it has survived in the same proportions as the service dress, examples of which can be found at the National Army Museum in London, as well as at the Royal Green Jackets Museum. The 1802 collation can be compared with that in the 1800 standing orders of the Rifle Corps (soon to become the 95th (Rifle) Regiment. The orders, which were actually published in 1801, although dated to the previous year, note that:

> The Officer's regimental dress is of two kinds; the full dress, and parade or service dress; the former consists in long coat, white breeches and black top boots, or regimental pantaloons and half-boots, hat cocked, pique front and rear; green feather and regimental cockade; coat hooked through the shirt under the stock, and about six inches of shirt frill appearing; the stock black polished leather, high necked and bound with velvet, or black silk plaited; the uniform sash worn over the sword-belt; regimental gloves and cane. The sash is never to be worn with shoes. The hair queued and powdered. It is optional with Officers to provide themselves with the full dress, it being solely necessary for attendance at court.[10]

The 1802 collation expands on the details of the full dress in a way that suggests a communication had passed from the adjutant of the Rifle Corps to the compiler of the collation. This level of detail is not found in warrants or other army level regulation, it appears much more akin to a description of a sealed pattern item, or a regimental order book.

---

9   AR108 and AR109, Archives of the Holburne Museum, Bath, (AHM), Relating to Captain Holburne.
10   W. Stewart, *Regulations for the Rifle Corps* (London: T, Egerton, 1901), Article X.

The full dress uniform coat for officers of a Rifle Corps is to be of dark green cloth, long skirts, and lined with white shalloon, the skirts turned back and fronted with white cassimere sewed down, and at the joining a circle of black velvet embroidered with silver. Lapel, collar, cuffs and wings black velvet. The lapels, rather short and made to button across the body at the fifth button, three inches in breadth at the bottom, and increasing gradually to three inches and a half at the top. A standing collar faced with green cloth, which with the cuffs are to be three inches in breadth. No slits in the cuffs. Cross pocket flaps. Ten buttons on each lapel, including one on collar; three on each cuff and pocket flap. The wings laced, and bullion and fringe besides epaulettes. The buttons set on at equal distances and all large excepting the collar and epaulettes. A flat plated button with a raised bugle horn and crown over it.[11]

Both of the progenitors of the Rifle Corps standing orders (Colonel Coote Manningham and Lieutenant Colonel the Honourable William Stewart) chose to have their portraits painted in the service dress, and there do not appear to be any portraits of rifle corps officers in the full dress, again indicating that the full dress long coat was not in general favour, despite the dashing description above. That the dress of the Experimental Rifle Corps was in flux at this point can also be inferred from a description and illustration that appears in *The British Military Library* of 1801.[12] This was another of those ephemeral unofficial military periodicals, featuring coloured plates of various regiments. Their plate of an 'Officer in Colonel Coote Manningham's Corps of Riflemen' is of the service dress, but this is here worn with the wings described for the full dress. Since the editors of the journal made a point of describing their plates as having been taken from life, this is likely to represent one of the earliest depictions of this later famous regiment.

Waistcoats

The difference between a jacket and a waistcoat technically is that a waistcoat is built from the front, and the back is derived from the front pieces. With a coat or jacket the reverse is true. A waistcoat therefore, can be sleeved or unsleeved. In the majority of cases in the 1802 collation, there are no mentions of sleeves. However, the dress waistcoats had longer skirts and pocket flaps, both of which were archaic, and therefore unfashionable, features. They were white or buff, according to the order of the regiment. The Rifle Corps had a green waistcoat for service dress, and a white one for full dress. These were likely to have been without sleeves, as they were paired with a jacket and coat respectively. The sleeved waistcoat of the other ranks could still be worn underneath the regimentals at the beginning of the century, although it was beginning to lose its sleeves to allow the coat to be cut closer. When the lapelled coat was abolished and the lace moved onto the body of the regimental

---

11 See Appendix 1, 1802 collation, Para 23A.
12 Anon., 'An account of the Rifle Corps', *The British Military Library, or, Journal: comprehending a complete body of military knowledge, and consisting of original communications, with selections from the most approved and respectable foreign military publications* (London: J. Carpenter, 1801), p.564.

'Officer in Corps of Riflemen, Officer of Marines', published 1801. Handcoloured engraving. Anonymous. This is one of the earliest representations of an officer of the Rifle Corp, from the British Military Library or Journal of 1801. The illustrations are described as 'from life' or 'from information given by officers of the corps.' The light cavalry sash and belt-plate are corroborated by items in the Royal Green Jackets Museum and at Edinburgh castle. The jacket is longer in the body than either of the two later surviving examples, and is adorned by an otherwise unrecorded pair of wings in black and silver. (Private Collection)

coat, the waistcoat was discontinued and instead mutated into the forage or fatigue waistcoat or jacket.

Great Coats

Regarding the greatcoats of officers, the 1802 collation is quite clear. Officers of all ranks and regiments, barring Rifle corps and the cavalry, were to wear a coat of dark blue cloth, double breasted, with two rows of buttons similar to their respective regimental buttons and a falling collar of scarlet cloth. The slit cuffs were blue and closed with four small buttons. Pockets to open at the plait; presumably behind.

Those of the rifle corps were to be of dark grey cloth, double breasted and with three rows of buttons, a falling collar and cuffs of green, slit as above and with four small buttons. The main buttons to be similar to those of the large size on the full dress coat. Pockets in the plait again. The degree to which regiments continued with this form of greatcoat for their officers will be more fully documented in Volume II.

Breeches

The breeches as described for the soldier are utterly contrary to prevailing civilian trends, and counter to the previous iterations of soldier's breeches, as well as to those of the officers. The description is quite clear however, so ought to be taken as gospel. It distinguishes a single regimental button on the leg, and tapes to tie the cuff. The usual form for officers and civilians was to have four or more buttons on the leg, and a cuff closure with buttons, and strings or tapes for morning dress and a buckle on the cuff for evening or full dress. This could be an example of a uniquely military style of breeches, connected to the use of long gaiters, which rendered a complicated cuff closure unnecessary because it would be invisible.

Reference to a set of regimental standing orders for the same period allows us to gauge the extent to which the 1802 collation is an accurate reflection of ongoing practice.

April 1802 Standing Orders of 2nd (Queen's) Regiment of Foot, second section

> Perfect uniformity in dress is a point that requires the constant attention of the officer in command of the regiment, and dress once appointed might as seldom as possible be changed. Should it be found necessary, the Adjutant is to be dressed, to have it in his power to give directions to the Corps.[13]

The adjutant of the regiment was the arbiter on matters of dress, taking instruction directly from the colonel, and ensuring conformity. In some regiments the adjutant worked with

---

13 Surrey History Centre, QRWS/1/8/1/8: April 1802 Standing Orders of 2nd (Queen's) Regiment of Foot, second section 1.

the quartermaster to ensure a supply of appropriate appointments and essentials for officers were maintained in house.

> That there might be no excuse for the want of that uniformity, the Quarter Master is always to have in store a certain quantity of every necessary articles of dress, such as lace, buttons, epaulettes, swords, sashes, plates from the tradesmen employed by the regiment, with whom accompts will be closed annually on the 24 December.[14]

The quarter master also held necessaries for purchase by the men. This would include items that were part of their uniform, such as gaiters, shoes, and shirts, as well as the miscellanea of gun oil and brickdust for cleaning arms. The extent to which this supply could constitute a monopoly varied from case to case, and was a matter of keen interest to the private men of the regiment. A quarter master who used his bulk buying power to supply articles cheaply was a blessing, one who enforced a monopoly to make a profit for himself was an object of loathing and complaint.

> The regimental coat according to His Majesty's order. Blue facings, cuffs and collar with white edging. A very narrow silver lace. 9 buttons on the front of the lapels, 4 on the cuffs, 4 on the pockets and 1 on the collar. The skirts also to be laced round on a blue edging, ending at the small of the back with two cross button holes parallel to one another. Silver spring [sic] epaulettes with a star and cross strap both on a blue ground and edging. Greatcoats blue with white edging, regimental buttons and a silver cord on the right shoulder.[15]

The extent to which the coat and greatcoat conform to the instructions of the 1802 collation is debateable. A reasonable assessment would be to say that they do not depart from the letter of the regulation, but they may exceed its parameters by blossoming into areas not mentioned as absolutely forbidden.

'Coats always hooked at the throat. This article to be particularly attended to in officers and men'.[16] This is a stricture frequently met with in standing orders of garrison and regiment. Leaving the collar open allowed for a greater profusion of neckcloth and shirt frill to be displayed. The absolute necessity of closing the collar being clearly enforced, as here, saw the frill displayed in other fashions. It became prone to burst out from the breast where several buttons could be left unopened. It also became the subject of starching and goffering to keep it rigid so it could be allowed to poke forth with such rigidity that it came to resemble the dimetrodon's fin.

'When not on public duty officers are to wear blue pantaloons and half boots or gaiters'.[17] The blue pantaloon was firmly established as an off duty form by 1802, being appropriate for marches as well, but not for parades. The half boot referred to is probably one of the earlier

14   SHC, QRWS/1/8/1/8: April 1802 Standing Orders of 2nd (Queen's) Regiment of Foot, second section, 2.
15   SHC, QRWS/1/8/1/8: April 1802 Standing Orders of 2nd (Queen's) Regiment of Foot, second section, 3.
16   SHC, QRWS/1/8/1/8: April 1802 Standing Orders of 2nd (Queen's) Regiment of Foot, second section, 4.
17   SHC, QRWS/1/8/1/8: April 1802 Standing Orders of 2nd (Queen's) Regiment of Foot, second section, 5.

forms of rear picqued boot to be worn outside the pantaloon. The later half boot would be ankle length, square topped and worn under a pantaloon, trowser, or gaiter.

> A black leather stock, a rosette on the hair and white leather sword knot with gold tassel to be considered as the uniform of the regiment. At the same time officers are always to be provided with every article of dress according to His Majesty's order.[18]

The 1802 collation specifies silk stocks, so the use of leather here is contrary to that specification, although by no means unusual. The most commonly encountered forms of stocks in orders are silk, velvet, and leather, although sometimes there are combinations of these three types. For instance a leather former covered with silk or silk velvet. The rosette on the hair is described as a rose in the collation. The sword knot described here is a regimental peculiarity, and utterly contrary to that described in the collation.

'Officers' and sergeants' sashes to be worn over the belt, tied as to hang down on the left thigh, the flankers as distinction over the right thigh'.[19] The wearing of the sash knot on the right by officers and serjeants of flank companies is another regimental peculiarity. The manner of wearing sashes lacked all homogeny at this time. Almost every regiment had a set of definitions on how and when the sash would be worn.

> Sashes to be worn only on Guard and regimental duty, Field days, musters, reading articles of war, and inspection of necessaries. This relates to sergeants as well as officers. The gorget always accompanies the sash.[20]

The use of the sash and gorget as marks of duty (the cartridge pouch took the place of the gorget in rifle corps service dress) had become so widespread as to be standardised. The wearing of the sash with shoes (and stockings) was almost entirely exploded by 1808, and yet there was still confusion. The 1802 collation bears several pencil additions on the subject, illustrative of the lack of clarity on this subject from Horse Guards:

> 'Query? How are the sashes to be tied, and on which side'. 'Sashes of officers & staff officers on the right side'. 'Query. Are not all staff officers considered cavalry?' 'Sashes to be considered a part of officers' uniform and only to be dispensed with when officers are permitted to appear in gaiters or boots'. 'Orders recently given out respecting Garrison staff officers'.[21]
>
> Dress of the men to be pointedly according with the King's orders, the hair of the flank companies and of the drummers to be plaited up. Where knapsacks are worn, the locks to be packed up, the hair tied clear and close to the head.[22]

18 SHC, QRWS/1/8/1/8: April 1802 Standing Orders of 2nd (Queen's) Regiment of Foot, second section, 6.
19 SHC, QRWS/1/8/1/8: April 1802 Standing Orders of 2nd (Queen's) Regiment of Foot, second section, 7.
20 SHC, QRWS/1/8/1/8: April 1802 Standing Orders of 2nd (Queen's) Regiment of Foot, second section, 8.
21 See Appendix 1, 1802 collation, notes to Para 36A. Further material on the wearing of the sash will be found in Volume II.
22 SHC, QRWS/1/8/1/8: April 1802 Standing Orders of 2nd (Queen's) Regiment of Foot, second section, 9.

The arrangement of the hair is according to regulation. The information on ensuring the hair is clear of the knapsacks is a valuable one, and indicates one of the difficulties that would be ameliorated by the long awaited cutting of the hair in 1808.

'Foraging caps worn in a polished leather case over the pouch, that of the drums fastened on above the drummer's case'.[23] The method of carrying the forage caps can be seen in images, 7.2 and 11.4 here, and in J.A. Atkinson's print of riflemen.[24]

'Gaiters to come up to the cap of the knee, fastened to a button on the breeches in the bend of the knee, by a small leather loop inside, not to be seen'.[25] This accords well with the instructions in the collation, which extend back to 1784.

'Pouches, or bayonet belts are on no account to be fastened or hooked to the jacket either before [in front of] or behind'.[26] This has no parallel elsewhere, and is presumably a corrective to malpractice.

'Drummers to have a white leather skin from the haunch to the lower part of the leg. At their own expense, the regiment having given the first set'.[27] There is no record of a similar appointment in the collation.

'Sergeants, bands and drums, to be always provided with white leather sword knots and gloves; the men with black leather cap for the hammer of the firelock'.[28] Again, these articles do not appear in the 1802 collation. The hammer-stall is known from illustrations and archaeological finds, and its continued use into the nineteenth century is rarely attested.

> Officers and men absent on leave or on the recruiting service where duties in regimentals are never to desist in any of the smallest particular from the ordered dress. The credit of the Corps is very much in the interest in the assurance of those members that are absent. Should this order be neglected by any, and it come to the knowledge of the regiment, they will be ordered forthwith to join, and the Adjutants will note that they do not at any future period meet the same indulgence.[29]

This order is at odds with other accounts of recruiting parties, where additions were made to entice recruits as described by Rifleman Harris:

> The serjeant-major was quite a beau in his way; he had a sling belt to his sword like a field officer, a tremendous green feather in his cap, a flaring sash, his whistle and powder flask displayed, an officer's pelisse over one shoulder and a double allowance of ribbons in his cap.[30]

23 SHC, QRWS/1/8/1/8: April 1802 Standing Orders of 2nd (Queen's) Regiment of Foot, second section, 10.
24 John Augustus Atkinson, *Picturesque representation of the Naval, Military, and Miscellaneous Costumes of Great Britain* (London: Miller and Walker, 1807).
25 SHC, QRWS/1/8/1/8: April 1802 Standing Orders of 2nd (Queen's) Regiment of Foot, second section, 11.
26 SHC, QRWS/1/8/1/8: April 1802 Standing Orders of 2nd (Queen's) Regiment of Foot, second section, 12.
27 SHC, QRWS/1/8/1/8: April 1802 Standing Orders of 2nd (Queen's) Regiment of Foot, second section, 13.
28 SHC, QRWS/1/8/1/8: April 1802 Standing Orders of 2nd (Queen's) Regiment of Foot, second section, 14.
29 SHC, QRWS/1/8/1/8: April 1802 Standing Orders of 2nd (Queen's) Regiment of Foot, second section, 11.
30 B. Harris, *Recollections of Rifleman Harris* (London: H. Hurst, 1848), p.245

On the whole the propensity of recruiting parties to enhance and exaggerate their regimentals appears to have been exceeded only by the elastic relation of their spiel to veracity. Below is a satire on the reported speech given by a recruiting party in Nottinghamshire, 1796.

I will lead you into a country
Where rivers consist of nut-brown ale,
Where the houses are built of hot roast beef,
And the wainscots papered with pancakes.

There, my boys, it rains plum-pudding every Sunday morning,
The streets are paved with quartern loaves,
And nice roasted pigs run about,
With knives and forks stuck in them, crying out,
"Who will eat me? Who will eat me?"[31]

31   James Granger, *Old Nottingham, Its Streets, People, &c.* (Nottingham: Nottingham Daily Express Office, 1904), p.59

8

Regulation of 1803

---

21 March, 1803. Order regarding garrison staff

Adjutant General, General Order to the army,
It is His Majesty's pleasure that in future officers serving upon the staff of garrisons shall respectively wear the uniforms undermentioned, viz.
A town major.
A scarlet coat, without lapels, blue cuffs and collar (infantry); plain white buttons at equal distances; two silver epaulettes, with a gold crown; and where there is a garrison badge, the device to be worn also with the words 'Garrison Staff' round; the sword and sword knots, the same as the regulation for the infantry officers, and suspended by a belt worn over the shoulder, the plate for the belt to be silver, with the crown, and badge as ordered for the epaulettes; white waistcoat, and breeches, cocked hat plain, with regulation feather, staff loop, and plain button.
A town adjutant.
The same as a town major, one epaulette on the right shoulder.
Provost marshal.
The same in gold, with one epaulette on the right shoulder.
Hospital Staff.
Plain scarlet coat lapelled, with yellow buttons, with the words 'Hospital Staff' round, crown in the centre, white waistcoat and breeches, military boots, plain cocked hat, infantry regulation swords and knots. No feather or epaulettes.
By Order of HRH, the Commander-in-Chief,
Harry Calvert Adjutant General.[1]

Horse Guards, 29 March, 1803,
It is His Majesty's Pleasure that in future Officers serving upon the Staff of Garrisons shall respectively wear the Uniforms undermentioned, viz.
A Town Major.

---

1   TNA, WO123/134/208: Army Circulars, Memoranda, Orders and Regulations. Adjutant-Generals Office, (Horse Guards).

'British Officer', 1800. Hand coloured engraving. Anonymous. The 1802 collation stipulates ten rows of lapel buttons to the waist, and this is in accordance with information from tailor's records. However, tailor's books sometimes stipulate a 'long' coat, or jacket requiring extra cloth and buttons. This officer, or a particular size has at least fifteen rows of buttons. (Anne S.K. Brown Military Collection, Brown University Library)

A Scarlet Coat, without Lappels, Blue Cuffs and Collar (Infantry); Plain White buttons at equal Distances; Two Silver Epaulets, with a gold Crown; and where there is a Garrison Badge, the Device to be worn also with the Words 'Garrison Staff' round; the Sword and Sword Knots, the same as the Regulation for the Infantry Officers, and suspended by a Belt worn over the Shoulder, the Plate for the Belt to be Silver, with the Crown, and Badge as ordered for the Epaulettes; White Waistcoat, and Breeches, Cocked Hat plain, with Regulation Feather, Staff Loop, and plain Button.

A Town Adjutant.

The same as a Town Major, one Epaulette on the right Shoulder.

Provost Marshal.

The same in Gold, with one Epaulette on the right Shoulder.

Hospital Staff.

Plain Scarlet Coat lapelled, with yellow Buttons, with the Words 'Hospital Staff' round, Crown in the Centre, White Waistcoat and Breeches, Military Boots, plain cocked Hat, Infantry Regulation Swords and Knots. No Feather or Epaulettes.

By Order of His Royal Highness,

The Commander-in-Chief.

Harry Calvert, Adjutant General.[2]

May, 1803. Submission to His Majesty

That the following be prescribed as the uniform for governors and lieutenant governors, viz.

A scarlet coat lapelled; a blue cuff and collar; gold epaulettes; yellow button with a crown embossed, and where there happens to be a garrison device, the same to be embossed, as likewise on the epaulettes.

White breeches and waistcoats, the buttons on the governor's coat to be placed in like manner as the heads of departments, and the lieutenant governors, as the deputies.[3]

4 June, 1803. General order on marking necessaries

In order to guard as far as possible against the pernicious practice of soldiers selling or pledging their necessaries, the Commander-in-Chief directs that officers commanding regiments, shall take care that every article of the soldiers regimental necessaries, that is capable of receiving a mark, shall be marked with the owners name, the letter of the company, and the number of the regiment to which he belongs.

These marks to prevent their being effaced are on all articles of line or cotton to be made with permanent ink. The shirts are to be marked on the bosom immediately under the frill. HRH enjoins all commanding officers of regiments to cause any person detected in purchasing, or receiving in pawn, soldier's necessaries to be prosecuted with the utmost rigour of the law.

Harry Calvert Adjutant General[4]

The passion for marking equipment could reach excessive lengths. James' *Military Dictionary* relates that:

Marshal Saxe, in his reveries, proposes that every soldier should be marked on his right hand, in order to prevent desertion. He recommends the composition which

---

2   TNA WO123/134/212, Army Circulars, Memoranda, Orders and Regulations. Adjutant-General's Office, (Horse Guards).

3   TNA, WO123/134/245, Army Circulars, Memoranda, Orders and Regulations.Adjutant-General's Office, (Horse Guards).

4   TNA, WO123/134/224, Army Circulars, Memoranda, Orders and Regulations.Adjutant-General's Office, (Horse Guards).

is used by the Indians; and grounds the propriety of his plan upon the custom which prevailed among the Romans, who marked their soldiers with a hot iron. We mention this as a suggestion grounded upon good authority; but we by no means recommend it as an adoption which would be palatable to an Englishman. Tastes and palettes, however, are seldom to be attended to in military matters; witness the hussar muff, and German whiskers.[5]

Although the branding or tattooing of soldiers upon enlistment never found official favour, branding as a punishment and distinguishing mark for misdemeanour did. The *Suffolk Chronicle*, 30 June, 1810 relates that:

If any soldiers, who shall have been tried by a court martial for desertion, and convicted thereof, shall again be tried and convicted of desertion, the Court may order such deserter to be marked on the left side, two inches before the armpit, with the letter D, and such letter not to be less than half an inch in length, and to be marked on the skin with some ink, or gunpowder, or some other preparation, so as to be visible and conspicuous, and not be obliterated.[6]

5 August, 1803 General order regarding bandsmen,

Adjutant General to the Army,
It is His Majesty's pleasure that, in regiments having bands of musick, not more than one private soldier of each troop or company shall be permitted to act as musicians, and that one non-commissioned officer shall be allowed to act as master of the band- these men are to be drilled and instructed in their exercise, and in case of actual service, are to fall in with their respective troops of companies, completely armed and accoutred. HRH the Commander-in-Chief desires that general officers commanding in districts, will immediately communicate the above order to the several regiments under their command and strictly enforce the observance.
Harry Calvert Adjutant General.[7]

This order concerning bandsmen has been included to illustrate the process by which private soldiers enrolled as bandsmen operated on service. The order states that they are to fall in armed and accoutred, but does not say whether they would wear their regimental suit, or their distinctive bandsmen's clothes if they had been provided with them by the colonel. This raises the comical suggestion of men serving in the ranks in some of the more outlandish band uniforms – for instance the Moorish style with turban and baggy trousers. Sadly, this possibility is too ridiculous to countenance, so one must assume that the bands' clothes travelled in the baggage if taken abroad on service (and inspection returns show they frequently were), and that those privates performing a dual role in their companies

5   James, *Military Dictionary*.
6   'Notes' Journal of the Society for Army Historical Research, volume XLIII, (1965), p.157.
7   TNA, WO123/134/245: Army Circulars, Memoranda, Orders and Regulations.Adjutant-General's Office, (Horse Guards).

Species of clothing to be provided; and claims of soldiers on account thereof:

Cavalry
1st articles of clothing for the Dragoon Guards ['and Heavy…' crossed out]
In a regiment of Dragoon Guards, or Heavy Dragoons, each serjeant, corporal, trumpeter and private man shall have for clothing.
Annually,
The hat; and one pair of gloves; and once in every two years
One coat;
One waistcoat; and one pair of breeches,

2nd articles of clothing for the Light Dragoons.
In a regiment of Light Dragoons, each serjeant, corporal, trumpeter and private man shall have for clothing.
Annually,
One pair of gloves; once in every two years,
One upper jacket,
One under jacket
One flannel waistcoat, and
One pair of leather breeches;
Once in every three years,
One helmet; and,
Once in every four years,
One watering cap.
The colour of the jacket for regiments serving in the East Indies, is to be grey, instead of blue.

3rd articles of clothing for the Royal Waggon Train. In Our Royal Waggon Train, each serjeant shall have for clothing.
A leather cap, laced with silver, to be supplied only when actually required,
And once in every three years
A blue jacket with silver lace.
A blue waistcoat with sleeves
A pair of blue plush breeches.
Each corporal shall have for clothing
A plain leather cap, to be supplied only when actually required, and once in every two years,
A blue jacket silver lace on cuff and collar
A blue waistcoat with sleeves
A pair of blue breeches.
Each private shall have for clothing,
A plain leather cap to be supplied only when actually required, and, once in every two years
A plain blue jacket
A blue waistcoat with sleeves.

A pair of blue plush breeches

sealed patterns of all the above mentioned articles are to be placed in the charge of the Inspectors of army clothing, who are hereby authorized to renew from time to time such of the patterns as are damaged or worn out, and the clothing is to be made up in strict conformity thereto.

But it is not required that the leather breeches and gloves should be shewn to the clothing Board, at the biennial exhibitions of patterns previous to the passing of assignments.

Infantry

4th Motives for the alterations in infantry clothing.

It is represented by our clothing Board that the breeches furnished as regimental clothing are made of materials inferior in quality and ill calculated to stand hard service or long marches;, that the annual delivery of a waistcoat front to soldiers in Europe and North America, is attended with less comfort to the men, than the practice of delivering a complete waistcoat with sleeves, which has been adopted in the West Indies: and that, although a very great and acknowledged advantage is achieved to the service from the delivery of shoes under the inspection of the clothing Board, yet that the arrangement in its present form is liable to objection in two points of view, in as much as, in the case of regiments at home the colonels, not having the means of making prompt payment for the shoes which they supply, are under the necessity of delivering to their regiments an article of inferior quality to that which the men can themselves purchase at the same perhaps at a lower price for their ready money, and as, in the case of regiments abroad the colonels expe-rience great difficulty and frequently losses in recovering from the soldiers, that portion of the cost of shoes, which according to the regulation hitherto in force each individual is to pay to his colonel.

In order, therefore, to remedy these evils, We are pleased to direct, that the clothing of our corps of infantry shall in future consist of the articles undermentioned viz: In a regiment of Foot Guards each serjeant shall have for clothing, Annually

A coat the sleeves unlined

A waistcoat with sleeves

A pair of breeches made of materials of the same quality as the coat and lined.

A pair of military shoes

A pair of gaiters and,

A pair of buck or doe skin gloves;

And once in every two years

A lackered felt cap, with a cockade and feather and tuft

Each corporal, drummer, and private man shall have for clothing, Annually

A coat the sleeves unlined;

A waistcoat with sleeves of milled serge,

A pair of breeches made of materials of the same quality as the coat;
A pair of military shoes.
A pair of gaiters; and
A pair of mitts, and once in every two years,
A cap as above

In a regiment of the line serving in Europe, North America, or New South Wales /
    Highland Corps excepted / each serjeant shall have for clothing
Annually
A coat the sleeves unlined
A pair of breeches made of materials of the same quality as the coat
A cloth waistcoat lined with sleeves of milled serge, and
A pair of military shoes, and once in every two years,
A cap as above

Each corporal, drummer and private man shall have for clothing
Annually
A coat the sleeves unlined
A pair of breeches made of materials of the same quality as the coat
A kersey waistcoat with serge sleeves, and
A pair of military shoes, and once in every two years;
A cap as above

In a Highland corps of the above station each serjeant shall have for clothing
Annually
A jacket the sleeves unlined,
A cloth waistcoat with serge sleeves,
A pair of military shoes,
The colonel is also to be at the charge of Highland appointments viz. bonnet,
    feathers, plaid and purse

Each corporal, drummer and private man shall have for clothing
Annually
A jacket the sleeves unlined
A kersey waistcoat with serge sleeves,
A pair of military shoes,
The colonel is also to be at the charge of Highland appointments viz bonnet,
    feathers, plaid and purse.

In a regiment of infantry serving in the West Indies (except for the 5th Batt of our
    60th regiment. and the regiments composed of people of colour) each serjeant
    shall have for clothing.
Annually
A coat partly lined,
A serge waistcoat with sleeves;

Two pair of Russian linen trowsers
A pair of flannel drawers; and once in every two years;
A cap as above

Each corporal, drummer and private man shall have for clothing
Annually
A coat partly lined,
A serge waistcoat with sleeves, with cuff and collar, the colour of the regt.
A pair of Russian linen trowsers
A pair of military shoes, and
A foraging cap, and once in every two years;
A lackered felt cap, as above.

8th In the 5th battalion of the 60th regiment and the 95th regiment of foot, or Rifle
    Corps, each serjeant shall have for clothing.
Annually
A jacket the sleeves unlined,
A waistcoat with serge sleeves,
A pair of pantaloons, and
A pair of military shoes, and
Once in every two years
A cap as above

Each corporal, drummer and private man, shall have for clothing.
Annually
A jacket lined, but not laced, with sleeves unlined
A kersey waistcoat with serge sleeves
A pair of blue pantaloons made of cloth of the same quality as the jacket, and
A pair of military shoes, and
Once in every two years,
A cap, as above.

The men are to be stopped the extraordinary charge of two shillings and three
pence on this clothing, in consequence of receiving pantaloons instead of breeches.

9th In the regiments composed of people of colour serving in the West Indies each
    serjeant shall have for clothing.
Annually
A jacket the sleeves unlined
A serge waistcoat with sleeves,
Two pair of Russian trowsers and
A pair of military shoes, and
Once in every two years
A cap as above,

A grey great coat of the same quality as now worn, but distinguished from the privates' great coats by cuffs, collar and Buttons of serjeants quality conformable to the Facings of the regiment.
Serjeants being Europeans, shall also have one pair of flannel drawers annually

Each corporal, drummer and private man shall have for clothing.
Annually
A round jacket, partly lined
Two pair of Russian linen trowsers
A pair of military shoes, and
Once in every two years;
A cap, as above, and
A grey great coat.

10th In a regiment of infantry serving in the East Indies I each serjeant shall have for clothing,
Annually
A great coat partly lined, and
Two pair of military shoes, and
Once in every two years
A cap, as above
In Lieu of other articles
Clothing adapted to the climate is to be supplied at the discretion of the commanding officer, to the amount of eighteen shillings and eight pence per annum, which will become an annual charge against the colonel.

Each corporal, drummer and private man shall have for clothing
Annually
A coat partly lined, and
Two pair of military shoes, and
Once in every two years;
A cap as above.
In lieu of other articles, clothing adapted to the climate is to be supplied at the discretion of the commanding officer, to the amount of Six shillings and seven pence Half pence per annum, which will become an annual charge against the colonel.
Certificates that articles to the amount above stated have actually been delivered to the serjeants, corporals, drummers and privates respectively of regiments in the East Indies are to be signed by the respective commanding officers and to be transmitted half yearly through the Adjutant General to Our clothing Board, care being taken to provide against accidents by sending a duplicate of each certificate by a subsequent opportunity.
Highland Corps serving in the East Indies are to discontinue while serving there, the Highland appointments.

11th In our Staff Corps each serjeant, corporal, drummer and private man shall
have for clothing.
Annually
A coat
A waistcoat or waistcoat Front.
A pair of blue cloth pantaloons
A pair of half boots and
Once in every two years;
A cap as above.
And further in consideration of the laborious nature of their service each serjeant,
corporal, drummer and private man shall have,
Annually
A Russia duck waistcoat with sleeves
And a pair of Russia duck pantaloons

12th Approved patterns of all of the above mentioned articles of clothing are to be
placed in the charge of the Inspectors of army clothing who are hereby authorized
to renew from time to time such patterns as are damaged, or worn out, and the
clothing is to be made up in strict conformity thereto.

13th Duties of the Inspectors of clothing
And whereas We have been pleased top order that the whole clothing of Our army
should be viewed by two permanent Inspectors of clothing, instead of being viewed,
as heretofore, by a general officer of the Clothing Board, and have appointed two
Inspectors of clothing accordingly: We do hereby authorize and direct the said
Inspectors or the Inspectors for the time being, to view, and compare with the
sealed patterns, the clothing of Our several regiments of cavalry and infantry, as
soon as the same shall have been prepared by the respective clothiers; and, if the
said clothing appear to be conformable to the sealed patterns, to grant two certificates of their view and approval thereof, one of which certificates is to be delivered
to the clothier to be sent with the clothing, to the Head Quarters of the Corps, and
the order to be issued by Our Clothing Board, as the necessary voucher for passing
the assignment of the allowance of said clothing.
    It is Our further will and pleasure, that the clothing be received and certificates
be signed by both the Inspectors, except in cases where the absence of one of them
shall be unavoidable, in all which cases, the cause of such absence is to be stated by
the other Inspector in his certificate of the view of the clothing.
    The Inspector shall follow such further Instructions as they may from time to
time receive from the Commander-in-Chief of Our forces, Our Secretary at War or
Our Clothing Board.

14th Sealed patterns of the clothing shall in future be sent to and remain deposited
at the headquarters of every corps, whether abroad or at home, in order that the
new clothing may be compared therewith, at any convenient time, by the general
officer commanding on their respective stations abroad and in the several districts

at home, or by the officers who may be appointed to inspect the said clothing and certificates of the conformity thereof to the sealed patterns, and of the same having been delivered in due time to the men, shall be in future transmitted by such general, or other officers as aforesaid through the Adjutant General to the Clothing Board: and to obviate any inconveniences that might otherwise arise form the want of such view of the clothing being taken at an early period it is hereby directed, that in each regiment abroad or at home, the commanding officer present with the corps when the clothing is received together with the two officers next in Seniority not under the rank of captain, do immediately on its arrival make a strict inspection into the same, and do cause to be drawn out an accurate state of the quantity, quality and condition thereof, which state he shall transmit, through the Adjutant General of Our forces to our Clothing Board: And it is Our pleasure that such state shall be entered into the regimental books for the future inspection of such superior officer as may be ordered from time to time to inspect or review the regiment.

15th The clothing of regiments on foreign stations is not to be furnished in materials, but is to be sent out made up; except in instances where We shall be pleased to grant a special dispensation, through our Commander in Chief or Secretary at War.

16th And whereas it appears highly expedient that an uniform rule should be laid down in regard to the claims of soldiers to clothing at stated times, or broken periods, and to the dates at which compensation shall be made in such cases as shall admit of payment in money, in lieu of the articles in kind under the restrictions herein after mentioned.

We do hereby declare and make known that, non-commissioned and soldiers dying or discharged before the completion of the period for which the clothing is assigned to last, reckoned from the usual day of delivery the same, have no demand whatever on account thereof.

If a serjeant is reduced to the ranks, his clothing is to be given in for the use of his successor and he himself will receive privates clothing equally worn or as nearly as may be with the clothing he has given in.

A recruit who comes into the regiment after the proper time of delivery of the clothing (if not raised for an augmentation, in which case he is to be furnished with new clothing complete as hereafter directed) shall be immediately entitled to clothing as good as that in wear by the rest of the regiment, and he shall be entitled to new clothing at the next period of the general delivery to the regiment.

17th It is the duty of the colonels and of those employed by them to take special care that the clothing be forwarded and delivered to their respective corps at the exact period when it is due and few cases ought to arise in which it should become a question, whether an allowance in money might not be substituted by the colonels, in lieu of delivering in kind the articles which by our regulation they are required to furnish but if from any extraordinary circumstances of the service, such an instance should be supposed to have occurred in any of our regiments, or detachments of regiments serving abroad, the grounds on which a commutation in money is proposed, shall be fully stated to the Commander in Chief of our forces or, where there is no Commander in Chief, to our Secretary of War, in order that our pleasure may be previously taken thereupon.

If We should think proper to signify Our approbation of the measures the following sums, being the estimated amount of what the colonels would have paid to their clothiers, after a reasonable deduction for incidental charges to which they are liable shall be given to the men.

In the Dragoon Guards and Dragoons

To each serjeant in lieu of:
   coat, waistcoat, breeches £5 12s
   2 hats, 2 pair gloves 12s
   Total £6 4s

To each corporal, trumpeter and private in lieu of:
   coat, waistcoat, breeches £3 6d
   2 hats, 2 pair gloves 9s
   Total £3 9s

Although some of the articles of clothing above specified belong exclusively to the Dragoon Guards and Heavy Dragoons it is to be understood, that the total rate of compensation applies equally to the Light Dragoons.

In the Infantry
   To each serjeant in lieu of clothing complete £3 12s
   To each corporal, drummer and private in lieu of clothing complete £1 16s 6d

18th Provision of necessaries
Whereas by our warrants of the 23th May 1797, for encreasing and regulating the pay of the non-commissioned officers and private men of corps of cavalry and infantry respectively serving at home, we therein ordered that a sum, not exceeding in the Dragoon Guards and Dragoons, two shillings and seven pence half penny per week, and in the infantry of the line, one shilling and six pence per week for necessaries should be retained from the pay of soldiers: and whereas lists of the necessaries to be provided out of the said stoppages, were by Our order annexed to Our clothing regulations of 20th May 1801, and 22nd December 1802, which lists now require alteration: We are pleased in lieu thereof to cause schedules to be annexed to this our warrant containing a specification both of the articles both of clothing and necessaries with which a soldier serving at home, is to be provided, and in which he is to be kept at all times complete: and we do hereby also authorise the like stoppage of 1s 6d a week for the necessaries of the same description from the pay of soldiers of infantry serving in any part of Europe or North America.

It is expected that all the articles of necessaries specified in the said schedules can be furnished of unexceptionable materials, and be kept in complete repair by the stoppages above mentioned, but in particular instances where the same shall not be found adequate, a regimental court of enquiry, or Court Martial, as the circumstances of the case may require is to be convened, for the purpose of authorising such further stoppages as may be judged expedient. And it is our express will and pleasure that no further stoppages for necessaries be made from the pay of soldiers, serving at home, or in any part of Europe, or North America without the sanction of such regimental Court of Enquiry or Court Martial.

We are further pleased hereby to authorize the like stoppages of 1s 6d per week for necessaries from the pay of soldiers of Infantry serving in the West Indies to be expended on articles suitable to that station.

19th Purchase of necessaries. The prices of the articles mentioned in the said schedules of necessaries are now purposely omitted, as liable to variation in a certain degree from temporary or local circumstances; but We do expect, that every officer in the command of a regiment, and every captain, or other officer commanding a troop, will feel it to be a most important part of his duty to take care, that, all articles are purchased for the soldiers, on the most advantageous terms and at steady prices; and that they are delivered to the men at prime cost, without any extra charge, then what, on some occasions may unavoidably be incurred for carriage and when regiments are on foreign stations, for freight and insurance.

If in the course of the year, any of the articles specified in the said schedules should not be wanted for the soldiers use, the money stopped for such articles shall be repaid him.

We do further think proper to declare that without derogating in any degree from the genial control and responsibility of the commanding officers of regiments both in the cavalry and infantry, or precluding them from directing the purchase of articles agreeably to Our regulations, and charging the same to the different troops and companies, whenever it evidently tends to the benefit of the soldier, it is nevertheless to the captains, or commanding officers of troops and companies that we do more immediately look for the due and punctual execution of Our royal intentions, in what regards the care of the clothing, and the provision and care of the necessaries of the men of their respective troops and companies.

And the captains or commanding officers of troops or companies are accordingly hereby made responsible that the necessaries provided for their men be of a fit and proper quality; that their complement be at all times complete; and above all, that such purchases as are necessary be made in the manner most likely to leave no cause of complaint to the soldier.

The captains, or commanding officers of troops, or companies are also responsible, that the persons furnishing the articles be settled with regularly and punctually, as the stoppages accrue.

20th Period of delivery of clothing
Whereas by our warrants of the 23rd April 1801 and the 22nd December 1803 [sic] We were pleased to establish a precise period for the delivery of the clothing to our regiments of Dragoon Guards and Dragoons, Foot Guards, and infantry of the line and to regulate the assignments of the clothing allowance in conformity thereto: and whereas we have since directed that our Royal regiment of Horse Guards should be subject to the provision on the above heads contained in the last mentioned warrant. We do hereby enjoin that the special directions contained in our said warrants, in regard to the intermediate assignments to be made for periods terminating on the 24th December 1801 and 1803 respectively, to the amount of compensation to soldiers for clothing during the said periods, and to the claims of colonels arising from the alteration of the period of clothing, be in every respect and duly attended to and fulfilled.

21st Date of delivery of clothing
In further conformity to the provisions of our said warrants, it is our pleasure that the 25th December 1803 shall be the day on which the next complete clothing of our Royal regiment of Horse Guards, and of our regiments of Dragoon Guards and Dragoons, Foot Guards, and infantry of the line shall be considered to be due, and upon the said day, or as near thereto as possible the same shall actually be delivered to the men of our said corps wherever stationed, in subsequent years also the 25th December shall be the date of delivery of the articles of clothing for our said forces, as the said articles become due respectively according to the periods assigned for their duration.

22nd Period of assignment
In order to correspond with the period of delivery, the next assignments of the allowance for the clothing of our said corps extending for two years in the cavalry, and for one year in the infantry, shall commence on the 25th December 1803 and the future annual or biannual assignments shall in like manner commence on the 25th December in succeeding years.

23rd The 23rd of this instant April shall be the day upon which the then colonels of our said corps shall be entitled to make an assignment for the period commencing the 25 December 1803, and on which they and their representatives shall have a vested interest therein. – In future years also, the 25 April preceding the commencement of the new assignment shall be the day on which the colonels title to such assignment shall become a vested interest.

24th Allowance to colonels on augmentation or new levies. Whenever augmentation to existing corps or new levies are placed on the establishment the like allowance of twenty four months off reckonings in the infantry shall be made to the colonel or commandant as heretofore: the proportion accruing between the date of the commencement of the augmentation or new levy on the establishment and the next general clothing period being uniformly granted under an assignment and the remainder issued in money.

25th Clothing of men raised for augmentation or new levies. Every man raised for such augmentation or new levy, shall upon being finally approved be furnished with complete new clothing: And at the commencement of the next assignment of the clothing allowance for the whole corps, every man without regard to the period at which he may have received his first clothing, shall become entitled to; and be supplied with another complete clothing; with the exception of such articles only, as, in the infantry, are appointed to last more than one year, and, in the cavalry more than two years.

26th Species and duration of cavalry appointments. The appointments to be furnished to the cavalry, exclusive of clothing and necessaries, shall consist of the undermentioned articles; which are to be provided in strict conformity to patterns lodged in the Office of the Comptrollers of the Accompts of Our army.

To the Dragoon Guards and Heavy Dragoons
Saddlery.
Boots shod with iron and nails at the toe
Cloaks with sleeves
Saddle with panel and pad in one, a web girth, with six roller buckles, pair of strap
    flaps
Martingale, breast plate, with roller buckles
Leather surcingles with roller buckles
Pair of stirrup leathers with roller buckles
Pair of stirrup irons
Bit and bridoon complete with head reins and nose band.
Pair of double forage straps with roller buckles
Pair of single forage straps with roller buckles
Firelock strap with roller buckle
Pair of holster straps
Holster and shoe case
Carbine bucket with picket ring
Cover for holsters
Leather cloak cover
Horse collar with iron chain
Buff accoutrements.
Pouch curved for thirty rounds
Pocket behind ditto
Roller buckles
Carbine belt, three inches wide.
Buckles with two brass tongues and tip
Brass slider and swivel
Sword waist belt two and a half inches wide

Brass plate and slide as a bar and double tongue
Bayonet frog, with buff leather
Sword knot of buff leather

To the Light Dragoons
Cloak with sleeves
Boots
Saddlery
Saddle complete, after the Dragoon Guards and Heavy Dragoons
Buff Accoutrements
Pouch curved for 30 Rounds
Pocket behind ditto
Roller buckles
Carbine Belt two and a half Inches wide
Buckles with two brass tongues and tip
Pairs of straps for the pouch to hang by
Brass slider and swivel
Sword waist belt one and a quarter inches wide
Sword carriages
Bayonet frog of buff leather
Sword knot of buff leather

To the Royal Waggon Train
Cloak
Boots

27th Duration of cavalry appointments. And whereas upon the report and representation of Our Board of General Officers, We were pleased by Our warrant bearing date the 13th August 1801 to annul the regulation dated 20th May 1736 by which fixed periods of duration had been assigned for certain articles of cavalry appointments as undermentioned viz.

Years of duration of appointments.
16 years.
Saddles
Holster Pipes
Buckets
Stirrup leathers
Stirrup Irons

12 years.
Bits

6 years.
Headstalls

Reins
Breast Plate
Cruppers
Girths
Surcingles
Straps

12 years.
Cloaks

6 years.
Boots

20 years.
Buff accoutrements

And whereas in process of time great and unexpected inconvenience was found to arise in the service from the disuse of such rule of conduct, under a sense of such inconvenience the Board of General Officers of Our cavalry, who were assembled in the year 1796, to consider of means for the better regulation of the clothing and appointments of the cavalry did, in their report made to Us, humbly remark, that although it is the duty of a colonel at all times to keep his regiment complete in its different appointments, yet it ought still to be expected, that the several species should last nearly the time prescribed by His late Majesty's warrant in the year 1736. And whereas since that time the general officers composing Our permanent Clothing Board, sensible of the continuance and bad effects of the same inconvenience, have also humbly submitted unto Us their opinion, that the revival of such a scale of duration as may reasonably be expected of cavalry appointments on home service, and as the colonels may be enabled to comply with would serve for a general guide in all future inspections, would assist much in checking negligence, and abuse and would restore that care, responsibility and attention of officers and men for their appointments which at all times, the service so essentially and necessarily demands and without which, no expence whatever can, in the field, preserve troops in an effective state: We are therefore pleased to order, that in conformity to the experiences of past times, and to ensure that care and attention which Our military service so essentially require, the regulation of 1736 above recited with regard to the expected duration of the before mentioned appointments shall be held in view in all annual inspections and be acted upon as far as possible in relation to the care and regimental economy of appointments during the ordinary course of home service: and as the duty of the colonel demands that he should at all times keep his regiment complete in its different appointments, so is the most strict attention to their proper care and preservation required from commanding troop officers which they are to enforce by every means in their power and to cause individuals to repair, or replace, such appointments as are lost or materially damaged by their neglect or mismanagement or otherwise than in the fair course of service.

28th Supply of great coats for the infantry.
And whereas by Our warrant of 23d April 1801 We are pleased to direct that each man of our regiment of Foot Guards, and infantry of the line (the regiments composed of people of colour, in which great coats form a part of the clothing supplied by the colonel and corps serving in the East Indies excepted) who was not then possessed of a great coat in good serviceable condition should forthwith be with one, according to a pattern lodged in the Office of the Comptrollers of the Accompts of the army, and that great coats of the like species should be supplied to the rest of the men of our said regiments as soon as the coats then in use become unserviceable, for which effect, we were pleased to authorise the colonels to provide at that time one complete set of great coats of an approved quality for the numbers borne on the establishment of their respective regiments. It is now Our pleasure that the following regulations be observed in the future supply of the said article.

29th Renewal of great coats
The great coats supplied as aforesaid shall be renewed at the expiration of every three years, from the time of their delivery, if necessary (but not oftener) agreeably to certificates to be from time to time transmitted to Our Secretary of War, specifying the number wanted and the periods at which those required to be replaced were originally delivered to the men.

30th Fund for replacing great coats
The expence of the future supplies of great coats shall be defrayed out of the fund established by Our warrant referred to, viz. An allowance from the public commencing from the 25 December 1801, and to be issued half yearly into the hands of the regimental agents, of three shillings per man per annum, and, in the case of corps using Highland clothing, of four shillings per man per annum for the full establishment of non-commissioned officers, drummers, and private men of each regiment of Foot Guards and infantry of the line at home and abroad (excepting as abovementioned regiments composed of people of colour, and corps serving in the East Indies) and a contribution for the colonels of said regiments (commencing also from the 25 December 1801) in corps using Highland clothing, of ten pence, and of other corps of one shilling and ten pence per annum for every man included in their assignments except warrant and contingent men: which allowance to contribution are to be continued as before.

31st Management of great coat fund
The fund so arising in each regiment shall be lodged in the hands of the regimental agent subject to the care and management of the commanding officer (not being under the rank of a field officer) who is to be accountable to Us for the proper expenditure of the same.

32nd Great coats to be considered as regimental necessaries
With the view of preventing great coats from being prematurely worn out by use or neglect, We do hereby declare Our pleasure, that they are to be considered as

'Second, or Coldstream Regiment of Foot Guards. 1801'. Of particular interest for the black over black top boots. Compare the method of attaching the gorget with the previous plate for evidence of regimental peculiarities. William Loftie. (Bibliothèque Nationale de France, 2018)

'An undress worn on the Expedition against Surinam in 1804'. 16th Regiment of Foot. This is possibly a self-portrait. Note the scarlet shoulder straps edged with silver lace instead of epaulettes. Although labeled as an undress, this is perhaps more properly to be considered a service dress with the officer wearing a regimental jacket, or single-breasted coat. The gorget is here suspended from the collar buttons, in a third variant. William Loftie. (Bibliothèque Nationale de France, 2018)

'16th or Buckinghamshire Regiment of Foot. Hompesch's Regiment of Mounted Riflemen. 22nd Regiment of Light Dragoons. Drawn in 1800'. The dress version of the 16th's uniform can be usefully contrasted with the service uniform in the previous plate. The Hompesch mounted riflemen is curiously labelled. Hompesch did carry this colour scheme over into other regiments with which he was involved, and it would had an influence on the facing colours adopted by the 5/60th. William Loftie. (Bibliothèque Nationale de France, 2018)

'XXXIst Regiment of Foot. 1801. Light Company'. The pantaloons and short gaiters are a typical service variant, here in a particularly highly coloured buff. The crested cap and non-regulation sabre are of a peculiar light company fashion. William Loftie. (Bibliothèque Nationale de France, 2018)

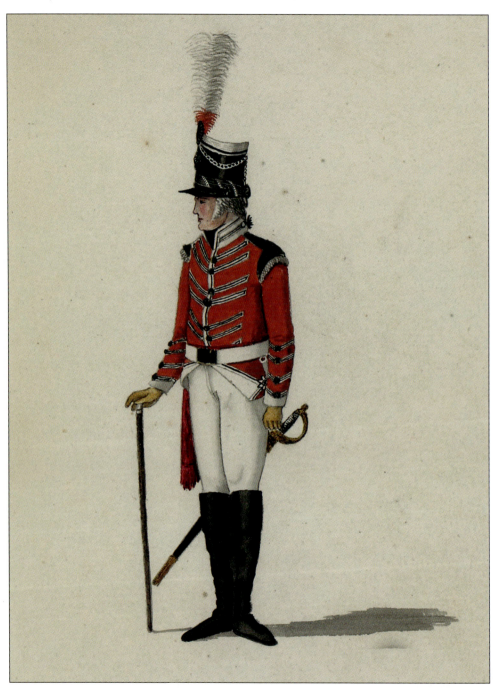

C6. 'VIth Regiment of Dragoon Guards or Carabineers. 1801'. The cane and top boots indicate a walking out dress, here combined with a presumed watering-cap that bears the turban and chains of the light dragoons' helmet-cap, combined with usual chaco features. William Loftie. (Bibliothèque Nationale de France, 2018)

'43rd or Monmouthshire Regiment of Foot. 1802'. The service dress blue pantaloons are here ornamented with Austrian knots. The centre ornament of the three on the pantaloons is very unusual, and the collar is red rather than matching the facings. Loftie has clearly distinguished the colour of the blue pantaloons from other examples in the series. It is here almost turquoise. William Loftie. (Bibliothèque Nationale de France, 2018)

'LVIIIth or Rutlandshire Regiment of Foot. Grenadier uniform as worn on their return from Egypt Feb 1802'.
The hessian boots are very high and tasselled. The creasing in the instep may be an attempt to imitate
the '*a la Souvorov*' style which was predominant on the continent but never much used in Britain. The
mamluke sabre and cordon sabre-carry were an affectation imported from Egypt by both the the French
and the British armies. Its principle advantage is in carrying the sabre high when mounted. William Loftie.
(Bibliothèque Nationale de France, 2018)

'95th or Rifle Regiment. 1803'. The rifles officer wears his moustache as permitted on service. Either the ends of his sash are knotted, or this is an early depiction of the corded 'light infantry' style sash. The shoulder belt plate appears to bear an oval plate rather than the later iconic lions head and whistle combination. Several examples of this belt-plates exist, but they are rectangular, rather than oval as here. William Loftie. (Bibliothèque Nationale de France, 2018.)

'Royal regiment of Artillery. 1802'. This classically correct depiction of the Royal Artillery uniform illustrates clearly the sloped shoulder effect that was the desired result of contemporary tailoring. Although epaulettes and wings were used in a military context to alter the silhouette to a more broad shouldered image, that emphasis ran contrary to the prevalent tailoring style. William Loftie. (Bibliothèque Nationale de France)

C17. 'Member of the Loyal North Briton's Association Riflemen'. Published 1807. Aquatint after F.C. Lewis engraved by Henderson. Among the less obviously startling elements of this uniform are the pique half-gaiters worn outside a pantaloon which is buttoned almost to the knee. This is a typical quasi-military style of the first five years of the century, and was mimicked by the regulars where possible. By 1807 it was drifting out of of fashion. (Version by Percy William Reynolds, V&A)

'Eighteen Cavalry Officers'. 1805. Robert Dighton Junior. Notwithstanding the title on the drawing, apart from the Life Guards and the Blues, who were not Dragoons, only Light Dragoons are shown. Uniforms from left to right: 23rd Light Dragoons; 1st Life Guards; 9th Light Dragoons; 16th Light Dragoons; 11th Light Dragoons; 22nd Light Dragoons; 14th Light Dragoons; 15th Light Dragoons; 8th Light Dragoons; 7th Light

Dragoons; 17th Light Dragoons; 10th Light Dragoons; 18th Light Dragoons; Royal Horse Guards (The Blues); unidentified (19th, 24th or 25th Light Dragoons?); 20th Light Dragoons; 21st Light Dragoons; 13th Light Dragoons. (RCIN 990002 Royal Collection Trust/ Her Majesty Queen Elizabeth II 2018)

'Sixteen Cavalry Officers. About 1806'. Robert Dighton Junior. Tentatively identified by uniform from left to right: 13th Light Dragoons; 8th Light Dragoons, 7th Hussars; 1st King's Dragoon Guards (or 1st Royal Dragoons, or 3rd Dragoons); 9th or 11th Light Dragoons; Royal Horse Artillery; General Officer of Hussars,

15th Hussars; 18th Hussars, Unidentified hussars; 9th or 11th Light Dragoons; Royal Horse Guards (The Blues); 18th Hussars; Aide de Camp to General Officer of Cavalry. (RCIN 916664 Royal Collection Trust/ Her Majesty Queen Elizabeth II 2018)

'Sixteen Cavalry Officers'. 1808. Robert Dighton Junior. Tentatively identified by uniform from left to right: 20th Light Dragoons; 7th Hussars; 12th Light Dragoons; 16th (?) Light Dragoons; Royal Horse Guards (The Blues); 10th Hussars; 16th Light Dragoons; General Officer of Hussars; 15th Hussars; Unidentified light

dragoons; 1st Royal Dragoons (or 1st King's Dragoon Guards, or 3rd Dragoons); 8th Light Dragoons; 9th or 11th Light Dragoons; 13th Light Dragoons; 18th Hussars; Life Guards. (RCIN 916665 Royal Collection Trust/ Her Majesty Queen Elizabeth II 2018)

'An officer in the Foot Guards taken from the life on the parade: Captain Winston'. Watercolour drawing, (created 1805-14). Robert Dighton. The hessian boots shown here are of a very soft leather, so the body of the boot relaxes into creases- a fashion distinct from the rigid hessians. The officer appears to be wearing his scabbard without a sword, a peculiar choice since his gorget and sash indicate he is on duty. (Anne S.K. Brown Military Collection, Brown University Library)

'An officer of the Life Guards'. Identified as Captain Neville. 1805-14. Robert Dighton. Bothe the knotting of the sash at centre back and the pendulant queue of the hair indicate a precise attention to regimental distinctions. The rattan cane appears to be accessorised with something akin to a sword knot. (Anne S.K. Brown Military Collection, Brown University Library)

'A design for a hussar masquerade costume'. 1783. Prince of Wales. The design is indicative of the profound nature of the Prince's early interest in military costume. (Anne S.K. Brown Military Collection, Brown University Library)

'Review on Blackheath of volunteers. Colonel de Blaquiere'. 1800. W.G. Elliott. Besides the accurate depiction of one of the more extreme variants of the cocked hat, the artist appears to have attempted to show the use of chevrons of lace upon the pantaloons. This style is usually associated with French officers in light cavalry dress. (Anne S.K. Brown Military Collection, Brown University Library)

'Review on Blackheath of volunteers. Colonel de Blaquiere'. Rear view. 1800. W.G. Elliott. The extraordinary length of the queue is here shown at its height in 1800. In the background several officers are escorting ladies around the review, and two of these officers wear the newly fashionable rifle dress. (Anne S.K. Brown Military Collection, Brown University Library)

'A Military inspector'. 1802-04. Robert Dighton Junior. The inspecting generals could naturally be expected to be exemplars of the regulated dress, here shown in service version with the unlaced coat, blue pantaloons and hessian boots that avoid the fashionable extreme. The general has made a sop to fashion by carrying a stylish 'military cane' with the associated silver lace cords and tassel. (Anne S.K. Brown Military Collection, Brown University Library)

'Views at Windsor, Major Packe'. 1805-14. Robert Dighton. It is useful to see two officers in full dress of the same regiment depicted together. The artist has shown the pantaloons in two different shades of buff, and the neck-ties are of two sorts. One officer is popping his frill, while the other has left the knotted ends of his necktie hanging loose.. These would appear to be personal fashionable choices- but only one of them can be according to regimental standing orders on dress. (Anne S.K. Brown Military Collection, Brown University Library)

9

Officers' Forage Caps

The great bar to an officer's taste was the want of forage in the country while on active service, which fell somewhat hard on the subalterns, who had to make do by contracting their baggage so as to deprive themselves of any chance of ostentation by variety. In fact they had to omit many articles necessary to their comfort or convenience. That something to wear, something to sleep on, something to eat with, and something with which to cook, were necessary for existence, and only one miserable animal permitted to carry all this between two was unfortunately the case. And so the minimum was carried. As a result, the expression of personal taste was necessarily confined to elaboration of those articles deemed essential and without which, no-one travelled. The regimental uniform was not an arena for personal expression, being instead a vehicle for the fancy of Horse Guards, with a very small modicum of the canvas allowed for a brushstroke from the colonel of the regiment. It was sacrosanct, and infringements on its canonical features were repressed. There were other items in the change of clothes that proved to be more fertile ground for the burgeoning genius of taste with which so many young officers fancied themselves to be abundantly endowed. These fields of endeavour were generally confined to: the undress clothes; the greatcoat; the forage cap; a waistcoat; and trousers or overalls.[1]

The regulated uniform of the Army was by its nature a hidebound and archaically styled beast. It was very slow to absorb changes in military fashion from the continent, and took even longer to reflect civilian fads, especially in those regiments where the taste of the colonel tended towards the old fashioned. This situation was to change with the advent of the Regency, when uniform would more closely reflect contemporary military trends, but pre-1811 the only colonels who had the weight to carve a path in opposition to the royal injunctions were those with a royal duke as regimental colonel, or a colonel wealthy and influential enough to stretch the limits of royal tolerance. Henry, Lord Paget, colonel of the 7th Hussars, was one of those who appeared able to transcend regulation. Even within the rarefied bounds of the members of the royal family there was variance: for every Prince of Wales blithely proceeding without regard to regulation, there was a Duke of Kent who was an absolute exemplar of the outdated Prussian style that George III admired and insisted

---

1   D. Roberts, *The Military Adventures of Johnny Newcome, with an account of his campaign on the Peninsula and in Pall Mall* (London:Methuen, 1904), p.14.

upon. However, the Army did not regulate everything, and, where gaps in army level regulation existed, they could be filled by the colonel's own ideas. Perhaps the area in which these possibilities were most easily expressed was the field of undress uniform, especially in relation to those articles actually described rather loosely, or not at all.

If officers' undress represents an area in which military style could more closely reflect contemporary taste, then forage caps, and also watering caps for the cavalry, were the most fertile ground for individualism to flourish. Whether that individualism began as the preserve of the colonel or not, it is apparent that on service it escaped any regulated confines and became subservient to 'la mode'. In 1800, company officers in a line regiment were expected to supply themselves with a dress cocked hat for full dress, and a cap for service dress. Field officers were initially not required to possess the regimental cap but continued in the cocked hat alone until 1812. Forage caps, and watering caps for cavalry, usually occupied a third and unusual category, where they could be worn with regimentals as a quarters cap, with undress as an undress cap, or as a third cap for service, usually with a greatcoat of regimental type, or of civilian/military cross over (see Volume II for a further discussion of these greatcoats).

Occasionally the undress cap also served as the forage cap, as was the case of the Experimental Rifle Corps, who used a helmet-cap (Tarleton, in modern usage) for service, parade, and undress in 1800,[2] but who had moved to a cap for service dress (like that of the men) by 1802. Images suggest that the mirliton cap enjoyed a considerable vogue in that regiment, but no forage cap seems to have been regulated until 1822.[3] The mirliton also served as a watering or undress cap for the dragoons and light dragoons at various intervals. Flank company officers and fusilier regiment officers could be required to have a wider variety of regimental headwear available. The standing orders of the Royal Fusiliers for 1798 detail the requirements for officers in that corps:

> A bearskin dress cap and upright white hackle feather to be provided at Wagner's Pall Mall. A helmet and white hackle feather to be provided at Wagner's. The officers belonging to the flank company, in addition to the whole of the above mentioned appointments with which they must also be perfectly complete, are to be always provided with a black leather dress cap and hackle crest feather belonging to that company.[4]

Despite the profusion of regulated hats and caps with which officers might be burdened, they still seem to have found room to deal with a forage, watering, or slop cap, in some cases several of these articles, as well as a night caps as considered necessary.

Tailors' pattern books are rather silent on the subject of forage caps, possibly indicating that tailors either tended not to be involved in the production and supply, or that the caps, being ephemeral and either unregulated, or loosely regulated, were not worthy of being

2   Lieutenant General Hon. Sir William Stewart, *Regulations for the Rifle Corps, formed at Blatchinton Barracks, under the command of Colonel Manningham* (London: T. Egerton, 1801), Article X.
3   Adjutant General's Office, *Regulations*, p.93.
4   Percy Sumner, 'Standing Orders of the Royal Fusiliers', *Journal of the Society for Army Historical Research*, vol.27, p.122.

recorded in the same way as pattern items of uniform, which were correspondingly more heavily regulated and required detailed tailors' notes. There are also hints that regimental tailors shouldered the burden for producing these items, for officers as well as for other ranks. Evidence that London tailors did participate in the supply of these whimsical creations is found in the ledgers of Meyer and Meyer, which are account, rather than pattern books, and thus give a different perspective, recording purchases rather than pattern items. That is not to say that the caps provided were not regimental patterns, but they were certainly not regulated at army level, as was the case with regimental uniforms.

The Meyer ledger has five illuminating entries. The first is for Surgeon Morrison of the 10th Light Dragoons (Hussars). It reads, '1811, January 1. Embroidering a forage cap 2s'. Note that the forage cap is being embroidered and not made. The second entry relates to Cornet Hoenes of the King's German Legion 1st Light Dragoons (Hussars). It reads, '1813, December. A Grey Cremer cap, gold band & tassel 3s 5d'. The Cremer referred to is Crimea fur, usually meaning fox. The third relates to Colonel Töbing, of the King's German Legion 3rd Light Dragoons (Hussars). It reads, '1809. Making a Superfine blue cloth cap. Silk lining & wadding 1s 9d. French braid 4s. Silver tassels, worsted braid 6s'. The fourth is for the same officer. 'Cloth. A rich silver bullion tassel for ditto 6s 6d'. The fifth is for Lieutenant Colonel Martin 2nd KGL light infantry. 'A superfine green cloth cap, lined with calico, black velvet round the bottom and a tassel. His own cloth. 8s'.[5]

Memoirs of the period occasionally record variants on the cloth or fur cap as recorded by Meyer's ledgers. Some samples are valid to see if there was further variety. Of interest is to discover whether forage caps were purchased purely according to taste, or in accordance with a regimental or battalion style in particular regiments. In the Meyer ledgers it can be seen that colour and lace conformed to expected regimental norms, based on the usual distinctive and lace colour. Evidence is elusive for the process by which regimental designs were regulated, it remains probably that regimental styles were treated in a similar way to hairstyles or necessaries. That is, the adjutant would be in possession of a pattern, sealed by the approval of the colonel, and this would be referred to by the officers when ordering their caps. Colonel Malet's history of the 18th Light Dragoons quotes a regimental letters book of 1810-12,

> The forage cap was of blue cloth with a white band, and the fur caps of racoon with scale chin straps. From the 1st of May white pantaloons were worn with jackets in place of pelisses. This did not prevent the wearing of the pelisse on full dress occasions.[6]

This type of regimental requirement may have been a typical experience for regimental officers. Even if some of them interpreted it as a launching point for fantasy, rather than a rigid injunction to adhere to type.

5   Archives of Meyer and Mortimer, Sackville Street, London: Ledgers of Meyer's Tailoring House.
6   H. Malet, *Historical records of the Eighteenth Hussars* (London: Clowes, 1869), p.186

'Hussars in the army of occupation, charging to a ball at Boulogne, sketched near Etaples'. Hand coloured engraving, published by S.W. Fores. The forage cap that has escaped the head of its owner may be the 7th Hussars regimental model mentioned by Mercer below. (Anne S.K. Brown Military Collection, Brown University Library).

Some regimental patterns were ubiquitous enough to be used as a model by those trying to pass themselves off as British officers. Mercer recounts his impression of a French spy in the Netherlands during the Waterloo campaign,

> He was dressed as our hussars usually were when riding about the country- blue frock, scarlet waistcoat laced with gold, pantaloons and forage cap of the 7th hussars. He was mounted on a smart pony, with plain bridle and saddle, was without sword or sash, and carried a small whip; in short his costume and monture were correct in every particular. Moreover he aped to the very life that 'devil-may-care' nonchalant air so frequently characterising our young men of fashion.[7]

A fortuitous survival is a small caricature of two hussars of the British Army of Occupation depicting a carriage accident near Etaples. The colouring suggests that of the three hussar regiments in occupied France, this represents the 7th Hussars. The model of forage cap shown falls into the category with a cloth body, a broad lace band, and a peak.

Cap and hat makers also provided forage caps, Captain Dyneley of the Royal Horse Artillery requested of his brother a foraging cap from Hawkes, 'Tell him to let it be much such another as Lieutenant MacDonald of Ross' troop had of him a short time since. If Hawke does not recollect, send me one "neat but not gaudy."'[8]

---

7   C. Mercer, *Journal of the Waterloo Campaign* (Edinburgh: William Blackwood and Sons, 1870), p.124.
8   T. Dyneley, *Letters Written by Lieuenant.-General Thomas Dyneley, while on active service between the years 1806 and 1815* (Godmanchester: Ken Trotman, 1984), p.23.

'Westminster Frolics.' From C.M. Westmacott, *The English Spy: an original work, characteristic, satirical and humorous*. The Westminster scholar's cap worn by the pranksters here, was one of the models for officers' forage caps as described below. (Private Collection)

The letters of William Thornton Keep of the 28th Foot, detail the difficulties of maintaining a fashionably up to date appearance while abroad on service. Keep records that after an initial unsuccessful foray into the world of good taste, he decided that being a leader of fashion was not for him. In 1813, he wrote home that,

> I have had a grey great coat made with a few marks of my vanity attached to it, and have set the tailors to work at a forage cap. Our noble commander I must tell you cares little how we equip ourselves, and leaves it entirely to our convenience and option. Among the vagaries this license admits of, I ordered the said article to be made of cloth similar to the coat but in the form of the Westminster scholar's caps – but after it was finished I was not so proud of it, as I expected to be, and thought it too grotesque and pedantic. Delmar has just arrived from England and has brought a forage cap with him, the gift of Robert Taylor that he wore at Berry Head [depot of the second battalion] and for that I have gladly exchanged my new and extraordinary one. It is of light grey, with a black tassel and broad band of velvet.[9]

In this instance it appears that Keep asked the regimental tailors to create a cap according to his own ideas, presumably one that was inspired by another example he had seen worn. Despite feeling under no military compulsion to conform in respect to his taste, he

9   I. Fletcher, (ed.), *In the Service of the King* (Staplehurst: Spellmount, 1997), p.132.

'Forage cap worn by Caesar Bacon'. This rare survival may be slightly later and reflect lancer influences, or it may be in the form of the 'scholar's cap' mentioned above. (Manx National Heritage Centre, photograph Dr David Blackmore)

nevertheless felt overtly singular when the cap was finished, and chose instead to revert to a type, worn by the second battalion at home. An example of peer pressure at work?

The style rejected by Keep can be identified. A number of Westminster scholars' caps of the period can be seen in an illustration for the English Spy, called, Westminster frolics. The cap is essentially a four cornered mortarboard type, the essence of the medieval scholar's cap, rather than the 19th century schoolboy cap.[10] The unusual nature of this cap is supported by one of the few well provenanced surviving caps from the period: the forage cap of the 23rd Light Dragoons, preserved in the Manx National Heritage centre as part of the kit of Lieutenant Caesar Bacon. This sort of corroboration is rather unusual, because so few caps, images of caps, or mentions of caps in textual sources survive that it is problematic to make any generalisation on styles, or on the popularity of each mode over time, or in any particular branch. It is possible to tentatively identify certain styles though the original names of these are lost, the tendency is always simply to describe, 'a cap,' or, 'a foraging cap'. It is one of the peculiarities of these caps that although foraging is an activity particularly concerned with the provendering of cattle, especially in this context those of the equine persuasion, the infantry, cavalry and artillery make equal use of this term to describe the caps worn when the regimental caps are discarded.

The mortarboard style was a recognisably British one, and its influence from scholars' caps suggests that this style predated the later adoption by lancer regiments of a similar but distinct mode, which rather derives from the Polish confederatka style, popularised as a lancer undress style by Polish officers, and adopted by French officers of lancer regiments under the First Empire.

There was at least one French fashion in forage caps that the British adopted with gusto, and it was derived from the *bonnet de police*, which was part of the continental tradition through much of the eighteenth century. Mercer, whose description of this cap as, 'The most

10   C.M. Westmacott, *The English Spy: an original work, characteristic, satirical and humorous* (London: Egan, 1825), p.66.

ungraceful head-dress that could well be devised' is quoted at length in Chapter 5, pinned the adoption of this version by his troop of the RHA to 1804, and believed some of the light dragoons to also be wearing it. The mode can be traced further back to the Egyptian expedition, when it achieved popularity among British infantry who were otherwise wearing the wedge cap, a specifically other-ranks forage cap that seems never to have been worn by officers. Versions of the *bonnet de police* cap with peaks can be seen in illustrations of the Egyptian period vying for popularity with the wedge. Its use seems to be recorded in the order books of the 13th Foot, for which see Chapter 11, and two examples survive: one for other ranks in the National Army Museum, and another for an officer in Bankfield Museum in Halifax. It may be that the use of the peak to shade the eyes from the Egyptian sun accounted for it sudden ascendance in popularity. The French and British forces alike suffered intolerably from ophthalmic related complaints in Egypt, and the use of the cap with a peak would have to protect the eyes.

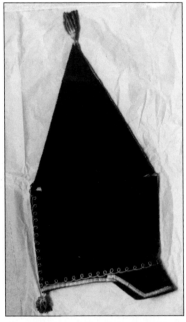

'Forage cap worn 1806-1808 by Ensign Vaughan of the 76th Foot. Photograph by Robert Cooper. (Bankfield Museum, Halifax) The officer's forage cap in the Bankfield Museum in Yorkshire belonged to Ensign Vaghan of the 76th Foot. In essentials, it is of the same type as that described as Mercer, and the surviving cap of Charles Grey, a private in the 10th Foot. This is the only style of forage cap that crosses rank barriers, being worn by privates as well as officers, although naturally the latter had a more distinguished, or gaudy, version, depending on one's point of view. The Vaughan cap dates from between 1806 and 1808.

'Forage cap worn by Private Charles Gray, 2nd Battalion, 10th (North Lincolnshire) Regiment'. The second forage cap of this style in the Bankfield Museum is an officer's model dated to 1806-1808. It is similar to this, with a black velvet body and velvet covered peak. The lower edge and peak are edged with silver lace, with a tassel to the rear of the bottom edge. The seams are ornamented with a repeated loop motif in silver *soutache*, and the *flamme* terminates in a second tassel. A further diagonal strand of *soutache* confines the *flamme* to the body when tucked under. (National Army Museum)

French influence could be even more direct, as witness this account of trading caps,

> In the course of the day, our men went down to a small brook, which flowed between the opposing armies, for water. One private of my own regiment [34th], actually exchanged forage caps with a soldier of the enemy, as a token of regard and good will.[11]

Generally there was little imitation between the privates and the officers, with the privates' forage caps following a separate line of development through the period (examined in more detail in Volume II). One account from 1812, of the storm of Ciudad Rodrigo, reveals an unusual cross fertilisation of style between the ranks, and is of added interest for its suggestion that non-commissioned officers might also upon occasion possess private items of clothing on service: 'My cocked hat was blown away, my clothes all singed; however the sergeant (of the 52nd), a noble fellow, lent me a catskin forage-cap'.[12] Catskin was not made from a skinned moggy, as one might expect. It was a name for a cheap form of silk velvet.

If French military influence can be traced in the adoption of the *bonnet de police* style, as Mercer suggests, there was another cross fertilisation during the Peninsular War, the adoption of the Spanish, Basque, or Pyrenean bonnet as the British Army traversed the Pyrenees. This was an example of a foreign civilian style being absorbed into the British military palette:

> The corps here presented a very novel appearance. From the great want of shoes, many of the men had been provided with the light hempen sandal, made and worn by the natives of this province, and well adapted to the steep and slippery heights by which they are surrounded; the becoming cap, too, of these mountaineers, was quite the fashion with our officers.[13]

In Spanish, the type of cap the Basque used is called a *gorra basca* or, more generally, a *boina*. Similar styles was known elsewhere in Spain. In Euskera, the Basque language, it is called a txapela and resembles a beret with a large and well developed crown. The adoption of local styles was a distinct feature of the Peninsular campaigns, The author of *Johnny Newcome* related that Major General Peacock, military governor of the forces at Lisbon, was compelled to take action against the sartorial excesses of the Belem Rangers, those officers so called because they hung around the rear echelons and depots at Belem, rather than moving up country with the army,

> With respect to the officers in Lisbon, who were there either on duty, on leave, or otherwise, the variety of their dress became at length so ridiculous that

11 Moyle Shearer, *Recollections of the Peninsula, An Officer of the 34th* (London: Longman, Hurst, Ress, Orme, Brown and Green, 1824), p.86.
12 Harry Smith, *The Autobiography of Lt-Gen Sir Harry Smith* (London: Murray, 1903) p.58
13 Sherer, *Recollections in the Peninsula*, p.186.

Major-general Peacock was obliged to issue a severe order, restricting them to the use of the regimental greatcoat and hat, or cap.[14]

Greater latitude was permitted to those with the army, and a particular mode of dress developed among the staff, who spread the mode by degrees to the regimental officers:

Lord Wellington, in consequence of the heat of the weather, indulged the officers in wearing loose greatcoats; but this was soon followed up with waistcoats of all sorts, and colours, with filigree gold , or silver buttons, and what were called forage caps, of all fancies and shapes. They only wanted the appendage of bells.

At Lisbon, Messrs Smith and Co opened a warehouse of English goods, where an officer might suit himself, paying rather dearly, with every article of wearing apparel, and furniture for his cattle.[15]

On his arrival with some other officers at Portsmouth in 1813 from Lisbon, Grattan of the 88th wrote:

We were all splendidly dressed with braided coats, handsome forage caps, rich velvet waistcoats appended to which were a profusion of Spanish silver buttons (some wore gold ones), and our pantaloons bore the weight of as much embroidery as poor Fairfield once said, would furnish a good sideboard of plate. Thanks to the German Tailor in Lisbon for this. But as we landed and saw the garrison of Portsmouth in their white breeches and black gaiters, and their officers in red coats, long boots and white shoulder belts we must have appeared to them, as they did to us, like men who formed part of an army of a different nation.[16]

Browne also recorded that the officers had their opportunities to refresh their kits, when the depots of the army moved from Lisbon to St Jean de Luz after 1813.

The town of St Jean de Luz thus became a sort of depot of the stores and clothing of the army. Shops were established in every house, and every sort of comfort and necessary very soon arrived from England, and so great was the number of speculators who arrived, that their competition rendered the price of articles much more moderate, than the necessities of the army would otherwise have forced them to pay.[17]

The knitted style of forage cap was clearly unknown to Browne in 1813, as he describes the locals of Bastan, near Pamplona (Basques), as wearing 'In place of hats, a dark blue worsted bonnet woven without a seam, such as is seen in some parts of the highlands of Scotland'.[18]

14   Roberts, *Johnny Newcome*, p.14.
15   Roberts, *Johnny Newcome*, p.33.
16   W. Grattan, *Adventures with the Connaught Rangers* (London: Edward Arnold, 1902), p.327.
17   T.H. Browne, *The Napoleonic War Journal of Captain Thomas Henry Browne* (London: Bodley Head, 1987), p.255.
18   Browne, *Journal*, p.251.

The role of the Highland bonnet as an undress cap has been extensively covered by Robert Cooper in his thesis on the Hummel bonnet.[19] Its use by officers seems to have been confined to Highland regiments.

> The full plumed bonnet was worn by the officers on guard, on parades, on the march and on fatigue duties. There was no regimental forage cap, though of course, an old bonnet without plumes, or some such headgear, was worn by officers in camp. The plumed bonnet is formed of feathers called, 'flats' and 'foxtails'. And in the 79th there were six of the latter pendant on the right side, (the bonnet of the 42nd had not these pendant feathers). Also a black cockade with silver sphinx in the centre of it, on the left side of the bonnet, and a leather peak on the front, placed above the black velvet binding. The bonnets of the serjeants and the privates were of the same form, but had not quite so many feathers. They were bound with patent leather, with a slit behind fastened with a ribbon, so as to admit of the bonnet being fastened to the head; also a black cockade and sphinx, and a peak in front. The hackle was white, red and white, or green, according to the company.[20]

This knitted type of cap seems to be unknown outside of Scottish regiments in the early period, although its use has been traced to some cavalry regiments in 1815.[21]

19 R.A. Cooper, *The Hummel Bonnet, an investigation of its production, design and significance in military uniform* (Thesis for the degree of Master of Philosophy by Research The Department of Archaeology, The University of Sheffield, May 2013).
20 H. Smith, 'A list of the officers of the 79th Foot 1800-1851', in McKenzie, *Historical Records of the 79th Queen's Own Cameron Highlanders* (London, Hamilton, Adams and Co, 1887).
21 Cooper, *The Hummel Bonnet*, p.165.

10

Regulation of 1804

The Royal Waggon Train was an extremely expensive innovation developed in 1802 under the control of the Quarter Master General's department. It was the latest attempt to bring transport of the equipment of the Army under military rather than civilian control, and was the most successful of those attempts to date. This letter from the clothiers Pearse illuminates the process of choosing the uniform for the new corps. Pearse explains that it was modelled on the fashion of the light dragoons, albeit at a cut rate price, and further that the fashion for the clothing was decided by the Duke of York.

29 February 1804, Letter on Royal Waggon Train

> Pearse Clothiers to Harry Calvert, Adjutant General,
> When the new patterns for the clothing of the waggon train were fixed upon by HRH the Commander-in-Chief, it was settled in respect to the Fashion of the clothing and the ornaments that the whole cost, should not exceed that of the regiments of light dragoons. We have therefore stated in the enclosed account, the price we charge for the clothing of the 15th regiment light dragoons, and also what we have charged for the Royal Waggon train, whereby you will see that it is done the cheapest for the waggon train. We have to request of you to lay this estimate before HRH and the clothing board, and trust it will be found satisfactory, and that you will be pleased to notify such approval to the Secretary at War for guide in passing our bill.
> J.N.& B. Pearse, clothiers.[1]

28 March, 1804. Extract from clothing board minutes

> Adjutant General to clothiers, Highland Regiments etc.
> The Adjutant General having stated that it is the Commander-in-Chief's wish that it should be declared by the board, what sum it is incumbent on the colonel of a Highland regiment to expend annually in the article of feathers for the bonnet of each soldier of his regiment, The board proceeded to take the subject into their

---

1   TNA, WO7/33/178, Departmental Out Letters, Board of General Officers.

Table 2 Estimate of the prices of clothing for the Royal Waggon Train 1804 (WO7/33/179)

Estimate of the prices of clothing for the Royal waggon train, 1804	Each	Total	Estimate if clothed as a regiment of light dragoons	Each	Total
188 private dress jackets.	22s 6d	£211 10s	188 privates and 12 artificers in privates dress jackets. (200)	25s 3d	£252 10s
12 serjeants ditto with chevrons.	44s	£26 8s	12 serjeants ditto with chevrons.	87s 6d	£52 10s
4 trumpeters ditto.	37s	£7 8s	4 trumpeters ditto.	80s	£16
8 farriers ditto including badge.	23s	£9 4s	8 farriers including badge.	25s 3d	£10 2s
12 artificers ditto .	23s	£13 16s	12 corporals including chevrons.	36s 9d	£22 1s
12 corporals ditto including chevrons.	34s 6d	£20 14s	188 privates and 12 artificers in privates dress jackets. (200)	15s	£150
188 private undress jackets.	17s 9d	£166 17s	12 serjeants ditto with chevrons.	27s 9d	£16 3s
12 serjeants ditto with chevrons.	29s	£17 8s	4 trumpeters ditto.	26s 3d	£5 5s
4 trumpeters ditto.	26s	£5 4s	8 farriers including badge.	15s	£6
8 farriers ditto including badge.	18s 3d	£7 6s	12 corporals including chevrons.	27s 6d	£16 10s
12 artificers ditto .	18s 3d	£10 19s	236 leather breeches.	24s	£283 4s
12 corporals ditto including chevrons.	27s 6d	£16 10s	236 flannel waistcoats.	3s 6d	£41 6s
220 private breeches blue shag.	15s	£165	236 cloaks.	37s	£436 12s
12 serjeants ditto ditto.	18s 6d	£11 2s			
4 trumpeters breeches, white shag.	15s	£3			
236 cloaks.	37s	£436 12s			
Packing expenses		£21 13s 6d	Packing expenses		£21 13s 6d
Grand total.		£1150 11s 6d	Grand total.		£1330 6s 6d

consideration, and after careful investigation of the cost attending the clothing of highland regiments compared with other regiments of the line, and recurring to the estimates of the years 1801 and 1803, the board is of opinion that the colonels of highland regiments can afford to expend for the article of feathers for each soldier, the sum of four shillings and ten pence annually on each suit of clothing without exceeding the estimate of clothing paid by colonels of other regiments of the line, and that neither a larger nor a less sum should be expended by them on this article.[2]

30 March, 1804. Circular Regarding Mourning

Adjutant General to Prince of Wales, Prince William Frederick, the Dukes of Clarence, Kent, Cumberland, Gloucester, Cambridge
HRH is most respectfully informed by the Adjutant General that from some difficulties that have occurred in arranging the funeral procession of the late General Sir William Fawcett from Great George Street to Chelsea, it is now determined that the procession shall commence at the Governor's lodge at Chelsea, and proceed from thence on foot to the place of interment.

The mourners and pall bearers to assemble at the state apartment in the governor's lodge tomorrow at half past one o clock PM. General and staff officers are to be in embroidered frock uniforms, other officers in their regimentals. The whole with crepes on the left arms.

Harry Calvert Adjutant General.[3]

11 April, 1804. General Order Regarding Medical Staff

Adjutant General to the Army,
It is His Majesty's pleasure that in future officers serving upon the medical staff of the army shall respectively wear the uniforms undermentioned, viz.

The Inspectors.
Scarlet coat, single breasted, with black velvet collar and cuffs, slashed sleeves and skirts, yellow hospital staff buttons, two epaulettes embroidered with gold on black velvet, with two gold embroidered button-holes on the collar, two on each cuff, and two plain on the sleeves;

Cocked hat, with black feather, black button, and black silk loop;

Blue pantaloons and half boots;

Black (waist) sword belt, regulation sword and sword knot, as approved for officers of infantry.

2   TNA, WO123/134/317: Army Circulars, Memoranda, Orders and Regulations. Adjuatant-General's Office, (Horse Guards).
3   TNA, WO123/135/307: Army Circulars, Memoranda, Orders and Regulations. Adjutant-General's Office, (Horse Guards).

Black (waist) sword belt, regulation sword and sword knot, as approved for officers of infantry.

Purveyors and deputy purveyors to wear the uniform of the physician and apothecary, with the exception of silver epaulettes and buttons for gold.

The Regimental surgeons and assistants to wear the uniform of the regiment, the coat to be straight, without facings, but with the regimental colour to collar and cuffs, and each one epaulette on the right shoulder.
    Harry Calvert Adjutant General[4]

17 September, 1804. Circular on waterproofing

Deputy Adjutant General to army agents,
The Commander-in-Chief directs that in future the great coats supplied to the army, are to undergo the process of being made waterproof previous to their being delivered to the regiments, for which purpose, you are requested to give the necessary instructions to the several army clothiers. I enclose for your information a copy of a letter received from the deputy Secretary at War which authorises the expence arising from making the coats waterproof agreeable to Messrs Duke's process being charged to the public.
    William Wynyard Deputy Adjutant General[5]

6 October, 1804. Circular on generals' uniforms

Deputy Adjutant General to Generals commanding districts,
I have the honour to enclose to you for the information of the brigadier generals in the district under your command His Majesty's pleasure with respect to the uniforms to be worn by those officers in future.
    William Wynyard Deputy Adjutant General.

[PS] It is His Majesty's pleasure that the uniforms of brigadier generals shall be the same as that of major generals, except that on the sleeves and pockets there shall be only three buttons placed two and one- one of the cuff.

The order of 30 October 1804 regarding caps for the 96th Foot throws some side light on the early caps of the period. It has been previously clear that there were new pattern caps for the infantry in 1800 (the first lacquered cap), 1806 (un-lacquered caps), and 1812 (the 'bang up' or Belgic cap). This letter suggests that a change was made between the introduction of the felt cap in 1800, and the commencement of a lacquered cap, which obviously occurred

4   TNA, WO123/134/320: Army Circulars, Memoranda, Orders and Regulations. Adjuatant-General's Office (Horse Guards).
5   TNA, WO123/134/371: Army Circulars, Memoranda, Orders and Regulations. Adjuatant-General's Office (Horse Guards).

before it became obsolete in 1806, and which we can now place prior to 1804 on the evidence of this letter.

30 October 1804. Letter regarding caps of 96th Foot

> Adjutant General to Francis Moore Esq
> I have had the honour to submit to the Commander-in-Chief your letter of the 29th instant with its inclosures, and am directed by HRH to state for the Secretary at War's information in reply to that part of Sir E Littlehales' letter which relates to the caps of the 96th regiment; that when the regulation respecting the lacquered caps for the army was established, His Majesty with a view to relieve the colonels of the regiments or the public from any extra expense, was graciously pleased to permit that in instances when at the period of issuing the regulation, regiments were entitled only to cap crowns for the ensuing year from having been supplied with completely new caps at the last delivery of their clothing, the regulations should not take effect until the expiration of the said year, for which they were to receive only the cap crowns, but whenever that period had expired, it became indispensable that every regiment should be furnished with the lacquered caps.[6]

13 December 1804. Circular to certain cavalry officers

> From the Deputy Adjutant General to Officers of certain regiments stationed at Windsor (Horse Guards), Chichester (Dragoon Guards), Exeter (Dragoon Guards), Piershill (dragoons), Canterbury, Colchester, Newcastle upon Tyne, Lewes, Brighton.
> I am directed to request that you will state for the Commander-in-Chief's information, whether the shag breeches furnished to the men as part of their regimental clothing, are found to last the time for which they are calculated to be in use, and if not, what means you resort to for providing the men with breeches til the next period of clothing. I am likewise to desire that you will state, for HRH's information, your opinion as to the expediency of continuing the use of shag for the breeches of the heavy cavalry and that you will mention the article you would recommend to be adopted in lieu of it, should your opinion incline to an alteration in this part of the regimental clothing.
> William Wynyard, Deputy Adjutant General.[7]

A further reference to caps comes in a letter written in reply to one from Coote Manningham, colonel of the 95th Rifles. The Adjutant General refused to countenance any change in the caps of the 95th Rifles as proposed by their colonel. We are left wondering what the proposed change may have been. In 1800 the standing orders of the regiment record two types of cap for the officers (a helmet cap, or Tarleton; and a cap like that of the men.) The men had the

6   TNA, WO3/152/420: Office of the Commander-in-Chief: Out-letters.
7   TNA, WO123/134/393: Army Circulars, Memoranda, Orders and Regulations. Adjutant-General's Office (Horse Guards).

standard 1800 cap, with a brass bugle horn instead of the universal plate, and green tuft and cap lines.

28 December 1804. Letter regarding caps of 95th

> Deputy Adjutant General to Brigadier General Manningham,
> I have not failed to submit to the Commander-in-Chief your letter of yesterday, and am commanded to inform you, the HRH cannot recommend to the King, any alteration in the caps approved by His Majesty for the 95th regiment.
> William Wynyard Deputy Adjutant General.[8]

1804, Stray document

> Assistant adjutant and quarter master general uniforms.
> Full dress.
> Scarlet coat, blue cape and cuffs.
> Twelve button holes on each side of the breast, including the cape, at equal distances, embroidered in silver, the same as aides de camp.
> Four embroidered holes on each sleeve, and skirts, at equal distances.
> Skirts sewed back and faced with white kerseymere, joined at the points with an embroidered ornament.
> Epaulettes embroidered on scarlet cloth, in like manner as aides de camp.
> Buttons, those of the adjutant and quarter master general and their deputies.
> Undress.
> The same as the above, without embroidered buttonholes.[9]

8   TNA, WO3/38/270: Office of the Commander-in-Chief: Out-letters.
9   TNA, WO123/134/334: Army Circulars, Memoranda, Orders and Regulations. Adjutant-General's Office (Horse Guards).

11

The Primacy of Regimental Orders

> The soldiers had a fashion distinct from the officers and they did not ape one another.[1]

It has been established elsewhere in this work that the most significant regulations on uniform were imposed at regimental level. The very existence of regimental orders which contravene Horse Guards orders is a demonstration of this principle. Army level regulation is significant. Local, brigade, or divisional orders have relevance, but the actual business of deciding which of the supra-regulation to follow, and which to suspend or omit, occurred primarily at battalion or regimental level. The colonel in chief, colonel commanding the regiment, or colonel commandant was supreme. Which had the upper hand varies from case to case. This can lead to extravagance in cases such as the 10th Hussars, which was in all practical aspects, immune to regulation above the regimental level. It can also be exhibited as excess, in the case of the 7th Hussars, where more was always more. In the fashionable infantry regiments, such as the 12th Foot, doyens of fashion in the line, or for the Coldstream Guards, it led to deviation from the norm in both quantity and style. A different expression of the colonel's primacy was expressed in the 1st Foot when their colonel was the Duke of Kent: the colonel's fancy was expressed as an absolute adherence to army regulation which was a peculiarity of its own. It is harder to establish the same theme in the artillery. There is some evidence, from Mercer for instance, that the artillery exhibited the same process at a lower level, and that company regulation was of a greater significance than it was in the infantry, where it was necessarily subordinate to the colonel's regulation, and usually suppressed by that same source. This peculiarity of the artillery was perhaps owing to their usual deployment being in companies or troops, rather than by battalion.

It might be useful here to examine the regimental orders of a line regiment that is not notable for its utter smartness, or relative slackness, but which falls somewhere in between. Finding relatively complete sets of regulation for particular regiments can be difficult. It is fortunate that there exists for the 13th Foot both standing orders, and regimental order books that significantly coincide chronologically. These enable us to provide a very thorough examination of what we can present with some confidence as an average regiment of

---

1   Blackmantle, *The English Spy*, p.177.

'Review at Brackley', 1803. Watercolour by Thomas Rowlandson. This illustration of a review shows the privates in white pantaloons, and the officers in the blue version with short hessian boots. All are wearing their long hair powdered. The light company captain wears his cap in contrast to the other officers in hats. (Anne S.K. Brown Military Collection, Brown University Library)

the period with an average approach to clothing and uniform. The records show a strong inclination towards utility, but are by no means immune to the influences of fashion, or the taste of the colonel. The extracts relative to clothing are presented here in their entirety, with occasional additional notes.

Some significant conclusions can be drawn. The colonel, Lieutenant General George Ainslie, consulted his officers on occasion concerning their preference for particular items. I hope it can be excused that he first of these is in 1798, immediately prior to the period under consideration, when the colonel observes that grey pantaloons have been chosen by the officers as an item to be worn in uniform, and as such, no further deviation will be tolerated.

There also appears at times an almost extraordinary variety of dress for the other ranks, who have multiple items of legwear, several regimental coats, undress waistcoats, and at least two forage caps and two regimental caps in use at the same time. This apparent superfluity is moderated by the absolute necessity of allowing nothing outside of these items to be owned, or carried by the men. The objective is to supply the men with everything practical that they will need for their various duties. Where the duty requires them to move more swiftly, or to preserve certain items for occasional use, the excess kit is withdrawn into regimental stores or heavy baggage, and re-issued as necessary. Many of the items thus reserved for occasional use are the old regimental clothing cut down or adapted. For instance, old regimental caps with the badges removed are used for certain duties, and old coats are turned or cut down into shells. The various duties reflect the typical life of an infantry of the line regiment in the period immediately before the Peninsular campaign. The 13th found themselves in Ireland in 1798, England in 1799, and then engaged in a series of assaults on the Spanish coats in 1800. In 1801 and 1802 they were engaged in the Egyptian campaign and subsequent garrison duty, from which they travelled to Malta and then Gibraltar. In 1805 they returned to England, and after occupying various stations in the south of the country they were removed to Ireland again in 1807, before sailing to Bermuda in 1808 where they would take part in the invasion and occupation of Martinique.[2]

The extraordinary variety of information to be found in these orders reinforces my conclusion that a serious study of the clothing in use by the Army can properly only be conducted at the regimental level. The distinct and particular nature of particular orders of dress, as well as hairdressing, and unique items of apparel observed here, are clear evidence of that particularity.

The sources for this study are the printed 1808 Standing Orders of the regiment, preserved in the Somerset Local Records Office,[3] and several sets of regimental order books, most of which are again in the records office, and further corroborating but shorter sets, preserved in a private collection. For convenience, I have presented the extracts here sequentially, and included a very few orders prior to 1800 and post 1808 where relevant.

6 June 1798

> The commanding officer is sorry to observe that such is the inattention of the officers to standing orders on the subject of dress, that any two appearing together can hardly be supposed to belong to the same corps, which is the less excusable, as the dress itself is so well adapted to the convenience of everyone: from this day every officer is positively forbidden to wear when in uniform any other pantaloons than the light pepper and salt mixture adopted by their own choice last August.

This is an example of a colonel taking steps to avoid the impact of the 'Tyranny of Taste' on the dress of his officers, not by imposing his own sartorial habits, or even those of Horse Guards, but by collaborating with his officers to find a common solution. The success of this measure can in part be judged by the necessity of issuing this order reminding the officers of their mutual decision. Is will be noted that the salt and paper pantaloons are an ephemeral fashion (if that is not a tautology in itself). The next mentions of pantaloons refer to several different colours, 'in the possession of the officers,' none of which are of this pattern. This is a useful reminder that the required regimental pattern may alter not only *with* the seasons, but as *frequently* as they do.

20 April 1800

> At morning drill and exercise, the men are not to wear their false tails, but are to have their hair combed clean through and tied close to the head. The men on guard

---

2   R. Cannon, *Historical Record of the Thirteenth, first Somersetshire; or Prince Albert's Regiment of Light Infantry* (London: Parker, Furnival and Parker, 1848).

3   Somerset Records Office. DD/SLI 6/5, X181-182: Regimental Orders of the 13th Regiment.

are also to take off their false tails, and have their hair similarly tied before they lie down on the guard bed at night.

29 April 1800

The new clothing is to be issued, and so there is a sufficiency of hats, ready-made. Extra breeches and leggings in the store. It is expected that every man will be fitted with them at evening parade.

4 May 1800

It is Lieutenant General Ainslie's orders that the officers' coats are not in future to be laced around the edging. As notwithstanding the brigade order to the contrary, some officers still wear their hair un-powdered, Lieutenant Colonel Colville will be under the necessity of reporting the first who comes undressed to parade to the Major General of the District.

He also disapproves most highly of the manner in which the grenadier officers generally wear their hair which has more the unmilitary appearance of a crop than of the plait which is ordered by His Majesty for the officers, as well as the privates of the grenadier company.

The lacing of the edge of coats was a recurrent bugbear for both Horse Guards and regimental colonels. The stricture against lacing turn backs in particular is still a common feature of inspection reports as late as 1810. It can be seen as a battle between the tailors, who insisted on deploying extra lace, the officers, who accepted it, and Horse Guards' natural inclination to deplore unnecessary extravagance.

21 May, 1800, Southampton

The taylors will march with the last division and be kept continually at work in the interim. Subsistence for them will be left in the hands of the master taylor.

1 May 1801, Alexandria

To save the clothing and great coats, as many taylors in addition to those now at work, as Corporal Gamble can employ, will be excused parades and all duties but guards, for the purpose of making fatigue jackets of the coarse cotton stuff of the country. To begin with those whose clothing was the first issued.

These jackets were a local issue, sourced locally by the regiment. At this point the regiment had been in Egypt a year, and was due new fatigue jackets. The last opportunity to be issued new ones was a year previously, and presumably those had expired, as the order implies greatcoats were being used for fatigues, or the regimental coats themselves. Regimental suits were expected to last a year, and it is probable that the fatigue jackets were worn more frequently than the red regimental coats, so the new jackets may have been long overdue. As items of necessaries, they would have been sourced by the regiment on home service, so there is nothing exceptional in the local provision of necessaries on foreign service.

11 May 1801

> It is hoped that officers will profit by the arrival of the fleet to provide themselves with such articles of dress as are essentially necessary for the appearance as such, and that some attempt at uniformity may be again made- pantaloons of either blue cloth, nankeen or Maltese stuff uniform with the men will be admitted- as the officers are supposed to have some of each on hand but of no other colour, as never before sanctioned in orders. Pantaloons are to be worn with the boots and not as fatigue trowsers. Such few officers as have adopted mustaches are desired to discontinue, as they carry an appearance not only of affected singularity but of want of cleanliness. It is particularly the office of the Major to enforce the uniformity of dress of the officers on parade, allowing for our present want of resources, and they are further requested not to allow of any deviation from it from officers who they may meet out of our immediate encampment.

Moustaches were lightly in vogue as an emblem of foreign service. Their use was normally limited to light dragoon regiments, and the light infantry at this time, although it remained unofficial. The Experimental Rifle Corps expressly permitted officers to bear moustaches on foreign service in their standing orders of 1800 but it appears the moustaches infrequently survived the return to the environs of Bond Street.[4]

The pantaloons are now of three types, the last of which, Maltese stuff, the officers shared with the men. Throughout the 18th century a heavy cotton serge was popular with sailors for trousers in the central Mediterranean area. The strong maritime tradition of Malta seems to have introduced the trousers to the Royal Navy, and the Mediterranean fleet was buying thousands of pairs in 1804.[5] This seems to be an earlier introduction, with the difference that the stuff was being used to make pantaloons. The Maltese fabric was usually indigo dyed solid blue but there are versions with fine white stripes. Sometimes wool or linen was blended with the cotton, but the fabric was generally stiff and hard wearing. Nelson considered it a cheaper and superior version of the Russia Duck beloved of British military contractors, which was an adequate fabric, but had the disadvantage of being supplied through a system with highly developed and entrenched methods of corruption. The Maltese were suppling a superior product and service.

4   Stewart, *Regulations for the Rifle Corps*, Article X.
5   L. Brockliss, J. Cardwell and M. Moss, *Nelson's Surgeon: William Beattie, naval medicine and the Battle of Trafalgar* (Oxford: Oxford University Press, 2005), p.90.

4 July, 1801

> No soldier, officer's servant excepted, do presume to appear in the streets without being properly dressed in regimentals, or white jackets and side arms. Foraging caps, if clean, and the flaps pulled over the eyes will be permitted.

There are very few surviving forage caps of other ranks for this period. Of the three main shapes used, only a single example of each of the first two exist, and barely two or three of the last. As luck would have it, the forage cap that is probably the earliest survival, belongs to the 10th Foot, who were in Egypt with the 13th in 1800–1801. This cap has a peak that can be worn up or down, which may correspond to the 'flap' mentioned above. It is tempting to draw the parallel that the 10th and 13th were using similar forage caps at this time.

16 July, 1801

> Officers on parade to wear their coats uniformly buttoned across, and without allowing any coloured waistcoat to be seen, they are to wear their white cross belts and feathers, which can be easily procured without red bottoms which for the present must be dispensed with.
> Being now in a stationary quarter, with many advantages denied to the rest of the army, gentlemen are to recollect that their dress greatly affects the general good appearance of the regiment, and that we have already and will have every day more and more the eyes of very observing people upon us to whom we ought to be anxious to shew the British troops to the best advantage.
> Such men's hair as requires it to be immediately cut according to regimental pattern.

17 October 1801, Preparations for marching Rosetta-Alexandria for embarkation

> The quarter master will immediately set the whole of the taylors with the exception of two for mending, at work upon the long leggings and no more Maltese trowsers are for the present to be made up.[6]

Throughout the period, one finds on board ship going home that the taylors were busy making breeches and gaiters up to replace those that were missing or inadequate. Long leggings here refers to gaiters, which would be part of the home service dress required should the British Isles be their destination. The reference to Maltese stuff appear to show that although the officers were using it for pantaloons to be worn inside boots, or long and tight over shoes, the other ranks were being supplied with trousers, which were presumably worn loose without gaiters (however, see below, 30 November 1801).

---

6   Somerset Records Office. DD/SLI 6/5, X182: Regimental Orders of the 13th Regiment.

'The death of General Sir Ralph Abercromby'. 1804 Engraving by Vendramini after Porter. This painting shows a wide variety of dress with headgear ranging from cocked hats through forage caps to the round hat used in the Mediterranean theatre. (Anne S.K. Brown Military Collection, Brown University Library)

22 November, 1801

> As the requisite materials for making up the regimental uniforms is not at present to be had, the Lieutenant-colonel allows of a jacket, but which must strictly conform to the pattern pointed out to the master taylor, it may for the present be worn on all duties, but officers are expected to have a good long coat for full dress when required, and are requested to supply themselves by the opportunity which offers, with round hats and regulation feathers to be worn on all parades. On the account of the scarcity of silver lace and buttons, they are dispensed with in the hat, and to be no longer considered uniform.

This order contains two dispensations from regulation on grounds of utility. The materials lacking for constructing new coats might be broadcloth, which would have to be imported to Alexandria. The jackets constructed may have been made from old uniform coats, or have been a completely different beast. The round hat, which was a relative of the modern top hat, was de rigeur for service in hot climates. The Royal Marines adopted it as their dress cap.

28 November, 1801

> Officers are requested to pay attention to the hint in Brigade Orders respecting uniformity in dress. The lieutenant-colonel has observed some officers in white

pantaloons, black, and other coloured waistcoats appearing from under the coat which are strictly forbidden.

Pantaloons had been authorised by the colonel in Maltese stuff (probably blue or striped), in blue, or in nankin (usually ranging from buff to yellow or pale brown). White was not an option, being here reserved for breeches for some reason. The coloured waistcoats are a demonstration of civilian fashion intruding into the uniform. An analysis of period fashion plates by Martin Lancaster has established that less than five percent of those shown were black, nearly half were white or off white, and some 34 percent were striped.[7] It seems likely that the civilian influence here followed these trends.

30 November, 1801

> The men will take their white breeches into constant wear from this evening, as it is probable that the Maltese stuff may again be worn, should the regiment remain in a hot climate, all the pantaloons, let them be ever so bad, to be washed and taken into the companies stores. They will at all events be serviceable on board ship.

There are several points of interest here: the Maltese stuff, although supposed to be hard-wearing and a relatively heavy cotton fabric, was considered as hot weather garments, as opposed to the broadcloth wool breeches which were now issued, it being November. The term pantaloon is here used to refer to the other ranks Maltese stuff legwear, which was described as trousers above. This creates a problem – were the colonel and adjutant using these terms interchangeably?

9 December, 1801

> If officers prefer the pantaloons as a more comfortable dress on duty at this season, he [the colonel] has not the slightest objection to their adoption, but must be previously assured that it is in the power of every one to conform to it. He has observed that several officers in making up their undress jackets, have deviated from the pattern, in having long button holes worked, which besides being contrary to the idea of the dress, takes up twice as much of the taylor's time as is necessary, and some are cut too short in front, and do not when buttoned up hide the waistcoat, flying off also ridiculously behind. The quartermaster will inform the master taylor that in future he will be made answerable for any deviation from the strict uniformity introduced into the dress of the officers (by himself or any of the regimental taylors) which includes lacing the full uniform lengthways, and if the undress, so simple a one in itself, cannot be made up with uniformity, it will be discontinued entirely, which will certainly be an inconvenience brought upon the whole by a minority. If others are to be purchased, the commanding officer requests that blue or other dark coloured gloves may not be worn on parade.

---

7   Martin Lancaster, 'Lecture on Fashion for Men.' Given at Spencerville Heritage Fair, USA, on 9 June, 2016.

These strictures combine the universal bugbear of the era, the additional lacing on the dress coat, with a useful reminder that adaptations for comfort made by the officers of a corps had to be adopted by all or none. The officers' sops to fashion included the addition of twist thread running outwards from the button holes on their undress jackets. This is seen in unlaced coats, for instance those of surgeons and of certain staff positions. The jackets were also being cut away behind, and made short to display the illicit coloured waistcoats. Combined with the use of fancy coloured gloves, an interesting picture of sartorial deviance emerges.

11 February, 1802, Valetta Harbour, HMS *Niger*

> Blue pantaloons and half boots are until further orders to be the constant dress of the officers, except when it may be their wish to appear of an evening (not at parades) in shoes, when the regimental standing orders as well as every other on that subject of uniformity is to be strictly attended to, this of course includes regulation sword belts, and must, now, sword knots and tassels for the round hats as ordered by General Fox. The undress jackets cannot be worn on guard, or at any full parade of the regiment.

28 April, 1802

> Such men as have long gaiters not of the proper regimental length, or such as are not worth laying by in store but are as good enough to be cut into short, are not to be returned as wanting new, but will have them altered by the regimental taylors, as the pantaloons are taken into use.

This suggests that short gaiters or half gaiters were being worn with the Maltese stuff pantaloons. These gaiters may have been worn inside the pantaloons, or more likely outside, as was more the fashion in 1802.

30 April, 1802, still at Gibraltar

> Commanding officers of companies will immediately compleat such of their men as may be in want of them with white jackets and loose trowsers of the uniform pattern. The regimental taylors cannot be spared for that purpose. A pattern piece of white stuff will be shown by the quarter master serjeant; which if approved of by Captains can procure on very reasonable terms. It is hoped that the men will in future wear their fatigue trowsers when they go to wine houses, and not carry their disgraceful marks of their drunkenness to parade with them'.

This would appear to mark a clear move from pantaloons to loose trowsers, implying that the Maltese stuff formerly used, had indeed been for pantaloons, rather than trowsers.

'Private of 3rd Foot Guards', 1800 (front view). Watercolour by J.A. Atkinson. The artist has faithfully recorded the appearance of the overalls that were common service wear throughout the period. (Anne S.K. Brown Military Collection, Brown University Library)

11 May, 1802

> It being many years since the edging of lace to the officers uniform was forbidden, it cannot be said that sufficient time has not been given for wearing out the coats so made up in those three or four officers who, either in new coats or turned old ones are now uniform must stand to the consequences of their opposition to a positive order, and the lieutenant-colonel thus pledges himself to take the most serious notice of any officer appearing contrary to that order after the 14th of this month. He has observed that some of the flank company's officers wear their epaulettes without the distinguishing mark of their rank.

It will be noted that the practice of wearing excessive quantities of lace on the coat was still being censured by Horse Guards' directives as late as 1810.

17 May, 1802

> The commanding officers of companies will give directions for having the woollen breeches washed, and such of the long leggings as required new dyed, previous to their being laid by in their companies store chests. The officers on parade will wear their coats hooked at the collar, and during the existence of the general order for wearing the sashes under the coat, the lapel to be left loose.

16 August, 1802

> Officers when on parade will wear their cocked hats with the cock full to the front, the side hanging over to the right.

25 August, 1802

> In order to save the men's good white shirts, they are to be provided with a check one each (constant work men, two) or to have their old white ones mended up so as to be fit, to be worn upon all duties of fatigue. The men are not to presume to wear them on other occasions. Nor are they to be worn by NCOs or drummers. Care must also be taken that the fatigue shirts are washed at the most after two days wear.

The checked shirts are an interesting departure. Later on there will be an injunction against wearing white false shirt fronts with checked shirts. This had become an undesirable practice directly derived from the toleration of checked shirts, which were usually considered working shirts.

28 August 1803

> The commanding officer has to signify that it is the Lieutenant Governor's intention that the officers of the garrison will wear plain blue cloth pantaloons when off duty from the 1st October.

buttonhole in the gaiters connecting them to the knee band button, was now closed, and a leather loop was attached to the gaiter to hold it to the knee band.

3 April, 1804

> As the regimental clothing is every hour expected the commanding officer does not wish any extra breeches to be made up for any man who can possibly do without them. commanding officers of companies will collect at the dinner parades of the three days next to come, the correctest states they can of what Russia duck jackets and fatigue trowsers are wanting to complete their men to one of each. The bad to be condemned, but kept for duties of fatigue.

The regimental clothing appears to be being delivered with a consignment of necessaries as well. The fatigue jacket and trowsers were both of Russia Duck at this time, which was linen and fairly heavy weight. A week later the regiment was parading in 'tongued pantaloons,' which were a form of mosquito trowser. These may have been the new undress trowser. Leaving the old duck trowsers to be used for heavy fatigues as is apparent in the following orders. At this time it is possible to see that the other ranks disposed of several pairs of legwear at any time. In this instance they had white breeches, white pantaloons for the summer, fatigue trowsers in duck for hard work, and tongued pantaloons for off-duty.

10 April, 1804

> The regiment to parade for exercise tomorrow at 11 O clock, in white jackets. Tongued pantaloons and side arms.

24 April, 1804

> Tongued pantaloons to be taken into wear by the men off duty commencing this day. The regiment to parade tomorrow at half past one O clock in watch coats, white jackets and fatigue trowsers.

27 April, 1804

> The officers will wear their white jean pantaloons at regimental parades, commencing this evening. The grenadiers will discontinue wearing the tassels and cord lately worn in their caps on the convent guard, as will Captain and Lieutenant Browne those worn by them, as not being according to the king's regulations, or uniform with the third officer of the company.

4 June, 1804 (still at Gibraltar)

> The gorget being the distinguishing mark of officers upon duty, is to be worn by those of the flank companies as well as the battalion, they are always to be worn by the orderly officers of the day. The swords, gorget and other appointments of

several officers, being thoroughly worn out, they are desired to provide themselves with others in town, or to give in their names to the quartermaster in the course of tomorrow, that others may be sent for from England.

7 June, 1804 – a recap for those re-joining

In points of dress the field officers are called upon to observe, that the regimental order for wearing the cocked hat (on parade) with the cock full to the front, the side a little to the right, to be enforced. Uniform leather gloves only, to be supposed on parade, the coat hooked at the collar, not to be dispensed with, and no more than the four upper button holes to be left unbuttoned. The sash to be wound twice round the body, confining the sword belt, close above the frog, the rolls passing one over the other, and kept opened out, pulled down a little before the front the coat, and hiding the meeting of the coat with the breeches.

The light infantry officers when next making up jackets will not have them so short, or so much cut off behind, as some worn at present. The epaulettes of flank companies officers to be always distinguished by the grenade and bugle. The looping worn by grenadier officers to be as pointed out by regulations.

26 July, 1804

The regiment will for the present parade in their white jackets, but every possible care must be taken of the red shells, as it is probable they may be again called into wear, on the change of season should not the regular clothing shortly arrive, at all events they will be wanted as a winter working dress.

The red shells may be reworked or cut down old regimentals used for undress or fatigue work. The regiment appear to have retained both the red shells and white fatigue jackets.

8 October, 1804

Officers to wear their blue pantaloons at parades until further orders.

29 December, 1804

In obedience to the garrison orders of yesterday officers are allowed to take all duties public as well as regimental in blue pantaloons and half boots and as this has often been the expressed wish of officers: it is hoped that the uniform appearance of the regiment will not be spoilt by their at any time appearing at this season in any other dress; the hatband pointed out in yesterday's orders will be accompanied by the button and loop as formerly worn in the regimental full dress and undress. Queues of the men will be most carefully laid up in company stores. The officers will also recollect that the caution which it is thought necessary to point out in this instance for the soldier holds good as to their own occasional appearance: cocked hat, queue, breeches and gaiters according to regulation. Dismounted officers will continue to wear their swords at all times in the shoulder belt until the uniform waist-belts are landed.

18 February, 1805

It appearing that the men's hair is falling off very fast most probably the effect of the late fever, the quartermaster will find a sufficiency of rum and oil to be well mixed in equal parts, and which under the direction of a NCO of a squad is to be well rubbed into the roots of the hair every day until further orders. The worsted footing being also found to cut the hair, a fold of thin linen must be either neatly rolled between the hair and it or a better length of ribband provided at the option of the soldier.

Given the penchant of the British soldier for rum, using it as an adulterant for hair oil appears to be a recipe for disaster.

18 March, 1805

As the new clothing and caps will be taken into wear on Sunday next, to prevent their being filthied by the oil which it has been found lately necessary to use for the men's hair, it must be all well washed out with soap and water on Wednesday. And instead of the 1st of the month, the hair of the whole regiment, (servants included) to be cut on Friday and Saturday. The commanding officer approving of the way in which James Ridolle of Captain Thornton's company has polished his new regulation cap directs that NCOs will make themselves acquainted with his mode of doing it and instruct their men in the same.

Infuriatingly it is not clear whether the method of polishing the cap referred to is for the cap peak only, or for the entire cap. Since this is the period of the model 1800 lacquered cap, it is reasonable to suppose that it is the entire cap body being polished.

24 March, 1805

Officers commanding companies will immediately inspect their men's old gaiters and when they find them sufficiently good, will direct them to be cut down to wear with the summer pantaloons. The men requiring it, are to be furnished from what officers servants and others can spare, with either a second coat or shell, in sufficient good repair to do occasional duties in, to save the new clothing. The quartermaster will allot six taylors to the business not of turning, but merely failing their inserviceable repair. Such old shells as commanding officers of companies may condemn as unfit to be any longer worn even on fatigues of which there are a great many, must be either burned or cut up into cloths. The men for working parties will wear their old regulation caps without the brass plate or tuft, as the leather foraging must be kept clean for to be worn with regimentals when off parade, according to garrison orders.

Here in a nutshell is a reason why the red coats of ordinary soldiers survive in such limited quantities. There may be no more than twelve privates' coats from regiments of regulars existing today. The 1802 collation allows for gaiters in linen or in cloth. It is not apparent which is indicated here, but the colonel's preference was for cloth for officers.

20 January, 1806, at Winchester

> Officers will parade for church on Sunday next in breeches and gaiters. The former of cloth, or the thickest double milled kerseymere. Cloth, it is believed, keeps its colour better.

20 March, 1806

> Servants or taylors must not be permitted, even on a march to wear any article of clothing not strictly regimental, the former may if they choose, carry their round hats over their packs and not vice versa as has been the case on several instances of this march. The attendance of soldiers on officers is entirely a secondary consideration, which must not interfere with the military appearance or duties required of them. Officers are expected to be provided with a small portmanteau or haversack, calculated to hold only such changes as they may want on the march, and such alone will be allowed to be moved by the men from the baggage waggons or stores to their billets.
>
> Upon the first threatening of rain, the greatcoats must be unfolded, and put on over the accoutrements.

31 March, 1806, Weymouth

> Officers who are having coats made up will have their epaulettes fastened by two holes cut into the shoulder of the coat. The silver cross loop to be discontinued.

29 May 1806

> Colonel Colville having noticed that the men's queues might be improved by adding one half inch to its length which allows of it being hung more regularly tapered from the tapes, he directed an alteration to be made in the standing orders, article two, section seven, to that effect. A pattern queue for each company and for the drummers, has been marked with his seal to which the whole are implicitly to comply in shape and length. The upper part of the flash is to be exactly even with the top of the queue which is to be at the length of the upper lace of the coat collar, supposing the latter to be well fitted to the neck. With this alteration it is impossible it can interfere with the pack or greatcoat if tied as is instructed so as to lay flat along the man's neck, for which there is to be no more padding used than merely sufficient to fill the uniform queue, when a man's hair is too thin. Nor should this occasion the smallest constraint or inconvenience to the soldier in the movement of his head. The queue is open for one half inch in the same, more readily to admit of the hair running through.

'Private of 3rd Foot Guards' 1800 (rear view). Watercolour by J.A. Atkinson. The artist has shown the hair taped and powdered. The other interesting aspects are the blanket roll which would contain a proportion of necessaries in instances when the knapsack was not carried. The forage cap is rolled above the cartridge pouch, and overalls are worn for service. (Anne S.K. Brown Military Collection, Brown University Library)

The serjeants will have the regulated length of the rolled great coats, that is, 15 inches, marked upon their pikes, to which as well as the pattern queues, the field officers are requested frequently to refer to see uniformity enforced.

31 July, 1806

Officer's servants and others having good coats of the last years clothing will produce them to the quarter master who will purchase from them at an equitable price, the rest not being of that description are immediately to be got rid of and false capes furnished for the whole regiment out of them.

7 August, 1806

Soldiers are only to carry on their backs the clothing of the year, and no old clothing will be allowed to be carried in the waggons but such as has been bought in by the quartermaster, according to the order of 31st July. Officers will therefore be particular in seeing that the yellow cloth for false capes has been resewed in obedience to that order.

15 August, 1806, Portsea Barracks

It appearing on Lt.-Col. Keane's inspection of yesterday, that with hardly any exceptions, the men have lost their kersey waistcoats, or rendered them useless by neglect and ill treatment, the quarter master will this day write to Mr Mitchell, clothier, of Titchfield, for such a number as will complete every man with one. They must be so fitted and stitched as not to require alteration and have a standing collar of such height only as will not be seen from under the cape of the coat.

Those waistcoats commanding officers of companies consider in sufficient good condition to wear without the coat to be immediately fitted with capes as described above.

17 August, 1806

A committee consisting of Captain Browne, and Thornhill, and Lt. Crespigney, assisted by the serjeant major and quarter master serjeant are desired in the course of tomorrow to examine patterns of different articles of sea equipment which will be necessary for the men should the regiment embark for foreign service, which they are now under orders to be prepared for. They will first of all inspect those directed by the commanding officer to be ready for them at the house of Messrs Gorden and Maille, and afterwards compare the price and quality with what may be had from other tradesmen in the town and neighbourhood making a written report by Wednesday next or sooner if possible.

3 January 1807

The Brigade will be formed precisely at 10 O clock tomorrow for divine service, and in light march order, but in breeches and long leggings, the 6th regiment will form three deep, regiments to bring parade states. The light marching order of the Brigade to be as follows: canteens, haversacks and packs, in which, besides the greatcoats neatly folded will be carried one shirt, one pair shoes, one pair stockings, razor and combs, brushes and blackball with a piece of soap.

30 March 1807

Some of the regiments in the Brigade being in the habit of wearing their foraging caps on night sentry, commanding officers of regiments are desired to give particular orders to the contrary, there being every service-like reason against it.

30 March 1807

> Sentries except in rain will not take their greatcoats or fatigue trowsers on the six
> O clock relief.

30 March 1807

> At five minutes before seven O clock a drum will beat, or bugle sound, at which
> companies will parade in their fatigue dress (except those warned for drill).

23 October 1807

> On account of the inspection tomorrow, the commanding officer of the Forces is pleased
> to permit the regiment to appear in their trowsers at this evening's garrison parade.

29 October 1808

> The regiment will parade for inspection of necessaries tomorrow at half past six in
> blue foraging caps and wearing their great coats over their white jackets.

The foraging caps mentioned over the entire eight year appearance include some with
folding peaks, others in leather, and both blue and white examples, the latter two running
concurrently. Allowing that this partial list may not even detail all of the changes, it appears
that the style changed fairly frequently.

30 October 1808

> Four of the best taylors being exclusively given up for officer's work that of the regi-
> ment must not be interrupted by officers employing any others.

30 October 1809

> The following articles are to be drawn tomorrow from the QM in addition to what
> companies have already received...
> 80 pairs of shoes per company,
> 40 pairs of soles,
> Pairs of stockings or half stockings,
> 3 dozen white shirts,
> One dozen check shirts,
> 50 pairs of shoe brushes,
> 2 dozen pairs of trowsers cut out but not made up,
> 50 cloth brushes,
> 2 dozen pairs of spats, cut out, but not made up.
> Thread for making ditto,

3 dozen button brushes,
50 combs,
60 worms and screws and 50 brushes and pickers,
50 spoons,
100 blacking balls.

This is an early use of the term 'spats' for gaiters, indicating that various terms were in use. The exact significance of spat here is not clear, but it possibly refers to half gaiters to be worn under a trowser, as opposed to short gaiters worn outside a pantaloon.

3 November 1808

Commanding officers of companies will on Wednesday next give in receipts for the clothing of the current year, agreeable to a form which may be seen at the office of the regimental clerk.

18 November 1808

Until every article of regimental clothing is completed the whole of the taylors are to be kept constantly at work; and exclusively for the men for whom the Quarter Master will be held responsible.

18 November 1808

Beginning on Sunday morning parades, officers will consistently appear until further orders in uniform round hats, blue pantaloons and half boots and hair out of powder.

19 November 1808

The regiment will embark in breeches and black leggings with trowsers over them. The dress to be worn on board is the white jacket with canvas frock over, trowsers and white foraging cap.

21 November 1808

Commanding officers of companies will be held responsible that each man takes with him a pair of flannel drawers of the materials for having them made on board. They are to be worn until further orders.

7 December 1808

With the exception of the field officers no individual of the regiment is to on shore [Barbados] until further notice. When such is given officers will wear their white pantaloons.

11 December 1808

The officers will be dressed in full uniform with sashes and gorgets. The men in blue foraging caps, the smock frock, trowsers and half gaiters for inspection by the Commander of the Forces tomorrow.

12 December 1808

It seeming desirable that in this climate the standing order should be dispensed with in that instance, officers will for the present allow the shirt collar to appear about half an inch above the black stock.

14 December 1808

The commanding officer has ordered Corporal Coleman on board from his marketing party a prisoner for appearing un-uniformly and otherwise improperly dressed in the streets and without his flannel waistcoat on. He has also observed officer's servants in the streets on similar occasions with silk handkerchiefs around their necks and otherwise un-uniform which he hopes will not again be the case.

14 December 1808

The flannel drawers are immediately to be tried on the men beginning with the largest, when the whole are complete and not until then, the commanding officer on board will order them into the possession of the men, but not to be worn until further order.

19 December 1808

In consequence of the general order of yesterday, the light marching order of the 13th will be as follows upon the present occasion, rolled up in a square piece of brown linen which will be provided by the Quarter master serjeant for the purpose.
    Conforming as much as possible to the regulated length of fold of the greatcoat and tied tight round with rope yarn, there will be a second check shirt, a second pair of good shoes, a comb, a razor, a piece of soap, and one brush- comrades carrying the one, that for the shoes; the other, that for clothes. No other articles whatever is to be admitted into the bundle, which when the greatcoat is slung, is to be carried in it.
    When unfolded, the straps are immediately to be buckled round the bundle so that in case of night alarm, there may be no excuse for leaving the articles behind.
    The companies on board each ship will parade in this mode every day, alternately until further orders, the greatcoat first slung, then unfolded and worn over the shoulders. In breeches, long leggings and with canteens and haversacks, the state of which must continue to be narrowly inspected.

Where the men have not regular socks or half stockings to land in, a pair must be cut of the worsted stockings, not unnecessarily to heat the leg underneath the long gaiters.

Should not the great coat straps be at present capable of sufficiently compressing the above described bundles, commanding officers of companies will take care that additional holes are first punched in them for that purpose.

As the most convenient dress for actual service, officers will immediately provide themselves with black waist belts, of a plain pattern in buckles and hooks.

25 December, 1808

The second buff straps to be immediately attached to and constantly worn with the tin magazine.

In 1784 a leather covered tin magazine had been added to infantry appointments to be issued and used only on active service. The 1802 collation describes the method in which this tin was carried. In 1808 the tin magazine was discarded with the advent of the sixty round cartridge pouch.[8]

26 December 1808

The board of survey having fixed the price of flannel drawers at 4s 11d sterling… and of the wrapper and cord for light marching kit at 1s 9d Bermuda Currency, of which the commanding officer approves. commanding officers of companies will take the steps they may think best for the security of the flannel drawers, which are not to be worn by the men till they take their linen trowsers into wear ashore, when they become an indispensable part of the soldier's dress, the colonel furnishing a second pair agreeable to His Majesty's regulations for the troops serving in the West Indies.

13 January 1809 [on board ship inspection]

Officers full dress'd, the men in blue caps, canvas frocks, trowsers and spats.

29 March 1809, Brigade Orders from Colonel Colville in capacity of Brigadier General

When they are used by troops under his immediate command, the Brigadier General cannot but express his dislike of check shirts worn with what the soldier calls a dickie of false frill, but wishes to be understood as not giving any order on the subject, not knowing to what extent or on what authority they may have been adopted in the instances he had occasion to notice at his inspection this morning.

---

8   See Appendix 1, 1802 collation, and also the illustration above showing a rear view of a private of the Foot Guards.

'Captn. Unett, Rl. Arty', 1804. Watercolour by unknown artist (Dighton?) A good representation of the longer and more rigid hessian that was to come to dominate the style. Note also the officer has exposed his fashionable fob ornaments below his sash. (Anne S.K. Brown Military Collection, Brown University Library)

velvet. White lining with slash sleeves and pockets. Flat gilt buttons with the crown, star, and words Commissariat Staff engraved thereon. Those for the commissary general to be placed three and three, and for the deputies two and two, for the assistants, one, and two epaulettes gold, straps embroidered on the cloth. The commissary general and deputies to have two. The assistants, one on the left shoulder.

Waistcoats and breeches. White.

Hat. With uniform button, regulation loop and band.

Sword. According to the staff regulation.

Harry Calvert Adjutant General.[6]

22 April, 1805. General order on horse furniture

Adjutant General to the army.

His Majesty having been graciously pleased to order a uniform horse furniture to be stablished for the staff officers of regiments of infantry, HRH the Commander-in-Chief desires that the commanding officers of regiments will give the necessary directions to their respective staff officers to provide themselves with regimental horse furniture as follows.

A housing or saddle cloth made in shape and size similar to that ordered for the general staff of the army of the colour of the facing of the regiment with a double row of the regimental lace round the edge.

The holsters to be covered with black bear skin, and the fronting of the bridle with ribband the colour of the housing.

Harry Calvert Adjutant General.[7]

7 May, 1805. Regulation for ADCs

From the Adjutant General.

Regulations for the dress of the ADC's to the King most Humbly submitted to His Majesty-

Full Dress embroider'd Coat to be worn at all Birth Days & Fetes given by their Majesties-

Plain Frock (with Epaulettes the same as the Full Dress embroider'd Coat) to be worn at all Field Days and Reviews.

White leather Pantaloons or Breeches, long Boots, Spurs, Regulation Staff Belt, Sword with steel scabbard & white Gloves.

The Lace Coat & Dress Horse Furniture to be worn only at Reviews, whereat His Majesty appears in Lace'd Uniform, and at levees and Drawing Rooms-

---

6   TNA, WO3/152/524: Office of the Commander-in-Chief: Out-letters. Letters to War Office and other Public Departments – Date: 01 January 1803–28 February 1805.

7   TNA, WO123/134/431: Army Circulars, Memoranda, Orders and Regulations. Adjutant-General's Office (Horse Guards).

On Ordinary Occasions, Blue Saddle Cloth with Gold Edge, Bridle front, and Roses
   of Garter Blue, and White Collars.
Approved by His Royal highness,
Signed, GR[8]

27 August 1805, Letter on mourning for insertion in the *London Gazette*

His Majesty does not require that the officers of the army should wear any other
mourning on the present melancholy occasion than a black crepe round their left
arm with their uniforms.
   Harry Calvert Adjutant General.[9]

The melancholy occasion was the burial procession of the remains of His Royal Highness
William Henry Duke of Gloucester, younger brother of King George III. A previous circular
letter from the Adjutant-General's office regarding mourning dating from 30 March, 1804,
relates the procedure for the funeral procession of the late General Sir William Fawcett:
'General and staff officers are to be in embroidered frock uniforms, other officers in their
regimentals. The whole with crepes on the left arms'.[10] It appears that other forms were
occasionally followed. James' *Military Dictionary* observes that there were fuller forms of
expression: 'Mourning is expressed, among military men, in the British service, by a piece
of black crape around the arm, and handle of the sword; and in some instances by a cockade
of the same'.[11]

4 November 1805, Circular to regiments of cavalry

From the Adjutant General to Officers commanding regiments of cavalry,
With a view to promote the comfort and health of the soldiers, His Majesty has
been graciously pleased to direct, that the cloaks of the non-commissioned officers
and private men of the regiments of cavalry, shall be rendered waterproof; and I
have received HRH the Commander-in-Chief's command, to inform you, that the
expence attending the process, will in future be admitted as a charge against the
public in the regimental accounts of the regiment under your command.
   Harry Calvert, Adjutant General[12]

---

8   TNA, WO123/134/435: Army Circulars, Memoranda, Orders and Regulations. Adjutant-General's Office (Horse
     Guards).
9   TNA, WO123/134/469: Army Circulars, Memoranda, Orders and Regulations. Adjutant-General's Office (Horse
     Guards).
10 TNA, WO123/135/307: Army Circulars, Memoranda, Orders and Regulations. Adjutant-General's Office (Horse
     Guards).
11 James, *Military Dictionary.*
12 TNA, WO123/134/485: Army Circulars, Memoranda, Orders and Regulations. Adjutant-General's Office (Horse
     Guards).

12 December 12 1805. Circular to certain officers

From the Adjutant General to the following, Sir John Moore, 52nd Regt, Sir [Henry] Wynyard, 1st Guards, Spencer, 40th Regt, Sir John Murray, 84th Regt, Stuart, 43rd Regt, Layard, 54th Regt, Mosheim, 60th Regt, Torrens, 86th Regt, O' Connell, 2nd West Indian Regt, Baron Rottenberg, 60th Regt.

In consequence of some representations which have been made to the Commander-in-Chief unfavourable to the lackered caps which are at present in use for the infantry of the army. HRH is desirous of availing himself of your sentiments on the subject and he requests that you will be so good as to state for his information whether from the observations you have been enabled to make, referring to the various climates and situations in which British troops are liable to be employed, you are of opinion that the caps now in use are preferable to the felt caps heretofore used and that you will add for HRH's consideration the grounds on which your preference for one or the other may be founded.

I am to request you will in addition mention the hatter by whom the caps of the – regiment are supplied.

Harry Calvert Adjutant General.[13]

---

13 TNA, WO123/134/491: Army Circulars, Memoranda, Orders and Regulations. Adjutant-General's Office (Horse Guards).

13

The Role of the Board of General Officer Reports in Regulating Fashion

The clothing of the army is generally called regimentals, every part of which should facilitate and not hinder, the various motions of the manual exercise. A soldier, without regard to fashion or taste, should be dressed in the most comfortable and least embarrassing manner possible; and the keeping him warm, and leaving him the entire use of his limbs, are objects always to be had in view.[1]

Report of the Proceedings of a Board of General Officers assembled by Order of the commander in Chief, at No.19 Great George Street Westminster on the 21 February 1810 to take into Consideration and frame a Code of Regulation on the Subject of Field Allowances, Camp Equipage, and Baggage, under the various Circumstances of Service which the British Army is liable to; also to Consider and report their Opinion upon other Matters referred to in the Papers laid before them.

President
Lieutenant General Ross
Members
Lieutenant Generals Sir Harry Burrard Bart
Sir David Baird Bart K.B.
Major Generals The Honourable Edward Paget
Sir Brent Spencer K.B.
Frederick Maitland
Earl of Dalhousie (Absent from the 27 February by permission of the Commander
    in Chief on Pressing Business in Hand)
James Thewles

Read a letter from the Adjutant general, dated the 13 February 1810, announcing the appointment of the Board, signifying His Majesty's Pleasure that Lieutenant

---

1   James, *Military Dictionary*.

'Halt of troops', 1808. aquatint by J. Hill after J.A. Atkinson. This depiction of soldiers on the march shows both trousers and breeches being worn, presumable by men on different duties. The mounted officer is in blue pantaloons, the common service dress variant both home and abroad. (Anne S.K. Brown Military Collection, Brown University Library)

General Ross should be President thereof, and calling the attention of the Board in the first instance, to certain Points represented as being more immediately connected with the Subject refer'd to their Consideration, and more particularly described in a letter from the Deputy Secretary at war to the Adjutant General Dated the 18 January 1810; which letter was also read, and it appeared therefore that His Majesty's Secretary at War, being desirous of obtaining precise information as to the Specific Articles of personal Baggage, Camp Equipage, and Necessaries, with which Officers of the several Ranks comprehending the Staff, both Military and Civil (and Classing the Officers of each in such a manner as may appear consistent with their relative situations) and Soldiers, should be provided when on actual service, in the respective cases of their being fully, or lightly equipped; and of ascertaining the reasonable Prices of the several Articles distinguishing in each case the Nature of the Tent from that of the other Articles of Camp Equipage – in order that the Amount of Indemnification to be granted, in the event of the Loss of the same, or of any part thereof, may be regulated thereby; as also the Sums which it may be proper to fix as a Compensation for the Loss of Horses of the several Classes, supposing the Horses to be purchased at Home, and not to be obtained at Inferior Prices in the Countries abroad where the Army may be serving, had requested the Commander in Chief to convene a Board of General Officers to consider the subject, and to report their Opinion thereupon.

The Report of a Board of General Officers assembled on the 22 of February 1805 for the purpose of considering the Subject of Field Equipments and Allowances in general; and a Paper containing suggestions under the head of 'Officers Baggage' &c. in which an Article relative to Women (wives of Soldiers) is strongly recommended by the Commander in Chief to the Consideration of the Board; were likewise heard.

The Board, aware of the importance of the Subject, submitted to their Consideration, both as it respects the Public and the Individuals immediately concerned, have endeavoured to keep that Circumstance distinctly in view throughout the whole of the Investigation and discussion which has taken place thereupon, and they trust it will be found that their Opinion upon every point has been formed with a due regard to the Public Interest on the one hand, and to the necessary Comfort and accommodation of the Officer and Soldier, on the other.

Before the Board proceed to detail the specific Articles of Baggage &c. with which the several Ranks of the Army should, in their opinion, be provided, when on actual Service, it will be necessary for them to offer some preliminary Observations upon such parts of the general Subject as may appear to require Explanation.

The difficulty of laying down positive Rules in regards either to the quantity or quality of the several Articles of an Officers Equipment, rendered it necessary for the Board to call for information of various kinds, and from different quarters, relative to both of these Points. They also Procured Patterns of certain Articles, particularly of Tents, Marquees, Bedsteads, Canteens and Portmanteau, together with Statements of the Prices charged by different tradesmen for each Article of Equipment supplied by them respectively; but finding that the Prices charged for many Articles of the same Description differed so materially in Amount as to render it impossible to form therefrom the proposed Scale of Allowances for the loss of such Articles; it was deemed expedient to obtain further and more satisfactory Information upon that head, and the Board accordingly directed that lists of the several Articles, which they considered necessary for the Equipment of Officers, should be sent to some of the principal Furnishers of such Articles, and that they should be desired to annex thereto the fair and reasonable Price of each Article supposing the same to be a good quality and not unnecessarily expensive. From the Information thus afforded, the Board have been enabled to fix, what they conceive may be considered as reasonable Average Prices for the several Articles, and the Sums specified against each Article in the annexed Schedule are calculated upon this principle accordingly.

The Board most cordially agree in opinion with the board that took into consideration the Subject of Field Allowances in the Year 1805, that the Tents for Regimental Officers, both of Cavalry and Infantry, should in future be furnished at the Public Expence: and the members of the Board, having upon every occasion, been Witnesses of the great inadequacy of the Allowances made for the Equipage of the Officers of the Army, under the heads of Bat, Baggage, and Forage Money, in order to prepare for taking the Field and for defraying their unavoidable extra expences during the first 200 Days of their being upon actual Service think it incumbent upon them to recommend, that, notwithstanding the Tents be furnished by the Public, no deduction should be made from the Allowances hitherto granted to them under any of the heads herein specified; and that such Allowances should in all cases be extended to the Cavalry, as well as to the Infantry.

It is likewise the Opinion of the Board, that the present Allowances of bat, Baggage and Forage Money should be continued to the Officers taking the Field in Great Britain or in Ireland and that a Sum of the same Amount, should be granted for Officers ordered to Embark for Foreign Service, under the denomination of Outfit Money to be considered as a separate Allowance, and distinct from any Allowance of Bat, Baggage or Forage Money which they may be entitled to on the particular Service whereon they are about to be employed. Officers who may follow their Regiments, to receive the same Allowances on Embarking, as those who preceded them, and the Passage of Officers who being detained by Duty, may not have embarked with their Regiments to be provided by Government or an Allowance to be granted, in aid of the expence thereof, according to the Rates specified in the existing regulations on that head- But this Indulgence not to be extended to Officers who may have obtained leave to remain behind their Regiments, for their own private accommodation.

The Board, after having inspected different Tents and Marquees for Officers, recommends one, made by Messrs Strachan and Thompson of Long Acre, of the following description and dimensions for Subalterns and Captains, viz.

A small Marquee, with a Gable Front. Ten feet five inches long (Six feet nine inches from Pole to Pole- three feet eight inches the Boot) Seven feet Six inches wide – Seven feet four inches high-Price Twelve Guineas; and for the Superior Ranks of Officers, a Marquee made by Messrs Lowndes of the Hay Market; Fifteen feet three inches long (six feet nine inches from pole to pole) Eight feet six inches wide- Eight Fett high.

The Board have likewise seen a light portable Iron Bedstead (invented by Messrs Strachan and Thompson) which, packed with its Bedding in the compass of a moderate sized Trunk (and weighing together Sixty Pounds) appears to be particularly well calculated for the use of all Officers upon Service: and they therefore recommend its being generally adopted.

The Canteens particularly recommended by the Board of Officers, are those shewn them by Messrs Strachan and Thompson, at Five Guineas and Eight Guineas the pair- the former for Subalterns and Captains, the latter for the superior ranks, under the rank of General Officers.

The Board having been informed that the 95th Rifle Regiment had provided, at their own expense, small camp kettles, to be carried by each soldier, conceived it to be a subject very deserving of consideration, whether, by some enlargement of the camp kettles it might not be rendered capable both of dressing the soldier's provisions, and also of carrying on a march, two days bread and meat, at the least, while at the same time it might be carried by the soldier without material inconvenience. In order to satisfy themselves fully on this point, they directed several patterns of canteens to be made up for their inspection, and they are so perfectly convinced that a canteen of the pattern which accompanies this report, would be found well calculated for securing the comfort of the soldier upon service, that they

'Suttling booth', 1808. Aquatint by J. Hill after J.A. Atkinson. This camp scene shows un-powdered tied hair, breeches with stockings, with gaiters and overalls. The forage cap is the wedge style that predominates in the infantry early period. (Anne S.K. Brown Military Collection, Brown University Library)

recommend its adoption for every regiment of infantry in the army. It will have the advantage of rendering entirely useless the haversack, in which the soldier's provisions have always been exposed to be injured by being bruised, or entirely destroyed by wet and inclement weather. A tin canteen of the pattern which accompanies the report for carrying water for the soldier on a march, is likewise recommended to be generally adopted.

The Board are of the opinion that the Camp kettles of the Cavalry cannot be carried by the Dragoon, and therefore recommend that the practice of carrying them on horses be continued.

It appearing to the Board that it would be attended with very considerable advantage to the Service were one kind of Package and of precisely the same dimensions, used for the conveyance of the Baggage of Officers upon all occasions; Messrs Strachan and Thompson have, at the suggestion of the Board, taken the trouble to make several Portmanteaus for their Inspection. The Pattern which accompanies the Report, and which the Board consider to be well calculated for all ranks of the Army when on actual Service, is therefore recommended for general adoption accordingly. It is two feet three inches long- eleven inches wide- nine inches deep- the weight when filled, about thirty six pounds- and the Price Two pounds Four Shillings. One of these Portmanteaus will contain the light Equipment, two the full Equipment of all officers below the Rank of Generals.

It being the Opinion of the Board that, as a Pair of Pistols forms a necessary part of the Equipment of General Officers- Aides de Camp-Majors of brigade- the Officers of the Adjutant general's and of the Quarter Master General's Departments- all Cavalry Officers- Field Officers and Adjutants of Regiments of Infantry- Officers of Rifle, or other Infantry regiments who are required by order to carry Pistols (Captains when ordered to be mounted, a Pair, Subalterns, one) – Provost Marshals, Deputy Provost Marshals – Fort or Town Majors – and Fort or Towns Adjutants: Indemnification should be granted for the same, if lost upon Service, at the rate of Five Guineas per Pair, in all cases.

The Commander in Chief having signified to the Board in reply to a question submitted to him upon the subject that he 'does not consider it necessary that Purveyors- the Officers of the Paymaster General's Department- or the Clerks of any of the Military departments, should be included in the Arrangements now under the Consideration of the Board; as, should it be necessary to indemnify any of the before mentioned Persons for Losses on any particular occasion, He is of opinion their Claims may be best determined at the time, according to the Circumstances of the Case, and that no General regulation should be established with respect to them. The Board have neither allotted any Articles of Baggage &c. nor proposed a scale of Indemnification for any Persons of these several descriptions, except in the case of the Clerks in the Commissariat Department, who apparently, by a Regulation lately issued under His Majesty's express Authority, to be placed on the regular Establishment of Officers of that Department.

The Board, considering the propriety and expediency of preserving, by every possible means, and upon all occasions, the several established Distinctions and Gradations of Military Rank, have thought it necessary (where practicable) with a view to mark that distinction as it respects the subject now immediately under their consideration, to make some difference (however small) in the quantity or proportion of Articles allotted to each Rank of Regimental Officers. Under the same impression and conviction, the Board have deemed it right wholly to separate the Military from the Civil Staff, instead of classing them together, and to allot to the Officers of the latter description such quantity or proportion of Articles of each kind as the relative Importance of their several Civil situations, and their comparative Rank with respect to each other, in their respective Departments, appeared to warrant: but without affording them any ground whereon to lay a claim to Military Rank, to which the Civil staff of an Army cannot in the opinion of this Board, have any pretension whatever.

It has not occurred to the Board, that it is necessary to propose a Light Equipment for the Gentlemen of any of the Civil Departments.

The Board are of Opinion, that Volunteers should be considered on the same footing, in regards to Indemnification for losses, as the Subalterns of the Regiments to which they belong, with respect to such Articles of Equipment as they are allowed to wear, while serving in that capacity.

Notwithstanding the amount of the estimated Value of the whole of the Baggage and Camp Equipage of Officers of the different Ranks exceeds, in some cases, the sums allowed by the existing Regulations for the loss thereof- a circumstance which the advance in the price of almost every Article renders unavoidable- The Board conceive there is no reason to conclude, that the future amount of Compensation to Individuals, for losses under those heads, will be greater (in many instances it will probably be less) than it has hitherto been; inasmuch as the whole of the Articles specified in the Schedule, and which include what the Officer Wears, can seldom, if ever, be lost under any circumstances whatever; and if proper precautions be taken, and due attention be paid by Officers to the Orders which it may be presumed will from time to time be issued, according to the nature of the particular Service on which an Army is to be employed, by the General officer Commanding with respect to the quantity of baggage &c. to be taken by the Officers serving under him; a small portion only of their personal Equipment will in general be exposed to the risk of being lost.

The number of Horses which the Board are of the Opinion should be allowed to each rank of Officers, Cavalry and Infantry and Staff, will not be found to differ materially from the number prescribed by the existing Regulations; but the Board have been under the necessity, in consideration of the very great Advance which has taken place in the price of Horses, to recommend that a considerable addition should be made to the rates of Allowance specified in the Regulation of the 1 March 1796, for the Indemnification of losses of this description; those Rates being evidently so inadequate to the Expence which must now be incurred by Officers in replacing their Horses, as to render further relief, in such case, and, in the opinion of the Board, to the full extent of the sums proposed absolutely necessary. The number of Horses to be allotted to each rank will of course occasionally vary, according to the nature of the Service, and from local and other circumstances to which no general Rules can apply, and must consequently, in such cases, be left to the discretion of the General Officer Commanding.

It only remains for the Board to observe, that the schedule embraces all the Article of Personal Equipment for Officers of every rank, Military and Civil, that of General officers excepted; whose claims for the loss of baggage and Camp Equipage, the Board are of opinion, should be decided on according to the same principle as those of other Military Officers; but without restricting them as to the precise number or quantity of any particular Articles they may find it expedient to take with them on Service, and which must of course depend upon Circumstances to which no general Rule can apply. It is therefore proposed that general officers losing the whole or any part of their Baggage, or Camp Equipage, shall make a return of the several Articles lost, and a charge for them, at the rates specified in the scale annexed to the Schedule, according to the actual extent of the loss, not exceeding in the whole, the following sums, viz.

A General -- Baggage £400 Camp Equipage £200 Total £600
Lieutenant General -- Baggage £330 Camp Equipage £170 Total £500
Major General -- Baggage £250 Camp Equipage £150 Total £400
Brigadier General Or Colonel Commanding a Brigade -- Baggage £200 Camp Equipage £150 Total £350

The Situation of a Commander of an Expedition, or of a Commander in the Field, is so different, upon different Services, that the Board do not feel themselves competent to give a satisfactory Opinion, as to the extent of the Allowances that should be liable to him for the loss of his Baggage, and Camp Equipage: But they think it their Duty to remark that the Allowance of *** thousand pounds which they understand has nee previously made to a General officer for equipping himself in *** station, is extremely inadequate for defraying the Expence which he must in general, unavoidable incur, under such Circumstances.

Schedule of the Articles of Personal Baggage and Camp Equipage, and of the number and description of Horses with which Officers, Military and Civil, and of the Articles of Necessaries with which Soldiers should be provided when on actual Service at Home and Abroad (including the Articles in wear) with the reasonable Prices of Value thereof.[2]

The entire mass of pages describing in detail the appropriate scales of equipment takes up rather a lot of space, so has been consigned to Appendix 2. Table Three illustrates the relative scales as applied to both captains and colonels of cavalry. This snapshot gives a useful impression of the quantities regulated. The prices found elsewhere in the material as compared with tailoring accounts for infantry officers appear realistic in comparison with these for fashionable cavalry clothing (see Table Six, Chapter 17) or those for the other ranks (see tables on legwear in Volume II).

2   TNA, WO7/56/1-59: Various Departmental, Out-letters. Board of General Officers. Reports Miscellaneous.

Table 3 Comparative Equipment Scales and Costs from Board of General Officers recommendations of 1810

Cavalry Colonel	Pound	Shilling	Pence	Cavalry Captain	Pound	Shilling	Pence
Full Equipment				*Full Equipment*			
One Helmet and Feather	4	4		One Helmet and Feather	4	4	
Two Jackets or Coats	24			Two Jackets or Coats	24		
Two Waistcoats	2	8		Two Waistcoats	2	8	
Two Pairs of Leather Breeches or Pantaloons	6	6		Two Pairs of Leather Breeches or Pantaloons	6	6	
Three Pairs of Drawers		10	6	Three Pairs of Drawers		10	6
One ditto Overalls	3	13	6	One ditto Overalls	3	13	6
One Great Coat	5	5		One Great Coat	5	5	
One Cloak	6	6		One Cloak	6	6	
Eighteen Shirts 21/	13	18		Eighteen Shirts 21/	12	12	
Two Black Stocks or Handkerchiefs 3/		6		Two Black Stocks or Handkerchiefs 3/		6	
Eighteen Pocket handkerchiefs 3/	2	14		Eighteen Pocket handkerchiefs 3/	1	16	
Eighteen Pairs of Stockings 3/6	3	3		Eighteen Pairs of Stockings 3/6	2	2	
Three pairs of Boots 48/	9	4		Three pairs of Boots 48/	9	4	
One ditto Spurs		9		One ditto Spurs		9	
Two ditto Shoes 12/	1	4		Two ditto Shoes 12/	1	4	
Three ditto Gloves 4/6		13	6	Three ditto Gloves 4/6		9	
Twelve Towels 1/6		18		Six Towels 1/6		9	
Six Table Cloths 10/6	3	3		Three Table Cloths 10/6	1	11	6
Brushes for Clothes and Shoes		5	6	Brushes for Clothes and Shoes		5	6
Razors, Combs etc.	1	1		Razors, Combs etc.	1	1	
One Regimental Sword	3	13	6	One Regimental Sword	3	13	6
One Light Sword	3	3		One Light Sword	3	3	
One Belt and Plate	2	2		One Belt and Plate	2	2	
One Sword Knot	1	1		One Sword Knot	1	1	
One Sabre Tasche	1			One Sabre Tasche	1		
One Pouch and Belt	1	1		One Pouch and Belt	1	1	
One Sash	3			One Sash	3		
One Writing Case	1	4		One Writing Case	1	4	
One Spying Glass	3	3		....			
Two Portmanteaus	4	8		Two Portmanteaus 44/	4	8	
Total Amount	116	5	6	Total Amount	102	12	6
Light Equipment				*Light Equipment*			
One Helmet and Feather	4	4		One Helmet and Feather	4	4	
Two Jackets or Coats	24			Two Jackets or Coats	24		
Two Waistcoats	2	8		Two Waistcoats	2	8	
Two Pairs of Leather Breeches or Pantaloons	6	6		Two Pairs of Leather Breeches or Pantaloons	6	6	

Cavalry Colonel	Pound	Shilling	Pence	Cavalry Captain	Pound	Shilling	Pence
Two Pairs of Drawers		7		Two Pairs of Drawers		7	
One Great Coat	5	5		One Great Coat	5	5	
One Cloak	6	6		One Cloak	6	6	
Nine Shirts	9	9		Six Shirts	6	6	
Two Black Stocks or Handkerchiefs		6		One Black Stocks or Handkerchiefs		3	
Nine Pocket handkerchiefs	1	9		Six Pocket handkerchiefs		18	
Nine pairs of Stockings	1	11	6	Six pairs of Stockings	1	1	
Two pairs of Boots	4	16		Two pairs of Boots	4	16	
One ditto Spurs		7		One ditto Spurs		7	
One ditto Shoes		12		One ditto Shoes		12	
Two ditto Gloves		9		One ditto Gloves		4	6
Six Towels		9		Two Towels		3	
Four Table Cloths	2	2		Two Table Cloths	1	1	
Brushes for Clothes and Shoes		5	6	Brushes for Clothes and Shoes		5	6
Razors, Combs etc.	1	1		Razors, Combs etc.	1	1	
One Regimental Sword	3	13	6	One Regimental Sword	3	13	6
One Light Sword	3	3		One Light Sword	3	3	
One Belt and Plate	2	2		One Belt and Plate	2	2	
One Sword Knot	1	1		One Sword Knot	1	1	
One Sabre Tasche	1			One Sabre Tasche	1		
One Pouch and Belt	1	1		One Pouch and Belt	1	1	
One Sash	3			One Sash	3		
One Writing Case	1	4		One Writing Case	1	4	
One Spying Glass	3	3		One Spying Glass	3	3	
One Portmanteau	2	4		One Portmanteau	2	4	
Total Amount	93	2	6	Total Amount	84	2	6

A comparison with the cost of equipping a hussar officer as illustrated in Table Six Chapter 17 reveals these cost estimates as hopelessly optimistic when contrasted with a fashionable regimental officer's capacity for conspicuous consumption. A more modest cavalry regiment would still struggle to equip its officers at the prices indicated. The prices for making up at regiment for the 16th Light Dragoons were recorded in the Long Military Papers now at the National Army Museum.[3]

This document gives a full analysis of the charges for making and the cost of materials employed for the various articles of uniform. The parts described are:

An Officer's Jacket. £20 5s 5d.
Making (Journeyman 8s, Master [illegible]. One and one eight of Blue Cloth at £1 8s yard- £2 11s 6d; Sleeve Linings and Pockets, 3s 6d; Cuff and Collars, 3s 2d?;

---

3   NAM, 1968-07-219: Papers of Lt. Gen. Robert Ballard Long, 1809-1825.

Director general of medical staff. 10 at 63s, plus 6 breakfast cloths at 31s 6d
Inspector of hospitals. 8 at 63s, plus 6 breakfast cloths at 31s 6d
Deputy inspector of hospitals. 6 at 63s, plus 4 breakfast cloths at 31s 6d
Physician. 4 at 63s, plus 3 breakfast cloths at 31s 6d
Commissary general. 12 at 63s, plus 8 breakfast cloths at 31s 6d
Deputy commissary general. 6 at 10s 6d.
Assistant commissary general 3 at 10s 6d

The numbers of tablecloths equate nearly to the numbers of stockings and shirts. Drawers were clearly infrequently worn, as a director general of hospitals has but six pairs, compared to 20 shirts, 20 pairs of stockings, and 16 tablecloths. The paucity of drawers is not altogether surprising, as the shirts used were long enough in the body to be gathered around the nether regions and used as underwear. The proportion of shirts and socks to tablecloths clearly has some significance though. We can infer that for the officer class, tablecloths were considered as important or nearly as important as clean shirts even under light equipment campaign conditions. It is something of a paradigm shift for modern sensibilities to appreciate that a clean tablecloth is of equal priority to a clean shirt.

Shipp's memoirs contain two useful observations on the uses to which table cloths could be adapted. He records that cloths were laid over the dressed table, 'It is the custom as you know, when the table has been laid to cover the things with a cloth to keep the flies away'.[5] Shipp also notes an unusual use of the cloths. On at least one occasion they served as winding cloths for the dead:

At last I got quite hungry, and thought that there would be no harm in helping myself to a biscuit or two. I turned back a corner of the (breakfast table) cloth; and there, staring up at me, was the face of the Colonel, laid out dead on his own breakfast table.[6]

It is tempting to see the tablecloths as part of a modular system, and consider that each cloth could be combined with others to create a larger dining area in conjunction with modular tables, enabling the host to adjust his hospitality on a sliding scale. It would be expected that superior officers would extend occasional or continual hospitality to their subordinates according to means.[7] Unfortunately the scale of tables provided does not support this hypothesis, unless it is accepted that each officer brought his own table, which is not something noted in the numerous memoirs. Officers liked to record occasions on which they dined with their superiors, and noted who kept an unusually good table, or a poor one, and although they sometimes relate the carrying of their own personal canteen to the host's table, they do not mention porting the table itself!

Further, the value of the tablecloths in both literal and implied terms exceeds that of the officer's canteen, which would include glassware, crockery, cutlery and all other items of table dressing and equipment.

5   Shipp, *The Path of Glory*, p.215.
6   Shipp, *The Path of Glory*, p.215.
7   J. Thornton, *Your Most Obedient Servant, Cook to the Duke of Wellington* (Exeter: Webb and Bower, 1985), p.22.

14

Regulation of 1806

16 April, 1806. Clothing for 5/60th

> Deputy Adjutant General to Board of General Officers,
> I have the honour to acquaint you for the information of the general officers composing the clothing board, that HRH the Commander-in-Chief has been pleased to approve of the 5th battalion 60th regiment being in future supplied with dark blue pantaloons, instead of light blue, as heretofore.
> William Wynyard Deputy Adjutant General.[1]

The adjustment in colour is a curious one, and a very uncommon detail to be found in Army level regulation. The use of pantaloons rather than trowsers by the 5/60th began as a feature of rifle corps, pantaloons being the dominant military fashion during the period around 1800 when rifle corps really began to flourish in Britain. The regular regiment of rifle corps, the 95th, would eventually make a transition from pantaloons to trowsers, but the 5/60th appear not to have followed them in this change.

Throughout the period 1800-1815 the line infantry regiments wore white breeches with long gaiters as their default wear. This was for parades, full dress, and for home service (with various alternatives for fatigues and second dress). Instead of breeches, the rifle corps (essentially the 95th and 5/60th) wore pantaloons with short gaiters worn inside or outside the pantaloon according to the prevailing style at any particular time. The pantaloons of rifle corps were a sort of extended full length breeches, snug to the leg.

The formalisation of the accepted practice of wearing alternative legwear on foreign service developed gradually, until official trials in 1809 on the Walcheren expedition resulted in a recommendation for the infantry to adopt short gaiters and grey trowsers for foreign service. When this recommendation was officially implemented, first by being phased in by general order in 1811, and then by warrant in July 1812, it specified grey pantaloons for infantry regiments when serving overseas (except certain stations). In September 1812 a new order was issued, superseding the relevant part of the warrant, and corresponding more closely to the original recommendation, by specifying grey trowsers instead of grey

---

1   TNA, WO7/33/438: Various Departmental, Out-letters. Board of General Officers, Clothing.

pantaloons. Since the next due date for clothing was 25 December 1812, there was time for clothiers to adapt to the new warrant. The main theatre effected by the new regulation would have been western Spain, which had a blanket exemption from the 1812 clothing issue until 25 December 1813. Since this was optional, trowsers may or may not have been substituted for pantaloons in some battalions on service with Wellington.

The rifle units were in a peculiar position, since they had both been put into their usual green pantaloons in the July 1812 warrant. If they were intended to be included in the new order of September, were they now supposed to move to grey trowsers, or to green trowsers, or to ignore the last order on the subject as being irrelevant to them? The information from the patterns room at the clothing office rather suggests that the 5/60th went one way, and the 95th another. The former having a pattern for pantaloons at the office, which unfortunately does not mention the colour (which could be either green or blue), and the 95th trowsers.[2] Again, the colour is not mentioned, but clearly, they are not grey, or a separate pattern to that of the regular grey infantry trowser would not have been required.

So, to what extent did the military trowser of late 1812 differ from the military pantaloon of earlier that year? Both were supplied, and so presumably worn with, short gaiters, and there is no alteration in these as far as we are aware, nor is a special pattern mentioned for rifle corps. So presumably both forms of legwear passed over the top of the gaiters, which seems to indicate a pantaloon that is wider at the cuff than the earlier pantaloons which are essentially an extended pair of breeches, often in web stocking with elastic properties, and held fast to the leg by a button closure at the ankle cuff. The author of an 1808 book on rifle corps deplored the use of the tight pantaloon, 'made to fit very tight and close,' to riflemen, usually issued with a white duck trowser as a change. He proposed instead, 'loose green pantaloons,' with a qualifier that, 'by loose, we do not mean to say trowsers equal in capacity to those of a sailor,' which would restrict movement by their bagginess, but merely, 'so loose as to allow of the foot being slipped with facility in', which was presumably not the case with the pantaloons. For length he suggested that they, 'hang easily down the leg and thigh, as low as mid leg.' Any longer and they would accumulate dirt. He also believed that they ought to be strapped and cuffed with leather, like cavalry overalls, and in addition to have a leather knee patch.[3] Something which was thankfully not considered by the Board of General Officers for Clothing. The accompanying illustration based on these precepts shows the proposed looser pantaloon, which to modern eyes looks very snug indeed, and which terminates just above the ankle.

20 October, 1806. Circular on caps

> Adjutant General to army agents,
> It having been represented to the Commander in Chief that the use of the lacquered cap which has been adopted for the Infantry of the Army has been found from experience to be attended with much inconvenience and prejudice to the troops, HRH has submitted the same to the King and His Majesty has been graciously

---

2   See Chapter 1.
3   H. Beaufoy, *Scloppetaria: Or considerations on the nature and use of rifle barrel guns* (Richmond: Richmond Publishing Company, 1971), p.243.

pleased to command that those regiments of infantry which are entitled to Caps for the Year commencing the 25 Dec 1806 shall have them made of felt in strict conformity to the pattern cap which is lodged at the Office of the Controllers of Army Accounts, the leather parts of which and brass plates are to be supplied once in two years and the felt crown and tuft annually as heretofore.

You will be pleased to make an early communication of the substance of this letter to the colonels of the regiments in your agency.

Harry Calvert Adjutant General[4]

The varnished or lacquered felt caps were finally discarded in 1806, for the reasons detailed in the circular letter above. Commentary on their in-utility had been growing since their introduction in 1800. An influential publication of 1806 noted that,

Not many months since a very fine battalion was seen to go through a field day, with the colours out, and the men with their foraging caps on, to preserve their varnished caps, lest they should be sullied, by dust, or the smoke of the powder.[5]

27 October, 1806. Circular regarding greatcoats

Adjutant General to Generals of Home districts, on foreign stations and to the Adjutant General of Ireland,

Application having been made to the Commander-in-Chief to authorise a difference to be established between the great coats of non-commissioned officers and privates, and HRH approving, as a mark of distinction, that serjeants should be allowed to wear on their present uniform great coats, collar and cuffs of the colour of the facing of their respective regiments, with the chevrons on the right sleeve, the same as on their regimental coats, and that corporals should wear the chevrons without any other distinction on their great coats; I have in consequence the honour to notify the same to you for the information of the several regiments within your command (or agency observing that regiments which adopt what is now proposed, or the individuals themselves, must be at the expence attendant; as the Commander-in-Chief cannot undertake to recommend any alteration in this respect in the established regulations.

Harry Calvert Adjutant General.[6]

---

4   TNA, WO123/134/552: Army Circulars, Memoranda, Orders and Regulations. Adjutant-General's Office (Horse Guards).

5   J. Russell, *A series of Experiments of attack and defence made in Hyde Park in 1802, under the sanction of His Royal Highness the Commander in Chief, with Infantry, Cavalry and Artillery; and in the Island of Jersey, in 1805* (London: T. Egerton, 1806), p.194.

6   TNA, WO123/134/558: Army Circulars, Memoranda, Orders and Regulations. Adjutant-General's Office (Horse Guards).

'British artillerymen pulling a gun', 1800. Unfinished ink sketch by Benjamin West. A curious feature is the gaiters, which have been left uncoloured by the artist. The long hair has been reversed back on itself to leave the tail shorter. (Anne S.K. Brown Military Collection, Brown University Library)

1 November, 1806. General order, dress of RHA

Master General of the Ordnance to officers RHA,
Except at dress parades, the blue regimental overalls are to be worn til dinner-time in place of the blue pantaloons, which is to be the afternoon dress when at home. At all parades, whether mounted or dismounted, and during the day, the black velvet stock is to be worn, with a quarter inch of shirt-collar over it; no other white to be shown.

In the evenings it is requested that black silk handkerchiefs may be substituted, with the same proportion of shirt collar over them.

When officers are dressed for a ball, evening party, or dine out, they are to wear the jacket open, white pantaloons, plain white waistcoat, with sash over it, light sword, regulation sword knot, black belt, with cocked hat and feather. In common a white leather swordknot is to be worn. Spurs with horizontal rowels to be worn at all times.

Lord Rawdon-Hastings Master General of the Ordnance[7]

---

7   TNA, WO55/574: Ordnance, Miscellaneous Entry books and Papers. Orders, General.

12 November, 1806. A letter regarding exemption

> Deputy Adjutant General to Lieutenant General Pigot, Colonel of the 82nd Foot,
> Having had the honour to submit to the Commander-in-Chief your letter of the
> 10th with the inclosures; I am commanded to signify to you that as it appears the
> lacquered caps were ordered and prepared for your regiment previous to the present
> regulation stablishing the felt cap, HRH approves in consequence thereof, of the
> lacquered cap being, in this instance, issued to, and worn by the 82nd regiment.
>   William Wynyard Deputy Adjutant General.[8]

24 November, 1806. Circular to army agents

> From the Adjutant General to Messrs Greenwood, Collyers, Hopkinson, Groasdaile,
> MacDonald, Bonner, Bownas, Copy sent to the Adjutant General of Ireland.
> I have the honour to signify to you, that the regulations contained in my circular
> letter of the 27 October last, respecting the mark of distinction on the greatcoats
> of non-commissioned officers, which the Commander-in-Chief had been pleased
> to approve should be adopted, are intended to apply, as well as to the regiments of
> cavalry, as infantry, which you are directed to notify accordingly.[9]

8   TNA, WO3/42/1: Office of the Commander-in-Chief: Out-letters. General letter.
9   TNA, WO123/134/564: Army Circulars, Memoranda, Orders and Regulations. Adjutant-General's Office (Horse Guards).

15

Of Powder Puffs and Bearded Brutes

The first fifteen years of the 19th century saw a transition in military hair styling from the formal powdered and queued look of the 18th century empire builders to the crop and whiskers of the 19th century romantic heroes. If the profusion of wigs in the 18th century provokes bewilderment today, the practice that followed the wigs of curling the side-hair, skinning the top, and then smothering the hair in rancid fat, before coating it in powder is perhaps even harder to understand. One never feels further away from the early 19th century than when reading Mercer's description, quoted in Chapter 5, of the stench of hair grease and rancid flour hanging over the military congregation in the chapel at Woolwich.

By 1800 the actual wig had already long been discarded by the Army. Wigs had drifted comprehensively out of fashion by 1790 and the influence of the French Revolution accelerated the process of decline until only the older and conservative, or hidebound, hung onto their wigs. They had been gradually diminishing in size during the latter half of the century, until even the military were forced to take notice. The Army as a body was renowned for adherence to archaic fashions, and so as the first step in the process of discarding the wig, they chose to dress the natural hair to resemble one. The practice of frizzing, plastering and powdering the hair until it was uglier than false hair was not an apparent transition from civilian style, but probably an importation from Prussia's army. What happened to all the wigs? The end was a long time in coming, but by 1815 wigs could be bought for six pence apiece in street markets by reaching into a barrel and taking whichever wig happened to emerge. The results of these lucky dip transactions were recycled as mop heads or polishing cloths.[1]

The fundamental changes of the period then, are from queues and powder to crops and whiskers. That much is clear, and on record, and yet the particulars of the initial and ultimate positions are unclear, even if the date of the transition is not. In fact, previous authors rather concentrate on the date of the transition as if that says it all, when the interesting elements are the precise style of hairdressing before and afterwards. The genesis of the change was the suspension of the use of hair powder. Although this was quickly reversed it heralded a decline in the number of occasions on which hair powder was used. Subsequent

---

1   R. Corson, *Fashions in Hair, the First Five Thousand Years* (London: P. Owen, 2001), p.276.

changes saw the loss of the side curls, the shortening of the queue, an increase in clubbing and tying up the hair under the cap, and then a final end to long hair in 1808.

Most of the information on this is gleaned from memoirs and regimental orders. The latter are the most interesting, and enable us to reconstruct the general orders on the early queue styles that no longer exist, and to get a little closer to the constraints imposed upon the crop, which was to be a precise mode and not a free for all. The evidence reveals the official hairstyle of 1800 through two identifications of regimental patterns with the official order, which is variously called King George's, or the Duke of Kent's. The Duke followed his royal father's edicts to the letter, and there are some grounds for considering the two styles to be the same thing by different names.

In 1795 the use of hair powder in the entire army had been temporarily suspended by general order.[2] The date coincides with the introduction of the tax on hair powder, from which officers, but not men, were exempted. The Revolution saw the end of powder in France and in England the end came with Pitt's government taxing it. Everyone wearing hair powder was required to pay a guinea a year, no matter how much or little they used. Revenue in the first year was £210,136, money that would usefully be put towards the war to convince the French to reinstate their King, who would presumably have in turn reintroduced the custom of wearing hair powder, a practice to which he never personally neglected to adhere.

The use of hair powder had reached some ridiculous excesses. In the *Monthly Magazine* of 1806, Fox is remembered as having his 'red heeled shoes and his blue hair powder'.[3] Early hair powder was white or grey, sometimes black or brown, very occasionally blond. Later it was tinted in various colours – red, pink, blue and lavender – and scented. Whatever the realities for the officer class, the powder of the men was always white, and often constituted of flour. The excessive use of flour in the composition of hair powder was the ostensible reason behind the hair powder tax in the first place, it being considered wasteful to use flour for purposes other than bread at a time when the country was at war:

> In the following year, 1795, a tax was imposed on hair powder. For some years this custom had been on the wane, and only worn by the elderly, the conservatives, officials, the clergy and the army; but each man in the army used about one pound of wheat flour a week on his hair, and this was more urgently needed for bread, during the wars. The 1795 tax was a guinea for those who wished to continue the custom; exempted were members of the Royal Family, the clergy, and officers of the army and navy.[4]

The 1795 tax dealt a deathblow to the use of hair-powder by all but the most reactionary civilians, but it was also a slow burning catalyst for the changes in the Army, paving the way for change, however tardy that change may have been in catching up with the shorthaired crop *a la Titus* of London and Paris.

2   TNA, WO3/14/71: Office of the Commander-in-Chief: Out-letters. General Letters, and TNA, WO3.28.103: Office of the Commander-in-Chief: Out-letters.
3   *The Monthly Magazine, or Register, 1806*, p.262.
4   N. Wraxall, *Memoirs of his own Time* (London: Richard Bentley, 1836), Volume I, pp.142-2.

'Certificate for payment of hair tax'. From the records of Major William Augustus Bygrave, 65th Foot. The certificate was issued gratis to those exempted from the tax for reasons of military service. (Rotherham Local Archives)

Standing orders of the 2nd Dragoon Guards dated 1795 insist that hair of officers and men will be powdered.[5] The 1795 Standing orders of the 106th Foot and the 115th Foot agree in this respect: powder was to be maintained.[6] The following year, the Royal Artillery was being instructed to queue their hair, as formerly,[7] and also in 1796 a circular from the Commander-in-Chief to cavalry regiments directed that, 'no officer, or soldier, should be permitted to cut his hair, so as to prevent it being worn queued, in the manner here directed'.[8]

So whilst it seems impossible to fix a date on which the temporary suspension on the use of hair powder was lifted, it was either largely ignored, quickly revoked, or both, and any attempt to extrapolate the suspension on the use of hair powder into a change away from the long hair and queue was quickly stamped out. The use of hair powder would endure until 1808, when the queue was abolished and powder was no longer required. The process of cutting hair short began with the hair powder tax, but took a very long time to overcome institutional resistance at Horse Guards, and it was still in general use for dress occasions throughout the army in 1808 when the general order to cut the hair arrived. The 1808 Standing Orders of the 13th Foot recognise that even though the colonel of the regiment

5   Anon., *Standing Orders, Forms of Returns, Reports, Entries, &c., of the Queen's Dragoon Guards* (London: J. Walter, 1795), p.4.
6   Anon., *Standing Orders for the Norwich; or, Hundred and Sixth Regiment* (Waterford: James Ramsey, 1795). p.2; Anon., *Standing Orders for Prince William's Regiment of Gloucester* (Gloucester: No Publisher, 1795), p.60.
7   TNA, WO55/677: Miscellaneous Entry books and Papers. Officers' orders books (Artillery).
8   TNA, WO3/29/32: Office of the Commander-in-Chief: Out-letters. General letters.

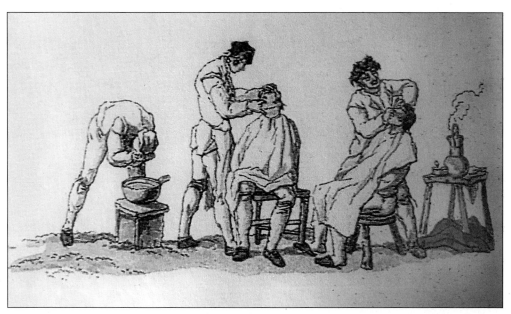

'Camp Barbers.' 1802, from Pyne's Micrococosm. In this context barbering related to shaving rather than hairdressing and setting. (Bristol Central Research Library).

was opposed to the wearing of hair powder by the men 'under any circumstances', it was still to be continued where garrison or other orders over ruled those of the regiment: a clear indication that local orders issued by superior officers would trump regimental practice in respect to hair. The Duke of York was notorious for his insistence on powdered hair, and he managed to preserve the use of hair powder and queues for those under his command until at least 1809. When the Duke of Kent was Governor of Gibraltar at the turn of the century, he issued a series of orders on dress. Mercer recalled that upon transport ships entering the harbour, the Duke's hairdresser boarded the ship with the pilot, and no officer was allowed to land until the hairdresser had approved or improved his coiffure.

The regime imposed by the Duke of Kent at Gibraltar was notorious and was recorded by many officers in their memoirs as an example of bad practice. Luard recalled,

> To such an excess was this carried during the command of the late Duke of Kent at Gibraltar, that when a field day was ordered, there not being barbers sufficient in the garrison to attend all the officers in the morning, the seniors claimed the privilege of their rank; the juniors consequently were obliged to have their heads dressed the night before; and to preserve the beauty of this artistic arrangement, pomatumed, powdered, curled, and clubbed, these poor fellows were obliged to sleep on their faces! It is said, that the adjutant's office of each regiment there was kept a pattern of the correct curls, to which the barbers could refer.[9]

9   Luard, *History of the Uniforms of the British Army*, p.101.

The orders of the Duke of Kent are so frequently referred to in memoirs that it is fortunate that several extracts from the 1802 orders of HRH the Duke of Kent when Governor of Gibraltar, have been preserved, so the memorialist's recollections can be compared with the actual document issued. Although it is mainly concerned with hair, it touches on other matters sartorial, and it is rare enough to need to be reproduced in full here,

> No.1 Officers to be allowed to wear whiskers, serjeants and soldiers not. The whiskers must be allowed to grow so as to come immediately forward into the face, but not to suffer them to grow more than half an inch below the bottom of the ear, nor to be longer than ¾ of an inch; at the same time they are desired not to shave between the whisker and the ear, nor otherwise to thin or clip them. NCOs and privates (except the drum-major and pioneers, by whom HRH desires them to be invariably worn) are on no account to wear side whiskers, but to have their hair shaved off perfectly square in a line with the top of the ear.
>
> No.2 Officers to appear at all times in white cross belts and regulation swords, with sashes. No dirks to be worn at all. The coat to be buttoned all the way to the neck, and no part of the shirt or waistcoat seen. The stock to be black leather with horizontal ribs, white breeches with regimental buttons and long boots, off duty. No short boots to be worn, or blue pantaloons.
>
> The hair to be cut and dressed according to the following form. The top hair to be cut so close as only to admit of its being turned with turning irons of the smallest size. The hind hair is to be parted from that of the top in the shape of a horse shoe, commencing from half an inch behind the ear, which is to be the extreme breadth of the top. This hair so parted off is to be combed back, and allowed to grow down in one even length, so that the whole of it may be in the queue. No part of the hind hair is to be thinned off and none of the short of the neck to be cut away. The hair being cut in this manner is to be dressed as follows, viz. the top to be turned with irons and combed from the ear upwards, the ear being left perfectly free from all powder. The queue to be tied at the distance of two inches from the head, the hair above the tie being moderately filled with powder and pomatum, but not so as to render it stiff or constrained. The regulation queue of which two are in the possession of the quarter master of the Royals, one for the officers, the other for the NCOs and men, which are so contrived as to enclose the hair to be at all times worn, except by grenadiers and fuziliers, when they are ordered to wear their bearskin caps, at which time they are to have their hair plaited according to the following directions.
>
> The hair in the first place to be tied with a string close to the head, then filled with powder and pomatum well mixed, next to be formed into these strands, which are to be braided as flat as possible, not to appear stiff, the plait to be turned up at the length of three inches from the tie, and fixed with a comb two inches in width which is to be placed at the top of the horse shoe, exactly where the back hair is separated from the front, the plait to cover the whole of the comb, and at the bottom to be half an inch wider than at the top. The string to which the hair is ties previous to its being divided for the purpose of being plaited is to be covered with a flash- particular care is to be taken that the hair is at all times thoroughly mixed

with powder and pomatum. Such officers whose hair is too short at present to tie, must wear the regulation queue fixed with a string round the head, but will on no account be permitted to wear a queue, as they do at present, sewed to their neck cloths, or to the collar of their coats.

Shoes never to be worn except at balls. On the 1st day of October, all officers must provide themselves with cocked hats, and further flank officers with regulation caps, patterns of which sealed with HRH seal, are to be procured on application to Mr Hawkes, accoutrement maker Piccadilly, until that period, during which round hats are still permitted to be worn, officers are desired to attend to wear them perfectly level on the head, and close down upon both eyebrows. Upon no account to press them so deep on the back of the head that the edge of the crown passes the top of the ear, by attending to which the hat will be even all round, and not sit lower behind than before, which is particularly disapproved of.

The surgeons are to wear black ribbed leather stocks 2 and a half inches broad, and whole boots that come within an inch of the knee, and to sit without a wrinkle. The artificers parade for work at half past three, remain at work 'til one, except an hour for breakfast, from one till four eat and dress, and from four 'til eight at drill. Every serjeant to show himself sober to the adjutant at 9 O clock, who is then to see every man is sober that mounts guard next morning.[10]

The process of preparing the hair was a complicated one and required the soldier to outlay on a profusion of necessaries. As with all necessaries these were required and enforced purchases, paid for by the soldier out of stoppages upon his pay, usually made from the regimental quartermaster, who would arrange supplies from approved tradespeople. A good description of the specialist equipment required to achieve the regimental hairstyles can be found in the memoir on fashion of Mercer of the Royal Artillery quoted in Chapter 5. The cavalry underwent a similar process:

Hard brush, soft brush, polishing brush, cloth brush, colouring brush, looking glass, powder-bag and puff. Two combs, large and small, one rosette, shaving box and razor. This is the equipment for the men. The horse has a separate set of brushes, combs, etc.[11]

The standing orders for the 3rd Dragoons further clarify the contents of the shaving box, 'a shaving box, brush and soap, a razor'.[12] This shaving box was omnipresent in every private soldier's equipment until the 1812 warrant, when the box was formally done away with, after an 1811 Board of General Officers report had recommended it be discontinued.[13] It appears that items of necessaries that were flammable were often used as fire-starting equipment on service, and the shaving box was no exception to this utilitarian approach to personal

10 Somerset Archives, Loose Manuscripts, DD/SLI/2/12.
11 Anon *Standing Orders in His Majesty's 1st (or Royal) Regiment of Dragoons,* 1799, p.22.
12 G. Mundy, *Standing Orders for the Third, or King's Own Regiment of Dragoons, issued by Lieut. Col. Godfrey Basil Mundy* (Dublin: J. Stewart, 1805), p.70.
13 TNA, WO7/56/97, Various Departmental, Out-letters. Board of General Officers. Reports Miscellaneous.

'Dragoons cleaning boots and harnesses.' 1802, from Pyne's Micrococosm. The extraordinary length of the tail of hair is apparent in this informal setting. (Bristol Central Research Library).

equipment. Some of the boxes also seem to have included a small looking glass, which would have been a useful addition in camp.

The first requirement was obviously that the soldier have sufficient hair to begin the process. There were strict injunctions to stop the soldiers from cutting their hair too short, and company barbers were instructed to cut and dress the hair according to patterns laid down by the adjutant:

> When a recruit is allotted to a troop, he must immediately be clothed, and provided with necessaries, and his hair cut by the man appointed for that purpose in the troop, according to the following directions, viz. Cut close on the upper part of the head, the whiskers level with the lower part of the ear. The hair cut away behind the ears a full inch, but none from the back part of the head, or under the queue, except the loose ones from the back of the neck.[14]

The unpleasant change from civilian hair to military was graphically recalled by John Shipp when he joined the 22nd Foot at Colchester in 1797:

> I went into the town to purchase a few things that I needed such as a powder-bag, puff, soap, candles, grease and so on. As soon as I got back I had to undergo the

14 Mundy, *Standing Orders*, p.103.

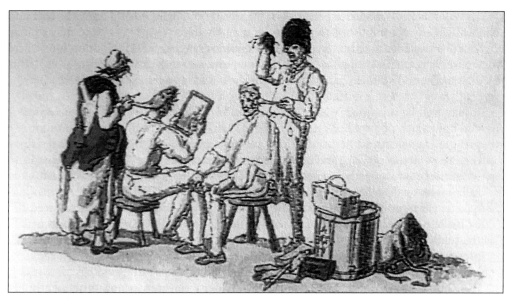

'Male and female camp hairdressers.' 1802, from Pyne's *Micrococosm*. Hairdressing was carried out by soldiers, professional hairdressers, and by women associated with the regiment. (Bristol Central Research Library).

operation of having my hair tied for the first time, to the no small amusement of the other boys. A large piece of candle-grease was applied first to the sides of my head, and then to the long hair behind. After this, the same operation was gone through with nasty stinking soap, the man who was dressing me applying his knuckles as often as the soap, to the delight of the surrounding boys who watched the tears roll down my cheeks. That part was bad enough, but the next was worse. A large pad, or bag, filled with sand, was poked into the back of my neck, the hair twisted tightly around it, and the whole tied with a leather thong, When thus dressed for parade, the skin of my face was pulled so tight by the bag stuck at the back of my head, that it was impossible so much as to wink an eyelid.[15]

As in other 'trade' appointments in a regiment, such as farriers, smiths, cobblers and tailors, a regimental barber would supervise the company principals, although it appears there was less formalisation of the hairdressing positions than in the other trades. A recruit skilled in the art of hair setting was naturally used in his ex-professional capacity in the regiment: 'Gibbons before he enlisted was a journeyman hairdresser, and become very useful in shaving, hair-cutting, and setting the razors of the officers'.[16] Private Gibbons is listed as a former wig maker in the regimental lists of the 33rd. It is probable that the end of the fashion for wigs meant an increased pool of hairdressers available for the army to recruit – an unexpected result of the hair-powder tax.

15 Shipp, *The Path of Glory*, p.37
16 F. Pattison, *Personal Recollections of The Waterloo Campaign* (Glasgow: Blackie and Co. 1870), p.4.

of leather, whalebone for officers or metal wire for the men, bound with black ribbon. Tufts of real hair were attached to the end. There was also a vogue for incorporating keepsakes of hair from sweethearts into the queue. The tuft would be tied into the ultimate portion of hair that emerged from the end of the tie. It was noted that this could provide an interesting contrast to the powdered or natural hair of the wearer, when the hair was a different colour.

Although the shifting nature of the styles of long hair mean that particular methods changed over the period, some general classification is possible, which means that when referring to particular accounts, the mode in use can be identified.

At the beginning of the century three main categories were used:

- The first was clubbing. For private soldiers, corporals, serjeants, and artillerymen. The hair was folded back on itself and tied behind at the base of the coat collar.
- The second was plaiting. For musicians and pioneers. The hair is braided into a pigtail and tucked up under the back of the cap, reaching from the base of the neck to the top of the head. Grenadiers and Light Infantry also used this method.
- The third was the queue. For battalion and staff officers. It was similar to clubbing but longer and the hair is folded back only at the very end, returning into the confines of the binding, leaving a loop of hair outside the binding.

By 1802 the mode had altered slightly, and we have a detailed rendering of the variants from the 1802 collation under the heading, 'Hair, how worn'. It suggests that the order of 21 July 1796 was still largely in effect. General officers, officers on the staff, and officers of infantry (excepting those of the grenadier and light companies) were to wear the hair queued and confined inside a ribbon. The ribbon began near the top of the collar of the coat and left about 1½ inch of hair out of the bottom. A rose of black ribbon covering the tie and queue about 11 inches in length. The flank company officers were to wear the hair plaited and turned up with a comb, with ends of ribbon hanging on the back from the tie:

> The Hair of the Serjeants and the Rank and File of Infantry throughout to be worn short at the Top and Sides, and the Hind Part queued (excepting the Grenadiers, Light Infantry, and Drummers). The Queue is to be 11 inches in length, the Ribbon to commence on the Hair at the Top of the Collar of the Coat, and to leave about 1 ½ inch of Hair out the bottom of the Queue; and the Fastening of the Ribbon to be covered by a Black Leather Rose. The Grenadiers, Light Infantry and Drummers to have the Hair short at the Top and Sides, and the Hind Part plaited and turned up under the Cap with a Comb, with three doubles and two Ends of Ribbon hanging down on the Collar of the Coat from the Commencement of the Plait.
>
> N.B. The Grenadiers. Etc. of some Regiments wear Black Leather cut in Form of a Ribbon. [23]

---

23 2006-11-50- National Army Museum, 'Descriptive View of the Clothing and Appts of the Infantry; bound and anno-
    tated manuscript copy dated 22 May 1802; inscribed inside cover in pencil, 'Copy of the Standing Regulations for the
    colours, clothing etc of the Infantry, to which are annexed the Guards, Rifle Corps etc'.

'Soldiers cleaning clothes.' 1802, from Pyne's Micrococosm. The specialist equipment or T-bar for suspending equipment is referenced in other barracks images. Its utility for keeping cleaned garments clear of the ground is clear. (Bristol Central Research Library).

An extract from the regimental orders of the 13th Regiment of Foot in 1807 indicates the state of affairs in a standard line regiment towards the end of the long hair period. The powder was to be avoided, except under exceptional circumstances. The use of grease was to be laid off, except when necessary for reasons of health. The side curls were gone, but replaced by 'frizzing', and the hair when queued was confined in three types of tying, according to whether upon a full dress, dress, or undress occasion.

The long hair was more popular in some quarters than in others. Surtees, best known as a memorialist of the 95th, recalled a moment of spontaneous haircutting from when he was a private in the 56th Foot. His regiment were on the beaches of the Low Countries in 1799, when he witnessed the false belief amongst the ranks that long hair could be dispensed with under active service conditions:

> Everything being ready for landing, we disembarked there on the 15th September, 1799. Among those regiments which landed, I remember the 35th was one. This regiment, after coming on shore, was drawn up close to us; they had not been long landed before the men began with their knives to cut of each other's hair, which then was worn in the shape of a club; this was done without any orders from their officers, and appeared to me, I confess, such a breach of discipline, as I could not have anticipated.[24]

24   W. Surtees, *Surtees of the 95th (Rifles)* (London: Leonaur, 2006), pp.14-15.

The privates were quickly disabused of this notion, but it was not an isolated incident, and sometimes these rumours were sponsored by authority, as was the case during the campaign in the Rio de la Plata:

> Although the fashion at that time was for soldiers to be smart, with long powdered hair, Sir Samuel Auchmuty believed they should be rough looking, with long beards and greasy haversacks. It was because of his dislike of dandyism that the fashion for powdered hair was done away with after we landed in South America. Of course it might have been that it was difficult to get the powder.[25]

Captain Ross-Lewin of the 32nd described an incident as early as 1797 when hair styles were changing, and a local commander made a unilateral decision to modernise the regiments under his command. Since clubbed hair was to replace the false tail, the soldier may not have been terribly pleased when the commanding general changed and he would have been liable to punishment for having cut his hair:

> The year 1796 was most auspicious for the army, as false tails and sandbags were condemned, and the pay was doubled. But so wedded do many people become to old customs, that some corps were to be seen dressed in this manner in '97. The Clare regiment were quartered that year at Waterford, and still continued to wear their hair clubbed. At length the general commanding there sent for one of the grenadiers to come to his room, and, as soon as the man made his appearance, the following colloquy commenced, 'My lad, how long does it take to dress your hair in this manner?' – 'An hour, plase your honour, to tie and be tied'. – And does it incommode you in doing your duty?' – 'Very much, sir; I can't turn my head without moving my body along with it, an' I'm afraid to eat after my hair is dressed, for fear of it's getting creased on me.' – 'Go,' said the general to his aide-de-camp, 'and get my dressing case'. The scissors were immediately in requisition, and the general cut off the grenadier's false tail, as well as the wings that projected over his ears.[26]

When the end finally came for the queue, it came suddenly. This gloriously martial but impractical appendage, which had caused the soldier much time and effort, was abolished by a General Order of 20 July 1808.[27] In future commanding officers were, 'To take care that the men's hair is cut close in their necks in the neatest and most uniform manner, and that their heads are kept perfectly clean by combing, brushing, and frequently washing them'.[28]

Several memorialists mention that the order was issued and then countermanded, but I have been unable to find any record of the countermanding in official records. It is possible that they have erred in following Gronow who mentions something of the kind:

---

25 W. Lawrence, *Autobiography of Sgt William Lawrence* (Staplehurst: Spellmount, 1995), p.24.

26 Ross-Lewin, *With The 32nd in the Peninsula*, p.105.

27 TNA, WO123/135/207: Army Circulars, Memoranda, Orders and Regulations. Adjutant-General's Office (Horse Guards).

28 Ross-Lewin, *With The 32nd in the Peninsula*, p.105.

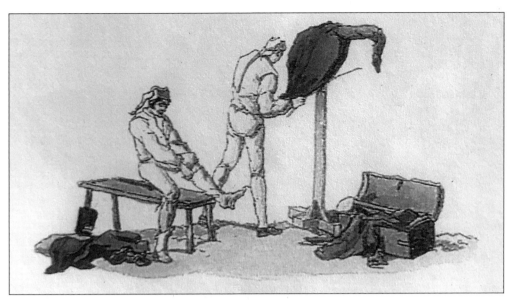

'Soldiers dressing.' 1802, from Pyne's Micrococosm. Again the T-bar reflects the importance given to the cleaning and care of garments. (Bristol Central Research Library).

The army was tormented with this preposterous and unwarlike method of dressing the hair, varying from club tails to macaroni tails and pig-tails. In the year 1804 the tails were ridiculous in length, an order was issued to reduce them to seven inches; and in 1808 the whole tails of the army were ordered to be cut off, an order that was obeyed with the greatest alacrity. The event was commemorated by numerous satirists. The day after the order to dock tails arrived, a counter-order came; it was too late, the tails were gone.[29]

In 1811, a Board of General Officers report on the proposed new warrants, which were to be issued in 1812, still detailed powder bag, powder and puff as dragoon necessaries at 2s and 6d. This is presumably carried over from the 1803 warrant, as the cavalry had lost the long hair at the same time as the infantry and artillery. The infantry were divested of their hair-dressing equipment at the same time as they lost their hair, being reduced from two combs to one, with fine teeth on one side only, and losing the hair leather and ribbons, instead being supplied with a sponge for cleaning the hair.[30]

There were occasional suggestions that certain regiments maintained the queued hair for a little longer than others. Although some regiments had a tradition of archaism, it seems improbable that a General Order could be resisted for long without an exemption order and survivals of the archaic mode of hairdressing can be measured in days rather than years:

29   Luard, *A History of the Uniforms of the British Army*, p.99.
30   TNA, WO7/26/132: Various Departmental, Out-letters. Board of General Officers. Clothing.

The 29th which on the day of our arrival at the mouth of the Mondego [1808] continued to wear the skirts of their coats hooked up in the old way, and their hats square instead of fore and aft [A reference to the officers]. The flank companies wore their hair turned up behind and made to rest on pieces of glazed leather, which were called flashes.[31]

It appears the 71st was another of the regiments that kept their hair long a little longer. This, from November 1808, near Salamanca:

It was one of the severest nights of cold I have ever endured in my life. At that time we wore long hair formed into a club at the back of our heads. Mine was frozen to the ground in the morning and when I attempted to rise my limbs refused to support me for some time.[32]

The first to cut their hair were those on home service. Lieutenant Thomas Henry of the 23rd Royal Welch Fusiliers describes the situation in a regiment that was proud of its fusilier distinctions in hirsute matters:

It was about this time that a general order was issued from the Horse Guards for the discontinuance of the use of powder on the heads of the soldiers, and directing that their heads should be closely cropped. It is natural to suppose that an order of this description would have been received by the men most gratefully, and that the officers would also rejoice at being permitted to disencumber themselves of so useless an appendage. No such thing, the order was obeyed in sulky silence by the officers, and particularly by those who had been distinguished by a luxurious plait. The colonel himself, who was one of these, was by no means pleased by the measure. We were seated at the Mess table, when the matter was talked over, and having perhaps taken an extra glass, by way of softening our vexation, one of the officers proposed that we should, there and then, cut off each other's plaits with a carving knife, and make a grand frizz of them in the fire. The first part of the proposition was acceded to, and I can vouch for its having been a rough and painful operation. The question of burning and frizzing our precious locks, was of a much more serious nature, and acceded to only by one or two old subalterns with whose heads time had taken its usual liberty of thinning and bleaching. The rest of us wrapped up our discarded tails in pieces of brown paper or pocket handkerchiefs, and carried them to our barrack rooms.[33]

The reaction in the barracks was of an altogether more serious nature:

With the men, the scene was far different, and the row which this order produced in the barrack yard amounted to very little short of mutiny. The women assembled

31 Ross-Lewin, *With the 32nd in the Peninsula*, p.105.
32 Hibbert (ed.) *A Soldier of the 71st*, p.21
33 Buckley, R, *The Napoleonic War Journal*,, p.114.

in groups of three or four, which after their respective stormy discussions, joined each other and added to the uproar. They swore by every oath that a soldier's wife has no difficulty in uttering, that the order should not be carried into execution, and that they would murder the first operator who should dare to touch a hair of their husband's head. They felt at once, that should the barbarous decree be carried into execution, they descended more than one step in the scale of female perfection, and that widowhood would inevitable be their lonely portion, in case of that event to which some of them looked forwards with complacency, and perhaps there were not wanting those who would have rather parted with their husband' heads, than that their claims to preservation of caste as wives should have been weakened by this cruel docking innovation.[34]

Fortunately for the discipline of the regiment, the colonel was more than equal to the situation, and despite his own sorrow, he provided an object lesson in how to break a fashionable habit:

Things were in this state of ferment when the adjutant waited on the colonel to report the state of confusion which prevailed in the barrack yard. He went there immediately and ordered out the first company... having done this he ordered them to take open order, and sending for benches from the barrack rooms had them placed behind each rank, and commanded the men to sit down. This they did in perfect silence, he then ordered off their foraging caps and sent for half a dozen haircutters, of which there are always plenty in every regiment. They were set to work and in less than ten minutes, nothing remained but the stump of the favourite club. The benches were then removed, ranks closed, and the company dismissed. The women assembled in groups and cursed and muttered, but the eye of the commanding officer subdued every other indication of mutiny'.[35]

The sequel demonstrates how quickly the adaptation was accepted after the initial reluctance to comply:

It was droll enough to see the men as they were dismissed to their barrack rooms, applying their hands to the back of their heads, to ascertain if it were a dream or reality. The soldiers however soon became reconciled to this great improvement, and the officers quickly perceived its good effects from the cleanliness which it produced. The women, I daresay, soon discovered some other foundation on which to build their hopes of perpetual wifehood, and in a few months, all the heads of the regiment were as quiet on the subject as if such a thing as a club had never been heard of.[36]

34   Buckley (ed.), *The Napoleonic War Journal*, p.115.
35   Buckley (ed.), *The Napoleonic War Journal*, p.115.
36   Buckley (ed.), *The Napoleonic War Journal*, p.116.

'Soldiers pulling on boots.' 1802, from Pyne's Micrococosm. The removal of boots, like the dressing of hair required the assistance of a comrade. Standing orders for light service suggest that necessities connected with grooming were sometimes limited to one set between two soldiers to reduce weight. (Bristol Central Research Library).

Costello's account is in contrast to almost all other information on the subject, which indicates that soldiers were expected to conform to regulations on shaving and hair dressing while on active service. The 95th were, however, one of the few infantry regiments to specify that officers could wear moustaches on service. The 1801 standing orders of the regiment on formation stated: 'The hair always queued according to the C-in-C's order; powder, side hair for two inches below the ear, and mustaches to be worn by those who choose on service'.[46] George Simmons of the 95th spoke of his brother when writing home to his mother indicating that moustaches were not considered *de rigeur* in the 95th: 'Joe is in high health. He is now very stout and cultivating a pair of moustaches, which amuse me no little'.[47]

More typical is this account of the 92nd Gordon Highlanders in 1813.

> Thinking ourselves secure of a resting place for the night, those whose chins required a little trimming set about that operation... everything was proceeding favourably... the razors running as quickly over our faces as the stiff and lengthy stubble would permit them- when, lo! the horn again sounded, not the note of preparation, but to fall in and be instantly off, and half shaved soldiers stood laughing at each other in every direction.[48]

46   Stewart, *Regulations of the Rifle Corps*, article X.
47   G. Simmons, *A British Rifleman* (London: Naval and Military Press, 2007), p.327.
48   J. Hope, *Campaigns with Wellington and Hill* (London: Leonaur, 2010), p.183.

The following passage from a letter written by George Simmons of the 95th to his father on 7 July 1815. It shows that at least one British officer did not find time to let a barber tend to him during the campaign:

> Having lost my baggage, my dress is rather ludicrous, a pair of shoes belonging to a French grenadier, a pair of blue trousers taken off a dead officer, shirt taken out of a portmanteau in the field, for the rest, it's pretty good and it holds together, but is black with blood, powder and which with my burnt hands and face, long hair and mous-tache and half my sabre scabbard taken off makes me rather a respectable figure.[49]

However, the style of wearing the moustache persevered in infantry regiments. It was still prevalent in the winter of 1813 and 1814 in the Netherlands:

> Every individual soldier in that army was as thickly covered in hoar frost as the trees which studded the plain; and the moustaches of those who cultivated the hirsute appendage, as a protection against the cold, soon found their breath freeze on the hair.[50]

The genesis of the moustache wearing fad are obscure, but a Germanic origin was anecdo-tally popular:

> During the time the Worcestershire Militia was quartered at Blatchington [early 1798], it is said to have been the first regiment in the British Army to introduce and wear the moustache, having copied it from the Austrians.[51]

This would have been a highly unusual and fashion driven novelty. Moustaches generally were considered a German or foreign affectation and so deplored or enthused over according to the onlooker's personal enthusiasm for innovation. An officer of the King's German Legion, a largely Hanoverian force in British pay recorded in 1809 that in Berkshire,

> We were regarded with infinite curiosity; every part of our equipment which bore foreign character being scrutinized with wondrous exactness and even our mous-taches commented on, as things of a nature almost miraculous. In fact the English military not patronizing these warlike appurtenances, I question if the good people of Wallingford had ever witnessed a previous example.[52]

The more conservative elements of the infantry as a whole, then, continued to shun the moustaches and whiskers, and if a light cavalry officer joined an infantry regiment, he

---

49   E. Macready, *Journal and opinions of Edward Nevil Macready, 30th Regiment of Foot* (London: Macmillan and Co. 1875), p.180.
50   Lieutenant Thomas Austin, quoted in A. Bamford, *A Bold and Ambitious Enterprise: the British Army in the Low Countries, 1813-1814* (Barnsley: Frontline Books), p.103.
51   R. Holden, *Historical Record of the Third and Fourth Battalions of the Worcestershire Regiment* (Harvard: Paul Trench, 1887).
52   J. Hering, *Journal of an officer in the KGL* (London: Leonaur, 2009), p.44.

was required to conform. Witness Edward Charles Cocks who moved from a cavalry to a Highland regiment, and wrote that 'I have shaved off my moustaches and most of my beard and turn out a smooth regular infantryman!'[53]

The artillery as usual followed the infantry, and suffered from the same exceptions on service, Mercer of the RHA in Flanders 1815 before Waterloo wrote:

> The Duke of Wellington was so indifferent to the manner in which officers dressed, that they indulged in all sorts of fancies. I remember, at this inspection, Ramsay wore the light-cavalry belt instead of a sash; Bull wore beard and mustache; so did Neland; I wore the mustache. [54]

Mercer's accounts of bearded artillerymen might appear mere aberration, were it not for a series of sketches in an 1813 German manuscript of several English officers with facial hair, including one remarkably hirsute artilleryman.[55]

The cavalry, naturally, operated under different rules, and moustaches were prescribed or proscribed according to the whim of the colonel of each regiment of hussars and dragoons, but they also suffered from the need to remove their hair when returning from service abroad. The 15th Light Dragoons regimental history relates that in March 1807:

> HRH the Duke of Cumberland directs that until further orders, officers will discontinue to wear the moustachios, it being difficult to preserve uniformity in this respect, from the frequent leaves of absence granted, when they are generally cut off.[56]

The unofficial practice of wearing whiskers and moustaches abroad but not at home gave rise to this laboured repartee, 'The son of a Scots Marquis, who had seen much service on the continent, was lately accosted by a friend in Bond Street, who facetiously desired, "that as hostilities were over, his whiskers might be put upon a peace establishment". His companion replied, "To that I have no objection, but I desire that at the same time your tongue may be put on the civil list!"'[57]

Finally, a reminder that cross-fertilisation works both ways. The returning soldiers clearly inspired some of the beaus of the Ton in their turn, and the author of Johnny Newcome laughed that in imitation of the army veterans, 'An enormous pair of Mustachios and Whiskers were frequently seen to protrude from the delicate countenances of some of our Bond Street beaus'.[58]

53 J. Page, (ed.), *Intelligence Officer in the Peninsula, Letters and Diaries of Major The Hon. Edward Charles Cocks* (London: Spellmount, 1986), p.180.
54 Mercer, *Journal of the Waterloo Campaign*, p.86.
55 Die Domizaer Bilderhandschrift 1813 (Hemmann)
56 R, Cannon, *Historical record of the Fifteenth, or the King's Regiment of Light Dragoons, Hussars: containing an account of the formation of the regiment in 1759, and of its subsequent services to 1841.* (London: Parker, 1841), p.71.
57 *Edinburgh Advertiser*, 14 May, 1802.
58 Roberts, *Johnny Newcome*, p.64.

16

Regulation of 1807

---

9 February, 1807. Waterproofing Army Clothing

Adjutant General to Clothing Board,
I have received the Commander-in-Chief's command to desire you will at the next meeting of the general officers comprising the clothing board submit to their consideration the enclosed letter from Sir James Cockburn covering by Mr Secretary Wyndham's directions a proposal from Mr Bowles, for rendering water-proof the raw material of which the army clothing is made and to signify to HRH's request that they will, after due consideration with the principal army clothiers, transmit the information they may receive together with their opinion as to the probable advantage to be derived to the public and to the army by the adoption of Mr Bowles' proposals.
Harry Calvert Adjutant General[1]

7 March, 1807. Letter regarding various waterproofing processes

Adjutant General to Clothing Board,
I am directed by the Commander-in-Chief to transmit the enclosed copy of a letter received from Messrs Duke and Co and am to signify that HRH considers it but just that their proposals with respect to rendering waterproof the greatcoats of the army should be taken into consideration by the general officers composing the clothing board at the same time as those of Mr Bowles.
Harry Calvert Adjutant General.[2]

13 March 1807. Letter regarding deviations owing to weather

Adjutant General to Lieutenant General Pennington, Colonel 10th Royal Veteran Battalion.

---

1   TNA, WO7/34/61: Various Departmental, Out-letters. Board of General Officers. Clothing.
2   TNA, WO7/34/64: Various Departmental, Out-letters. Board of General Officers. Clothing.

Agreeably to your request, I have submitted to the Commander-in-Chief your letter of the 12th and have in consequence received HRH's commands to signify for your information, that a portion of watch coats and warm overalls being allowed in Canada for the men on duty, the arrangement proposed with respect to the great coats of the 10th Royal Veteran Battalion is rendered unnecessary. With respect to the men wearing Russia sheeting trowsers in summer, the Commander-in-Chief is not aware that such a deviation from the regulations of the army can be at all necessary, and HRH desires that the battalion under your command will strictly conform to what His Majesty's regulations require with respect to dress and clothing.

Harry Calvert Adjutant General.[3]

14 March, 1807. Letter to form Board of General Officers on hussars' clothing

Adjutant General to Lord Paget,
I have the honour to inform your lordship that it is the Commander-in-Chief's pleasure, that a board of officers , of which you will be the president, should assemble, for the purpose of preparing for HRH's consideration, a statement of the different articles of clothing and equipment, which it may appear advisable to substitute in those regiments which are at present, or may hereafter, by His Majesty's permission, be allowed to adopt the appointments and clothing of hussars, for the articles of the same description, which are in use in the regiments of British light dragoons. The officers named in the margin [certain officers of the 15th LD, 7th LD, 10th LD, and 2nd LD KGL], are those to whom, in conjunction with your lordship, the Commander-in-Chief is pleased to confide this service, and they will be directed to meet your lordship at the times you may appoint, and if you approve it, a room will be provided for your accommodation at no.19 Great George Street.

I am directed to observe, that in making the required statement, it is necessary that the board should bear in mind the expenditure allowed for the corresponding articles in a regiment of British light dragoons, and conform themselves as closely as possible thereto, in the recommendation they may make of the articles to be substituted in regiments allowed to use hussar clothing and appointments, in which the duration of the articles must be equally considered, as their original cost. The whole must be drawn up in a manner to give a comparative view of the expenditure in both services, and in terms which may furnish materials for a warrant, which will afterwards be prepared for His Majesty's final approval, and for his royal signature,

Harry Calvert Adjutant General.[4]

---

3   TNA, WO3/42/308: Office of the Commander-in-Chief: Out-letters. General letters.
4   TNA, WO3/42/322: Office of the Commander-in-Chief: Out-letters. General Letters.

'Cavalrymen Passing Through a Stream, Being Mustered by a Trumpeter'. Undated watercolour by J.A. Atkinson. The use by the cavalry of caps of various patterns for 'watering-order' indicates an additional level of service dress or undress. There is some cross over between the two modes. (Yale Center for British Art)

7 April, 1807. Letter for 51st clothing

> Pulteney to Clothing Board,
> In addition to my predecessor's letter of 10th of February last, I am to acquaint you for the information of the clothing board that the 51st Regiment of Foot is destined for service in Ceylon and the 19th and 66th for service at Madras, and that patterns of their clothing for the ensuing year should now be sealed accordingly.
>   John Pulteney.[5]

The carefree and devil-may-care nature of Georgian military bureaucracy is never more clearly exemplified than in the trivial correspondence regarding the substitution of milled kersey breeches for those of shag in the dragoon regiments. In one of those curious survivals, almost a complete correspondence on the matter has survived in the letter books of the Board of General Officers clothing, where a conscientious clerk decided to copy out the letters by rote rather than just suggest their gist, as was normal in letter books. The result is a riveting blow-by-blow account of the mischievous jockeying between the Board of General Officers clothing, the army comptrollers, and the Adjutant General's office. The 1807 part of the story unfolds in May, and the first two letters of that period have been reproduced in full, dealing with the proposal for the substitution and its recommended trial. The trial

---

5   TNA, WO7/34/67: Various Departmental, Out-letters. Board of General Officers. Clothing

of kersey was not compulsory, although all colonels of dragoon regiments were permitted to make it if they were keen to experiment beyond a basic shag. The next communication was a letter from March 1807 in which the colonel of the 4th Dragoon Guards elaborated on an independent trial of one year commenced in February by a rough rider from his regiment. This man had 'constantly rode in them' and they were still found to be serviceable, having had just one new web strap repair in that period. A further letter from the clothiers Pearse accompanied a pattern set of kersey breeches (pattern no.2) that had been delivered as an experimental test sample in 1805. They were seated with webbing and cost 13s, or 14s 3d with a second seating of webbing. Pearse notes further that shag breeches had been at 15s between 1805 and 1807, but had subsequently risen to 17s 6d owing to the 'enormous increase in the price of coarse woll'. Here the correspondence ceases, and this window into the trial process closes, although subsequent warrants reveal that the era of shag was indeed drawn to a close, ending a curious period when the heavy cavalry had breeches, and the light cavalry jackets, made out of something that very much resembled the shag pile carpet of the 1970s.

12 May 1807. Circulars

> Horse Guards,
> Sir, the Bearer will deliver to you a Pair of Milled Heavy Cloth Breeches which have been proposed for the use of the Regiments of Dragoons instead of the Shag Breeches which are now worn. And I am to signify the commander in Chief's desire, that these Breeches may be submitted for the examination of the Board of General Officers, who will be pleased to Report their Opinion whether it appears desirable that the Milled Kersey should be adopted instead of the Shag breeches. I take the opportunity to enclose for the information of the Board the accompanying letter from the Clothiers who have provided the Breeches, as likewise a Certificate from the Officer commanding the 4th Dragoons, a Man of which Regiment has for some time past been wearing a pair of these Breeches in order to prove their durability.[6]

Comptroller's Office to Harry Calvert Adjutant General, 5 June 1807

> Copy of minutes of Clothing Board meeting. Approval of HRH as soon as possible please so Clothiers can complete if necessary for next issue.[7]

Harry Calvert Adjutant General to above, 8 June

> A circular letter has been sent to Colonels of Dragoon Regiments permitting them to substitute kersey for shag breeches, 'in the event of their wishing to make the experiment whether they are preferable.[8]

6   TNA, WO7/34/56: Various Departmental, Out-letters. Board of General Officers. Clothing.
7   TNA, WO7/34/56: Various Departmental, Out-letters. Board of General Officers. Clothing.
8   TNA, WO7/34/56: Various Departmental, Out-letters. Board of General Officers. Clothing.

Letter from Lieutenant Colonel Teesdale

> Manchester 31 March 1807
> The pair of Kersey wove Cloth Breeches ordered by Adjutant Haveley were taken
> into wear by a Rough Rider on the 9 February 1806 since which time he has
> constantly rode in them, they are still serviceable, they had one new web strap in
> the above period.
>   H Teesdale, Lt-Col 4th Dn Gds.[9]

Letter from Clothiers

> No.41 Lothbury, London, 21st April
> Sir, Agreeable to your desire we send herewith a pair of Dragoon Breeches made of
> the milled Kersey Cloth to pattern no.2 delivered you in the year 1805 as an experi-
> ment. The price of Breeches made to patterns sent herewith,
>   Sealed with webbing is 13s
>   To allow a second seating of webbing 1s 3d
>   Total 14s 3d
> For your further information we add that 'til the Clothing 1805 to 1807 the Shag
> Breeches were charged at 15s, but on account of the enormous increase in the price
> of coarse wool and consequently the increased price of Shag they were then charged
> to the Colonels at 17s 6d and from what we can learn from the Manufacturers there
> is no prospect of a reduction in the price of the Shag for the next clothing period.
>   JN&B Pearce.[10]

5 June, 1807, Letter on milled breeches

> Clothing board to Comptroller's office, Adjutant General copied,
> Having laid before the general officers who compose the clothing board your letter
> dated 12th ultimo accompanying a pair of milled kersey breeches proposed for the
> use of the regiments of dragoons instead of the shag breeches which are now worn:
> I am directed to transmit to you a copy of the minutes of the board as far as relates
> to the subject and to request that you will be pleased to communicate to me as early
> as is convenient the pleasure of HRH as to substituting the milled kersey instead of
> the shag breeches for the ensuing two years of clothing, in order that the clothiers
> may be informed which patterns will be allowed to be sealed.
>   Thomas Fauquier Clothing Board.[11]

9   TNA, WO7/34/56: Various Departmental, Out-letters. Board of General Officers. Clothing.
10   TNA, WO7/34/57: Various Departmental, Out-letters. Board of General Officers. Clothing.
11   TNA, WO7/34/57: Various Departmental, Out-letters. Board of General Officers. Clothing.

23 June, 1807. Letter reporting on waterproofing

> Adjutant General to Clothing Board,
> Having laid before the Commander-in-Chief your letter of the 3rd with the several enclosures, (herewith returned) I received HRH's directions to communicate with the officers commanding the regiments named in the margin for the purpose of ascertaining their opinion of the waterproof greatcoats as to their use and efficiency agreeably to the suggestion of the general officers composing the clothing board, and I have the honour to transmit for their information the accompanying letters which have been received from the officers containing their opinions on the subject referred.
> 2nd Foot Guards,
> 3rd Foot Guards,
> 4th Foot,
> 14th Foot,
> 25th Foot.
> Harry Calvert Adjutant General[12]

26 June, 1807. Letter regarding extinct regiment

> War Office, Foreign Departments, to Clothing Board,
> His Majesty having been pleased to command that the Regiment of Fraberg [sic] should on account of its late mutiny be immediately disbanded, I am to acquaint you therewith for the information of the clothing board and to request that the assignment of off-reckonings for the clothing of the corps above mentioned for the year commencing the 25 December 1807 be not passed.
> J. Pulteney.[13]

In December 1803, three years after the French occupation of Malta was brought to an end by the combined efforts of the Maltese population and British forces, a certain Count Froberg was granted a Letter of Service by Britain's Secretary at War to raise a regiment in Germany for service in Malta. Such Letters of Service were frequently issued to British agents in Europe during the Napoleonic Wars. Froberg was a French Royalist whose real name was Gustave de Montjoie, and according to Adam Neale, writing in his 1813 work *Travels Through Some Parts of Germany, Poland, Moldavia and Turkey*, he had 'passed himself upon the British government' as the German Count Froberg.[14] The spurious count immediately set about recruiting for the Froberg Levy, as the regiment came to be called, in Albania and the Christian parts of Turkey, and had managed to assemble a force consisting of about 500 men by 1806, when the levy first arrived in Malta.

---

12   TNA, WO7/34/80: Various Departmental, Out-letters. Board of General Officers. Clothing.
13   TNA, WO7/34/83: Various Departmental, Out-letters. Board of General Officers. Clothing.
14   A. Neale, *Travels Through Some Parts of Germany, Poland, Moldavia and Turkey* (London: Longman, Hurst, Rees, Orme, and Brown, 1818), p.233.

The recruitment practices employed by Froberg were dubious to say the least, and Neale remarks that 'the most unprincipled deceit and falsehood were employed to obtain recruits'.[15] The resulting regiment consisted of a motley group of Germans, Poles, Swiss, Albanians, Bulgarians and Greeks. With such a miscellaneous assemblage of nationalities, each with its own language, religions and customs, the successful future of the regiment could certainly not be taken for granted. Furthermore, many of the rank and file of the regiment had been enticed to join up as ensigns and captains with promises of high pay and allowances. When they arrived in Malta, however, they were forced to do duty as privates, receiving much lower wages. Sure enough, there was great discontent among the men, and things came to a head soon after their arrival in Malta, eventually leading to a most inglorious end for Froberg's Regiment.[16]

2 July, 1807. Letter on pattern cap

Deputy Adjutant General to Clothing Board,
I have the honour to send herewith by direction of HRH the Commander-in-Chief a pattern felt cap which His Majesty has been pleased to approve and which is hereafter to be adopted throughout the infantry of the army in lieu of the lacquered felt cap hitherto used; and of which I am to request you will inform the general officers composing the clothing board.
     William Wynyard, Deputy Adjutant General.[17]

9 July, 1807. Letter regarding test items

Clothing Board to War Office,
A gentleman of the name of Green having called upon me this morning and (as he says by authority from Sir James Pulteney) requesting that the papers contained in his letter of the 6 of April last relating to the appointments for the 42nd Regiment may be officially returned to the war office as he is sensible the board of general officers was not the proper quarter to refer them to. I hereby return them accordingly: and at the same time transmit to you a letter from the Secretary at War dated 9 March last enclosing a state of the particulars of a set of rifle appointments for the 95th Regiment referring the same to the clothing board for their opinion, 'as to the propriety of the species of the several articles and the reasonableness of the charges'. On which points the board have not thought themselves competent to decide and desired the Adjutant General to return the papers to the WO which General Calvert did accordingly. They have, however, been again sent to the office of the clothing board, and are now returned with the account of the appointments of the 42nd regiment.
     Thomas Fauquier, Clothing Board.[18]

15   Neale, *Travels*, p.233.
16   *Times of Malta*, 1 February, 2015.
17   TNA, WO7/34/85: Various Departmental, Out-letters. Board of General Officers. Clothing.
18   TNA, WO7/34/86: Various Departmental, Out-letters. Board of General Officers. Clothing.

9 October, 1807. Letter on great coats

> Having laid before the Commander-in-Chief the enclosed letter from Messrs Pearse respecting the great coats provided for the regiments composed of men of colour, I have received HRH's commands to desire that it may be submitted to the next clothing board to take the suggestion of Messrs Pearse into consideration and report their opinion thereon for the information of the Commander-in-Chief by whose directions I am to add that frequent representations have been received from the West Indies respecting the badness of the quality of the cloth of which the present greatcoats are made.
>
> Harry Calvert Adjutant General[19]

4 November, 1807. Warrant concerning shoes

> Regulation for the supply of shoes to His Majesty's regiments of infantry serving in the East Indies (having reference to pages 439 and 440 of the General Collection published 25 April, 1807.)
>
> Whereas the Commander-in-Chief of our forces, and the general officers composing with him our permanent clothing board, have had under their consideration the reports of sundry officers conversant with the nature of the service in the East Indies; from which it appears that the shoes sent out from this country as part of the regimental clothing are less adapted to the use of the soldier, than the shoes made by the natives of India; which latter can also be procured at a comparatively low rate: And whereas it has in consequence been recommended to us by our said clothing board, that an alteration be made in our regulation for the clothing of the army, bearing date the 22 of April 1803, so far as regards the future supply of shoes to regiments serving in India: our will and pleasure is, that notwithstanding any directions contained in our said regulation, one pair of shoes only, per man, be in future forwarded for the use of our regiments serving in the East Indies, along with the annual regimental clothing, and that the value of a second pair of shoes be allowed to each serjeant, corporal, drummer and private on that station, and the amount laid out as the commanding officer of our respective regiments shall deem expedient, in shoes made by the natives of that country, or in such other necessaries as shall be judged most advantageous for the service; certificates of the delivery of such necessaries, being duly forwarded through the Adjutant General of our forces, to the clothing board.
>
> For which this shall be to all whom it may concern a sufficient warrant, authority and direction.
>
> Given at our court at Saint James's this fourth day of November, 1807, in the forty-eighth year of our reign.
>
> By His Majesty's command, James Pulteney[20]

---

19   TNA, WO7/34/109: Various Departmental, Out-letters. Board of General Officers. Clothing.
20   TNA, WO123/117/100: Army Circulars, Memoranda, Orders and Regulations. Army Regulations, etc from Various Sources.

24 Nov, 1807. Letter on waterproofing gaiters

Adjutant General to Board of General Officers clothing,
I have received the Commander in Chief's commands to request you will be pleased to submit to the Clothing Board the enclosed letter from Messrs Duke & Co on the subject of rendering waterproof the Gaiters of the non-commissioned officers and privates of the Army, and I am further to request after the Board shall have taken the same into consideration that they will be pleased to report their opinion thereon for the information of His Royal Highness.
　　Harry Calvert Adjutant General.[21]

29 November, 1807. General order, dress of artillery

Master General of the Ordnance to officers of artillery,
The officers' great coats, of the marching battalions, are to be of plain blue cloth, with a single row of flat metal buttons.
　　Lord Rawdon-Hastings, Master General of the Ordnance[22]

17 December, 1807. Letter on great coats

Clothing Board to Adjutant General,
In obedience to the commands of HRH the Commander-in-Chief signified to me in your letter dated the 9 October last. I yesterday laid before the clothing board of general officers the letter which you enclosed from Messrs Pearse respecting the great coats provided for regiments composed of men of colour, which the board having duly considered I have received their directions to communicate to you, for the information of HRH the result of their deliberations on the subject. Viz.
　　That with a view to the soldiers of the regiments of colour serving in the West Indies being furnished with, "a sufficient great coat the same as is worn by the soldiers of the regiments of the line calculated to last three years. It is submitted for the Commander-in-Chief's consideration that the colonels of the West India regiments should pay annually as a fund for supplying great coats to their regiments the sum of five shillings and seven pence halfpenny, being half the expense of the great coats at present furnished by them which are to last two years and that from this fund, government should provide great coats of a quality equal to that worn by the rest of the infantry of the army".
　　At the same time it appears to the board that it would be satisfactory to receive the opinion of the general officers commanding the Leeward Island and Jamaica stations as to the sufficiency of the great coats at present furnished by the colonels of the West India regiments as well as whether the great coat worn by the line which is calculated to last three years is applicable to the West India regiments.
　　Thomas Fauquier, Clothing Board.[23]

21　TNA, WO7/34/119: Various Departmental, Out-letters. Board of General Officers. Clothing.
22　TNA, WO55.574 (RJM, p.33): Ordnance Office and War Office: Miscellaneous Entry books and Papers. Orders.
23　TNA, WO7/34/110: Various Departmental, Out-letters. Board of General Officers. Clothing.

18 December, 1807. Letter regarding gaiters

> Thomas Fauquier, Board of General Officers clothing to comptroller's office, Adjutant General copied,
> On the subject of rendering waterproof the gaiters of the non-commissioned officers and privates of the army, I laid the same before the Clothing Board of General Officers on Wednesday last and the Board having duly considered the proposal of Messrs Duke & Co submit their opinion to His Royal Highness that there being no fund from which the additional expense can be defrayed it is not feasible to adopt it- unless Government shall enable the Colonels to pay the same.
> Thomas Fauquier[24]

24 December 1807. Memo on clothing for Royal York Rangers

> Adjutant General to Lieutenant Colonel Gordon,
> That it be submitted to His Majesty that the uniform of the Royal York Rangers which has heretofore been red with blue facings, be changed to that of green, faced with red.
> Harry Calvert Adjutant General.[25]

31 December 1807. Letter concerning surgeons' dress

> Deputy Adjutant General to J Knight Esquire,
> I have the honour to acknowledge the receipt of your letter of the 16th instant and to acquaint you in reply that it is understood that the medical officers whether of cavalry or of infantry are to wear a similar uniform to the other officers of their respective corps, with this exception, that the medical officers are to be distinguished by wearing a black feather.
> William Wynyard Deputy Adjutant General.[26]

24   TNA, WO7/34/120: Various Departmental, Out-letters. Board of General Officers. Clothing.
25   TNA, WO3/194/19: Out-letters. Letters to Public Departments.
26   TNA, WO3/194/34: Out-letters. Letters to Public Departments.

17

The Rise, Wobble, and Triumph of the Hussar Craze in the British Army

---

> Muffeteers. A name given to such regiments of dragoons as have been ordered to wear the furred caps, particularly the 7th and 15th light dragoons. The name is so far appropriate, because the caps of these corps resemble the common muffs worn by the females in Great Britain, and by the effeminate males on the continent.[1]

The Prince of Wales can be considered the most ardent advocate of the hussar against the jackboot prejudice of his father. He had been made colonel of his own light dragoon regiment in 1793, but that did not stop him trying to adopt a hussar regiment in 1796. The regiment that seduced his interest was the Hompesch Hussars, an émigré corps compose of deserters from the French service, and other continental outcasts. They had arrived in England from the West Indies, and were awaiting disbandment at Southampton when the Prince noticed them. He invited them all to a colossal party, and having feasted them, was impressed enough to deck them out in his own personal button, which featured his ostrich feathers and motto. This partiality did not save the regiment from their fate of disbandment, and having refused the opportunity to enlist in a British light dragoon regiment they dissolved away into other émigré units.

Serjeant Landsheit of the Hompesch Hussars, recalled the attempts of the recruiting party of the 25th Light Dragoons, who he found to be a poor contrast to his own regiment's prodigious dandies. The English equivalent by contrast were,

> Dressed in dirty grey jackets, leather helmet caps fearfully blackballed, white leather breeches, and shoes and long gaiters. They wore white feathers thrust into the sides of their helmets, and sabretaches tucked up so as to descend no lower than the hips. On the whole, we had never seen such spectacles.[2]

---

1 James, *Military Dictionary*.
2 N. Landsheit, *The Hussar: A German Cavalryman in British service throughout the Napoleonic Wars* (London: Leonaur, 2008), p.52.

The continental hussar style was a very different creature to the rather poor looking British hybrid that the light dragoon had evolved into. The rather fascinating and beautifully distinctive series of uniforms sported by the light dragoons at the start of the French Revolutionary wars had been superseded by a new kit. This had been proposed by a Board of General Officers composed in 1796 to conduct a wide ranging enquiry into all facets of the cavalry service, from horses and horse breeding, to clothing, saddlery, and equipment. A short waisted jacket had replaced the light dragoon's former charming combination of sleeved waistcoat and sleeveless 'shell', or outer waistcoat. This brought the light dragoon regiments closer in some respects to hussar dress, but in France and Germany it had long been the thing for swaggering hussars to trail their sabres on the ground, and their sabretasches were worn pendent just inches from their boot soles where they were always in danger of tripping over them. The pragmatic British approach of wearing the sabretasch on the hip failed to find favour with those used to true hussar panache. Ultimately some of those Hompesch men enlisted in a new émigré corps, the York Hussars, along with emigres and prisoners from the hulks. The regiment's largely German speaking crew of ruffians found favour with the King, and this may have been a partial step towards his allowing British regiments to convert to hussar dress. It is certain that by June 1802, with peace reductions stripping out the army, the York Hussars came to an ignominious end, with the majority of the regiment electing to return home to Germany rather than take service in a regular British cavalry corps.

There the matter may have rested, with the British continuing to spurn the hussar trend, had not the entreaties of a combination of various royal princes forced the issue. As a concession to their pressure, from early 1803 two royal colonels were each allowed to re-uniform a single troop of their light dragoon regiments as a hussar troop.[3] Presumably this was a merely sartorial distinction, as there is no record of there being any intention that these troops would be in any way trained differently. Each of these two colonels – the Prince of Wales in the 10th and Prince Ernest, the fifth son of George III, colonel of the 15th Light Dragoons – began immediately to re-equip his new plaything. The Prince of Wales was ably assisted by Captain Quentin, who would later head the 10th. Quentin had many officer-like qualities, and importantly, besides his mores serious accomplishments, he, 'knew how the pelisse should be slung, and the proper cut of the hessian boot'.[4]

The hussar troop of the 10th were soon re-equipped with mirliton caps, fur trimmed pelisses, knotted barrel sashes and Hungarian saddles. The Prince also bought forty of Ezekiel Baker's new rifled carbines, which were cousins of those rifles being used by the newly raised Rifle Corps of Coote Manningham, then training at Shorncliffe under Sir John Moore. Like the Rifle Corps, the embryonic hussars had a period of gestation to fulfil before they would see service.

In 1805, with Nelson having postponed the imminent invasion threat with his victory off Cape Trafalgar, the country braced itself to recommence the land war in earnest. It may be that the presence of two regiments of light dragoons equipped as hussars in the King's German Legion in a camp at Ipswich impressed the King with their efficiency for in

3   R. Liddell, *The Memoirs of the 10th Royal Hussars* (London: Naval and Military Press, 2015), p.25.
4   W. Lennox, *Celebrities I Have Known* (London: Hurst and Blackett, 1877), Volume I, p.194.

February of that year an order came down from Horse Guards that, 'His Majesty permits the 10th of Prince of Wales's Own Light Dragoons to wear Hussar appointments'.[5] Although the King had belatedly permitted the change in dress, he baulked at letting the regiments call themselves hussars, so what he gave with one hand, he withheld with the other, and for many years they continued to appear in the army lists as Light Dragoons (Hussars), a somewhat mean-spirited distinction. Three other regiments began to be converted at this time, the 7th, 15th, and 18th Light Dragoons. The conversion took some eighteen months to be effected. Lord Paget's 7th were ready first in September 1806. The 10th, 15th, and 18th were largely complete by July 1807. And as soon as the last moustache had been grown, the regiments prepared for service.

Two of the regiments concerned were headed by royal princes, and the others by two of the wealthiest peers in the Kingdom. Three of these colonels were also leaders of the Bon Ton, which was London's, and therefore the whole country's, fashionable world or considered themselves so, and it is not surprising that their regiments had a reputation as 'smart' corps. The concept of 'smartness' or 'fineness' was idiomatic to the beaus of the ton, and as closely coveted as the epithet of being, 'a crack corps' was to become later in the 19th century. To earn the epithet, a regiment had to be exceptionally well clothed, mounted, and armed. It also needed an air of uniqueness and exclusivity, and the hussar vogue conveyed those qualities to a tee. Hussars were smart not only because they had an expensive and exotic dress, but because they were new and experimental in nature. The 95th Rifles was to enjoy some of the same exclusivity, but being infantry they never attracted many nobles or leaders of the fashionable world in the way that the hussar regiments would.

Hussar Dress, outlandish, outrageous, and foreign, was an ideal vehicle for the expression of the Prince of Wales's rebellion against his royal father. He was not alone in his enthusiasm and Lord Petersham; the two Lord Manners; and the notorious Beau Brummell all served at one time or another in the 10th. They were attracted by the exclusivity of the hussar craze which chimed most neatly with the prevailing ethic in the Ton. The same drive for singularity would result in the rise of the Dandy, although strictly speaking that was a post-1815 term for the exclusive set of trend setters and their often rather odious acolytes.

After the success of the Hussar revolution in dress, a wobble occurred in 1809. The hussars had performed well on service in Spain in the campaign of Sir John Moore, but suffered with the rest of the army in the scrambled retreat over the mountains to the re-embarkation points at Vigo and Corunna. Almost all of the horses were destroyed at Corunna rather than be abandoned to the French and a great deal of equipment went the same way. The effect of this hard campaigning was that the black leather bridles and tack were exchanged for brown, which was easier to keep presentable in the field, and the rain sodden top heavy fur caps were relegated to full dress, being replaced by an un-peaked cap or chaco. A chaco, chacot, or shako was properly distinguished by being a cylindrical or near cylindrical cap with a leather top part to the crown.

At the same moment as the expeditionary army was limping home from the Spanish debacle a scandal was breaking in London over the head of the Commander-in-Chief of the

5   TNA WO123/161/367: Army Circulars, Memoranda, Orders and Regulations. Adjutant-General's office, Horse Guards.

Army, the Duke of York. There was an enquiry in the House of Commons into corrupt practices, after the Duke's mistress was accused of selling promotion in the army, by slipping names into the lists after the Duke had approved them. The Duke was eventually acquitted of corruption, but his mistress had sung like a canary and public opinion had turned fatally against him. The Duke of York, who had proved himself an energetic and capable reformer, resigned as Commander-in-Chief, and was replaced by Sir David Dundas, a pedagogic placeholder whose natural inclination was against the flash and panache of light troops in general and hussars in particular. Although Dundas's tenure in the Commander-in-Chief's seat was to be sound in principle and brief in duration, the King was irritated with the Duke of York, and as usual, furious with the Prince of Wales, and lashed out against what he saw as the pet projects of his two errant sons. One of these was, 'the dressing our light dragoons like mountebanks, and calling them hussars'.[6] According to Lord Moira the King promptly censured and altered several of the Duke of York's regulations, but little trace remains in the official record of this volte-face on hussars, which must have been rendered nugatory by the calm veteran Dundas. It was rather late in the day to allow the King's spleen to wreck sensible reforms, and the vagaries of fashion also survived. The King also had a, 'disposition… to make all the Light Dragoons heavy again' and mercifully that also fell between the cracks, the bureaucracy of State having learnt methods of managing and diluting the Royal Command owing to the episodic nature of the King's sanity in these unfortunate years.

There was some truth in the opinion that hussars were merely expensively dressed light dragoons, and there was a proposal in 1811 that showed the prejudice against hussars was still bubbling over. Typical of this reaction was a plan submitted to the Prince Regent and to the Commander in Chief for a levy of 'rough hussars' who would displace the function of hussars to yet another variation of the light cavalry model:

> Lieutenant-General Money humbly begs leave to lay before His Royal Highness the Prince Regent a proposition he has this day submitted to the Commander in Chief.
>
> Lieutenant-General Money has observed in Lord Wellington's last official letter, and in private letters, how superior, in point of numbers only, the enemy are in cavalry; it is therefore devoutly to be wished, that those fine regiments we have now in Spain should be as complete as possible, and fit for service, which cannot be done but by relieving them from the harassing duties of a camp, which render at least one fourth not in a state to come into contact with the enemy. Much less to follow them in critical moments, when great advantages might with reason be expected from them.
>
> Lieutenant-General Money (in order to keep our whole force of cavalry always in a state to act) begs leave to propose to HRH raising immediately six hundred rough hussars, mounted on Welch horses, by men below the army standard; such a corps as this, raise at no great expense, would not only release our best cavalry from all the fatiguing duties of the camp, but may be advanced on piquets that are not meant to be supported, and do the greater part of the patrolling duties etc. etc. Should this proposition meet HRH's approbation, Lieutenant-General Money

6   J. Mollo, *The Prince's Dolls* (London: Pen and Sword, 1997), p.88.

will pledge himself to raise four hundred of them in England and Ireland, and to be ready for embarkation within four months, on any conditions HRH may think proper to prescribe.[7]

The influential author of *James' Regimental Companion*, Charles James of the Royal Artillery, was another voice against the fashion,

Agreeing as we most cordially do, with the opinion of this respectable and able officer, who has seen much service, and witnessed the utility of the death hussars of Prussia during the seven years war, and from having been present at our disasters in America, and during the most trying moment of the French revolution equally engaged upon the continent, is competent to bear his theory out by practical knowledge, we have thought it right to preserve this document; and, in so doing, we sincerely hope, that some alteration will take place in the care, management and even in the outfit of our dragoon regiments. We shall waive all comment upon the unfortunate whim that first introduced the muff and the sabretache- one calculated only to receive the icicles in winter, and to oppress the head like as gorged sponge in rainy weather, or to blind the men by a collection of dust in summer; and the other to serve as a convenient instrument, by which a daring foot soldier may drag his mounted antagonist from his horse, and shoot or bayonet him as he falls. HRH the Prince Regent, (whose exalted mind has been naturally imbued with the best military notions, and is constantly directed towards every object, however minute or apparently trifling, that can add to the comfort or security of a soldier;- who is himself above all petty prejudices, and feels that common sense, though perhaps unpractised in the field, is competent to suggest the best ideas from the closet,) has lately, we understand, suggested a helmet for dragoons, that possesses every quality which can be wanted. It is light, easy, and so contrived, that the principal parts of the head, face and neck are protected.[8]

Having thus cursorily touched upon the outward dress and trappings of the men, we shall take the liberty to repeat what we have often heard confirmed by the most experienced officers abroad and at home, that our horses are too tenderly brought up for continental warfare, or indeed for any species of warfare which requires the endurance of hard weather. By a late order, the curry comb is less used, and the animal is allowed to preserve that oily moisture upon the skin that prevents him from catching cold in a rainy season; nor are his feet allowed to be pared so close, and to be compressed too much that the least hard work makes him tender footed. Perhaps if cavalry horses, but most especially artillery horses, were kept more in the open air at all seasons of the year, we should not constantly see verified the following observations regarding our cavalry on service: Nothing can be more

---

7   James, *James' Regimental Companion*, Vol.III, p.466.
8   A footnote to the original reads 'The hussar saddle, which seems made for no other purpose than to gall and cramp the withers of a horse, to rupture the recruit, and to embarrass the made soldier, will probably also fall under HRH's consideration.'

ground, again figured a skull and crossbones. The people of London, not easily aston-ished, so accustomed were they to all sorts of eccentricities, were simply astounded by this masquerader. It was rumored that this fantastical person was no other than Murat, whose reputation in Britain equaled that of Durow, a clown at the Astley circus who supported, at arm's length, a platform on which eighteen grenadiers performed maneuvers. But on inquiry being made, it was found that the visitor was a Hungarian officer, named Baron Geramb; and that he had come to submit to the British government a sure fire way of crushing Napoleon's power in five months.[12]

Similar vogues erupted at various times for Highlanders, and later on, for cossacks. In 1813, when a Russian officer brought a Cossack to London in his retinue, he became a celebrity in society and launched the craze for Cossack trowsers. Society was always eager for new sensations, and any excuse would serve to excite a new fashion. The Cossack, one Alexander Zemlenutin of the Don regiment, was written up at length in the *Morning Chronicle*, given a grand tour of London by the Mayor, and finally exhibited to the public at the London Royal Exchange.

The July 1813 edition of *Ackermann's Repository* featured in addition to its fashion plates a 'Letter from a Young Lady in London to Her Friend in the Country,' a letter replete with information on the latest in urban fashion. Some key shifts in fashion our lady reports were, 'The adoption of the Cossack coat and Pomeranian mantle, in place of the spencer and French cloak'. It is possible to trace the arrival of an exotic novelty from sensation, to ball or masque dress at parties, through male and female civilian fashion, and on into military fashion. The Hussar was in company with the Moor, the Cossack, and the Highlander in this transition.

The introduction of the hussar dress into the Army was achieved by an inspired piece of bureaucratic deception. In order to convince the King that his government would not incur extra expense it was necessary to show that equipping a regiment in hussar dress was comparable in value and cost to that of a regular light dragoon regiment. This was clearly not the case, but it did not prevent Horse Guards from acquiescing in this self-deception.

In order to accomplish the skulduggery, a careful analysis was drawn up showing the comparative cost and duration of light dragoon and hussar clothing. In almost every item, hussar clothing cost more.

Table 4 Comparison of Prices, Hussar and Light Dragoon Uniforms

Hussar Pelisse.	£1 17s 6d		
Hussar dress jacket.	£1 11s	LD dress jacket.	£1 6s 9d
Hussar cap.	£1 1s	LD helmet-cap.	19s
Hussar pantaloons.	£1 8s	LD leather breeches.	£1 5s
Total	£5 17s 6d	Total	£310s 9d

The imbalance in cost was corrected by expressing a belief that hussar clothing lasted longer and thus represented better value. Four years for a hussar's pelisse, dress jacket, and cap, as

---

12 Lenotre, *Romance of the French Revolution*, p.266.

opposed to two years for equivalent light dragoon clothing and cap. This meant that the cost per year was intended to be roughly equivalent: a piece of trickery, if ever there was one, but it was passed. It was only required to convince Horse Guards of the relative expenses of the clothing supplied by the King of course. Where hussars were possessed of other superfluous items of equipment these were detailed as necessaries to be charged to the soldiers' personal accounts, or lost in the vagaries of accoutrements and appointments.

Once the clothing for privates and non-commissioned officers had been passed off as incurring no greater expense than that of a light dragoon private, the greatest hurdle to the adoption of hussar regiments was passed. Where the officers were concerned it was impossible to conceal the extravagance intended, and the only restraining factor was the influence of the colonel (usually a negative factor in this context), and the pocket of the officer concerned. It is useful at this point to look in more depth at a particular regiment to see quite what went on in the name of fashion.

The 7th Light Dragoons (Hussars) are particularly well represented in period tailoring books, not least in the account books of Meyer's, who were the colonel's primary preferred and recommended tailors. Remarkably, Meyer's still exist today, in the form of Meyer and Mortimer, and they have been generous with access to their records. The Meyer Ledger contains the following entries for the 7th.[13]

Captain Pipon. Three separate entries.

First Entry.
17 November 1809. Pair of 6 thread mixed milled stocking pants. £3 10s
20 November 1809. Superfine black cloth coat. £5 8s
20 November 1809. A black cassimere waistcoat. £1 9s
20 November 1809. Pair of black single cassimere breeches. £2
21 November 1809. A blue second cloth coat. Crest buttons for servant. £3 5s
21 November 1809. A scarlet second cloth waistcoat. £1 4s 6d
21 November 1809. Sleeves for ditto. 4s 6d
7 January 1811. A buff cassimere waistcoat, single breasted, gilt buttons. £1 5s 6d
7 January 1811. A buff cassimere waistcoat, single breasted, gilt buttons. £1 5s 6d
28 January 1811. Repairing a drag great coat for servant. 2s
21 December 1812. Two and three quarter yards blue superfine cloth for a pelisse great coat. £4 16s 6d
17 yards French braid. £1 9s 9d
16 silk olives. 7s 4d
6 tassells gimp and fringe. 15s 6d
4 and a half yards of shalloon 15s 9d
Link (mink?) fur trimming £2 14s
4 yards figuring braid.
Making the great coat and pockets. £1 18s

Second entry water-damaged. 1809?

13   Ledgers of 1809-1827. Meyer and Mortimer at Sackville Street, London.

Olive cloth great coat faced with silk, (extra in cloth). Silk sleeve lining, silk serge. £8 10s 6d

Blue cloth coat. £4 4s

White Marcella waistcoat £1 3s

Cassimere waistcoat bound gilt buttons. Returned.

Pair of cotton stocking pantaloon drawers. £1 10s

Pair of milled cloth stocking pantaloons. £3 10s

One buff cassimere waistcoat. £1 11s

Pair drab coloured single cassimere breeches. £1 10s 6d

Superfine green cloth coat with plated buttons £5 8s

Lengthening(?) a blue regimental jacket and adding lace. £1 5s

20 yards royal cord at 5s 6d, 4 yards of figuring at 1s 3d, 14 yards Russia braid at 6d £1 2s

3 small buttons, three eights of a yard of cassimere. 12s 6d

Leather for the bottom. 2s 9d

Cloth coat, calico sleeve lining. £5 8s

Single black cassimere breeches £2 7s 12d

Black cassimere waistcoat £1 9s

Lengthening/strengthening(?) a blue regimental jacket, adding lace. £1 6s

3 yards silver royal cord at , Russia braid. £1 8s 3d

3 yards of stout figuring, 4 yards of fine figuring, cassimere. 14s 6d

A buff cassimere waistcoat with gilt buttons. £1 11s

A buff cassimere waistcoat. £1 11s

Superfine blue cloth coat, plain gilt buttons. £5 8s

Miscellaneous civilian items.[14]

Third entry. 1814

22 July 1814. A black(?) coat cassimere waistcoat and ditto pantaloons. 96 £9 3s

13 August 1814. A regimental jacket and pelisse. 108 £56 14s

13 August 1814. A ditto waistcoat and pantaloons. 108 £15 4s

14 September 1814. A suit of livery and crest dies. 157 £8 8s 6d

16 September 1814. A brown cloth great coat. 159 £7 8s

28 September 1814. A pair of fustian overalls. 163 £1 2s

11 November 1814. A pair of regimental pantaloons. 183 £7 18s 6d

24 December 1814. A blue coat, quilted waistcoat and calico ditto. 217 £5 14s

Total £127 13s

Lieutenant Grenfell.

25 July 1814. A white quilt waistcoat and ditto pantaloons. 99 £3 18s

15 August 1814. A regimental jacket and pelisse. 116 £56 14s

15 August 1814. A ditto waistcoat and two pantaloons. 116 £21 16s 6d

14 Ledgers of 1809-1827. Meyer and Mortimer at Sackville Street, London.

19 August 1814. A brown coat and two buff cassimere waistcoats. 138 £8 1s
19 August 1814. A white quilting waistcoat. 138 £1 8s
20 December 1814. A scarlet coat, ditto regimental waistcoats. 210 £10 17s 6d
Total £102 15s

Lieutenant Peters.

1814. A blue cloth great coat, trimmed. 111 £12 12s
1814. A regimental jacket and pelisse. 117 £56 18s 6d
1814. A regimental waistcoat and pantaloons. 117 £15 4s
1814. A pair of undress regimental pantaloons. 169 £6 12s 6d
1814. A light hussar regimental wallet £5 15s 4d
Total £135 8s 5d

Cornet/Lieutenant Maddison, two separate entries.

First Entry
11 July 1810. Pair of drab ribbed stocking pantaloons plain. £2 2s
21 July 1810. 2 pairs of patent white stocking pantaloons plain. £5 2s
25 July 1810. Superfine blue regimental jacket laced with silver. £14 11s 6d
13 August 1810. Pair of patent white cotton stocking pantaloons, plain. £2 7s
31 August 1810. Pair of Superfine blue mixed cloth pantaloons plain. Returned.
5 September 1810. Pair of India nankeen trousers. £1 8s
8 September 1810. Pair of India nankeen trousers. £1 8s
10 September 1810. Pair of superfine blue mixed cloth pantaloons, plain. £2 17s
21 November 1810. Superfine blue regimental pelisse, fox quill fur trimming. £26 1s 3d
23 March 1811. Two pairs of stocking pantaloon drawers. £1 10s
25 Match 1811. Two pairs of patent white cotton stocking pantaloons plain. £4 14s
30 March 1811. Two pairs of cotton stocking pantaloon drawers. £1 10s
1 April 1811. A superfine blue regimental jacket. £14 6s 6d

Second entry.
27 August 1814. A regimental jacket and pelisse. 147 £56 14s
27 August 1814. Repair of a pelisse. 453 3s 6d
12 September 1814. A regimental waistcoat and two pantaloons. 155 £21 16s 6d
Total £113 13s 10d

Lieutenant Meyer.

19 August 1814. A regimental jacket and pelisse. 139 £56 14s
3 September 1814. Repair of a pelisse. 453 3s 6d
15 September 1814. A scarlet cassimere dress waistcoat. 458 £7 5s 6d
16 September 1814. A blue cloth coat. 159 No charge.
Total £64 3s

Lieutenant Stone.

11 April 1809. A scarlet cassimere regimental waistcoat (extra long) £4 18s 6d

11 April1809. Extra long, and cap. 18s 6d

2 May 1809. Superfine blue regimental jacket laced with silver (extra long and cloth) £15 13s 9d

5 June 1809. A white Marcella waistcoat, three rows of thread buttons. £1 8s

6 June 1809. Two white Marcella waistcoats, three rows of thread buttons £2 16s

7 June 1809. A white Marcella waistcoat laced with silver (to be charged to Colonel Vivian.)

8 June 1809. A white Marcella waistcoat, three rows of thread buttons. £1 8s

11 September 1809. Pair superfine grey mixed cloth overalls. £3 13s 6d

11 September 1809. Pair of chains. 9s 6d

11September 1809. Extra advance on cloth 17s 6d

20 September 1809. Turning the lace of a blue regimental pelisse. £1 7s 6d

20 September 1809. New fox quill fur trimming £3 3s

20 September 1809. Half a yard of silk to repair the lining. 4s

25 September 1809. Black cassimere waistcoat. £1 3s 6d

30 September 1809. Extra advance on cassimere 6s

2 October 1809. Strip rattinet waistcoat, gilt buttons bound with black. £1 3s 6d

2 October 1809. Superfine scarlet cloth hunting jacket, single breasted, plain gilt buttons. Callico sleeve lining, extra advance on cloth, scarlet velvet collar.

7 February 1810. Superfine plain black cloth coat. £5 5s

8 March 1810. Pair of patent white cotton stocking pantaloons plain. £2 7s

8 March 1810. Pair of patent white cotton stocking pantaloons plain. £2 7s

29 April 1810. Superfine blue regimental jacket. £15 13s 9d

Cornet/Lieutenant Wildman, two separate entries.

First Entry

1 February 1809. A pair of superfine mixed cloth overalls, bone buttons. £3 13s 6d

1 February 1809. A pair of chain for ditto. 9s

13 March 1809. A white Marcella waistcoat. £1 3s

13 March 1809. Pair of fawn coloured 4th stocking breeches, silk facings. £1 10s

18 March 1809. A pair of superfine mixed cloth overalls, strapped with cloth. £4 9s

18 March 1809. Pair of chain to ditto. 9s 6d

21 March 1809. Superfine scarlet regimental dress waistcoat. £4 18s 6d

29 March 1809. Altering a blue regimental great coat. 5s 6d

8 September 1809. 5 and a half yards of blue second cloth for horseman's cloak. £5 15s 6d

4 yards of white rattinet for body lining. 19s

Blue shalloon for cape lining. 4s 6d

Plated buttons and materials. 10s

Share of cap etc. 2s 6d

8 November 1809. 4 pair of patent white cotton stocking pantaloons plain. £9 8s

8 November 1809. A pair of superfine grey mixed cloth overalls, strapped with cloth, and brown leather at bottom, scarlet on the sides. £3 13s 6d

8 November 1809. Pair of chains. 9s 6d
17 November 1809. Superfine blue regimental pelisse laced with silver. £22 2s 9d
Fox quill fur trimming. £3 3s
11 May 1810. Superfine blue regimental jacket laced with silver. £14 14s
12 May 1810. New strapping a pair of mixed overalls and repairing. 7s 6d
12 May 1810. Superfine mixed cloth for the strapping. 10s 6d
12 May 1810. Drab coloured leather for the bottom. 6s 6d
13 May 1810. Put silver lace on the sides on a pair of mixed overalls and alter. 4s 6d
4 and a quarter yards of rich silver lace for above. £2 8s 10d
Put silver lace on a pair ditto and alter. 4s 6d
4 and a quarter yards of rich silver lace for above. £2 8s 10d

Second entry.
Made Lt.
8 November 1811. A pair of patent white cotton stocking pantaloons, plain. £2 7s
9 November 1811. Altering a regimental jacket made less in the body. 18s
9 November 1811. Altering a regimental pelisse ditto. 10s
9 November 1811. A superfine blue regimental jacket laced with silver. £16 4d
9 November 1811. 4 pairs of patent white cotton stocking pantaloons. £9 8s
9 November 1811. Altering a regimental jacket. 18s
9 November 1811. A pair of superfine grey mixed cloth overalls, strapped with the same, black leather at bottom, no chains. £4 10s
9 November 1811. 4 and three quarter yards rich silver lace for the sides of the above. £2 17s
9 November 1811. Another pair of overalls ditto with lace ditto. £7 7s
11 November 1811. 2 pairs of patent white cotton stocking pantaloons. £4 14s
12 November 1811. Altering two pairs of white stocking pantaloons. 7s
12 November 1811. A pair of blue broad ribbed stocking pantaloons. £2 10s
12 November 1811. Altering two pairs of white stocking pantaloons. 7s
12 November 1811. Making a husoollantto and regimental jacket and lining the jacket 8s 6d
12 November 1811. New calico body lining. 4s 6d
26 December 1811. A superfine blue regimental pelisse lined with crimson plush and laced with silver. £23 12s
Fox quill fur trimming for above. £3 3s

Ternor, Captain. (Now Major)

2 September 1809. Changing the lace of a blue regimental pelisse. £1 18s
2 September 1809. Crimson silk sleeve lining to ditto. 17s
2 September 1809. Crimson plush for collar lining, and for adding the sleeves. 7s 6d
2 September 1809. Silver royal cord for ditto. 11s
2 September 1809. Fox quill fur trimming for a blue regimental pelisse. £3 3s
Total. £6 16s 6d

Captain Robins.

A scarlet cassimere regimental waistcoat, laced with silver. £5 10s

Cornet Shirley.

8 April 1811. Superfine blue cloth regimental jacket. £15
Richly laced with silver, 2 and a half yards of cord, 3 yards of something else. £1 4 and a half d
13 April 1811. Superfine blue cloth regimental jacket. £16 4 and a half d
13 April 1811. Pair mixed cloth milled stocking pantaloons. £3 3s
30 April 1811. Superfine blue cloth regimental pelisse lined with crimson plush, neck. Linen lining. £22 18s 3d
30 April 1811. Extra lace for above. 13s 10d
30 April 1811. Quill fox fur trimming. £3 3s
30 April 1811. A scarlet cassimere regimental; waistcoat. £5 5s 6d
30 April 1811. Pair of superfine blue stocking pantaloons. £2 2s
30 April 1811. Pair of superfine grey mixed cloth overalls strapped with the same, leather at bottom. £4 10s
30 April 1811. Pair of chains for above. £9 6d
30 April 1811. 6 pars of white patent cotton stocking pantaloons. £10 2s
30 April 1811. A blue second cloth horseman's cloak, lined with white rattinet, velvet collar lining. £9 8s 9d
30 April 1811. A superfine blue cloth great coat looped with French braid and olives, faced with silk. £14 11s 3d
5 November 1811. A superfine blue regimental pelisse laced with silver. £23 12 1d
Fox quill fur trimming for ditto £3 3s

Major Hodge.

12 February 1814. A blue cloth regimental jacket. £28 15s 4d
12 February 1814. A pair blue stocking pantaloons, laced. £8 10s 12d
12 February 1814. Altered a gal. slin [illeg.] to a regimental jacket old pattern. 17s 6d
18 February 1814. A blue cloth regimental pelisse. £34 18s 10d
18 February 1814. Altering a pelisse and jacket. No cost.
11 May 1814. A scarlet cassimere waistcoat, laced. £11 19s 2d
11 May 1814. Alter figure on blue stocking pantaloons. 18s 3d
1 June 1814. Altering a regimental jacket. No charge.
8 June 1814. Altering stocking pantaloons. 11s 3d
9 June 1814. Ditto ditto. No cost.
11 June 1814. Alter 7 uniforms. £8 11s 4d
28 June 1814. A pair blue stocking dress pantaloons. £8 10s 2d
6 July 1814. A buff cassimere waistcoat. £1 10s
22 July 1814. Altering fur of a pelisse. £5 2s
6 August 1814. A blue cloth coat. £5 5s

19 August 1814. Altering a regimental pelisse. £1 1s
23 December 1814. Two pairs pantaloons, regimental. £10 16s 6d
23 December 1814. Altering a pair ditto. 18s

Lieutenant O'Grady.

13 August 1814. A blue cloth greatcoat trimmed. £12 12s
13 August 1814. A regimental jacket and pelisse. £56 14s 6d
13 August 1814. A regimental waistcoat and pantaloons. £15 8s 6d

Cornet/Captain O'Hagerty/O'Haggerty.

9 May 1814.
10 May 1814. A blue cloth regimental jacket and stocking pantaloons. £24 4s 7d
8 June 1814. A blue cloth pelisse. £23 15s 9d
10 June 1814. Altering a regimental jacket. £2 2s 9d
18 June 1814. A scarlet cassimere dress waistcoat. £7 4s 6d
20 August 1814. Putting fur to a pelisse. 9s 6d
20 August 1814. A pair of dress pantaloons. £7 18s 6d
March 1815. Altering jacket and pelisse. £2 3s 10d
31 March 1812. Grey Bey overalls. £6 13s 10d
30 October 1813. Plush silk. £1 5s
18 June 1814. Waistcoat. £6 3s 6d

Captain Heileger.

29 June 1814. A regimental jacket. £25 18s 6d
1 July 1814. A regimental pelisse. £30 15s 6d
13 July 1814. A regimental dress waistcoat and pantaloons. £15 4s
2 September 1814. A regimental great coat. £12 12s
24 September 1814. A pair blue cloth laced overalls. £6 6d
6 October 1814. A pair of undress pantaloons. £6 12s 6d
13 December 1814. Altered regimental waistcoat. £5 15s 4d

Colonel Kerrison.

30 June 1814. A regimental jacket and pelisse. £63 14s 2d
4 July 1814. A dress waistcoat and pantaloons. £20 4s 10d
10 August 1814. A plain undress pantaloons. £8 10s 2d
30 August 1814. A blue silk waistcoat laced. £5 19s
17 November 1814. A scarlet cassimere regimental dress waistcoat. No charge.
25 November 1814. A regimental pelisse. £35 3s 4d
20 December 1814. A pair of dress pantaloons. £8 10s 12d
20 December 1814. A gold neck line. £5 5s
To lace undercast in gymp. DB (?) £15
Greatcoat(?) as above. £60(?)

Captain J.J .Fraser.

>11 July 1814. A regimental jacket and pelisse. £56 14s
>18 July 1814. A regimental dress waistcoat and pantaloons. £15 14s
>16 September 1814. A pair blue undress pantaloons. £15 4s
>21 November 1814. Altering regimental waistcoat and pelisse. 16s
>21 November 1814. Ditto a regimental jacket. 12s 6d
>25 November 1814. Ditto(mistake?) a regimental waistcoat £5 14s

Lieutenant Gordon.

>15 July 1814. A blue coat and white quilting waistcoat. £6 13s
>22 July 1814. A white quilting waistcoat and a buff cassimere waistcoat. £2 18s
>25 July 1814. A white quilting waistcoat. No charge.
>2 August 1814. A pair black superfine pantaloons and two drawers. £4 1s
>6 August 1814. A green shooting jacket, cassimere waistcoat and quilted waistcoat.
>   £8 1s
>6 August 1814. A blue cloth coat. No charge.
>14 September 1814. An olive cloth greatcoat. £8 8s 3d
>14 September 1814. A blue cloth coat. £5 9s 6d
>4 October 1814. A regimental waistcoat and pantaloons. £15 4s

In addition to the accounts of individuals, there exist a number of records related to regimental accounts with the tailoring house. The 7th was one of those regiments accustomed to making up most, or all, of the privates' clothing regimentally, rather than the normal practice of purchasing it ready made from an army clothing contractor, and then subsequently refitting it to the men at headquarters. This deviation from standard practice required an annual dispensation to be made from the Commander-in-Chief, but the indulgence was granted to a substantial number of regiments. The most common dispensation granted to infantry regiments was for the breeches to be made up by the regiment. Presumably this was for reasons of economy. Since breeches were intended to be fitted to the man, any despatched in standard sizes would have to be ripped down and remade under normal circumstances. As a result it was probably cheaper to make them 'in-house' from materials provided by the contractor handling the regimental clothing, or by purchase from another source. The 7th, being a highly fashionable regiment, preferred to cut out the middleman. The costs of making up in house to their demanding standards were not inconsiderable as the following table from February 1815 shows.

Table 5 Costs of Tailoring work

	Made by Praters, clothiers.	Made by regimental tailors.
Private's pelisse.	£2 2s	£1 17s 5 1/2 d.
Private's dress jacket.	£1 15s	£1 11s 8d
Private's undress jacket.	16s 9d	14s 4 1/2d
Pantaloons.	£1 8s 6d	£1 5s 7 1/4d

The Meyer entries for regimental accounts are as follows.

Regt Account 7th Hussars
1809 cont. from page 37 (missing?)
24 March 1809 delivered. 266 pair of overalls at 29s. £385 14s
16 May 1809. 10 yards of mixed cloth.
16 May 1809. 10 yard of brown linen.
30 August 1809. 18 pairs of mixed overalls at 29s. £26 2s
30 August 1809. 23 and a quarter yards mixed cloth at 9s 6d.
30 August 1809. 24 yards mixed cloth at 9s 6d.
30 August 1809. 23 and a half yards mixed cloth at 9s 6d.
30 August 1809. 23 and a half yards mixed cloth at 9s 6d.
30 August 1809. 23 and a quarter yards mixed cloth at 9s 6d.
30 August 1809. 23 and a half yards mixed cloth at 9s 6d.
30 August 1809. 23 and a quarter yards mixed cloth at 9s 6d.
30 August 1809. 25 yards mixed cloth at 9s 6d.
30 August 1809. 24 and a half yards mixed cloth at 9s 6d.
30 August 1809. 11 and a half yards mixed cloth at 9s 6d.
30 August 1809. 49 gross of buttons at 2s 2d. £5 6s 2d
30 August 1809. 311 and a half yards of linen at 1s 4d. £20 15s 4d
30 August 1809. 210 pairs of leather strapping. £73 10s.
Total £626 16s 9d
29 September 1809. 4 rich sable fur skins (direct to adjutant major). Returned.
3 October 1809. A regimental jacket for pattern. £1 9s
3 October 1809. A regimental pelisse for pattern. £1 17s 10d
3 October 1809. 10 pairs of overalls as above.
16 July 1810. Related lists for mixed cloth, damping, strapping and linen, £89.[15]

Further evidence comes from other tailors books and records. The Hawkes tailoring book has three entries comprising: a detail of the officers' pantaloons braiding; a long pelisse or greatcoat design; an image and description of the officers' waistcoat and overalls; and an image and description of an officer's regimental jacket.

12 June 1815 for lieutenant. Blue superfine cloth jacket. Blue collar and cuffs, lined throughout with white cassimere, yellow leather round the bottom part in the streamers and a bt pocket slit in the band. 4 hooks and eyes. Captains exactly the same, only a ½ inch French braid all round and on the side seams instead of round back. 23 or 24 loops.

No date. Dress waistcoat, scarlet cassimere, gold royal cord round the edges and ½ inch French braid. Loops gold royal cord, large and small trimming braid. 15 loops. Eight shown

---

15   Ledgers of 1809-1827. Meyer and Mortimer at Sackville Street, London.

No date. 7th overalls blue cloth strapt with the same, no cuff, 2 gold laces down each side seam, gold loops at the bottom. A leather strap under the foot.[16]

Percy William Reynolds notes that the private's 7th jacket formerly in the Cotton collection at Waterloo has exactly the same pattern braiding in the knotwork on the sleeve as the Hawke's officer's example. It lacks only the fine soutache work.[17]

The Stothard tailoring book contains four entries for 1813. They comprise a jacket, dress-coat, waistcoat, and a pelisse. There are descriptions just for two items.

A plain waistcoat for the 7 Royal hussars, cord round the edges, breats of round cord all in a piece, eyes at the back and eyes up the front, 3 eyes between each hook to the shoulder seam, no pockets, silk back laced, silk linings throughout, 11 hooks and eyes, buttons on the left forepart 3 eyes between the first loops and the bottom, long eyes end of the loops. Field Marshals made the same except inch L all round.[18]

A jacket made of superfine blue cloth, white cuff and collar royal cord breast edged all round, with Roushay(?) round back. Figures in braid in the Brii.. Roushay round back, down the sideseam and from the knot at the hip. Figure in braid down the sideseam eyes four times down a hook on each side, something like a sheeps horn with a diamond of half inch braid on the top and end of the collar. Ditto cuff, no edges to the cuffs Roushay round back top of the cuff above the alfinch [half inch] lace, to go all round and up the slit. A catch pasters(?) top side of the sleeve, 4 hooks and eyes, eyes part back of the same stated on. Hungary knot, 4 eyes on each side the knot, top the cuff, braid to die at the bottom. Three rows of buttons, yellow leather bottom, calico linings pockets straight across, crows feet at the end, French braid round the collar.[19]

Although other tailoring books are useful for descriptions of the uniform and images of the details, the Meyer ledger is the most useful for its actual figures and costs. It is possible to gauge some of the variation in this comparison of relative costs which has been extrapolated from the Meyer tailoring accounts.

Twenty two officers are represented in the table. A typical parade state for a light cavalry regiment would be twenty six officers, so although the date range spans five years, allowing for multiple changes in personnel, the data is representative enough to allow some useful comparison. A number of conclusions can be drawn from this analysis of officers' expenditure. Firstly the pattern officer's pelisse was eleven and a half times as expensive as that of the enlisted men. Despite that disparity, not one of the officers recorded failed to exceed the price of the pattern garment. So in principle the range of comparison between the cost of a private's pelisse and that of an officer falls between 12 and a half times and 19 times as much. The former reflects the pocket of the cheapest cornet, and the latter that of the colonel commanding. Lord Paget as colonel presumably spent even more in order to maintain his

---

16 National Army Museum, (NAM), Archives: 2004-06-92, Military tailor's pattern books 1800-1817.
17 Reynolds, *Military Costume of the Eighteenth and Nineteenth Centuries*, Vol. IX, p.160.
18 Stothard, *Tailoring Book*, Unpublished manuscript, Anne S.K. Brown Military Collection.
19 Stothard, *Tailoring Book*, Anne S.K. Brown Military Collection.

Table 6 Tailoring Bills of the 7th Light Dragoon (Hussars)

Rank	Regimental jacket	Jacket and pelisse	Regimental pelisse	Regimental waistcoat	Dress p'loons	Undress p'loons	Overalls	Waistcoat and p'loons	Date	Name	Source
Private	£1 9s		£1 17s 10d						1809	Pattern	Meyer
			£22 3s 10d				29s		1804	Pattern	Plas N.
Cornet	£14 11s 6d		£26 1s 3d (with fox)						1810–1811	Maddison	Meyer
Cornet	£14 6s 6d								1810–1811	Maddison	Meyer
Cornet	£14 14s		£25 5s 9d (with fox)	£4 18s 6d			Mixd sfine £3 13s 6d (2)		1809	Wildman	Meyer
Cornet							" strapped £4 9s		1809	Wildman	Meyer
Cornet							" with lace £7 7s (2)		1811	Wildman	Meyer
Cornet	£16 4d (rich)(2)		£26 15s 2d (fox, rich)(2)	£5 5s 6d			Grey sfine £4 10s		1811	Shirley	Meyer
Cornet	£16 6s 6d		£23 15s 9d	£7 4s 6d	£7 18s 6d (2)		Grey bey £6 13s 10d		1814	O Haggerty	Meyer
Lieutenant	£16 4d		£26 15s (with fox)				" £4 10s lace £2 17s (2)		1811	Wildman	Meyer
Lieutenant		£56 14s						£21 16s 6d (2 p'loons)	1814	Maddison	Meyer
Lieutenant		£56 14s						£21 16s 6d (2 p'loons)	1814	Grenfell	Meyer
Lieutenant		£56 18s 6d		£7 5s 6d		£6 12s 6d		£15 4s	1814	Peters	Meyer
Lieutenant		£56 14s							1814	Meyer	Meyer
Lieutenant	£15 13s 9d (long)			£4 18s 6d (extra long)			Grey sfine £3 13s 6d		1809	Stone	Meyer
Lieutenant	£15 13s 9d (long)								1810	Stone	Meyer
Lieutenant		£56 14s 6d						£15 8s 6d	1814	Grady	Meyer
Lieutenant								£15 4s	1814	Gordon	Meyer
Captain		£56 14s		£5 10s	£7 18s 6d		Fustian £1 2s	£15 4s (2)	1814	Pipon	Meyer
Captain										Robins	Meyer
Captain	£25 18s 6d		£30 15s 6d			£6 12s 6d	Blue cloth laced £6 6d	£15 4s	1814	Heileger	Meyer
Captain		£56 14s		£5 14s		£15 4s		£15 14s	1814	Fraser	Meyer
Major	£28 15s 4d		£34 18s 10d	£11 19s 2d	£5 8s 3d (2)				1814	Hodge	Meyer
Colonel	£63 14s 2d		£35 3s 4d		£8 10s 12d	£8 10s 2d		£20 4s 10d	1814	Kerrison	Meyer

status as one of the 'beaus' of the army. The overalls follow a similar pattern, regarding officers and men, but there is a sharp distinction between prices of different officer's overalls that seems to be based on varying qualities, perhaps reflecting that utilitarian overalls were coexisting with overalls that were superseding the pantaloons as articles of display for dress.

In general, increased rank means increased expenditure, but this is not an absolute measure. We can see big-spending cornets and economically minded captains. There are also outliers in each section where the general trend is followed, but specific items are more indulgent, or more restrained than the normal and fall outside the standard range. For instance, Major Hodge bought the most extravagant regimental waistcoat in the regiment, outspending the colonel, but reined his purse in on dress pantaloons, where he spent less than a cornet would. The most fertile ground for expression of wealth and taste may be this regimental waistcoat (in this case a sleeveless under-waistcoat) where there is a wide price differential that does not reflect the difference between ranks. It may be that the waistcoat was exempt from the general trend of rank reflecting ornamentation, and it was considered fair ground for displays of ostentation.

A side-by-side comparison can be made with the officers and privates of a light dragoon regiment to see to what extent the hussars are more expensive, without including the misleading weighting of the flawed Horse Guards figures on relative periods of wear. Information is available for the 16th Light Dragoons for the period 1806-08. The light dragoons, of course, were still referring to over and under jackets on their official returns, even though these garments had been dropped as early as 1796 in most cases, and the regiments had adopted hussar style short pelisses with fur as tailoring accounts make plain. The continued use of standard forms marked under and over jacket has given rise to the erroneous belief that the pelisse was worn over the regimental jacket, whereas in fact the two items were equivalent garments worn in winter and summer respectively, exactly as in continental forces.[20] Where no pattern item cost is known, I have used the lowest recorded figure for an individual. Additional data from the 15th Light Dragoons immediately prior to their conversion to hussars is included where it exists. The 16th Light Dragoons had adopted a pelisse contrary to regulation.

Table 7 Further Price Comparisons, Light Dragoons and Hussars

7th Hussars	Jacket	Pelisse	Waistcoat	Dress pantaloons	Undress pantaloons	Overalls
Officer	£14 11s 6d	£22 3s 10d	£4 18s 6d	£5 8s 3d	£6 12s 6d	£3 13s 6d
Private	£1 9s	£1 17s 10d				29s
16th LD						
Officer	£10 5s 5d	£12 4s 0d	£1 10s 10d	£3 18s 3d	£2 13s 11d	£1 10s 10d
Private	£1 0s 2d	£1 0s 2d				
15th LD						
Private	£1 5s 3d			£1 4s 3d		

---

20   T.H. MacGuffie, TH, 'Light Dragoons, details of clothing,' *Journal of the Society for Army Historical Research*, 26, (1948-49), p.42.

In 1810, Horse Guards had produced a series of tables detailing the proposed reasonable costs for officers' dress and equipment according to branch, rank and department.[21] This was initially conceived as a corrective to excessive expenditure after the country was stung by some pretty excessive compensation claims after the debacle of the Corunna campaign ruined officers through the loss of their equipage abandoned on the retreat or destroyed on the beaches. It was timely, comprehensive and fairhanded, being composed solely of officers of experience, some of whom had suffered in the 1809 campaign. All of the items of equipage were tested, and priced by clothing contractors and tailors.

It is instructive to see to what extent the proposed sums for compensation would serve should the officers of the 7th Hussars gave found themselves experiencing losses such as those of the Corunna retreat. It was proposed and expected that a cavalry captain would expend £24 on his two jackets. We can see that no captain in the 7th paid less than £56 and 14s for his two jackets. Waistcoats were to be compensated at the rate of £1 and 4s. The captains of the 7th paid upwards of £5 10s for theirs. The same levels of extravagance were exhibited at ranks below and above that of captain.

In conclusion, it is hard to present the alteration in dress made to the light dragoon regiments converted to hussars as anything other than an expensive decision made purely on grounds of fashion. The increase in expenditure fell on the state through the increased contributions to regimental clothing fraudulently misrepresented as savings or equivalents. It fell on the men, who were charged for additional and largely useless necessaries, such as sabretaches, and fur dress caps, and it fell hardest on the officers, who at least, had nobody except themselves to blame, having either chosen their corps, or having the opportunity to exchange out of it.

---

21   TNA, WO7/56: Various Departmental, Out-letters. Board of General Officers. Reports Miscellaneous.

18

Regulation of 1808

9 January, 1808. Letter on facings for 23rd Light Dragoons

> Adjutant General to Clothing Board,
> I have the honour to acquaint you for the information of the clothing board that
> His Majesty has been pleased to approve of the facings of the clothing of the 23rd
> light dragoons being changed from blue to crimson according to the enclosed
> sealed pattern.
> Harry Calvert, Adjutant General[1]

21 April, 1808. Letter regarding preserving caps

> Adjutant General to Thomas Fauquier, secretary of clothing board,
> I have the honour to transmit to you the inclosed letter, received from Mr John
> Stand, relating to a certain process whereby he proposes to preserve and improve
> the felt caps now in use by the army, and I am to request by the Commander-in-
> Chief's direction, that you will submit the same to the general officers composing
> the clothing board, that their opinion of its utility may be obtained for HRH's
> information.
> Harry Calvert Adjutant General.[2]

The exact process referred to is not clear. It may be that this was a movement towards
returning to a lacquered preparation applied to the felt body of the cap. If so, it was unlikely
that the request met with success, since it was only two years since the lacquered cap had
been discarded on grounds of inutility.

---

1 TNA, WO7/34/127: Various Departmental, Out-letters. Board of General Officers. Clothing.
2 TNA, WO3/194/255: Office of the Commander-in-Chief: Out-letters. Letters to public departments.

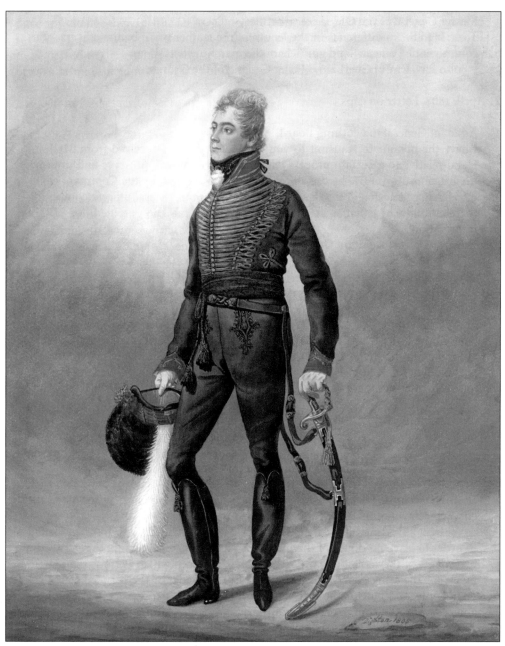

'Officer of the Royal Horse Artillery', 1805. Watercolour by Robert Dighton. The bow tied to the hair is just visible behind the collar. The sash appears to be neither the hussar barrel sash, nor the infantry sash, but the form with plaited tails that became associated also with the light infantry. (Anne S.K. Brown Military Collection, Brown University Library)

5th The staff serjeants to be dressed according to regulations; the serjeant major and quarter master serjeant to be distinguished only in the manner therein pointed out.

6th The bugle horn players to be dressed as the drummers of the regiment.

7th The men are to carry their greatcoats at inspections and reviews, as likewise all duties.

8th Regiments not provided with grenadier caps and pioneer accoutrements are to be immediately supplied.

9th The plates on the caps of some corps and the serjeants swords and sashes (the latter being entirely crimson) are reported to be contrary to orders. They must be in strict conformity to the King's regulations, and the general officers will give orders accordingly, and see that they are complied with.

10th The clothing is to be made up in strict conformity to the sealed patterns; and general officers, when inspecting regiments are enjoined to pay particular attention on this head, and to report any deviation therefrom, for which commanding officers will be made responsible.

It appeared some time back on an inspection being made of the clothing of the militia, that the coats of many regiments were so tight, particularly in the sleeves, as not to admit of the waistcoat being worn, which was supposed to be the cause of the sickness that prevailed at the close of the last winter and in the early part of the spring.

The colonels must be cautioned with respect to the ensuing clothing; and the general officers will be careful to see that the men have on the proper waistcoats with sleeves, which are always to be worn except in very hot weather.

Several of the confidential reports of the general officers, notwithstanding the orders on this subject, have been found unsatisfactory and not to answer the purpose intended. General officers in command of brigades will be pleased to refer to the orders of the 5 December 1798, 20 November 1806 and 25 may 1807, which have been given out for their guidance, and the general officers in command of districts are not in future to forward any of these reports, for the purpose of being submitted to the Commander-in-Chief, unless made agreeably to HRH's instructions.

H Calvert Adjutant General.[12]

1 July 1808. Letter on Russia Duck for the West Indies

Deputy Adjutant General to Board of General Officers,
Should any difficulty arise in procuring Russia duck for the trowsers of regiments serving in the West Indies, HRH the Commander-in-Chief approves of the men being supplied with trowsers made of blue kersey agreeable to the patterns already approved.

William Wynyard Deputy Adjutant General.[13]

---

12 TNA, WO123/135/197: Army Circulars, Memoranda, Orders and Regulations. Adjutants-General's Office (Horse Guards).

13 TNA, WO7/54/35: Various Departmental, Out-letters. Board of General Officers. Reports on Clothing.

8 July, 1808. Letter regarding blue trowsers

> Clothing Board to Adjutant General,
> Having laid before the clothing board of general officers which was held here on Friday last your letter of the 31 of May with one from Mr Gilpin of the 28th of that month, the board for the reasons stated in Mr Gilpin's letter, and on the authority of a letter from the deputy adjutant general signifying the approbation of HRH the Commander-in-Chief that the regiments serving in the West Indies should be supplied with trowsers made of blue kersey according to patterns already approved, were pleased to allow the patterns to be sealed for those regiments which were brought in by Mr Gilpin.
> Thomas Fauquier Clothing Board.[14]

20 July, 1808. General order regarding hair

> From Adjutant General to the army.
> The Commander-in-Chief directs it to be notified, that in consequence of the state of precaution for immediate service, in which the whole army is at the present moment to be held, His Majesty has been graciously pleased to dispense with the use of queues until further orders.
> HRH desires the commanding officers of regiments, will take care that the men's hair is cut close to their necks in the neatest and most uniform manner, and that their heads are kept perfectly clean by combing, brushing, and frequently washing them; for the latter essential purpose it is His Majesty's pleasure that a small sponge shall hereafter be added to each man's regimental necessaries.
> Harry Calvert Adjutant General.

Attached note:

> On the 23rd July letters were addressed to General Lord Heathfield and to the officer commanding the Royal Regiment of Horse Guards, stating that this order did not apply to His Majesty's Life Guards or to the Royal Regiment of Horse Guards.[15]

The order of 20 July 1808 is the first intimation of the army's intention to abandon the queued hair that was a relic of the fashions of the previous century. This change had been arriving in increments, with the use of powder being occasionally suspended and the queue itself shortened and simplified in 1803. It is notable that this order is merely a temporary suspension of the practice, and two regiments are specifically excluded and ordered to retain their queues. In practice, of course, once the queues were gone, there was no turning back, with most of the army welcoming the end of this onerous and unhygienic practice. There were a few holdouts – but mostly, as always, commanding officers lacked the clout to flout a general

---

14 TNA, WO7/34/208: Various Departmental, Out-letters. Board of General Officers, Clothing.
15 TNA, WO123/135/207: Army Circulars, Memoranda, Orders and Regulations. Adjutant-General's Office (Horse Guards).

order, unless they were royal dukes. In 1802 the Duke of Kent was appointed to command the garrison at Gibraltar, after a series of mutinous incidents on the Rock. He immediately took the situation firmly in hand and restored something like order to the garrison. The governor's residence was still being repaired from the damage it had sustained during the last siege in 1783, so he took up residence near it, and from this lofty vantage point he felt sufficiently secure to enforce a regime of hairdressing in splendid isolation from, and in contradiction of, the rest of the Army. It was unusual, and contrived enough to attract the attention of several memorialists and diary writers, who often felt aggrieved that even the briefest sojourn ashore in Gibraltar from a troop transport ship calling there, required them to conform to the Duke's conception of military elegance.

5 August, 1808. Deputy Adjutant General to army agents

> I have the Commander-in-Chief's commands to desire you will make known to the clothiers of regiments in your agency, that, in consequence of His Majesty's order for the soldiers to wear their hair short, it is HRH's pleasure that the collars of the regimental jackets should be made higher in the neck, so as to entirely cover the clasp of the stock.
> Wynyard, Deputy Adjutant General.[16]

The order regarding extending the collar of regimental coats upwards to cover the stock buckle is interesting in the light of the trend in archaeological discoveries in the Peninsula which appear to indicate that the stock buckle changed between 1808 and 1812 from a scalloped shape to a rectangular one some thirty percent smaller than the first type. The bulk of finds of the former are in Spain and Portugal, whereas the latter shape predominates in the Pyrenees.

The order to modernise the hair significantly updated the appearance of the army, and was broadly met with approval.

> I could not help observing the difference between their [the French] troops and ours, for certainly they had by far the most military appearance, looking like men, with their moustaches and cropped heads, while we, with our smooth chins and abominable queues, were more like the white faced monkey.[17]

The modernisation did not entirely do away with the urge of some to make themselves conspicuous. In at least one case this took the retrograde form of aping the previous incarnation of hairstyle: 'In the paroxysm of a wish to be singularly singular, a friend of mine shaved all the hair off the crown of his head, and he was decidedly the most outre looking man among us, and consequently the happiest'.[18]

16   TNA, WO123/135/209: Army Circulars, Memoranda, Orders and Regulations. Adjutant-General's Office (Horse Guards).

17   T. St Clair, *A Soldier's Recollections of the West Indies and America* (London: Bentley,1834), Volume II, p.346.

18   Grattan, *With the Connaught Rangers*, p.50

14 December, 1808. General order on recruits' clothing

The Commander-in-Chief is pleased to direct that the articles of clothing speci-
fied in the margin shall be furnished to all recruits who are hereafter raised for the
infantry and general service, in the several recruiting districts.
White kersey jacket 6s 4d
White cloth breeches 6s 2d
Pair gaiters 3s
Stock and clasp 9d
Cap and plume 3s 1d
Total £1

Supplies of these articles will accordingly be sent to the Head Quarters of each
district in Great Britain, in order that they may be delivered to every recruit, on
his being intermedially approved, and the cost of them, is to be defrayed out of the
bounty payable at that period.
    It is the Commander-in-Chief's command that the levy money shall hereafter be
disposed of in conformity to the annexed schedule.
    Harry Calvert Adjutant General.[19]

The full text of the 31 March 1808 warrant on hussars

Warrant for regulating the clothing and appointments of regiments of dragoons
equipped as hussars.
    (Having reference to page 433 of the general collection published 25 April, 1807.)
    Whereas we have thought proper to direct that certain of our regiments of light
dragoons, instead of using the ordinary articles of clothing and appointments for
our cavalry, as described in our clothing regulation of the 22 April, 1803, should
be clothed and appointed as hussars; and whereas a board of officers has been
summoned by order of the Commander-in-Chief of our forces, to report their
opinion on the most eligible patterns of hussar appointments, and on other points
connected with this measure: our will and pleasure is, that the following regulations be established, founded on the said report.

I.
In regiments of cavalry authorised to wear hussar clothing and appointments, each
    man shall have for clothing.
Annually,
One pair of gloves,
Once in every two years,
One undress jacket,

---

19 TNA, WO123/135/252: Army Circulars, Memoranda, Orders and Regulations. Adjutant-General's Office, (Horse
    Guards).

One flannel waistcoat,
One pair of pantaloons,
Once in every four years,
One pelisse,
One dress jacket,
One hussar cap,
Once in every eight years,
One sash.

II.
The articles of accoutrements and saddlery to be furnished to the said regiments
    are to be as follows,
Belt swivel and pouch,
Saddle flaps, seat etc.,
Holsters and straps,
Bucket,
Stirrup leathers,
Ditto irons,
Bit and curb,
Cloak,
Sword belt and sling,
Shabraque,
Carbine strap,
Headstall, and reins,
Breast plate,
Crupper,
Girth and strap,
Surcingle,
Baggage strap,
Cloak straps,
Boots,
Collar head, and leather rein,
Spurs,
Swordknot,
Shabraque strap,
Sabretasche and straps.

III.
In the said regiments the curry comb and brush now provided by stoppage out
of the dragoon's pay shall be laid aside, and with the saving to the dragoon on
this article, together with the allowance of 1s 8d per annum for horse cloths, the
dragoon shall provide a saddle blanket.

IV.

For the said regiments, two leather bags in the holster of the saddle shall be supplied instead of the ordinary haversack; and in lieu of the water deck as at present supplied, sheepskins shall be adopted, to be provided out of the present allowance for water decks.

V.

All the above articles of hussar clothing and appointments shall be made up in precise conformity to patterns approved by us, and lodged in the charge of our inspectors of army clothing.

For which this shall be to all whom it may concern, a sufficient warrant, authority and direction.

Given at our Court of St James's this 31st day of March, 1808, in the forty-eighth year of our reign.[20]

25 August, 1808, Warrant concerning greatcoats

Whereas it hath been represented unto us, that the great coats at present supplied as an article of clothing to our regiments of people of colour, and intended to last two years, are insufficient for that purpose, and that it would be advantageous to our service, if the species of greatcoat worn by the infantry of the line, generally, were adopted by the above regiments; our will and pleasure is, that in lieu of the greatcoats described in the tenth article of our clothing regulations of the 22 April, 1803, the colonels of our regiments composed of people of colour, do supply each serjeant, corporal, drummer and private man thereof, with a great coat of the regulation pattern approved for the infantry of the line; which great coats are to last three years.

Of which the general officers of our clothing board, and all others whom it doth or may concern, are to take notice and govern themselves accordingly.

By His Majesty's command, J.A. Pulteney.[21]

---

20 TNA, WO123/117/110: Army Circulars, Memoranda, Orders and Regulations. Army Regulations, etc from Various Sources.

21 TNA, WO123/117/125: Army Circulars, Memoranda, Orders and Regulations. Army Regulations, etc from Various Sources.

Appendix I

The 1802 collation with annotations of Carman

The following article was first published in the *Journal for the Society of Army Historical Research* volume XIX (no.76) 1940 by W. Y. Carman. It is reproduced in full here, with the permission of the present Journal editor. One of the original documents, held in the War office Library when Carman consulted them, is now held in the National Army Museum. The whereabouts of the other is unknown. The manuscript has been consulted, but since it was found unnecessary, and indeed impossible, to improve upon Carman's presentation, and in particular his notation of the complicated alterations, I have followed his version substantially, with minor revisions, where errors in transcription may have occurred, and have been exposed by examination of the original. Spelling and grammar have in places been simplified or modernized to homogenise with the rest of the text in this book. Where the meaning is unclear, the original manuscript has been followed.

In the first MS book the items are dealt with one by one, using various paragraphs of the 1768 warrant as a basis, these being followed by the date of the amending regulations, and then, in another column, by a full revised description of the clothing regulations as was presumed to be in force in 1802. Various corrections are appended to this latter column, the resulting amended account being reproduced in the second MS book.

The title of the first and larger MS book is 'View of the standing regulations for the colours, clothing, etc., of the infantry, to which are annexed the guards, rifle corps, etc. etc'.

The second and smaller book bears the same title and in pencil is written 'This is an Amended Copy of the 'Descriptive View of the clothing and Appointments of the infantry' dated 22 May 1802'.

This article on the clothing regulations of 1802 contains the bulk of the material found in the first book, including all the pencil annotations and corrections, and where the amended reproduction in the second book (called 'z' in the article) differs from the first book, this also is specially noted.

At the end of both books are given out in detail 'The devices and badges of regiments' and also 'The general view of the facings'.

The earlier part of the first book is tabulated in five columns with the following headings, and these headings are represented in this article by the letters shown against them:

A. Articles.
B. By regulations of 19 December 1768.
C. Dates of alterations made from time to time.
D. As the regulations are supposed to stand at present.
E. For observations and improvements.

The separate paragraphs, which are numbered here for convenience, given under these five headings in the first book, are as follows:

(Para. 1) (Columns B and D) No colonel is to put his arms, crest, device or livery on any part of the appointments of the regiment under his command. Z.[1] (Para 2 and 3) A. colours (A[2] *of the 3 regiments of Foot guards, colours of the regiments of the line.)* Z.

(Para 3) B. D. The second colour to be the colour of the facings of the regiments with the Union in the upper canton, except those regiments which are faced with red, white or black. The second colour of those regiments which are faced with red or white to be the red cross of St. George in a white field and the Union in the upper canton. The second colour of those regiments which are faced with black is to be St. George's cross throughout, Union in the upper canton, the other three cantons black. In the centre of each colour is to be painted or embroidered in gold roman characters the number of the rank of the regiment within a wreath of roses, and thistles (D.—[5 Nov. 1800, C.][3] and the shamrock) on the same stalk, except those regiments which are allowed to wear any devices or ancient badges, on whose colour the rank of the regiments is to painted or embroidered towards the upper canton. The size of the colour to be six feet six inches (D.—six feet two inches[4]) flying and six feet deep on the pike. The length of the pike, spear and ferrule included, to be nine feet ten inches. The cords and tassels of the whole to be crimson and gold mixed. Z.

(Para 4) A. Drums. Z.
B. D. The drums to be of wood (D.—*except by application*). The front to be painted with the colour of the facing of the regiment, with the King's cypher and crown, and the number of the regiment under it. Z.

(Para 5) A. bells of arms
B. bells of arms to be painted in the same manner.
(D.—['During this War,' C.] 'None used with the present camp equipages.
Qv'. Should this article by kept up in the regulations?'[5])

1 The letter Z indicates that column D (or Column A in certain instances is reproduced without any further alteration in the second MS book.
2 Additions in pencil in either volume are here shown in italics within brackets, preceded by the letter indicating the column in which the corrections were made.
3 Where column D contains additions or corrections to the information given in column B, this is inserted in round brackets, the whole being preceded by the letter D, which is followed by a square bracket containing the date of the amending regulations as noted in column C.
4 'By information from Mr. Horne'.—D.
5 The note under column D has been crossed out in pencil, and the whole of Para 5 has been omitted in Z.

(Para 6) A. Camp colours. Z.
B. D. The camp colours to be eighteen inches square and the colour of the facing of the regiment upon them. The poles to be seven feet six inches long, except those of the quarter and rear guards, which are to be nine feet. (D.—The camp colour for the regimental guards is to be the Union of the same size, and the poles the same.) Z.

(Para 7) A. A general's full dress uniform coat. (Z. Qv. *'field marshal's buttons & coat.*) Z.
B. 'No regulation inserted'.
(D.—[21 July 1786, C.] The grand or full dress uniform coat for a general, is to be of scarlet cloth, long skirts, lined with white silk. No lapels, small round cuffs *of blue cloth,*6 short standing *scarlet* collar, cross pocket flaps, one row broad gold lace round the coat and pockets, and three rows round each cuff, the upper most of which, is to be half the breadth of the two below it, but of the same pattern. The narrow lace to go round the collar. Two epaulettes, which, with the lace, are to conformable to patterns approved by His Majesty. The general officers' button, set on, at equal distances, which is a gilt button, nearly flat, ornamented with a sword and truncheon, encircled with a wreath of laurel.) Z.
   (East *More information required apply to a Taylor Mr. Munroe (?) Shepherd.*)

(Para 8) A. Their half dress or embroidered coat. Z.
B. 'No regulation inserted'.
(D.—[28 Oct. 1797: 26 May 1798, C.] The half dress, or embroidered uniform coat of a general, is to be of scarlet cloth, long skirts made to hook back, and lined with white kerseymere, standing collar of scarlet cloth, with small cuffs of blue cloth, lapels of the same colour as the cuffs, 3 inches in breadth and made to button over the body down to the waist.7 The cuffs ---- inches in breadth and indented. The uniform buttons set on at equal distances upon lapels, sleeves and skirts. No pocket flaps.
   The button holes embroidered, and on the sleeves and skirts double, sloping inwards till they meet, where the buttons are set on, with one of the cuff. *Two* embroidered button holes on the back between the hip buttons, ten buttons on each lapel including the one on the front of the collar, four on each sleeve and skirt. The pockets in the plait or at the Inside, and the epaulettes embroidered, or a similar pattern as the button holes.) Z.
   (East *Apply to Mr. Shepherd or Mr. Davison*).

(Para 9) A. Their plain or undress coat. Z.
B. 'No regulation Inserted'.
(D.—The undress or plain uniform coat of a general, to have embroidered epaulettes and to be similar in every respect, as the half dress uniform, excepting that the button holes throughout are to be without embroidery.) Z.

---

6   D originally read: 'Small round cuffs, short standing collar, and both or dark blue cloth' (presumably the 1786 regulation), and was altered in D in pencil to read as above, which alteration was reproduced in Z.
7   Instead of kerseymere, D originally read silk/shalloon but was altered in pencil to cassimere.

(Para 10) A. The Lieutenant generals' full dress uniform coat. Z.
B. 'No regulation inserted'.
(D.—[21 July 176, C.] The great or full dress uniform coat for a lieut.-general is to be similar throughout, as that described for a general, excepting that there are only two broad laces round the cuffs, without the third narrow lace above them.) Z.

(Para 11) A. Their embroidered and undress coat.
B. 'No regulation inserted'.
(D.—[28 Oct. 1797; 26 May 1798, C.] The half dress or embroidered and undress or plain uniform coats, are in like manner similar as those described for a general excepting that the buttons are to be set on 3 and 3.) Z.

(Para 12.) A. The major-generals' full dress coat. Z.
B. 'No regulation inserted'.
(D.—[21 July, 1786, C.] The great or full dress uniform coat for a major general is to be similar throughout, as that described for a general, excepting that there is only one broad lace around the cuffs, without the narrow lace above it.) Z.

(Para 13.) A. Their embroidered and undress coats. Z.
B. 'No regulation inserted'.
(D.—[28 Oct 1797; 26 May 1798, C.] The half dress or embroidered and undress or plain uniform coats, are in like manner similar as those described for a general excepting that the buttons are to be set on 2 and 2.) Z.

(Para 14.) A. Adjutant-general, Quarter-master general & Barrack-master generals' embroidered and undress coats. Z.
B. 'No regulation inserted'.
(D.—[31 January 1799, C.] The uniform coats for the Adjutant-general, Quarter-master general, and the Barrack-master general, to be the same in silver as those described for the embroidered and plain uniform coats for a lieutenant general.) Z.

(Para 15.) A. Deputy Adjutant-general, deputy Quarter-master general & deputy Barrack-master general, embroidered and undress coats. Z.
B. 'No regulation inserted'.
(D.—[31 January. 1799, C.] The uniform coats for the deputy Adjutant general, deputy Quarter-master general and the deputy Barrack-master general to be the same in silver as those described for the embroidered and plain uniform coats for a major-general. Any of these officers being general officers are permitted to wear in silver the button appropriated to officers of that rank, instead of the raised staff button which is commonly worn.) Z.

(Para 16.) Z. Aides de camp's embroidered and undress coats. Z.
B. 'No regulation issued'.
(D.—[31 Jan. 1799, C.] The embroidered uniform coats for aides de camp to general officers to be of scarlet cloth, long skirts made to hook back and lined with white shalloon *or kersey-mere,* No lapels and made to button over the body down to the waist. A falling collar and

small cuffs of blue cloth – Ten embroidered button holes on each front of the coat, including the one on the collar, and Three double embroidered button holes on each sleeve, including one on cuff, and the same numbers on each skirt. No pocket flaps, and the pockets to open in the plait, two embroidered button holes on each back skirt between the hip buttons. Plain flat gilt buttons set on 2 and 2, excepting one on each cuff and the upper one on each skirt. The undress or plain uniform coats for aides de camp are similar to the above excepting that there is no embroidery but on the epaulette). Z.

(Z only: *There should be a reference to the article epaulette.*) (D. *'King's ADC vide Mem 7 May 1805, page 435 C. Book'.*8) (Z. *King's aides de camp wanting'.*)

(Para. 17) A. Assistant adjutant-generals, Assistant quarter-master generals & majors of brigades embroidered and undress coats. Z.
B. 'No regulation Inserted'.
(D.—[31 Jan. 1799, C.] The embroidered or plain uniform coats for Assistant adjutant-generals, Assistant quarter-master generals, or for deputy-assistants and for majors of brigades are to be the same in silver as those described for aide de camps to general officers. These uniforms are appropriated exclusively to the officers herein specified, and His Majesty is graciously pleased to permit generals the staff officers above mentioned to appear in the field in plain uniforms.) Z. (D. *Vide page 334 circular book 1804'.*9)

(Para 17A.) (A. *uniform town majors & adjutants.*) Z. (*This additional information is in Z only:* The uniform coat for a town or fort major to be plain scarlet with blue cloth lapels, a gilt button with the word 'staff' and the addition of the name of the garrison to which he belongs encircled on it; And two gold lace epaulettes. A town adjutant the same uniform, but with one epaulette. *Some alteration is to made in this, query'.*)

(Para 18.) B, D and Z. The number of each regiment to be on the buttons of the uniforms of both officers and men.

(Para 19.) A. Officers of the guards full dress uniform coats. Z.
B. 'No regulation inserted'.
(D.—['Supposed to be at the present time,' C.] The full dress uniform coat for the officers of the guards to be of scarlet cloth, long skirts, lined with white silk/shalloon and sewed back. lapels and cuffs of dark blue cloth – The lapels 3 inches in breadth throughout and reaching down in a line with the pocket flaps. To be sewed down and not made to button over the body. 10[10] buttons on the lapels set on at equal distances. Cross pocket flaps, on which a narrow gold lace. On the upper part of the flaps, and round them on the skirts, a broad gold lace, double the breadth of the narrow, and which nearly covers this part of the skirts. Three buttons set on the skirt and nearly covered by the flap. A standing collar of scarlet cloth,

---

8   This refers to page 435 of 'general orders, circular Letter, 1800-1806' (in War office Library), which give the 'regulations for A.D.C's to the King' dated 7 May, 1805.
9   See 'Asst. Adjutant& Q.M.G's uniforms' of 1804, contained in p. 334 of 'general orders, circular Letters, 1800-1806' (in War office Library).
10   D gives 11/10. Z had 11/10 but altered to 10.

lined with white silk and laced round with the narrow lace similar to that on the lower part of the pocket flaps. The button holes on the lapels looped with the same lace, and the outer side of the lapels and skirts edged with the same, and part of the skirts on both sides edged to where they meet on being sewed back. At the joining of the skirts to be a small oval like piece of blue cloth richly embroidered. Three laced loopings as button holes as on each of the back skirts, beginning the hip buttons and joined to the lace on the skirts round cuffs and no slits 31/2 inches in breadth, 3 buttons on each and two rows of lace: the lower on broad similar to that on the lower part of the pockets, the upper row narrow and similar to that on the collar and lapels. Laced scarlet wings on the coats of the officers of grenadiers at light infantry with bullion and fringe beside the epaulettes. Embroidered grenades instead of the blue cloth ovals on the skirts of grenadiers and bugle horns on the of the light infantry.) Z.
  (East *Apply to Mr. Davison.*)

(Para 20.) A. Officers of the guards frock uniform coat. Z. (D.—['Supposed to be at the present time,' C.] The frock uniform coat of the officers of the guards to be of scarlet cloth, lined with white shalloon, long skirts and sewed back. Lapels & cuffs of dark blue cloth. The lapels three inches in breadth throughout and made to buttons over the body down to the waist. Round cuffs and no slits, 3 ½ inches in breadth, and a standing collar of scarlet cloth. No lace on the buttons holes, but the collar and cross pocket flaps laced round with gold lace, the out edge of the lapels and skirts laced with the same to the bottom. The upper part of the skirts to be laced on both sides and a row of lace from the hip buttons down the plait of the skirt to where it joins the part turned back and an edging of blue cloth on the skirts on each side of the lace. A small oval like piece of blue cloth embroidered set on each skirt where they meet. Officers of grenadiers, scarlet wings, laced & fringed besides epaulettes and embroidered grenades of the skirts. Officers of light infantry to have jackets ; the skirts short turned back and fronts with white cassimere. The pocket flaps to slope diagonally. The cuffs collar & lapels similar, and laced similar to the battalion, but bugle horns on the Points of the turnbacks of the skirts. Small buttons on the jackets for light infantry, large ones on the coats for grenadiers & battalions, and to be set on equal distances 2 and 2, or 3 and 3 according to the Regt...) Z.

(Para 21.) A. Uniforms of officers of regiments or corps of infantry. Z.
B. The coat to be lapelled to the waist, with cloth the colour of the Facing of the regiment and the colour not to be varied from what is specified hereafter. They may be without embroidery or lace, but if the Colonel thinks it proper to have either gold or silver embroidered or laced button holes these are permitted. To have cross pockets and sleeves with round cuffs and no slits. The lapels and cuffs to be of the same breadth as ordered for the men.
(D.—[28 Oct. 1797; 26 May 1798, C.] The uniform coats for officers of regiments or corps of infantry to be scarlet cloth, long skirts made to hook back and line with white or buff *kerseymere or* shalloon, according to the regiment lapels, cuffs and collar of cloth the colour of the facings of the regiments, which is not to be varied from what is particularly specified hereafter. The lapels 3 inches in breadth throughout and made to button over the body down to the waist. Round cuffs and no slits, 3 ½ inches in breadth; *turned down* collar;[11] cross pocket

flaps for the grenadiers, and battalions, for the light infantry to slope diagonally. 10 buttons on the lapels, including one on the collar, four on the cuff and on pockets and set on at equal distances, 2 and 2 or 3 and 3 according to the regiment 2 worked button holes on each of the back skirts where they break off at the hips. *It is to be observed that officers appearing at court are to have the lapels buttoned back.* The jackets for light infantry, short skirted, the front skirts turned back and faced with cassimere the colour of the lining. Small buttons on the jackets for light infantry and large ones on the coats of the grenadiers and battalions.

Scarlet wings for grenadiers and light infantry with bullion and fringe besides epaulettes.

An embroidered grenade on the skirts of the grenadiers and a bugle horn on those of the light infantry. The button holes may be without embroidery or lace, but if the colonel thinks proper, gold or silver embroidered or laced button holes are epaulettes are permitted.) Z.

(Para 22.) A. Uniforms of officers of highland regiments
B. 'No regulation inserted'.
(D.—[28 Oct. 1797; 26 May 1798, C.] The uniform coats for officers of highland regiments are of the same description as those for other corps of infantry excepting that the skirts are short and the part turned back is sewed and fronted with cassimere like light infantry, and of the same colour as the lining, and that they have but eight buttons on the fronts and three on sloping pocket flaps.) Z.

(Para 23A.) A. Full dress uniforms of officer of rifle corps. Z.
B. 'No regulation inserted'.
(D.—['Supposed to be at the present time,' C.] The full dress uniform coat for officers of a rifle corps is to be of dark green cloth, long skirts, and lined with white shalloon, the skirts turned back and fronted with white cassimere sewed down, and at the joining a circle of black velvet embroidered with silver.[12] Lapel, collar, cuffs, and wings black velvet. The lapels, rather short and made to button across the body at the 5th button, 3 inches in breadth at the bottom, and increasing gradually to 3 ½ inches at the top. A standing collar faced with green cloth, which with the cuffs are to be 3 inches in breadth. No slits in the cuffs. Cross pocket flaps. Ten buttons on each lapel, including one on collar; Three on each cuff and pocket flap. The wings laced, and bullion and fringe besides epaulettes. The buttons set on at equal distances and all large excepting the collar and epaulettes. A flat plated button with a raised bugle horn and crown over it.) Z.
(E. *To be decided hereafter.*)

(Para 23B.) A. The service uniform of officer of rifle corps. Z.
B. 'No regulation inserted'.
(D.—['Supposed to be at the present time,' C.] The undress or service uniform for officers of the rifle corps to be a jacket of dark green cloth, without lapels or skirts, and made to button over the body down to the waist. The breast fronted with green cloth, lined with green silk or shalloon. A black velvet standing collar lined with green cloth. Cuffs black velvet 2 ½ inches in breadth, pointed and to open with 5 buttons. A double row of buttons on one front and a

---

12 In Z altered to 'gold or silver'.

single row with button holes on the other. 22 buttons in each row and the same number of looping of black silk twist on each front between the rows with a knot on the outer side; the looping 7 ½ inches in length at the top and reduced gradually to 2 ½ inches at the bottom, and in which forms the buttons are set on. A loop of twist on each front of the collar, a row of the same down the seams from the shoulders to the hip buttons, and a double row on the fronts instead of pocket welts. Black velvet wings and straps with bullion and fringe, besides a silver[13] chain on the wings and straps. The buttons throughout of a round form like a ball and set on at equal distances. The lace and epaulettes silver.[14]) Z.

(Para 24.) A. Uniform of officers of corps not numbered. Z.
B. 'Altered stated in folio 4' (*i.e.*, D).
(D.—[28 Oct. 1797; 26 May 1798, C.] The *form of the* uniform coats for officers of the Queens Rangers,[15] the S. Wales corps,[16] are[17] *to be* similar to those for officers of regiments of infantry.) Z.

(Para 25.) A. Uniforms of officers of regiments of people of colour.
B. 'No regulation inserted'.
(D.—['Supposed to be at the present time,' C.] The uniform coats for officers of regiments of people of colour are to be of scarlet cloth, long skirted, and every way similar to those described for officers of regiments on infantry, excepting that they are to have half lapels, which are to be 3 inches in breadth at the bottom and to increase gradually to 4 at the top and a standing collar of scarlet cloth. The colour of the facings, cuffs, etc., according to the order for the regiment.[18]

(Para 26.) A. Epaulettes. Z.
B. officers of grenadiers to wear an epaulette on each shoulder. Those of the battalion to wear one on the right shoulder. They are to be of embroidery or lace, with gold or silver fringe.
(D.—['Supposed to be at the present time,' C.] The straps of the epaulettes for general officers (excepting for the full dress coat) are to be gold embroidery on scarlet cloth according to the pattern for the button holes, which with a rich bullion and fringe forms the epaulette. Those for their aides-de-camp are to be embroidered on dark blue cloth according to the pattern of their button holes, with a rich bullion and fringe. Those for the Adjutant-General, the quarter-master general and the Barrack-master general, and also for their deputies, are to be in silver embroidery on scarlet cloth, similar in pattern as those for general officers. Those for Assistant Adjutant-generals, Assistant quarter-master generals and Deputy assistants to both, and of majors of brigade, are to be silver embroidery on dark blue cloth with rich

---

13 In Z altered to 'silver or gilt'
14 In Z altered to 'silver or gold'.
15 'This corps is understood to be in green clothing' added in D in ink and crossed out in pencil. Not given in Z.
16 In D it is here stated 'and the one in Africa as also of the Garrison battalions and companies of Invalids'. This was crossed out in pencil' and is not included in Z.
17 In D 'supposed' was inserted here, but afterwards crossed out in pencil. Not given in Z.
18 In column E is, 'The same as the officers of other regiments,' and the whole of column D is crossed out in pencil. Para 23 is not reproduced in Z

bullion and fringe Similar in pattern to those for aide-de-camps. Those for officers of the guard to be gold lace with rich bullion and fringe. Those for officers of all other regiments or corps of infantry to be of gold or silver embroidery of lace with rich bullion and fringe, according to patterns approved by their respective colonels.) Z.

(Para 27.) A. How worn. Z.
B. 'No regulation inserted'.
(D.—[31 Dec. 1791; 31 Jan. 1799, C.] The Adjutant general and quarter-master general of the Forces, the in England & their respective deputies, as also the aides de camp of His Majesty & of His Royal Highness the Commander in Chief, are distinguished exclusively by wearing two epaulettes. All other Adjutant-generals, quarter-master generals and Barrack-master generals with their deputies, wear one epaulette on the left shoulder.[19] Aides de camp to general officers of cavalry wear one epaulette on the left shoulder. Those attached to general officers of cavalry wear one epaulette on the left shoulder. Those attached to general officers of infantry one epaulette on the right shoulder. Assistant Adjutant-generals & Assistant quarter-master generals wear two epaulettes and majors of brigades one. These are to be similar to aides de camp but in silver.

When a major of brigade in attached to cavalry, the epaulette to be worn on the left shoulder and when attached to infantry on the right shoulder. Effective field officers of the guards and of regiments or corps of infantry and officers of fusilier regiments are to wear two epaulettes. All other officers of the above corps are to wear but one epaulette, which is to be on the right shoulder, excepting the adjutants of the guards who are permitted to wear two, with a small deviation in the bullion, as are also officers of the grenadier and light infantry companies and all the officers of the rifle corps when in full dress. The epaulettes for officers of grenadiers to have an embroidered grenade on the broad end of the strap and those for light infantry and rifle corps to have an embroidered bugle horn.) Z.

(Para 28.) A. Waistcoats for general officers, officers of the guards and of the infantry & rifle corps. Z.
B. The waistcoats to be plain, without embroidery or lace.
(D.—['No alterations made'. 'Upon Establishing of rifle corps,' C.] The waistcoats for the full dress uniform of general officers and of officers of the guards are to be single breasted and of white cloth or cassimere. The skirts rather short and with flaps to the pockets and 3 or 4 buttons on the skirts. Those for the frocks or undress are to be of similar materials and form, but without skirts or pocket flaps. All other officers of regiments or corps of infantry are to have waistcoats of similar materials and form as those for the generals' undress, but to be white or buff according to the order for the regiment. The full dress waistcoat for officers of a rifle corps are to be white and of similar materials and form as for officers of infantry. The service waistcoat for officers of a rifle corps is to be of dark green cloth, like the jacket, cut rather short and without skirts, a standing collar which with the breast are to be faced with green cloth, and the pockets made at the breast, 22 buttons on one side of the fronts and

---

19 *'Vide order 1804,'* in pencil, in E only.

button holes at the Other. The buttons on all waistcoats to be small and a uniform button similar to those on the coats. No lace or embroidery, and to be quite plain.) Z.

(Para 29.) A. Breeches, pantaloons, kilts and trowsers. Z.
B. 'No regulation inserted'.
D.—['No alteration made'. 'Upon establishing of the rifle and other corps,'
C.] The breeches for general officers, officers of the guards, officers of regiments or corps of infantry, and for the full dress of officers of a rifle corps, are to be of the same materials and colour of their waistcoats. *Officers of the foot guards are permitted to wear white leather breeches with regimental buttons with their frock uniforms.*[20] The service dress for a rifle corps is dark green pantaloons with a row of black twist down the seams. Officers of the highland corps are to wear the kilt, purse and hose similar to their men. Officers of the Royal staff corps[21] are permitted to wear blue cloth pantaloons similar to their men.[22] *Officers belonging to regiments serving in the West Indies are permitted to wear trowsers similar to their men.* Z.

(Para 30.) A. great coats. Z.
B. 'No regulation inserted'.
(D.—['Supposed to be at the present time,' C.] The great coats for general officers, officers of the guards, officers of regiments or corps on infantry and of highland regiments are to be of dark blue cloth, double breasted, with two rows of buttons and a falling collar of scarlet cloth. Blue cuff with slits and to open with 4 small buttons. The pockets to open at the plait. Buttons similar to their respective uniforms or regimentals. The great coat for officers of a rifle corps are to be of dark grey cloth, double breasted, and with three rows of buttons, a falling collar, cuffs with slits and 4 Small buttons – The collar and cuffs of dark green cloth. The pockets to in the plait and the buttons similar to the large size of the full dress coat.[23]) Z.

(Para 31.) A. stocks. Z.
B. 'No regulation inserted'.
(D.—['Supposed to be at the present time'. C.] White stocks to be worn by general officers and officers of the guards in their full dress uniforms and black silk stocks when in their frocks or undress uniforms. Black silk stocks are also to be worn by all other officers of either infantry, rifle or staff corps. And by the staff throughout.) Z.

(Para 32.) A. Hair, How Worn. Z.
B. 'No regulation inserted'.

20 A pencil note: 'general and staff officers – leather breeches with boots'.
21 In D was here written 'it is supposed'. This is crossed out, 'are permitted to' was substituted in pencil, followed by 'Query' and 'Yes'.
22 In D was here added: 'and it is supposed that the officers of the regiments of people of colour are to wear Trowsers like their men and likewise officers of other regiments when serving in the West Indies'. But this is crossed out in pencil and omitted in Z.
23 A pencil note in E reads: '*Some regulation appears necessary respecting the mode of wearing the swords and Sashes with the great coat,*' and a subsequent note states, '*on the outside,*' but Z gives in ink, following at the end of Para 30, 'with great coats the sword and Sash is to be worn on the Outside'.

(D.—[21 July 1796 'Supposed to be at the present time; an order has been issued since the above date but cannot find it,' C.] general officers, officers on the staff, and officers of infantry throughout (excepting the grenadier and light companies.) are to wear the hair queued. The ribbon beginning near the top of the collar of the coat and leaving about 1 ½ inch of hair out of the bottom. A rose of black ribbon covering the tie and queue about – inches in length. The officers of grenadier and light infantry to wear the hair plaited and turned up with a comb, with ends of ribbon hanging on the back from the tie.[24]) Z.

(Para 33.) A. 'Hats and helmets'. Altered in Z to 'hats and feathers'.
B. 'The hats to be laced with gold or silver as hereafter specified and to be cocked uniformly'.
(D.—[4 May 1796, C.] The uniform hat for officers throughout is to be without lace with a crimson and gold cord round the crown with crimson and gold rosettes or tufts brought to the edge of the brim. A black cockade and their uniform button with a gold or silver lace loop according to their regiment of corps. The officers of battalions to have a white feather with red at the bottom; those of grenadiers to be all white, and those of light infantry and of the rifle corps to be dark green. General officers and those on the staff to wear a white feather with red at the bottom, and the loop of the hat to by in gilt of silver Scales. The feather for the whole to be the Cock's Hackle.
   The hat to be cocked with uniformity according to a pattern hat left at the Comptroller's office for army accounts. The officers of the guards are to have gold lace hats and the usual feather when in full dress uniform. The officers of the highland corps to wear the Scots Bonnet and black Ostridge feather similar to their men. Officers of the rifle corps, when in service uniform, to wear *caps like their men*25 Z.

(Para 34A.) A. Swords, sword knots and belts. Z.
B. The swords of each regiment to be uniform and the sword knots of the whole to be crimson and gold with stripes. The hilts of the swords to be gilt or silver according to the colour of the buttons of the regiment.
(D.—[29 April 1786; 6 July 1789; 4 May 1796, C.] The uniform sword for general officers, officers on the staff,[26] officers of the guards and of regiments of corps of infantry is to be the same; it is to have a brass guard, pommel, & shell, and gilt, with the grip or handle of silver twisted wire. The blade straight and made to cut and thrust, one inch at least broad at the shoulder and to be strong and substantial. The scabbards black, with gilt mounting. The sword for officers of the highland corps to be[27] *according to a particular pattern at the Comptroller's office* and that by the rifle corps to be a sabre similar to light cavalry. The sword knot to be crimson and gold in stripes.) Z.

---

24   In D follows this sentence: 'These ends to be – inches in length'. This is crossed out in pencil, and is omitted from Z.
25   In D was written in ink 'helmets with a hair cockade and green feather and a silver crown and bugle engraved on the right side of the helmet'. This was crossed out in pencil, and '*caps like their men*' was substituted. In Z a pencil note adds: 'the 5th regiment claim the privilege of wearing white feathers, a distinction gained (it is said) in action'.
26   Pencil note in Z states: '*Error in Regard to the sword of generals and the staff*'.
27   In D the original wording here was 'the broad sword'. This was crossed out and the words in italics substituted, with a reference 'Adjutant-generals letter, 10 Dec. 1798'.

(Para 34B.) A. How worn and no other arms in use by officers, excepting rifle corps. Z.
(D.—[6 July 1789; 21 July 1792, C.] The sword to be carried in a white[28] belt round the waist, but over the coat, by general officers and by officer on the staff, on which there is to be a clasp according to a pattern at the Comptroller's office. By all other officers (excepting the rifle corps) it is to be carried in a buff[29] belt of the same breadth and colour as the men's with a silver or gilt plate or buckle according to their lace. When on Duty, the belt is to be worn on the right shoulder & over the coat, when off Duty to be under the coat and over the waistcoat. The officers of the rifle corps are to carry their swords in a black leather belt round the waist on which the Mounting is to be silver, the belt to be of the same breadth as their men's'.) Z.

(Para 35A.) A. Espontoons.
B. The battalion officers to have Espontoons. (D.—[29 April 1786, C.] No longer used.[30]
(D.—[8 May 1792, C.] No other arms to be carried by officers of infantry but swords.)

(Para 35B.) A. Officers of rifle corps to carry a small pistol. Z.
(D.—['On Establishing the rifle corps,' C.] Officers of the rifle corps besides their swords are to carry a small pistol in a pouch worn with a black leather belt across the left shoulder, the flap of the pouch ornamented with a silver lion's head and a chain with a green ivory whistle on the front of the belt at the breast.) Z.

(Para 35.) A. Sashes and gorgets. Z.
B. The Sashes to be on crimson silk and worn round the waist. The King's arms to be engraved on the gorget, also the number of the regiment. They are to be either gilt or silver according to the colour of the buttons of the uniform. The badges of those regiments which are entitled to any, are also to be engraved.

(Para 36A: 'Sashes'.) (D.—['Supposed to be at the present time,' C.] The sashes for general officers, officers on the staff and all officers of infantry are to be of crimson silk and to be worn round the waist but over the coats, excepting the highland corps. Those on the generals and staff officers are to be worn under the waist belt, and those by all others to be on the outside of the shoulder belts, with the knot and ends on the left side. The officers of highland corps to wear them across the left shoulder, outside the belt, with the knot and ends on the right side.) Z.[31]

(Para 36B: 'Gorgets'.) (D.—[4 May 1796, C.] The gorget is to be of the same size and form throughout and gilt with the King's cypher and crown over it engraved on the middle, and

---

28 'buff' originally inserted in D and Z, but crossed out.
29 'leather' inserted here in ink in Z.
30 crossed through in pencil in D and not reproduced in Z.
31 In pencil in Z is the following: 'Query? How are the sashes to be tied, and on which side'. 'Sashes of officers & staff officers on the right side'. 'Query. Are not all staff officers considered cavalry?' 'Sashes to be considered a part of officers' uniform and only to be dispensed with when officers are permitted to appear in gaiters or boots'. 'Orders recently given out respecting Garrison staff officers'.

to be worn with a ribbon and tuft or rosette at each end of the colour of the facings of the regiment or corps, excepting by those which are faced with black, who wear them with a red ribbon. The gorget to be fastened to the upper button and the lower part of it not to come below the 5th button.[32]) Z.

(Para 37A.) A. Caps for grenadier officers. Z.
B. officers of grenadiers to wear black Bear Skin caps and [see Para 37B]. (D.—['Supposed to be at the present time,' C.] Grenadier officers and officers
of fusilier regiments to wear black bear skin caps, the ornaments gilt,[33] but in dimensions and every other respect similar to those hereafter specified for the men. Officers of light infantry to wear[34] caps of the same materials as a hat and of similar formations. Those ordered for the whole infantry of the army with a dark green feather and a bugle horn *in the front.35* The officers of grenadiers *and fusilier corps* are to wear these sort of caps with a white feather and a grenade at occasional parades, But when not required They are to wear hats as already specified (excepting with a gilt or silver grenade instead of button and) with a white feather. The battalion officers of fusilier regiments are also to have these sort of caps for occasional parades with a red and white feather, but when not particularly ordered they are to wear hats in a similar manner as other regiments.[36])

(Para 37B.) A. Fusil and pouches.
B. [continued from Para 37A] 'to have fusils and shoulder belts and pouches. The shoulder belt to be buff or white according to the colour of their waistcoats.
(D.—[8 May 1792, C.] fusils and pouches abolished. But the rifle corps wear a pouch, as already stated.[37])

(Para 38.) A. Gaiters. (Z. Boots, gaiters & pantaloons.)
B.I. No regulation for boots inserted.
D.I. ['Supposed to be at the present time,' C.]
B.II. The whole to wear black linen gaiters with black buttons and small stiff tops, black garters and uniform buckles.
No regulation for white gaiters inserted.

32   In D was here inserted: 'Effective field officers and adjutants who are to be on horseback not to wear gorgets. It is supposed neither do the officers of rifle corps or light infantry'. This is crossed out in pencil and in E column there is a pencil note 'I do not recollect any regulation which exempts these officers from wearing gorgets'. None of this is reproduced in Z.
33   In D was originally written here 'or silver according to the lace of the regiment'. This was crossed out in pencil and was not reproduced in Z.
34   In Z is here written 'at all time'. Not given in D.
35   The sentences which follow from here to the end are crossed out in pencil in D and in their place is substituted in Z: 'The officers of grenadier. & fusilier corps are allowed to wear hats with the distinguishing feather & button when the men appear in felt caps'.
36   In E is a pencil note as follows: 'I conceive it to be His Royal Highness's intention that the grenadier caps shall be fronted with brass consequently those of the officers will be gilt without any preference to the lace of the regiment'. 'Yes'. The whole of this is crossed out in pencil and is not reproduced in Z.
37   All crossed out in pencil and not reproduced in Z.

D.II.—[21 July 1784, C.]
B.III. No regulation for trowsers or pantaloons inserted.
(D.III.—['Supposed to be at the present time,' C.] D. General officers, staff officers, officers of the Foot guards, effective field officers and adjutants of regiments or corps of infantry to wear black topped boots, officers of the rifle corps and of the staff corps half boots. All other officers of regiments or corps of infantry, serving in Europe, America or at The Cape of Good Hope,[38] excepting the highland corps, are to wear black cloth woolen gaiters with small white metal buttons & are to be of a similar formation as the men's. Those officers belonging to regiments serving in the East & West Indies[39] to wear trowsers similar in form to the men. Officers of the guards when in full dress uniform to wear white linen gaiters reaching up to the top button of the knee with small black *leather40* buttons and black silk[41] Garters below the knee. On a march or on out duties, officers are permitted to wear dark blue cloth pantaloons *and no other colour will be permitted.*) Z.

(Para 39.) A. Serjeants coats of the guards. Z.
B. 'No regulation inserted'.
(D.—[24 Nov. 1770; 15 Nov. 1773[42]; 'Supposed to be at the present time. N.B. – The first alteration in the form appears to be 28 Oct. 1797[43]; 11 July 1774.[44] C.] The coats for serjeants of the guards to be of scarlet cloth, lined throughout with white serge, short skirted, The front skirts sewed back and faced with serge, and an edging of blue cloth close to the lace. No lapels, but made to button over the body down to the waist. Both fronts edged with gold lace and ten looping of the same sort of lace on each front (excepting the 3rd regiment) The holes looped with gold lace and one row of lace round each cuff. Cross pocket flaps for the grenadiers and battalions. And to open *outside.* For the light infantry they are to slope diagonally and toe open at the plait, 4 buttons on each flap. (excepting the 3rd regiment) The holes looped with lace and a row of lace round the flaps on the skirts. Each skirt and the turnback of the front-skirts to be laced to the bottom. A diamond of lace under the hip buttons, and another in a line with them on the joining of the back skirts which are to fold well over. Blue cloth wings for the grenadiers and light infantry and on each five darts of lace. The wings of the light infantry are also laced round and those of the grenadiers a row of lace on the bottom. The wings of each have likewise a gold fringe, and gold lace epaulettes with fringe to be worn on each shoulder of the grenadiers and light infantry. One similar sort of epaulette to be worn on the right shoulder of serjeants of the battalions and on the left shoulder a laced strap with gold fringe.
[11 July 1774 C.] The 3rd regiment of guards to have but 9 buttons on the lapels and 3 on each cuff and pocket flap. The button on the pocket flaps and hips of the grenadiers and

38 'Or at the Cape of Good Hope' crossed out in pencil in both D and Z.
39 In D there is the following footnote to this sentence: 'NB.—Trowsers being the regulation for the men in the West Indies, it is supposed that the dress of officers on duty is to be the same'. This has been crossed out in pencil and omitted from Z.
40 In D 'leather' was substituted in pencil for 'horn'. Leather in Z.
41 In D 'leather' is given as an alternative to 'silk,' but has been crossed out in pencil and not given in Z.
42 These two dates are opposite the sentence dealing with collar, cuffs and shoulder-straps.
43 This comment is opposite the sentence dealing with pocket flaps.
44 This date refers to the buttons of the 3rd regiment, referred to later.

battalions to be large, on the other parts of their coats they are to be small, as are the whole on the jackets for light infantry. The buttons to be set on at equal distances, 2 and 2 or 3 and 3 according to the regiment[45]) Z.

(Para 40.) A. serjeants coats of regiments or corps of infantry when serving in Europe, North America or at the Cape of Good Hope.[46] Z.
(D.—[4 Feb. 1769; 15 April 1781; 28 Oct. 1797; 9 April 1800; 23 April 1801; 20 May 1801, C.] The coats for serjeants of regiments and other corps of infantry (excepting the highland corps) which are serving in Europe, North America or at the Cape of Good Hope, to be of scarlet cloth lined throughout, the sleeves with linen, the other parts with white or buff serge according to the orders for the regiment short skirted. The front-skirts sewed back and faced with serge, with and edging of white lace. 10 loops of lace on each front of the coat, with buttons on one front and holes on the other. No lapels but made to button over the body down to the waist. The loops to be four inches in length at the top and reduced gradually to three inches at the bottom.[47] The cuffs, collar and shoulder straps the colour of the facings of the regiments which is not to be varied from what is specified hereafter. A standing collar 3 inches in breadth which with the shoulder straps are to be laced round. The cuffs 3 ½ inches in breadth with 4 buttons and loopings on each. Cross pocket flaps for the grenadier and battalions, and to open on the outside. For the light infantry they slope diagonally and to open in the plait. On each pocket flap 4 buttons and loopings. The buttons on the cuffs, pocket flaps and hips of the grenadiers and battalion to be large; on other parts of their coat to be small as are the whole on the jackets for the light infantry. The wings of the grenadiers and light infantry to be scarlet cloth, with 6 darts of lace on each; besides which the grenadiers have a row of lace on the bottom of the wings, and those for the light infantry are to be laced round; a diamond of lace between the hip buttons, over the joining of the back skirts which are to fold well over. The buttons to be set on at equal distances, 2 and 2, 3 and 3 according to the order for the regiment. The serjeants lace is a white worsted braid. NorthB.—The serjeants of the Royal staff corps are similar to the above, but without loopings & feathered with white on the collar, cuffs and straps.) Z.

(Para 41.) A. serjeants' coats of highland regiments in Europe, &c. Z.
B. 'No regulation inserted'.
(D.—[7 July 1790; 28 October 1797; 9 April 1800; 20 May 1801, C.] The coats for serjeants of highland regiments are to be similar to those described for other regiments, excepting that they are to have but 8 buttons on the fronts of the coats and 3 on each pocket flap, which is to open and slope diagonally like those for light infantry. The lace for the 42nd is white silk instead of worsted.) Z.
(Para 42.) A serjeants' coats of regiments or corps of infantry in East or West Indies.
B. 'No regulation inserted'.
(D.—[7 Jul. 1790; 8 Jul. 1791; 30 Nov. 1796; 28 Oct. 1797; 20 May 1801, C.]

---

45 'Chevrons instead of epaulettes & knots'. This is a note in pencil in Z, immediately preceding para 39, but appears to be a general note and not with reference to Para 39 only.
46 'Or at the C. of G. Hope' has been crossed out in Z and also in D.
47 'and set on horizontally' has been added here in Z.

The coats for serjeants of regiments or corps of infantry (excepting those of people of colour) which are serving the East or West Indies are to be similar in every respect as for those regiments which may be in Europe, excepting that they are to be without lining. In lieu of which the inside of the fronts of the coats are to be faced with scarlet cloth, as far back as the looping are set on.) Z.

(Para 43.) A. serjeants coats of rifle corps in Europe, &c. Z.
B. 'No regulation inserted'.
(D.—['1 Dec. 1800 and supposed to be at the present time,' C.] The jackets for serjeants of rifle corps are to be of dark green cloth without lining, except the sleeves, but the Inside of the fronts are to be faced with green cloth. Rather short skirted and not turned back, but cut to slope off behind. No lapels and made to button over the body down to the waist. Standing collar which with the cuffs are to be of black cloth and feathered with white. Three rows of buttons on the fronts of the jackets and 12 in each row; two rows on one side and one row and holes on the other, The buttons set on at equal distances but the rows 7 ½ inches apart at the top and reduced gradually to 2 ½ at the bottoms. The cuffs 2 ½ inches in breadth and Pointed, opening at the Hand with 4 buttons. The pockets pretty high on the fronts of the jackets and the welts set on sloping. A button on each hip and the back skirts made to fold well over. The buttons small throughout, being very much raised, with a bugle horn and crown over it engraved. NB.—No provision made for this corps if serving in the West Indies.) Z.

*Query: Whether it will not be expedient to fix on general uniform for rifle corps or companies permitting no other variation than with respect to the buttons & facing*48 As there are more than one rifle corps, and the dress of each different, it appears to be requisite to mention that the description given has been solely for Colonel
Manningham's corps. The following are the dresses for the private men of the 5th battalion of the 60th regiment and also for the rifle companies of the five other battalions of this regiment no uniform could be seen but for the privates.

5th battalion of the 60th regiment. The jackets of the private men of the battalion are of green cloth, without lapels or lining, but the fronts of the jacket faced with green cloth, and made to button over the body down to the waist with 9 buttons. The skirts rather short and lined with green serge. The hind skirts fold over between the hip buttons and also turned back to meet the front skirts, with a button in the joining, and each have a slip of red cloth along the edge of the skirt lining. 6 darts of lace on each wing, which with a red standing collar are laced round. The cuffs, red cloth made pointed, and to open at the wrist with 2 buttons. The shoulder straps of green cloth with a red feathered edge. No pocket flaps, and the pockets to open at the plait. The whole of the buttons small. The lace a scarlet worsted binding. A white milled serge waistcoat with sleeves and blue cloth pantaloons.

The rifle corps of the 1st, 2nd, 3rd, 4th & 6th battalion of the 60th regiment. The jackets for the rifle corps of the above battalions are of green cloth without lapels or lining except the sleeves. The inside of the breast fronts (faced) with red cloth, and made to button over the body down to the waist with 10 buttons, short skirts, not turned back, but cut to slope off

---

48   Appended to E in the same writing, but in ink, is the note which follows. These noted in E are not reproduced in Z.

behinds, with the pocket flaps sloping like light infantry & the pockets in the plait. Round cuffs with 4 buttons on each and without slits. The cuffs, shoulder straps and a standing collar of green cloth, No wings or lace, but the edges of the whole jacket feathered with red cloth. The back skirts to fold well over between the hip buttons, and all the buttons on the jacket small.

A white milled serge waistcoat with sleeves. Green cloth breeches, and black cloth woolen gaiters.

(Para 44.) A. Serjeants jackets of regiments of people of colour. Z.
B. 'No regulation inserted'.
(D.—[24 April 1795; 30 Nov. 1796; 9 April 1800; 20 May 1801. C.] The jackets for serjeants of regiments of people of colour to be of scarlet cloth, very short skirted and not made to turn back, but cut to slope off behind. No sleeves linings and only part of the body lined. Half lapels and made to button over the body down to the waist. A standing collar of scarlet cloth. The lapels, cuffs, and shoulder straps the colour for the facings of the regiment and not to be varied from what is specified hereafter. 3 buttons, and loopings on each lapel. The lapels 3 inches in breadth at the bottom and increasing gradually to 4 at the top. The cuffs 2 inches in breadth, pointed and opening at the Hand with 2 buttons. The collars, cuffs and shoulder straps laced round and one button on each hip and the back skirts to fold well over. The buttons small throughout and set on at equal distances. The lace of the whole to be white silk.) Z.

(Para 45.) A.B.C.[49] 'NB.—No regulation for the clothing of the Queen's Rangers which appears by Letter of 18 Nov. 1781, To be green with blue cuff and cape. No mention of breeches and waistcoats'.

D.—[50]North B.—The 33rd regiment have white shoulder straps (this is struck out in pencil) and custom has made most regiments put on the wings of the grenadiers and light infantry a very full worsted fringe, as also a grenade on the skirts of the grenadier coats and a bugle horn on those of light infantry.

Query. Whether it would not be expedient expressly to allow the use of these articles or else discontinue them.
Z.[51] NB.—The grenadiers and light infantry at the option of the colonel of regiments are permitted to wear, the former a grenade, the latter a bugle on the turn back of the skirt of the coats. They are also permitted to wear worsted fringe on the wings which must however be made in strict conformity to the patterns lodged at the officer of the Comptrollers of army accounts.

49 This note occurs at the foot of the page and underneath, but not in, columns A B C. It is not reproduced in Z.
50 This note occurs at the foot of the page. It is not reproduced in Z, but instead appears the two sentences that follow note 51.
51 This explains the note mentioned in footnote 50.

(Para 46). A. Corporals and private men's coats & jackets. Z.

b. The coats of corporals to have a silk epaulette on the right shoulder. The coats of the grenadiers to have the usual wings of red cloth on the point of the shoulder, with six loops of lace of the same sort as the button holes and a border on the bottom. The men's coats to be looped with worsted lace, but no border, the ground of the lace to be white with coloured stripes. To have white buttons. The breadth of the lace to make the loop round the button hole to be about half an inch. Four loops to be on the sleeves, and four on the pockets, with two on each side of the slit behind.

The breadth of the lapels to be three inches, to reach down to the waist, and not to be wider at the top than the bottom. The sleeves of the coats to have a small round cuff without and slit, and to be made so that they may be unbuttoned and let down.— The whole to have cross pockets, The flap to be sewed down, and the pocket to be cut in the lining of the coat. The cuffs of the sleeves which turns up, to be three inches and a half deep.

(D.—['Similar dates as stated for the serjeants,' C.] The coats for corporals & private men of the guards and regiments or corps of infantry in every country (excepting of rifle corps) are to be of red cloth instead of scarlet and of inferior quality to the serjeants and on every service they are to be exactly similar in the colour of the facings, in the formation, turning back or sloping off the skirts, and in setting on the lace, buttons, shoulder straps, & pocket flaps as also the wings of grenadiers, and light infantry as already described for the serjeants of their respective regiments or corps. The lace is to be throughout a white worsted ground with distinguishing stripes or worms as per general view of the facings, etc. The corporal's knots to be white silk varied something like the lace, excepting for the guards, whose knots and lace are to be entirely white. The knots to be silk, the lace worsted and about ½ inch in breadth. The corporals and private men of the guards to have their coats lined throughout with white serge, those in regiments the Royal staff corps, or other corps of infantry serving in Europe or North America[52] are to have no sleeve linings. In every other respect, in Europe or on any other Station, they are lined, the Inside with serge or faced with cloth, and the skirts turned back and faced, etc. with white or buff serge in a similar manner as those for serjeants, but of a coarser quality. The corporals of grenadiers and light infantry are to wear two epaulettes or knots; those of the battalion to wear one on the right shoulder. The regimental button to be white throughout. The jackets for corporals & private men of the rifle corps are to be of dark green cloth, inferior in quality to the serjeants', but in formation, colour of the collar, cuffs & shoulder straps, and in the buttons, etc. etc. exactly similar to the serjeants. Each corporal is to wear 2 epaulettes or knots which are to be of green and black worsted instead of silk.) Z.

(E. *Chevrons proposed viz. 2 for the corporals, 3 for the serjeants.*)

(Para 47.) Serjeant's waistcoats when serving in Europe, North America, Cape of Good Hope or West Indies, with the compensation, while serving in the East Indies. Z.

B. The buttonholes or the waistcoats to be plain, and without braid looping. (D.—[15 April 1781; 14 Nov. 1782; 9 April 1800; 23 April 1801; 20 May 1802,

---

52 'or at the cape of Good Hope' was written in D and Z, but crossed out in both.

C.] The waistcoats for serjeants of the guards and regiments or corps of infantry serving in Europe, and North America are to e of cloth nearly similar in quality to their coats, and in colour white or buff as the linings of the coat, They are to be single breasted with 8[53] small buttons on one side and button holes on the other without lace. Are to be short and without pockets or skirts. The first waistcoat issued to a serjeant Is to be complete after which he is to be annually entitled to the fronts of a waistcoat only. The waistcoats for serjeants of regiments or corps serving the West India (excepting regiments of people of colour) consist of white milled serge and are to be at all times issued complete, the back being supplied in lieu of lining of the coat. They are to be serge in formation similar to those in Europe but in addition they are to have serge sleeves with cuffs and collars as the facings. For which each serjeant will have to pay 1s./10d. annually and the sleeves are to be considered as part of their regimental necessaries. The waistcoats for serjeants in highland regiments are in quality similar to other regiments, according to their station of service, but rather shorter on account of the kilt. The waistcoats for serjeants of the rifle corps are to be of dark green kersey, and issued at all times complete. To be single breasted with 12 buttons on one side and holes on the other, without loopings.

The fronts rather short and no skirts or pockets. The buttons, the small uniform ones similar to those on the jackets. The serjeants in regiments or corps of infantry serving in the East Indies receive a credit in money in lieu of waistcoats as will be specified hereafter. The serjeants in regiments of people of colour are not to have waistcoats and receive a compensation as will be stated under the article of breeches.) Z.

(Para 48.) A. Serjeants breeches when serving in Europe, North America or at the Cape of Good Hope and the compensation when serving in the East or West Indies. Z.
B. 'No regulation inserted'.
(D.—[4 February 1769; 15 April 1781; 14 Nov. 1782; 28 Oct. 1797; 9 April 1800; 23 April 1801; 21 May 1801, C.] The breeches for serjeants of the guards and of regiments or corps on infantry servicing in Europe, North America excepting the Royal staff corps, are to be of[54] cloth similar to their coats and of the same colour as the lining.

They are to be made to come well up on the hips, and below the knees as far as the calf of the leg, unlined except the waistbands, and the seams covered, on the inside, on the fork, with one pocket on the right side. One small regimental button, and white tape strings at each knee and another button behind, set on above the knee band, to keep up the garters. The serjeants in regiments or corps of infantry serving in the West Indies excepting the people of colour are to receive annually I pair of linen trousers in lieu of breeches. The serjeants in regiments or corps of infantry serving in the East Indies are to have the following compensation in lieu of waistcoat and breeches, etc., *viz.*

For fronts of waistcoats and buttons	4s. 11d.
For a pair of breeches	10s. 9d.
For lining of the coat	1s 2.
16s. 10d.	

---

53   '8' is in Z only.
54   'white' is here written in D and crossed out. Not inserted in Z.

This sum to be annually credited to their accounts at the time of delivering the clothing, and in consequence, they are to be provided and charged with the expense of the proper substitute for these articles which is to be obtained in that country. The serjeants of the highland corps when serving in Europe, North America,[55] are annually to receive on the delivery of the clothing, 4 pairs of hose, besides which they are to receive[56] *at the rate of 12 yards of plaid*[57] *in 4 years* and a purse once in every seven years. When these corps are serving in the East or West Indies they are to lay aside the highland dress altogether, and are to receive clothing in every respect similar to the other regiments of infantry that are serving in those climates. The serjeants of the rifle corps serving in Europe, North America are to wear green cloth pantaloons similar in quality and colour to their coats. They are to be made to come down to the ankles. The serjeants of the Royal staff corps when serving in Europe, North America are to wear dark blue cloth pantaloons. They are to be made to come down to the ankles.[58] The serjeants in regiments of people of colour are to wear Russia duck trowsers of which they are annually to receive two pairs in lieu of waistcoats & breeches &c., *& the staff corps when serving in the West Indies come under the regulation of regular corps serving in that climate.*) Z.

(Para 49.) A. Corporals & private men's breeches, etc. Z.
B. 'No regulation inserted'.
(D.—['Similar dates as stated for the serjeants,' C.] The breeches for corporals and private men of the guards and regiments of corps of infantry serving in Europe, North American are in like manner as the serjeants to made of cloth in quality equal to their coats, and of the same colour and formation, etc., as the serjeants of their respective corps.[59] The corporals & private men in regiments or corps of infantry in the West Indies (excepting regiments of people of colour) receive annually as the serjeants a pair of linen trowsers in lieu of breeches. The corporals and private men in regiments or corps of infantry serving in the East Indies are to have the following compensation in lieu of waistcoats and breeches, *viz.*

For fronts of waistcoats & buttons	1s 9d.
For pair of breeches	4s 6d.
For lining of coat	1s 0d.
7s. 3d.	

This sum to be annually credited to their accounts, and the proper substitute for these articles to be provided as directed for the serjeants. The corporals and private men of highland

---

55   In D is here stated 'or at the Cape of Good Hope are not to wear breeches and in lieu, they'. This is crossed out and does not appear in Z.

56   In D is her stated '6 Yards of plaid once in two years'. This is crossed out and is penciled '*At the rate of 12 yds. In 4 years*'.

57   A pencil note in E reads: '*Query. Whether this allowance of plaid is intended solely for the purpose of making the kilt. Is the use of the plaid in other forms discontinued? I thought it was continued as an article of dress, though the great coat was substituted on service*'. '*Certainly & the difference may be made up by the colonel furnishing… [Illegible.]*'

58   In D is here inserted: 'N.B. No provision made for the rifles and staff corps when in the East or West Indies,' and crossed out in pencil. It is not in Z.

59   In D is here written: 'but in wearing, the waistcoat is to be inside the waistband of the breeches and the buttoning of the coat to come down to prevent the waistcoat from being seen'. This is crossed out and does not appear in Z.

regiment serving in Europe and North America are to be provided with hose, kilt and purse in the same manner as directed for serjeants, and when serving in the East or West Indies they are to be provided with similar clothing throughout, as other regiments of the line serving in these climates. The corporals and private men of a rifle corps serving in Europe, North America are to be provided with green cloth pantaloons in Lieu of breeches, in a similar manner and form as directed for serjeants. The corporals & private men of the Royal staff corps serving in Europe, North American are in like manner to be provided with dark blue cloth pantaloon as directed for serjeants.[60] The corporals and private men of regiments of people of colour are to be provided annually with two pairs of Russia duck trowsers in lieu of waistcoats and breeches as stated for the serjeants'. Z.

(Para 50A.) A. drummers coats of the guards and of Royal regiments and regiments of the line when in Europe, North America or at the Cape of Good Hope. Z.
B. The coats of drummers & fifers of all the Royal regiments are to be red, faced and lapelled with blue and laced with Royal lace. Those for the drummers and fifers of the regiments which are faced with red, are to be white, faced, lapelled & lined with red. Those of all other regiments are to be of the colour of the facings of their regiments faced and lapelled with red. To be laced in such manner as the colonel shall think fit. The lace to be of the colour of that on the soldiers coats. The coats to have no hanging sleeves behind.
(D.—['Similar dates as stated for the serjeants,' C.] The coats for drummers and fifers of the guards and of all Royal regiments or Royal corps of infantry serving in Europe, North American are to be of red cloth similar in quality and colour as for the rank and file. For those corps that are faced with red or black there are to be of white cloth and for all other corps or regiments the coats are to the colour of the facings of the regiments and of a superior quality to the rank and file. They are to by short skirted and lined throughout. Those regiments that are faced with white, red, black, or buff are to have red linings to their coats. The guards and all other regiments or corps are to have white linings. The front-skirts turned back and faced as the linings and the edge laced; those of the guards with a blue feathered edge under the laced.

No lapels but made to buttons over the body down to the waist. Both fronts of the coats looped with laced and ten buttons (or in proportion for boys) set on one side and holes on the other. The lace set on the fronts as stated for their regiments. The cuffs, collar, wings, and shoulder-straps for the guards and for all Royal regiments or corps to be of dark blue cloth. For all other regiments or corps they are to be of scarlet cloth. The pocket flaps and buttons set on as stated for the respective regiments and, where the size of the boys will admit, to have the same number. The seams of the coats to be laced, but the bars of lace on the sleeves to be in the option of the colonel. The cuffs of the drummer of the guards to be indented, for all other regiments or corps to be round and without slits. The drummer of the guards to have three rows of double lace down each front of the coat and two rows of single lace down the back between the rows of lace on the seams. The fronts of the coats to be edges with lace (besides the loopings) as also the skirts and pockets flaps in the same manner as their

---

60   In D is here written: 'N.B.. No provision made for the rifle and staff corps when in the East or West Indies'. This is crossed out and does not appear in Z.

regiments. The wings of the drummers of the guards to have darts of white silk lace, and with the collar is laced round with the same Sort of lace, besides which both have a white silk fringe. The whole of the other lace on the coats for the drummers of the guards and for the drummers of Royal regiments or Royal corps comes under the denomination of Royal lace, and consists of blue and white, or blue white and yellow worsted, considerably raised above the common lace. The lace for drummers of all other regiments is raised in the same manner and is a mixture of coloured worsted approaching nearly to the colour of the lace of the rank and file, but the pattern of it is various and has been in the option of the colonel.[61] The coats for drummers in the highland corps are to be similar to those described for other regiments excepting that there are to be but eight buttons on the front of the coats and three on each pocket flap, which are to slope diagonally.) Z.

(Para 50B.) A. Drummers' coats or jackets when serving in the East or West Indies. Z.
B. 'No regulation inserted'.
(D.—['Similar dates as stated for serjeants,' C.] The coats for drummers in regiments or corps of infantry serving the East or West Indies (excepting those of people of colour) are to be in colour as directed for other regiments but to be without lining, the fronts of the coats beings faced with cloth as already stated. The coats for drummers of the Royal staff corps to be similar to those regiments of the line that are faced with blue. The jackets for drummers of regiments of people of colour are to be in the colour similar as directed for other regiments, but to have half lapels, which with the cuffs and wings, are to be of scarlet cloth as other corps, and a standing collar of the same colour as the body of the coat which is to be laced round. The buttons and loopings to be set on similar as directed for the regiments with the addition of lace on the wings and down the seams of the coat and sleeves. The lace is at present white and the option of the Colonel.) Z.

(Para 51.) A. Buglers' jackets for the rifle corps. Z.
B. 'No regulation inserted'.
(D.—['The same,' C.] The jackets for buglers of the rifle corps are to be of dark green cloth: in the formation, number of buttons, and setting them on, etc., to be similar to the rank and file, with the collar, cuff, shoulder straps and wings of black cloth. The seams throughout to be feathered with white, and a black and white worsted fringe on each wing.

(Para 52.) A. Armourers' jackets for the rifle corps
B. 'No regulation inserted'.
D.—['The same,' C.] The jackets for the armourers of the rifle corps to be of dark grey cloth, and in the formation, number of buttons etc. and setting them on to be similar to the rank and file. The cuffs and collars to be of dark green cloth and the seams throughout feathered with green.[62]
    (East *I believe it is intended that the armourers should be serjeant-armourers, consequently their dress should correspond with their rank in the regiment.*)

---

61 In D is here inserted: 'N.B. In the lace for the Coldstream regiment of guard the clue is represented to be the Flower of Luce'. This is crossed out in pencil and '*Yes*' is added in pencil. It is omitted from Z.
62 The whole of D has been crossed out in pencil. Not any part of Para. 52 appears in Z.

(Para 53.) A. Waistcoats and breeches for drummers & fifers. Z.

B. The waistcoats & breeches of the drummers & fifers of all the Royal regiments are to be of the same colour as that which is ordered for their respective regiments. Those of regiments faced with red, buff or white to have red waistcoats & breeches, and those of all other regiments, are to be of the same colour as the men.

(D.—['Similar dates as stated for the serjeants,' C.] The waistcoats and breeches, or the articles substituted for them, for the drummers and fifers of the guards and regiments or corps of infantry as also for the buglers and armourers[63] of rifle corps, to be exactly similar to what has been already specified for the rank and file of their respective regiments according to the service or Station they may be upon. The compensation of money in lieu of waistcoats and breeches for drummers and fifers serving in the East Indies, and the substitute to be provided for them, to be also similar to the rank and file as heretofore stated for corps serving in that country.) Z.

(Para 54.) A. Great coats. Z.

B. 'No regulation inserted'.

(D.—[28 Oct 1797; 23 April 1801, C.] The non-commissioned officers, drummers, fifers and private men in the guards and regiments or corps of infantry serving at home or abroad (excepting those in the East Indies and in regiments of people of colour) are from 25th December 1802 to be constantly supplied with great coats. They are to be of a dark grey woolen stuff kersey wove, loose made, to come well up about the neck, have a large falling cape to cover the shoulders, and they are to reach down to (or below) the calf of the leg, as per pattern great coat left at the comptrollers officer for army accounts. And as they are to be supplied from a fund principally created by a gratuitous bounty from the public, they are to last not less than three years and are to be considered as regimental necessaries or appointments. And in order that a strict attention shall be given to the preservation of them and to prevent their being lost or prematurely worn out by abuse or neglect each individual in whose possession they ought to be at the time, shall be responsible and liable by a stoppage from his pay to make good the loss or damage that may occur by neglect or misconduct, during the said period of three years, which time these great coats ought to last with but common attention and care. The price of each great coat is 14s./6d., created by annual saving of 1s./10d. made by the present disuse of lapels and formation of the clothing for the army. To which is added an annual donation of 3s./-- thereby forming the sum of 14s./6d. in three years.—And as the annual donation on the clothing of a highland regiment is but /10d. the donation to these corps in annually 4s./-- to enable them to have a similar great coat fund as to other regiments. In consideration of which these corps are to be supplied with great coats similar to other corps and are to lay aside the plaid usually worn by them, *except as articles of parade.*64 And as it is proper that the strictest economy and attention should be paid to the disposal of the fund for supplying and keeping in repair the great coats and to guard against profusion or mismanagement of the same, 'It is to be put under the special care and direction of the officer who is commanding the regiment or corps (he not being

---

63   The word 'armourers' is underlined in both D and Z.

64   In E there is added: '*Query. The plaid is supposed to be laid aside altogether*'.

under the rank of a field officer) on the 25th of December. Which account is (to) be signed upon honour. As is more particularly specified by a special warrant bearing date the 22nd of April 1801'. And as a similar saving by the disuse of lapels and in the formation of clothing arises to the regiments or corps of infantry serving in the East Indies, the disposal of the same for the benefit of the men is to be complied with by the officer commanding the regiment or corps, as specified in the said warrant of the 22nd April 1801. Great coats for the regiments of people of colour are considered as forming part of their regimental clothing, and to be supplied by the colonel (as mentioned in the said warrant of 22nd April 1801) once in two years for each man.) Z.

(Para 55.) A. felt caps.[65] Z.
B. The hats of serjeants to be laced with silver. Those of corporals and private men to have a white tape binding. The breadth of the whole to be one inch and a quarter; and no more to be on the back part of the brim, than what is necessary to sew it down. To have black cockades. (D.—[4 Feb. 1769; 21 Oct. 1783; 21 July 1784; 16 July 1787; 1 March 1790; 8 July 1791; 15 Dec. 1793; 24 Feb. 1801, C.] Caps made of felt and leather with a brass plates, cockade and tuft (conformable to a pattern left at the Comptroller office for army accounts) to be worn, instead of hats, by the non-commissioned officers, drummers, fifers and privates of the guards and by every description of corps of infantry, excepting the highland corps, who are, when in Europe, North America, to continue to wear the highland bonnet, but when in the East and West Indies, are to wear the felt caps similar to other regiments. They are to be made of sufficient size to come completely on the head. To be worn straight and even and brought well forward over the eyes.
The felt cap and the tuft is to be supplied annually. The leather part, brass plate & leather cockade once in every two years. It is permitted to engrave the number of the regiment on each side of the lion, on the lower part of the brass fronting and those regiments that are entitled to badges are permitted to bear them in the centre of the Garter. The grenadiers who are allowed to wear these caps occasionally may also bear the grenade in the same manner as other regiments wear their badges. The tufts worn by the battalion to be white with a red bottom, by the grenadiers to be all white and by the light infantry to be dark green. The whole to wear the button of their respective regiments in the centre of the cockade, excepting the grenadiers who are to have a grenade. The rifle corps not to wear the brass fronting on their caps, but in lieu to have a bugle & crown with a green cord round the cap.[66] The serjeants, buglers, and rank and file to wear green feathers.) Z.

(Para 56.) A. Grenadiers bear skin caps. Z.
B. [This is the same as D except that D states 'the badge of the Royal regiments is to be white,' and badges of other line regiments are not mentioned.]

65 In Z is added in pencil: 'To be altered to the new regulation'.
66 In D is here stated: 'The serjeant and buglers to wear green feathers, the rank and file and armourers a green tuft similar to light infantry'. This sentence is amended in D and reproduced in Z as above.

(D.—['No alteration,' C.] The caps of the grenadiers to be of black bear skin. On the front, the King's crest[67] *in brass* on a black ground with the motto 'Nec aspera terrent'. A grenade on the back part, with the number of the regiment on it. The Royal regiments and the six old corps are to have the crest and grenade, and also the other particulars specified hereafter. The badges of the regiments are to be white and set near the top of the back part of the cap. The height of the cap (without the bear skin which reaches beyond the top) to be twelve inches.) Z.

(Para 57.) A. Caps for the officers and men of regiment of fusiliers. Z.
B. [same as D, but exclusive of the last sentence.]
(D.—['No alteration,' C.] The regiments of fusiliers to have black bear skin caps. They are to be made in the same manner as those which have been ordered for the grenadiers, but not so high, and not to have a grenade on the back part of the cap.

These regiments are also to wear the felt cap on common parades like other regiments and with similar tufts.) Z.

(Para 58.) A. Drummers and fifers caps. Z.
B. [same as D before alteration.]
(D.—['No alteration,' C.] The drummers and fifers to have black bear skin caps, on the front the King's crest of[68] *brass* on a black ground, with trophies of colours and drums. The number of the regiment on the back part as also the badge if entitled to any as ordered for the grenadiers.)[69] Z/

(Para 59.) Black leather stocks. Z.
B. 'No regulation inserted'.
(D.—[8 July 1791, C.] Black leather stocks to be worn by the non- commissioned officers, drummers, fifers and privates of the guards and by every other description of regiments or corps of infantry.) Z.

(Para 60.) A. Serjeants sashes. Z.
B. The sashes to be of crimson worsted, with a stripe of the colour of the facing of the regiment, and worn round the waist. –Those of the regiments which are faced with red, to have a stripe of white.
(D.—[12 August 1799, C.] The sashes for the serjeants of the 1st regiment of Guards are to be of crimson worsted with a white stripe, for the Coldstream regiment to be crimson worsted throughout, and for the 3rd regiment of the Guards to be in three stripes of crimson, white and blue worsted. Those for regiments or corps of infantry that are faced with red or purple

---

67 In D was written here 'of silver plated metal'. This was crossed out and amended in pencil to 'in brass' which was reproduced in Z. In E was the following in pencil, 'Query. *With respect to the colour of the plate I believe it is His Royal Highnesses intention that the whole shall hereafter be of brass*'.
68 In D was originally written here, 'silver plated metal'. This was altered in pencil to 'brass' which was reproduced in Z.
69 In D was here written: 'N.B. The drummers caps of the Coldstream Regiment of Guards have a drum on the back part of the cap and the whole wear their feathers with the bearskin caps' (the last phrase is underlined). This paragraph is crossed out in pencil and in E appears a note in pencil: '*I do not understand this*'. It does not appear in Z.

to be crimson worsted with a stripe of white in the middle. For other regiments or corps to be crimson also with a stripe down the middle of the same coloured worsted as the facings of the regiment. Those for the rifle corps to be stripes of black, crimson and green worsted. They are to be worn over the coat round the waist, and outside the shoulder belt, with the tie and ends hanging on the left side; excepting the highland corps, who are to wear them over the left shoulder with the tie and ends hanging on the right side.) Z.

(Para 61.) A. Quantity of ammunition; magazine; pouch; badges on pouches. Z.
B. 'No regulation inserted'.
(D.—[21 July 1784; 13 Aug. 1798, C.] Sixty rounds of ammunition to be carried by each rank and file of the guards and regiments or corps of infantry when upon actual service, Twenty-four of which are to be in a tin case furnished on such occasions by the Board of Ordnance. This magazine is to be covered with black leather and delivered complete with buff straps and buckles to be occasionally fastened to the bayonet belt. The remaining 36 rounds are to be carried in a pouch in which there is to be a double box of wood bored with this number of holes. The flap of the pouch is to be plain (excepting the guards) and the bottom part of the corners rounded and fastened underneath the pouch by a strap and button. There is also to be attached to the pouch and covered by a flap a small leather pocket for carrying spare flints, turn-screws, etc. The regiments of guards wear their badges, or other ornaments on the flaps of the pouch.) Z.

(Para 62A.) A. Pouch & bayonet belts for the guards and regiments of infantry. Z.
B. The breadth of the shoulder belt to be two inches and three quarters; that of the waist belt to be two inches; and those regiments which have buff waistcoats are to have buff coloured accoutrements. Those which have white waistcoats are to have white.
(D.—[1 July 1784; 13 Aug. 1798, C.] The belts for the pouches and bayonet are to worn cross-ways over the shoulders and to consist of buff leather of equal breadth *viz:* 2 1/8 inches which are to be coloured white for all regiments excepting those which are faced with buff; for these corps they are to be of that colour. The belt is to be fastened to the pouch by two small buff straps and buckles under the pouch and to admit of being shortened or lengthened according to the size of the man. The plate of the bayonet belt to have the number of the regiment and to be placed so as to cover both belts where they meet on the breast. On the Inside of the bayonet belt there are to be two Ds to which the magazine straps are to be occasionally buckled.[70] *The belts of people of colour are to be of black leather the same breadth as regiments of the line.*) Z.[71]

---

70 In D is written: 'N.B. The belts for the line at 2 1/8 inches in breadth are thought by the accoutrements makers too narrow for the weight of the 60 rounds of ammunition'. Also the following note: 'The belts of the guards are broader than the line, and the bayonet belt narrower than the pouch belt, on being 2 ½ inches, the other 2 1/4. Besides this difference with the line the pouch belt has (exclusive of Fastening underneath) two oblong brass buckles and brass tips on the ends of the belt. These buckles appear to be about 6 inches above the pouch and cause the pouch belt to be in three pieces'. This is crossed out in pencil, as are also the following pencil notes which appear in E: 'I believe this observation applies only to the Coldstream regiment'. 'This is deferred till a reference is had to general officers'. Not any of this footnote is reproduced in Z.

71 In D is written: 'N.B. There does not appear to be any order relative to the Regt. Of People of Colour. It is therefore concluded that they are to be similar to other Regiments although they have Black Leather Belts at present'. This is

(Para 62B.) (D.—['1 July 1784; supposed to be intended,' C.] The magazines are not to be worn on the common marches at home, but only to be used on actual service. No regiment or corps of infantry to embark for a foreign station without being in possession of these magazines.) Z.

(Para 62C.) A. Firelock sling. Z.
B. 'No regulation inserted'.
(D.—[13 August 1798, C.] The sling for the firelock to be of buff leather 1 ½ inches in breadth and to be the same colour as the pouch and bayonet belts.) Z.

(Para 63A.) A. Pouch and pouch belt, horn, etc., for rifle corps. Z.
B. 'No regulation inserted'.
(D.—['1st December 1800 and date of establishment,' C.] The pouch for a rifle corps to have wooden box boxed for 12 rounds, and another tin capable of holding 24 rounds. The flap of the pouch without ornaments and rounded at the corners and fastened underneath with a strap and button. The pouch belt to be of black leather 2½ inches in breadth and fastened to the pouch by straps and buckles similar to the line.
   They are also to have a powder horn laying nearly on the outside top of the pouch, which is suspended by a green cord that passes over the belt and across the left shoulder; likewise a small powder flask kept on the breast and suspended from the neck by a green cord.) Z.[72]
F. 'Colonel Manningham's corps'.

(Para 63B.) A. Waist-belt for ditto. Z.
B. 'No regulation inserted'.
(D.—['1st December 1800 and date of Establishment,' C.] The sword bayonet belt to be also of black leather and the same breadth as the pouch belt It is to be worn round the waist and over[73] the jacket, to which the carriage for the sword bayonet is fixed, as also a ball bag which hangs nearly in the front of the body'. Z.

(Para 63C.) A. Rifle sling. Z.
B. 'No regulation inserted'.
(D.—[1 December 1800, C.] The sling for the rifle is likewise to be of black leather and 1 3/8 inches in breadth.) Z.

(Para 64A.) Long gaiters. Z.
B. The serjeants, corporals, drummers, fifers and private men to have black linen gaiters of the same sort, as is ordered for officers; also black garters and uniform buckles.
(D.—[21 July, 1784, C.] Black woolen cloth long gaiters to be worn by non- commissioned officers, drummers, fifers and private men of the guards and regiments or corps of infantry

---

crossed out in pencil, and in E is a pencil note: '*Query. I should imagine Black Belts are better adapted to their use*'. '*Yes*'. This is also crossed out, and in E is written: '*The Belts for Regiments. Of People of Colour are to be of Black Leather the same as Regiments. Of the Line*'. This latter sentence only appears in Z

72   In E is written in ink: 'Query. Are the lt. infantry to carry Hatchets and Powder Horns?'
73   In D was written 'under/over,' but 'under' was crossed out.

serving in Europe, North America (excepting by the highland corps, the rifle corps, and the Royal staff corps). They are to come up over the breeches to the edge of the cap of the knee and to be rounded off so as to cover the knee band of the breeches behind, without appearing to have crease or a wrinkle and be fastened behind to a regimental button set on sufficiently high above the knee band to prevent any opening from appearing between the gaiters and the breeches. The gaiter buttons to be small, of white metal and set on at equal distances.) Z.

(Para 64B.) A. Highland kilt & hose. Z.
B. 'No regulation inserted'.
(D.—['Established custom,' C.] The highland regiments are to wear the kilt and hose as already stated.) Z.

(Para 64C.) A. Linen trowsers. Z.
B. 'No regulation inserted'.
(D.—[9 April 1800; 20 May 1801, C.] These corps when serving in the West Indies are to wear linen trowsers, as already provided instead of gaiters and breeches.) Z.

(Para 64D.) A. Short gaiters. Z.
B. 'No regulation inserted'.
(D.—[1 Dec. 1800 and Date of Establishment,' C.] The serjeants of the rifle corps to wear half boots and the rank & file, buglers, and armourers are to wear black woolen cloth short gaiters, with small white metal buttons, and to come up sufficiently high above the ankles to prevent any opening from appearing between them and the pantaloons.) Z.

(Para 64East) A. Half boots. Z.
B. 'No regulation inserted'.
(D.—[9 April 1800; 20 May 1801, C.] The non-commissioned officers, drummers and private men of the Royal staff corps are to wear half boots, which are to come up sufficiently high above the ankle to prevent an opening from appearing between them and the pantaloons.)[74] Z.

(Para 64F.) A. Russia duck trowsers. Z.
B. 'No regulations inserted'.
(D.—[9 April 1800; 20 May 1801, C.] The regiments of people of colour are to wear Russia duck trowsers as already provided for.) Z.

(Para 64G.) A. Regiments in the East Indies. Z.
B. 'No regulations inserted'.
(D. [9 April 1800; 20 May 1801, C.] The regiments or corps of infantry serving in the East Indies as already stated are to be provided with the proper substitutes in that country.] Z.

---

74 In D is appended the following note: 'N.B. No regulation stated for either the rifle corps or Royal staff corps if serving in the West Indies'. This is not given in Z.

(Para 65A.) A. Serjeants swords. Z.

B. All the serjeants of the regiments, and the whole grenadier company to have swords. The corporals and private men of the battalion companies (excepting the regiment of Royal highlanders) to have no swords.

(D.—['6 July 1782; Supposed to be at the present time,' C.] The swords for serjeants of the guards and of infantry throughout (excepting the rifle corps) to be the same. They are to have a brass hilt, and the grip or handle to be of brass twisted wire, which, with the blades, are to be in the dimensions and form exactly similar as stated for the officers; and are to be worn above the coat across the right shoulder in a buff[75] belt of the same breadth and colour as the men's, with a buckle or plate on the breast.) Z.

(Para 65B.) B. 'No regulation inserted'.

(D.—[8 May 1792, C.] The serjeants of light infantry not to wear swords.) Z.

(Para 66.) A. Drummers swords. Z.

B. All the drummers & fifers to have a short sword with a scimitar blade. (D.—['Supposed to be at the present time,' C.] The swords for drummers to have a straight blade 24 inches in length, with the hilt, grip, and mounting similar to serjeants.[76] N.B. Patterns of the serjeants and drummers swords belts etc. to be left at the Comptroller's office of army account.) Z.

(Para 67.) A. Pikes. Z.

B. The serjeants of grenadiers to have fusils, pouches & caps. Those of the battalion to have halberds & no pouches.

(D.—[7 April 1792; 8 May 1792, C.] Pikes to be carried (instead of halberds) by the serjeants of the guards and regiments and corps of infantry (excepting by the serjeants of light infantry and of the rifle corps). The serjeants of light infantry are to carry fusils and bayonets. Their pouches to be smaller than the men's but of the same form and quite plain; the belts the same breadth as the men's. The serjeants of the rifle corps are to carry a rifle and a sword bayonet. The pouch smaller than the men's and the flap ornamented with a brass lion's head. The belt similar to the men's. They are to have a green ivory whistle, like the officer's, and a powder flask and horn like the men. The sword belt worn round the waist, and to be of the same form and breadth as the men's.) Z.

(Para 68.) A. Pioneers appointments. Z.

B. Each pioneer to have an axe, a saw, and an apron; a cap with a leather crown, and a black bear skin front, on which is to be the King's crest in white, on a red ground; also a saw and an axe. The number of the regiment to be on the back part of the cap.

(D.—['No alteration,' C.] The Pioneers to have an axe, a saw and an apron, exclusive of accoutrements, and arms like the rank & file. They are also to have caps with a leather crown

---

75   'leather' is inserted here in Z.

76   In E is inserted: 'By information from the accoutrement makers'. Not given in Z.

and black bear skin fronts on which are to be the King's crest in white, [white deleted & *brass* inserted] on a red ground, also an axe and a saw. The number of the regiment to be on the back part of the cap. The pioneers are also to have felt caps similar to the battalion.[77])

East *'I believe it is to be H.R.H.s intention to make some alteration in the appointment of the pioneers on the model of those furnished to the Dutch corps'. 'Refer to General Dundas'.*

(Para 69.) A. Hair of the non-commissioned officers, drummers & private men. Z.
B. 'No regulation inserted'.
(D.—['No orders appears relative to hair, but the annexed is inserted as it relates to the soldier under arms, and is supposed to be the present order for the hair,' C.] The hair of the serjeants and the rank and file of infantry throughout to be worn short at the top and sides, and the hind part queued (excepting the grenadiers, light infantry and drummers). The queue is to be 11 inches in length, the ribbon to commence on the hair at the top of the collar of the coat, and to leave about 1 ½ inch of hair out the bottom of the queue; and the fastening of the ribbon to be covered by a black leather rose. The grenadiers, light infantry and drummers to have the hair short at the top and sides, and the hind part plaited and turned up under the cap with a comb, with three doubles and two ends of ribbon hanging down on the collar of the coat from the commencement of the plait.[78]) Z.

(Para 70.) A. Firelock and bayonet, also rifle and bayonet sword. Z.
B. 'No regulation inserted'.
(D.—['Supposed requisite to be inserted,' C.] The rank and file of the guards and of regiments or corps of infantry to be armed with a musket and bayonet. The bayonet --- inches in length, and the whole of the muskets of the same bore. The rank and file of the rifle corps to be armed with a rifle gun and sword bayonet --- inches in length.) Z.

Devices and badges of the royal regiments and of the six old corps, also what have been granted to other regiments.

This space to be left for the guards.[79]

---

77 This is left blank in Z and in its place is the following not: *'To be fixed upon by a Board of General Officers'*.
78 In D is here added: 'N.B. The grenadiers etc. of some regiments wear black leather cut in form of a ribbon'. Crossed out in pencil and not given in Z.
79 This is written in pencil in both MS books. In the first MS book it is followed by this note, also in pencil: *'At the present the badges on the colours are so different and the colours so numerous, there being one for each company, it was judged better to leave the whole Blank until something was defined. The 1st battalion of the Coldstream and the 1st battalion of the 3rd regiment are entitled to the Egyptian badge'.*

First, or Royal Regiment.	In the centre of their colours, the King's cypher, encircled with the collar and crown over it. In the three corners of the second (or regimental colour) a thistle and a crown within the circle of St Andrew and the number of each battalion attached to a label where the wreathe oif roses and thistles unite. On the grenadiers' caps, the King's crest, also the King's cypher, withgin the circle of St Andrew, and crown over it with its appropriate motto. The drums (and bells of arms if to be preserved in the regulation) to have the same device as the caps painted on them and the number of each battalion and rank of the regiment underneath it. The 2nd battalion is also to have the the Egyptian badge. (z. 'Not fixed upon yet.') N.B. This description is taken from the Adjutant-General's letter of 24 November 1801. Vide the printed regulations and the letter. Where there is already a badge on the colours that intended for (Z. Egypt etc.) will require something more particular than when it may happen to be the only badge.
Second, or Queens Royal Regiment.	In the centre of each colour, the Queens cypher on a red ground within the Garter and crown over it. In the three corners of the second colour the Lamb, being the ancient badge of the regiment. On the grenadiers' caps, the King's crest, also the King's cypher and crown over it as in the colours. The drums (and bells of arms, etc.) to have the Queen's cypher painted on them in the same manner and the rank of the regiment underneath. The Egyptian badge.
3rd Regiment, or Buffs.	In the centre of their colours, the dragon, being their ancient badghe, and the rose and crown on the three corners of their second colour. On the grenadiers' caps, the King's crest, also the dragon. The same badge of the dragon to be painted on their drums (and bells of arms) with the rank of the regiment underneath.
4th or King's Own Royal Regiment.	In the centre of their colours the king's cypher on a red ground within the garter and crown over it. In the three corners of theiur second colour the lion of England being their ancient badge. On the grenadiers' caps, the King's crest, also the King's cypher and crown, as in their colours. The drums (and bells of arms) to have the King's cypher painted on them, in the same manner and the rank of the regiment underneath.
5th.	In the centre of their colours, St George killing the dragon, being their ancient badge and in the three corners of the second colour the rose and crown. On the grenadiers' caps the King's crest also St George and the dragon to be painted on their drums (and bells of arms) with the rank of the regiment underneath.
6th.	In the centre of their colours the antelope, being their ancient badge, and in the three corners of the second colour. On the grenadiers' caps the King's crest also the antelope. The same badge of the antelope to be painted on their drums (and bells of arms) with the rank of the regiment underneath.
7th, or Royal Fusiliers.	In the centre of their colours, the rose within the garter, and the crown over it. The white horse in the corners of the second colour. On the grenadiers' caps the King's crest, also the roise within the garter and crown as in the colours. The same device of the rose within the garter and crown on the drums, (and bells of arms). Rank of the regiment underneath.
8th, or King's Regiment.	In the centre of their colours the white horse on a red ground within the garter and crown over it, in the three corners of the second colour the King's cypher and crown. On the grenadiers' caps the King's crest, also the white horse as in the colours. The same device of the white horse within the garter on the drums (and bells of arms). Rank of the regiment underneath. The Egyptian badge.
9th or East Norfolk Regiment.	The badge of Britannia. N.B. The mode of placing the badge of the colours of the 9th regiment is not stated in the Adjutant-General's letter of 9th July 1799.

10th or North Lincoln Regiment.	The Egyptian badge. N.B. One of the regiments from India.
12th or East Suffolk regiment.	The word(s Minden and) Gibraltar upon their grenadier and light infantry caps and upon the plates of their accoutrements and drums and likewise upon their second colour just underneath the number of the regiment. Adjutant-General's letter 28th July 1784.
13th of 1st Somersets regiment.	The Egyptian Sphinx.
14th or Bedfords regiment.	The black bear skin caps of the grenadiers and drummers to be fronted with red. The motto and the horse white metal.
18th or Royal Irish.	In the centre of their colours, the harp in a blue field and the crown over it, and in the three corners of the second colour, the lion of Nassaus, King William III's arms. On the grenadiers [caps], the King's crest, the same manner on their drums (and bells of arms) and the rank of the regiment underneath. The Egyptian badge.
20th or East Devon regiment.	The Egyptian badge (and Minden).
21st of Royal North British Fusiliers.	In the centre of the colours the Thistle within the circle of St. Andrew and crown over it, and in the three corners of the second colour, the King's cypher and crown. On the grenadiers' caps. The King's crest also the Thistle as in the colours. On the drums (and bells of arms) the Thistle and crown to be painted as in the colours. Rank of the regiment underneath.
23rd or Royal Welsh Fusiliers.	In the centre of their colours, the device of the Prince of Wales. Viz. Three feathers issuing out of the Prince's coronet. In the three corners of the second colour, the baadges of Edward the black prince, viz. The rising sun, the red dragon, and the three feathers in the coronet. Motto: Ich Dien. On the grenadiers' caps the King's crest, also the feathers as in the colours. The same badge of the three feathers and motto Ich Dien on the drums (and bells of arms). Rank of the regiment underneath. (This regiment is also entitled to Minden and the Egyptian badge).
24th or Warwick Regiment.[1]	The Egyptian badge. (This regiment was part of the reinforcements).
25th or Sussex Regiment.	Minden. The Egyptian badge. (This regiment was part of the reinforcements).
26th or Cameronian Regiment.	The Egyptian badge. (This regiment was part of the reinforcements).
27th or Enniskillen Regiment.	Allowed to wear in the centre of their colours a castle with three turrets, St George's colours flying in a blue field and the name Enniskillen over it. On the grenadiers' caps the King's crest also the castle and name, on the drums (and bells of arms). Rank of the regiment underneath. Egyptian badge.
28th or North Gloster Regiment.	The Egyptian badge.
30th or Cambridge Regiment.	The Egyptian badge.
37th Regiment.	Minden. The Egyptian badge.
39th Regiment.	The word Gibraltar upon their grenadiers and light infantry caps and upon the plates of their accoutrements and drums as likewise upon the second colour just underneath the neame of the regiment.

42nd or Royal Highlanders.	In the centre of their colours the King's cypher within the Garter and crown over it, under it St. Andrew with the motto Nemo me Impune lacessit, in the three corners of the second colour the King's cypher and crown. On the grenadiers' caps the King's crest also St Andrew as in the colours. On the drums, (and bells of arms), the same device with the rank of the regiment underneath. Egyptian badge.
51st Regiment.	The Egyptian badge.[2] I think Minden. [In Z, 'The Egyptian Badge' has been crossed out and 'Minden' substituted for it.]
44th or East Essex Regiment.	The Egyptian badge.
50th or West Kent Regiment.	The Egyptian badge.
54th or West Norfolk Regiment.	The Egyptian badge.
56th or West Essex Regiment.	The word Gibraltar upon their grenadier and light infantry caps and upon the plates of their accoutrements and drums as likewise upon their second colour just underneath the name of the regiment.
58th or Rutland Regiment.	The word Gibraltar upon their grenadier and light infantry caps and upon the plates of their accoutrements and drums as likewise upon their second colour just underneath the name of the regiment. The Egyptian badge.
60th or Royal Americans.	In the centre of their colours the King's cypher within the Garter and crown over it, in the three corners of the second colour the King's cypher and crown. The colours of the second battalion to be distinguished by a flaming ray of gold descending, from the upper corner of each colour towards the centre. On the grenadiers' caps the King's crest also the King's cypher and crown as in the colours. On the drums and bells of arms the King's cypher printed in the sme manner and the rank of the regiment underneath.
61st or. S. Gloster Regiment.[3]	The Egyptian badge.
79th regiment.	The Egyptian badge.
40th Flank companies only.	The Egyptian badge.

N.B. Whenever the Egyptian badge is decided upon the mode of placing on the colours, drums etc., will have to be expressed.

Notes
1   N.B. These three regiments were part of the reinforcements.
2   In Z 'The Egyptian badge' has been crossed out and 'Minden' substituted for it.
3   Two other regiments (88th and 92nd?) and also a 'Detachment' are also given here in the first MS book, but the names of the regiments are lost owing to the paper being torn.

Colour of the body of coats for rank and file	Colour of the facings of the coats for rank and file	Rank and Title of Regiment	Distinction in the same colour	If gold or silver lace for officers	Colour of the linings and breeches	Colour of lace for rank and file	Buttons, how set on coat
Red	Blue	First Regiment of Guards		Gold	White	White	Equal distances
"	"	Coldstream Guards		Gold	White	White	2 and 2
"	"	3rd Regiment of Guards		Gold	White	White	3 and 3
"	"	1st or the Royal		Gold	White	White with blue double worm	
"	"	2nd or Queen's Royal		Silver	White	White with blue stripe	
"	"	4th or the King's Own		Silver	White	White with blue stripe	
"	"	7th or Royal Fusiliers		Gold	White	White with blue stripe	
"	"	8th or King's		Gold	White	White with blue and yellow stripe	
"	"	18th or Royal Irish		Gold	White	White with blue stripe	
"	"	21st or Royal Fusiliers		Gold	White	Whitw with blue stripe	
"	"	23rd or Royal Welsh Fusiliers		Gold	White	White with red, blue and yellow stripes	
"	"	42nd or Royal Highlanders		Gold	White	White with red stripe	Equal distances
"	"	60th or Royal Americans: 1st,					
"	"	2nd and 3rd battalions		Silver	White linings only	White with two blue stripes	
"	"	4th battalion		Silver	White linings only		
"	"	6th battalion					
Green	Red	60th or Royal Americans: NB one rifle coy to each batt					
Red	Yellow	6th, or 1st Warwick	Deep yellow	Silver	White	White with yellow and red stripes	
"	"	9th or East Norfolk		Silver	White	White with two black stripes	
"	"	10th or North Lincoln	Bright yellow	Silver	White	White with blue stripe	
"	"	12th or East Suffolk		Gold	White	White with yellow, crimson and black	
"	"	13th or 1st Somerset	Philemot yellow	Silver	White	White with yellow stripe	
"	"	15th or East York Riding		Silver	White	White with yellow and black worm and red stripe	
"	"	16th Buckinghams		Silver	White	White with crimson stripe	
"	"	20th or East Devon	Pale yellow	Silver	White	White with red and black stripe	
"	"	25th or Sussex	Deep yellow	Gold	White	White, with blue, yellow and red stripe	
"	"	26th or Cameronian	Pale yellow	Silver	White	White with blue and two yellow stripes	

Colour of the body of coats for rank and file	Colour of the facings of the coats for rank and file	Rank and Title of Regiment	Distinction in the same colour	If gold or silver lace for officers	Colour of the linings and breeches	Colour of lace for rank and file	Buttons, how set on coat
Red	Yellow	28th or North Gloster	Bright yellow	Silver	White	White with one yellow and two black stripes	
"	"	29th or Worcester		Silver	White	White with two blue and one yellow stripe	
"	"	30th Cambridge	Pale yellow	Silver	White	White with sky blue stripe	
"	"	34th or Cumberland	Bright yellow	Silver	White	White with blue and yellow worm and red stripe	
"	"	37th or North Hampshire		Silver	White	White with red and yellow stripe	
"	"	38th or 1st Staffords		Silver	White	White with two red and one yellow stripe	
"	"	44th or East Essex		Silver	White	White with blue, yellow and black stripes	
"	"	46th or S Devon		Silver	White	White with red and purple worms	
"	"	57th or West Middlesex		Gold	White	White with black stripe	
"	"	67th or South Hampshire	Pale Yellow	Silver	White	White with yellow, purple and green stripes	
"	"	75th	Deep yellow		White	White with two yellow and one red stripes	
"	"	77th			White	White with black stripe	
"	"	80th				White with two red and one black stripe	
"	"	82nd or Prince's own				White with black stripe	
"	"	83rd				White with one red and one green stripe	
"	"	84th				White with two scarlet stripes by twos	
"	"	84th				White with two scarlet stripes by two	
"	"	85th or Buckingham's				White with two red worms and two black stripes	
"	"	86th				White with two yellow and two black stripes	
"	"	88th	Pale yellow		White	White with two black, two red & one yellow stripe	
"	"	91st				White with one black stripe and black dart	
"	"	92nd				White with one blue stripe in edges	
"	"	93rd				White with one yellow stripe	
Red	Green	5th or Northumberland	Gosling green	Silver	White	White with two red stripes	

Colour of the body of coats for rank and file	Colour of the facings of the coats for rank and file	Rank and Title of Regiment	Distinction in the same colour	If gold or silver lace for officers	Colour of the linings and breeches	Colour of lace for rank and file	Buttons, how set on coat
Red	Green	11th or North Devon	Full green	Gold	White	White with two red and two green stripes	
"	"	19th or 1st York N Riding	Deep green	Gold	White	White with stripes, red and green	
"	"	24th or Warwick	Willow green	Silver	White	White with one red and one green stripe	
"	"	36th or Hereford		Gold	White	White with one red and one green stripe	
"	"	39th or East Middlesex		Gold	White	White with light green stripe	
"	"	45th or Nottingham	Deep green	Silver	White	White with green stripe	
"	"	49th or Hartford	Full green	Gold	White	White with two red and one green stripe	
"	"	51st or 2nd York W Riding	Deep green	Gold	White	White with green worm stripe	2 and 2
"	"	54th or West Norfolk	Popinjay green	Silver	White	White with green stripe	
"	"	55th or Westmoreland	Dark green	Gold	White	White with two green stripes	
"	"	63rd or West Suffolk	Very deep green	Silver	White	White with very small green stripe	3 and 3
"	"	66th or Berkshire	Yellowish green		White	White with 1 crimson and green and 1 green stripe	
"	"	68th or Durham	Deep green	Silver	White	White with yellow and black stripes	
"	"	69th or S Lincoln	Willow	Gold	White	White with one red and two green stripes	
"	"	73rd	Dark green			White with a scarlet edge	Equal distances
"	"	79th	Dark green			White with one yellow and two red stripes	
"	"	87th				White with red stripe	
Red	Buff	3rd the Buffs, or East Kent			Buff	White with yeloow, black and red stripes	
"	"	14th or Bedford		Silver	Buff	White with blue and red worm and buff stripe	
"	"	22nd or Cheshire	Pale buff	Gold	Pale buff	White with blue and red stripe	
"	"	27th Enniskillen		Gold	1 buff	White with blue and red stripe	Equal distances
"	"	31st or Huntingdon		Silver	Buff	White with blue and yellow worm and small red st	
"	"	40th or 2nd Somerset		Silver	Buff	White with red and black stripe	
"	"	48th or Northampton		Gold	Buff	White with black and red stripe	

Colour of the body of coats for rank and file	Colour of the facings of the coats for rank and file	Rank and Title of Regiment	Distinction in the same colour	If gold or silver lace for officers	Colour of the linings and breeches	Colour of lace for rank and file	Buttons, how set on coat
Red	Buff	52nd or Oxfords		Silver	Buff	White with red worm and orange stripe	
"	"	61st or South Gloster		Silver	Buff	White with blue stripe	Equal distances
"	"	62nd or Wiltshire	Yellowish buff	Silver	Yellowish buff	White with two blue and one straw coloured stripe	2 and 2
"	"	71st			Buff	White, red stripe	
"	"	78th				White with green stripe	
"	"	81st				White with blue and scarlet edges	2 and 2
"	"	90th	Deep buff			White with blue and buff stripe	
Red	White	17th, or Leicesters	Greyish white	Silver	Greyish white	White with two blue and one yellow stripe	
"	"	32nd, or Cornwall		Gold	White	White with black worm and black stripe	
"	"	43rd, or Monmouth		Silver	White	White with red and black stripe	
"	"	47th, or Lancashire		Silver	White	White with one red and two black stripes	
"	"	59th, or 2nd Nottingham		Silver	White	White with red and yellow stripes	
"	"	65th or 2nd York, N Riding			White	White with red and black worm and black stripe	
"	"	74th				White with red and blue stripe	
Red	Red	33rd or 1st York West		Silver	White	White with red stripe in the middle	
"	"	41st		Silver	White	White with black worm	
"	"	53rd or Shropshire		Gold	White	White with red stripe	
"	"	76th				White with black stripe	2 and 2
Red	Purple	56th, or West Essex		Silver	White	White with pink colour stripe	
Red	Black	50th, or West Kent		Silver	White	White with red stripe	
"	"	58th or Rutland		Gold	White	White with red stripe	
"	"	64th or 2nd Staffords		Gold	White	White with red and black stripe	
"	"	70th or Surrey		Gold	White	White with narrow black worm stripe	
"	"	89th				White with red and blue stripe on edge	
Red	Orange	35th, or Dorset		Silver	White	White with one yellow stripe	
Red	Yolk	72nd				White with green stripe	
Green	Red	60th, 5th battalion (rifle)				Feathered with red	

Colour of the body of coats for rank and file	Colour of the facings of the coats for rank and file	Rank and Title of Regiment	Distinction in the same colour	If gold or silver lace for officers	Colour of the linings and breeches	Colour of lace for rank and file	Buttons, how set on coat
Green	Black	Manningham's Rifles		Silver		Feathered partly with white	
		Queen's Rangers					
Red*		Scotch Brigade					
		New South Wales					
		Royal Staff Corps		White	White	Feathered*	
		Frazer's African Corps					
		Invalid Comps					
Red*	Blue*	7 Royal Garrison battalions		Gold*	White*	White*	Equal distances
Red	White	1st West India				White with one black stripe	Equal distances
Red	Yellow	2nd West India				White with green, yellow, and purple stripe	Equal distances
"	"	3rd West India				White with one large black stripe	Equal distances
"	"	4th West India				White with one blue and two yellow stripes	Equal distances
"	"	6th West India				White with black stripe	Equal distances
"	"	7th West India				White with brown, yellow and scarlet stripe	Equal distances
"	"	9th West India**				White with two blue and one yellow stripe	Equal distances
Red	Grey	8th West India**				White, with red, yellow, and black stripe	Equal distances
Red	Green	5th West India	Dark green			White	Equal distances
"	"	11th West India**				White, with a narrow green edge	Equal distances
Red	Buff	10th West India**				White with scarlet and black edge	Equal distances
"	"	12th West India**				White with scarlet and black edge	Equal distances

* Only given in 1st MS. book and in pencil
** Only given in 1st MS. book.

Appendix II

Material Extracted from report in Chapter 13

Schedule of the Articles of Personal Baggage and Camp Equipage, and of the number and description of Horses with which Officers, Military and Civil, and of the Articles of Necessaries with which Soldiers should be provided when on actual Service at Home and Abroad (including the Articles in wear) with the reasonable Prices of Value thereof.

Cavalry
Field Officer, or Colonel doing Duty as Field Officer.
Baggage.
Full Equipment
One Helmet and Feather
Two Jackets or Coats
Two Waistcoats
Two Pairs of Leather Breeches or Pantaloons
Three Pairs of Drawers
One ditto Overalls
One Great Coat
One Cloak
Eighteen Shirts
Two Black Stocks or Handkerchiefs
Eighteen Pocket handkerchiefs
Eighteen Pairs of Stockings
Three pairs of Boots
One ditto Spurs
Two ditto Shoes
Three ditto Gloves
Twelve Towels
Six Table Cloths
Brushes for Clothes and Shoes
Razors, Combs etc.
One Regimental Sword
One Light Sword
One Belt and Plate

One Sword Knot
One Sabre Tasche
One Pouch and Belt
One Sash
One Writing Case
One Spying Glass
Two Portmanteaus

Light Equipment:
One Helmet and Feather
Two Jackets or Coats
Two Waistcoats
Two Pairs of Leather Breeches or Pantaloons
Two Pairs of Drawers
One Great Coat
One Cloak
Nine Shirts
Two Black Stocks or Handkerchiefs
Nine Pocket handkerchiefs
Nine pairs of Stockings
Two pairs of Boots
One ditto Spurs
One ditto Shoes
Two ditto Gloves
Six Towels
Four Table Cloths
Brushes for Clothes and Shoes
Razors, Combs etc.
One Regimental Sword
One Light Sword
One Belt and Plate
One Sword Knot
One Sabre Tasche
One Pouch and Belt
One Sash
One Writing Case
One Spying Glass
One Portmanteau

Camp Equipage
Full Equipment:
One Marquee
One Light Portable Iron Frame Bedstead
One Mattress
One Bolster

Brushes for Clothes and Shoes
Razors, combs, &c.
One Sword
One Sword Knot
One Belt and Plate
One Gorget
One Sash
One Writing Case
One Spying Glass
Two Portmanteaus

Light Equipment Price or Value
One Hat & Feather (or Caps at 31/6d) 70 7 0 0
Two Coats 8 16 0 0
Two pairs of Epaulettes 6 12 0 0
Two Waistcoats 24 2 8 0
Two pairs of Breeches or Pantaloons 36 3 12 0
Two pairs of Drawers
One Great Coat
One Cloak
Nine Shirts
Two Black Stocks or Handkerchiefs
Nine Pocket Handkerchiefs
Nine pairs of Stockings
Two pairs of Boots
One pair Spurs
One pair Shoes
Two Pairs Gloves
Six Towels
Four Table Cloths
Brushes for Clothes and Shoes
Razors, combs, &c.
One Sword
One Sword Knot
One Belt and Plate
One Gorget
One Sash
One Writing Case
One Spying Glass
One Portmanteaus

Camp Equipage.
The same as for a Field Officer of Cavalry.
Horses
Two Chargers £32.10 each.

One Bat Horse £21
One additional Bat Horse for a Colonel.

Captain.
Baggage. See Table.
Camp equipage. The same as for a captain of cavalry.
Horses. Two bat horses at £21 each.
Subaltern.
Baggage.
Full equipment: The same as for a captain omitting one table cloth at 10s 6d and a writing case at 24s and deducting 36s from the price of the epaulettes. Total £80 9s 6d.
Light equipment: The same as for a captain, omitting the writing case at 24s and deducting 36s from the price of the epaulettes. Total £64 11s.
Camp equipage. The same as for the subalterns of a troop of cavalry.
Horses. One bat horse each £21.
Paymaster.
Baggage and camp equipage: The same as for a captain.
Horses. One saddle horse at £31 10s
One bat horse at £21
Adjutant.
Baggage and camp equipage: The same as for a subaltern with a writing case at 24s.
Horses.
One charger at £52 10s
One bat horse at £21.
Quarter master.
Baggage and camp equipage: The same as for a subaltern with a writing case at 24s.
Horses.
One saddle horse at £31 10s
One bat horse at £21.
Surgeon.
Baggage and camp equipage. The same as for a paymaster.
Horses.
One saddle horse at £31 10s
One bat horse at £21.
Assistant surgeon.
Baggage: The same as for a subaltern.
Camp equipage. The same. One marquee being for their joint use.
Horses.
One bat horse each at £21.
Military Staff.
General.
Baggage £400
Camp equipage £200
Horses.
Six chargers at £63 each.

Ten draught and bat horses at £21 each.

Lieutenant-General.
Baggage £330
Camp equipage £170
Horses.
Four chargers at £63 each.
Eight draught and bat horses at £21 each.

Major General.
Baggage £250
Camp equipage £150
Horses.
Four chargers at £63 each.
Six draught and bat horses at £21 each.

Brigadier General, or colonel commanding a brigade.
Baggage £250
Camp equipage £150
Horses.
Four chargers at £63 each.
Four draught and bat horses at £21 each.

Adjutant general and quarter master general, having the rank of colonel.
Baggage, camp equipage and horses: The same as a major general.
If of inferior rank only four draught and bat horses.
Deputy adjutant general and deputy quarter master general, at the head of their respective
    departments.
Baggage and camp equipage: According to their regimental rank.
Horses.
Four chargers at £63 each.
Four draught and bat horses at £21 each.
If under a superior.
Two first chargers at £63 each.
Two second chargers at £36 15s each.
Two bat horses at £21.

Assistant adjutant general and assistant quarter master general.
Baggage, camp equipage and horses: According to their regimental rank.
If not field officers.
Two first chargers at £63 each.
One second charger at £36 15s.
Two bat horses at £21 each.

Deputy assistant adjutant general and deputy assistant quarter master general.

The same. Omitting one bat horse at £21.

Military secretary.
Baggage and camp equipment according to his regimental rank.
Horses: One first chargers at £63 each.
One second charger at £36 15s.
Two bat horses at £21 each.

Aide de camp.
Extra aide de camp when regularly sanctioned, and major of brigade.
Baggage and camp equipment according to their regimental rank.
Horses: One first chargers at £63 each.
One second charger at £36 15s.
One bat horse at £21 each.

Deputy judge advocate.
Baggage and camp equipment according to his regimental rank.
One saddle horse at £31 10s
One bat horses at £21 each.

Inspector of foreign corps.
Baggage and camp equipment according to his military rank.
Horses: Two first chargers at £63 each.
Two second charges at £36 15s.
Three bat horses at £21 each.

Chaplain.
Baggage, camp equipment and horses: The same as for a regimental surgeon.

Surgeon to the general commanding.
Baggage, camp equipment: The same as for a regimental surgeon.
Horses.
Two saddle horses at £36 15s
Two bat horses at £21.

Baggage master general.
Baggage and camp equipment: The same as for a captain of infantry or according to his regimental rank.
Horses.
Two saddle horses at £36 15s
Two bat horses at £21.

Assistant baggage master general.
Baggage and camp equipment: According to his regimental rank.
Horses.

One saddle horse at £36 15s
One bat horse at £21.

Captain of guides.
Baggage and camp equipment: According to his regimental rank.
Horses.
Two saddle horses at £36 15s
Two bat horses at £21.

Assistant captain of guides.
Baggage and camp equipment: According to his regimental rank.
Horses.
Two saddle horses at £36 15s
One bat horse at £21.

Town or fort major.
Baggage and camp equipment: According to his regimental rank.
Horses.
Two saddle horses at £36 15s
Two bat horses at £21.

Town or fort adjutant.
Baggage and camp equipment: According to his regimental rank.
Horses.
Two saddle horses at £36 15s
Two bat horses at £21.

Provost marshal.
Baggage and camp equipment: As a captain of infantry.
Horses.
Two saddle horses at £31 10s
One bat horse at £21.

Deputy provost marshal.
Baggage and camp equipment: As a subaltern of infantry.
Horses.
One saddle horse at £31 10ss
One bat horse at £21.

Civil staff.
Medical department
Director General
Baggage Price or Value
Two hats & black feathers at £3 3s- £6 6s
Two uniform coats with epaulettes at £14- £28

Two waistcoats at £1 4s- £2 8s
Two pairs of breeches at 36s-£3 12s
Six pairs of drawers at 3s 6d- £1 1s
One great coat £5 5s
One cloak £2 12s 6d
Twenty shirts at £1- £21
Three neck handkerchiefs at 3s-9s
Twenty pocket handkerchiefs at 3s-£3
Twenty pairs of stockings at 3s 6d-£3 10s
Two pairs of boots at 48s-£4 16s
Two pairs of shoes at 12s-£1 4s
Two pairs gloves at 4s 6d- 9s
Twenty towels at 1s 6d- £1 10s
Ten table cloths at 63s- £31 10s
Six breakfast clothes at 31s 6d- £9 9s
Brushes for clothes and shoes 5s 6d
One sword £3
One sword knot 9s
One belt and plate £1 15s
Writing and dressing boxes £5 5s
Three portmanteaus at 44s- £6 12s
Total: £143 8s
Camp equipage
One marquee £21
Bedstead and bedding as in the preceding cases £14 8s 6d
Camp table and stools £6 6s
Kitchen utensils £15
One pair of canteens £15 15s
Total £51 92 6d
Horses
Two saddle horses at £52 10s each.
Four bat and draught horses at £21 each.

Inspector of hospitals.
Baggage Price or Value
Two hats with black feathers at £3 3s- £6 6s
Two uniform coats with epaulettes at £14- £28
Two waistcoats at £1 4s- £2 8s
Two pairs of breeches at 36s-£3 12s
Three pairs of drawers at 3s 6d- 10s 6d
One great coat £5 5s
One cloak £2 12s 6d
Eighteen shirts at 21s- £18 18s
Three neck handkerchiefs at 3s-9s
Eighteen pocket handkerchiefs at 3s-£2 14s

Eighteen pairs of stockings at 3s 6d-£3 3s
Two pairs of boots at 48s-£4 16s
Two pairs of shoes at 12s-£1 4s
Two pairs gloves at 4s 6d- 9s
Eighteen towels at 1s 6d- £1 7s
Eight table cloths at 63s- £25 4s
Six breakfast cloths at 31s 6d- £9 9s
Brushes for clothes and shoes 5s 6d
One sword £3
One sword knot 9s
One belt and plate £1 15s
Writing and dressing boxes £5 5s
Two portmanteaus at 44s- £4 8s
Total: £131 9s 6d
Camp equipage
One marquee £21
Bedstead and bedding as in the preceding cases £14 8s 6d
Table and stools £4 4ss
Kitchen utensils £12 12s
One pair of canteens £10 10ss
Total £41 14s 6d

Horses
Two saddle horses at £52 10s each.
One bat horse at £21 each.
Two draught horses at £21 each.

Deputy inspector of hospitals.
At the head of a department on service.
Baggage and camp equipage the same as an inspector.
If under a superior,
Baggage Price or Value
Two hats with black feathers at £3 3s- £6 6s
Two uniform coats with epaulettes at £14- £28
Two waistcoats at £1 4s- £2 8s
Two pairs of breeches at 36s-£3 12s
Three pairs of drawers at 3s 6d- 10s 6d
One great coat £5 5s
One cloak £2 12s 6d
Twelve shirts at 21s- £12 12s
Three neck handkerchiefs at 3s-9s
Twelve pocket handkerchiefs at 3s-£1 16s
Twelve pairs of stockings at 3s 6d-£2 2s
Two pairs of boots at 48s-£4 16s
Two pairs of shoes at 12s-£1 4s

Two pairs gloves at 4s 6d- 9s
Twelve towels at 1s 6d- 18s
Six table cloths at 63s- £18 18s
Four breakfast cloths at 31s 6d- £6 6s
Brushes for clothes and shoes 5s 6d
One sword £3
One sword knot 9s
One belt and plate £1 15s
Writing and dressing boxes £5 5s
Two portmanteaus at 44s- £4 8s
Total: £113 6s 6d
Camp equipage
One marquee £21
Bedstead and bedding as in the preceding cases £14 8s 6d
Table and stools £3 3s
Kitchen utensils £10 10s
One pair of canteens £8 8s
Total £36 9s 6d
Horses
Two saddle horses at £52 10s each.
One bat horse at £21 each.
Two draught horses at £21 each.

Physician.
Baggage and camp equipage the same as the deputy inspector, omitting two table cloths at
    63s each, one breakfast cloth at 31s 6d and kitchen utensils 42d and from the marquee,
    £8 8s.
Horses
Two saddle horses at £52 10s each.
Two bat horses at £21 each.

Surgeon.
Baggage, camp equipment and horses the same as a physician.

Apothecary.
Baggage and camp equipment the same as a regimental surgeon.
Horses. Two saddle horses at £52 10s each.
Two bat horses at 21s each.

Hospital mate.
Baggage and camp equipage the same as assistant surgeon.
Horses.
Two saddle horses at £52 10s each.
Two bat horses at £21 each.

Purveyor.
Baggage, camp equipment and horses the same as assistant surgeon.

A deduction at the rate of £6 per pair for epaulettes to be made in cases where that article is not worn by the officers of the departments, or if one epaulette be worn, £3 to be deducted from the sum of £14, the price of the coat and epaulettes.

Commissariat department.
Commissary general.
Baggage Price or Value
Two hats at 63s- £6 6s
Three uniform coats with epaulettes at £14- £42
Three waistcoats at 24s- £3 12s
Three pairs of breeches at 36s-£5 8s
Six pairs of drawers at 3s 6d- £1 1s
One great coat £5 5s
One cloak £2 12s 6d
Two pairs of overalls at £3 13s 6d- £7 7s
Twenty-four shirts at £1- £24
Four neck handkerchiefs at 3s-12s
Twenty-four pocket handkerchiefs at 3s-£3 12s
Twenty-four pairs of stockings at 3s 6d-£4 4s
Three pairs of boots at 48s-£7 4s
Two pairs of shoes at 12s-£1 4s
Three pairs gloves at 4s 6d- 13s 6d
Twenty-four towels at 1s 6d- £1 16s
Twelve table cloths at 63s- £37 16s
Eight breakfast clothes at 31s 6d- £12 12s
Brushes for clothes and shoes 5s 6d
One sword, belt etc. £5 5s
Writing and dressing boxes £5 5s
Four portmanteaus at 44s- £8 16s
Total: £188 6s
Camp equipage
One marquee £30
Bedstead and bedding as in other cases £14 8s 6d
Table and stools £6
Kitchen utensils £20
One pair of large canteens £21
One cart £12
Total £73 8s 6d
Horses
Two saddle horses at £63 each.
Two saddle horses at £36 15s each.
Six bat and draught horses at £21 each.

Deputy commissary general.
Baggage Price or Value
Two hats at 63s- £6 6s
Two coats complete at £14- £28
Two waistcoats at 24s- £2 8s
Two pairs of breeches at 36s-£3 12s
Three pairs of drawers at 3s 6d- 10s 6d
One great coat £5 5s
One cloak £2 12s 6d
One pair of overalls £3 13s 6d
Eighteen shirts at 21s- £18 18s
Two black stocks or handkerchiefs at 3s-6s
Eighteen pocket handkerchiefs at 3s-£2 14s
Eighteen pairs of stockings at 3s 6d-£3 3s
Three pairs of boots at 48s-£7 4s
Two pairs of shoes at 12s-£1 4s
Three pairs gloves at 4s 6d- 13s 6d
Twelve towels at 1s 6d- 18s
Six table cloths at 10s 6d- £3 3s
Brushes for clothes and shoes 5s 6d
One sword, belt etc. £5 5s
Writing and dressing boxes £5 5s
Two portmanteaus at 44s- £4 8s
Total: £105 14s 6d
Camp equipage
One marquee £21
Bedstead and bedding as in other cases £14 8s 6d
Camp table and stools £4
One pair of canteens £8 8s
Total £26 16s 6d
Horses
Two saddle horses at £52 10s each.
One bat horse at £21.

Assistant commissary general.
Baggage Price or Value
Two hats at 63s- £6 6s
Two coats complete at £14- £28
Two waistcoats at 24s- £2 8s
Two pairs of breeches at 36s-£3 12s
Three pairs of drawers at 3s 6d- 10s 6d
One great coat £5 5s
One cloak £2 12s 6d
Twelve shirts at 21s- £12 12s
Two black stocks or handkerchiefs at 3s-6s

Twelve pocket handkerchiefs at 3s-£1 16s
Twelve pairs of stockings at 3s 6d-£2 2s
Two pairs of boots at 48s-£4 16s
Two pairs of shoes at 12s-£1 4s
Two pairs gloves at 4s 6d- 9s
Six towels at 1s 6d- 9s
Three table cloths at 10s 6d- £1 11s 6d
Brushes for clothes and shoes 5s 6d
One sword, belt etc. £5 5s
Writing and dressing boxes £5 5s
Two portmanteaus at 44s- £4 8s
Total: £89 3s
Camp equipage
One small marquee £12 12s
Bedstead and bedding as in other cases £14 8s 6d
Table and stools £3
One pair of canteens £5 5s
Total £22 13s 6d
Horses
One saddle horse at £31 10s each.
One bat horse at £21.

Deputy assistant commissary general.
Baggage. The same as for an assistant commissary general omitting one table cloth 10s 6d,
    writing and dressing boxes at £5 5s in lieu of the latter a writing case £1 to be allowed.
Camp equipage. The same deducting £1 from the camp table and stool.
Horses. One bat horse £21.

Clerk.
Baggage. The same as the deputy assistant commissary general.
Camp equipage. The same between two clerks or between himself and the deputy assistant
    commissary general.
Horses. One bat horse £21.

Commissary of accompts.
Baggage and camp equipment. The same as a deputy commissary general.
Horses. Two saddle horses at £36 15s each.
Three bat horses at £21 each.

Deputy Commissary of Accompts.
Baggage and camp equipage the same as assistant commissary general.
Horses. Two saddle horses at £36 15s each.
Two bat horses at £21.

Assistant commissary of Accompts.

Baggage and camp equipage the same as deputy assistant commissary general.

Horses. One saddle horse at £36 15s each.

One bat horse at £21.

A similar observation to that at the end of the medical department relative to epaulettes.

Personal Necessaries of Soldiers.

Cavalry Private. Serjeant (where different.)

One pair of saddle bags 18s 6d

One stable jacket 14s 6d

Extra pair of leather breeches of the same quality, and to be in wear with those furnished by the colonel £1 5s

Ditto of plush breeches 15s

One pair of breeches slings 1s

One ditto trowsers 7s

One ditto overalls £1 1s 6d

Three shirts £1 1s £1 4s

One black stock 9s

Three pairs of stockings 6s 7s 6d

Two pairs of shoes 14s

One pair of shoe clasps 4s

One pair of long gaiters 4s 4s 6d

One foraging cap 3s 6d

One button stick and hook 6d

One comb and sponge 6d

One razor and soap 1s

One set of brushes 2s

One blacking ball 4d

One turnscrew 5d Not for sjt.

One worm and picker 7d Not for sjt.

One carbine lock case 1s 9d Not for sjt.

One nose bag 1s 8d

One watering bridle at 6s and log 6s 6d

One mane comb and sponge 7d

One curry comb and brush 3s 1d

One horse picker and scissors 1s 4d

Total: Privates £8 12 4d Serjeants £8 14s 7d

Infantry. Private Serjeant (where different)

One knapsack 10s 6d

One extra pair of breeches 7s 7s 6d

One pair of breeches slings 1s

Three shirts £1 1s £1 4s

One black stock 9d

Three pairs of stockings 7s 7s 6d

Two ditto shoes 14s

One ditto long gaiters 4s 4s 6d
One foraging cap 2s 2s 6d
One button stick 3d
One comb and sponge 6d
One razor and soap 1s
One set of brushes 2s
One blacking ball 4d
One turn screw 5d
One worm and picker 7d
Total. Privates £3 12 4d Serjeants £3 16s 9d
Servants not being soldiers the same as for a serjeant of infantry.

Scale of Prices or Value of Articles of Baggage, Camp Equipment and Horse Equipment for Officers of All Ranks, Military and Civil.
Baggage
Hat and feather for general officers £4 4s
Hat and feather for the inferior ranks. £3 10s
Hat and feather for medical and commissariat departments £3 3s
Helmet and feather £4 4s
Cap for officers of light infantry £1 11s 6d
Jacket for cavalry £12
Embroidered coat for a general and for a lieutenant general including epaulettes £28
Ditto for a major general £25
Coat for regimental officers and officers of the civil department (if for a general officer £1 more) £8
Epaulettes for general and field officer per pair £6
Epaulettes for captain (single) £2 10s
Epaulettes for subaltern (single) £1 12s
Waistcoat £1 4s
Breeches £1 16s
Leather breeches or pantaloons for cavalry £3 3s
Drawers 3s 6d
Overalls (for mounted officers only) £3 13s 6d
Great coat £5 5s
Cloak for general officers and officers of cavalry £6 6s
Cloak for other staff officers and infantry officers of all ranks £2 12s 6d
Shirt £1 1s
Black stock or handkerchief 3s
Pocket handkerchief 3s
Stockings 3s 6d
Long gaiters (for regimental officers of infantry) 10s 6d
Gloves 4s 6d
Towel 1s 6d
Tablecloth for general officers and superior staff officers, the medical and commissariat department £3 3s

Breakfast cloth ditto £1 11s 6d
Breakfast cloth for the inferior ranks 10s 6d
Boots £2 8s
Spurs for all mounted officers 7s
Shoes 12s
Brushes for clothes and shoes 5s 6d
Regimental sword or sabre (for cavalry) £3 13s 6d
Light sword for ditto £3 3s
Sword for infantry and staff officers £3 3s
Knot (cavalry) £1 1s
Sabretache (cavalry) £1
Knot (infantry) 9s
Sword belt 14s
Belt plate £1 1s
Waistbelt and furniture for cavalry and staff officers £2 2s
Pouch and belt £1 1s
Sash £3
Gorget 10s 6d
Dressing box and writing box £5 5s
Writing case £1 4s
Spying glass £3 3s
Portmanteau £2 4s
Camp equipage.
Marquee for general officers £30
Marquee for field officers £21
Marquee for captain and subaltern £12 12s
Marquee for director of hospitals £21
Marquee for principal and deputy inspectors £21
Marquee for Commissary general £30
Marquee for deputy ditto £21
Marquee for commissary of accompts £21
Marquee for other staff officers £12 12s
Table £1 stool 6s
Privates tent £8
Light iron trunk bedstead £7 10s
Mattress £1 14s
Bolster 11s
Pillow 10s
Three blankets at 7s 6d- £1 2s 6d
Coverlid 15s
Two pairs of sheets at 21s 3d- £2 2s 6d
Two pillow cases 3s 6d
Canteens for general officers £21
Canteens for field officers £8 8s
Canteens for captain and subaltern £5 5s

Canteens for director of hospitals £15 15s
Canteens for principal inspectors £10 10s
Canteens for deputy ditto and physician £8 8s
Canteens for Commissary general £21
Canteens for deputy ditto and for commissary of accompts £8 8s
Horse equipment.
Saddle complete £8 18s 6d
Bridle complete £2
Set of horse furniture for the different ranks of officers who are allowed chargers £7 7s
Pair of pistols £5 5s
Harness for a draught horse £3 3s
Harness for a bat horse £5 5s
Saddle etc. for a servant £3 3s
Bridle ditto 16s

Field Officers of Cavalry and Infantry and Staff Officers upon the same footing to be allowed a Soldier's Tent for Servants and Baggage.

The Articles under the Head of Horse equipments, though not mentioned in the Schedule, must of course be considered as constituting a part of the Personal Equipment of Officers for which, if lost on Service, they are entitled to Indemnification. The number of Articles of each description necessary for the different Ranks will depend upon the number of Horses of Each Class, respectively allotted for them.

The Board conceive that two sets of Horse Furniture are necessary for General Officers-one set for the Inferior Ranks; and that this Article is requisite for those Officers only who are allowed Chargers.

On an Emergency, Officers of all ranks may be supposed to have only an Opportunity of carrying with them, in addition to their Provisions,

A Cloak, Shirts, pair of Stockings, A pair of Shoes, Shaving Box, Towel.

The board having considered that part of the Adjutant General's Letter which relates to Women (Wives to Soldiers) are of Opinion that no Woman or Child should be allowed to embark with regiments to be employed upon active Service in Europe, and that in all cases the Commanding Officers of Regiments should have signed Lists of the Women and Children left behind; but in recommending the adoption of a measure which, though obviously calculated to promote the general advantage of the Public service may appear harsh to the Soldiers, The Board conceive that some relaxation in favour of their Feelings, by allowing an additional number of Women beyond the former usage to each regiment, where it can be done without essential injury to the Service, may be permitted, and they therefore recommend that one Woman should be allowed for every Ten Men, to regiments embarking for the East or West Indies, North America, the Cape of Good Hope, or for Garrisons in Europe.[1]

---

1   TNA, WO7/56/1-59: Various Departmental, Out-letters. Board of General Officers. Reports Miscellaneous.

Bibliography

Archival Sources

The National Archives (TNA):

WO3/10 Office of the Commander-in-Chief: Out-letters. General Letters (Series 1-1767-1800) – Date: 01 March 1791–31 October 1792.

WO3/14 – Office of the Commander-in-Chief: Out-letters. General Letters (Series 1-1767-1800) – Date: 01 June 1795–31 December 1795.

WO3/28 – Office of the Commander-in-Chief: Out-letters. General Letters (Series 2-1765-1801) – Date: 01 August 1793–31 May 1796.

WO3/29 – Office of the Commander-in-Chief: Out-letters. General Letters (Series 2-1765-1801) – Date: 01 May 1796–31 December 1796.

WO3/38 – Office of the Commander-in-Chief: Out-letters. General Letters (Series 3-1801-1857) – Date: 01 September 1804–30 April 1805.

WO3/42 – Office of the Commander-in-Chief: Out-letters. General Letters (Series 3-1801-1857) – Date: 01 November 1806–30 April 1807.

WO3/152 – Office of the Commander-in-Chief: Out-letters. Letters to War Office and other Public Departments – Date: 01 January 1803–28 February 1805.

WO3/158 – Office of the Commander-in-Chief: Out-letters. Letters to War Office – Date: 01 November 1811–31 March 1813.

WO3/194 – Office of the Commander-in-Chief: Out-letters. Letters to Public Departments – Date: 01 December 1807–31 May 1808.

WO3/367 – Office of the Commander-in-Chief: Out-letters. Letters to Regimental Officers – Date: 01 July 1814–31 October 1814.

WO6/25 – War Department and successors: Secretary of State for war and Secretary of State for War and the Colonies, Out-letters. Continent. Helder Expedition. Date: 1794–1803.

WO7/26 – War Office and predecessors: Various Departmental, Out-letters. Board of General Officers. Clothing. Date: 1757–1767.

WO7/32 – War Office and predecessors: Various Departmental, Out-letters. Board of General Officers. Clothing. Date: 1800–1802.

WO7/33 – War Office and predecessors: Various Departmental, Out-letters. Board of General Officers. Clothing. Date: 1802–1806.

WO7/34 – War Office and predecessors: Various Departmental, Out-letters. Board of General Officers. Clothing. Date: 1806–1810.

WO7/54 – War Office and predecessors: Various Departmental, Out-letters. Board of General Officers. Reports on Clothing. Date: 1806–1828.

WO7/56 – War Office and predecessors: Various Departmental, Out-letters. Board of General Officers. Reports Miscellaneous. Date: 1810–1816.

WO26/38 – War Office: Entry Books of Warrants, Regulations and Precedents. Date: 1799–1802.

WO26/39 – War Office: Entry Books of Warrants, Regulations and Precedents. Date: 1802–1805.

WO26/40 – War Office: Entry Books of Warrants, Regulations and Precedents. Date: 1805–1807.

WO27/135 Office of the Commander-in-Chief and War Office: Adjutant General and Army Council: Inspection Returns. From 51 Foot. Date: 1815.

WO30/55 – War Office, predecessor and associated departments: Miscellaneous Papers. Defences of Great Britain. Military Description of partes of England and Ireland, by General Roy. Date: 1765.

WO55/574 – Ordnance Office and War Office: Miscellaneous Entry books and Papers. ORDERS. General. Date: 1790–1815.

WO55/677 – Ordnance Office and War Office: Miscellaneous Entry books and Papers. Officers' Orders Books (Artillery). Date: 1775–1804.

WO123/117 – Ministry of Defence and predecessors: Army Circulars, Memoranda, Orders and Regulations. Army Regulations, etc. from Various Sources. [Vol.1] Date: 1789–1809.

WO123/118 – Ministry of Defence and predecessors: Army Circulars, Memoranda, Orders and Regulations. Army Regulations, etc. from Various Sources. 1806–1809 "Appendix to Vol. 1 various, pre 24 Dec 1809, but not bound in" I-XIV (Contents listed).

WO123/120 – Ministry of Defence and predecessors: Army Circulars, Memoranda, Orders and Regulations. Army Regulations, etc. from Various Sources. [Vol.1] Date: 1811–1813.

WO123/128 – Ministry of Defence and predecessors: Army Circulars, Memoranda, Orders and Regulations. Adjutant General's Office (Horse Guards). General Orders. Nos 1-79. Date: 1792 -1804.

WO123/131 – Ministry of Defence and predecessors: Army Circulars, Memoranda, Orders and Regulations. Adjutant General's Office (Horse Guards). General Orders. Nos 235-326. Date: 1813 1816.

WO123/134 – Ministry of Defence and predecessors: Army Circulars, Memoranda, Orders and Regulations. Adjutant-General's Office (Horse Guards). General Orders and Circular Letters (original MS), paginated and listed at front or back. Date: 1800–1806.

WO123/135 – Ministry of Defence and predecessors: Army Circulars, Memoranda, Orders and Regulations. Adjutant General's Office (Horse Guards). General Orders and Circular Letters (original MS), paginated and listed at front or back. Date: 1807–1812.

WO123/161 – Ministry of Defence and predecessors: Army Circulars, Memoranda, Orders and Regulations. Adjutant General's Office (Horse Guards). General Orders and Circular Letters (original MS), paginated and listed at front or back. Date: 1805–1824.

The Royal Collection (TRC):
Carlton House Papers. 2236-2241 and 2257-2260 Carlton House Armoury Inventories.

The National Library of Scotland (NLS):
ACC 9074.23 – Original letters and despatches, misc. papers home service 1804–1810.

The National Army Museum (NAM):
1968-07-126 – Smith, Charles Hamilton, Military Manuscripts.
2004-06-9 – Bound photographic record of the contents of the military pattern books of Thomas Hawkes, latterly Hawkes Moseley and Company, London, 1800–1817; associated with the Wars of the French Revolution (1793–1802) and the Napoleonic Wars (1803–1815).
1968-07-209-3 – Macready E, Journal and opinions of Edward Nevil Macready, 30th (Cambridgeshire) Regiment of Foot, 1814–1830.
2006-11-50 – Descriptive View of the Clothing and Appts of the Infantry; bound and annotated manuscript copy dated 22 May 1802; inscribed inside cover in pencil, 'Copy of the Standing Regulations for the colours, clothing etc of the Infantry, to which are annexed the Guards, Rifle Corps etc'.
1968-07-219: Papers of Lt. Gen. Robert Ballard Long, 1809–1825.

British Library (BL):
BLL01018405879: Standing Orders for Prince William's Regiment of Gloucester. (Gloucester: 1795).
BLL01016752043: Standing orders for the Norwich; or, Hundred and Sixth Regiment. (Waterford: James Ramsey, 1795).
BLL01001095773: Standing Orders, Forms of Returns, Reports, Entries, &c., of the Queen's Dragoon Guards. (London: J. Walter, 1795).
BLL01001095807

Anne SK Brown Military Collection. (ASKB):
Stothard, Military tailoring book.

Victoria and Albert Museum, National Art Library (NAL):
86.LL.09. Reynolds, P, Military Costume of the Eighteenth and Nineteenth Centuries, Vol. IX.
MSL/1933/2993. Pattern Book of military, naval, militia, yeomanry and volunteer uniforms, 1795–1809.

Meyer and Mortimer at Sackville Street, London. (M&M):
Ledgers of 1809–1827.

Somerset Records Office (SRC):
DD/SLI 6/5, X181 – Regimental Orders of the 13th Regiment of Foot.
DD/SLI 6/5, X182 – Regimental Orders of the 13th Regiment of Foot.

Liddell RS, *The Memoirs of the 10th Royal Hussars* (Uckfield: Naval & Military Press, 2015).

Luard J., *A History of the Dress of the British Soldier* (London: Clowes, 1852).

MacDonald J, *Instructions for the conduct of infantry on actual service* (London: No Publisher, 1807).

MacDonald, R.J., *The History of the Dress of the Royal Regiment of Artillery* (London: Southeran, 1899).

MacGuffie, T.H., 'Light Dragoons, details of clothing,' *Journal of the Society for Army Historical Research*, volume 26 (1948).

MacGuffie, T.H., 'Light Dragoons, details of clothing,' *Journal of the Society for Army Historical Research*, volume 27 (1949).

Malet, H., *Historical records of the Eighteenth Hussars* (London: Clowes, 1869).

Maxwell, H., *The Creevey Papers 1768-1838* (New York: E.P. Dutton, 1904).

Mercer, C., *Journal of the Waterloo Campaign* (Edinburgh: William Blackwood and Sons, 1870),

Mercer, C., 'Military reminiscences of latter end of eighteenth and beginning of nineteenth centuries', in McDonald, R, *The History of the Dress of the Royal Regiment of Artillery* (London: Sotheran, 1911).

Milne, S., *The Annals of the King's Royal Rifle Corps, Appendix volume* (London: Murray, 1913).

Mollo J., *The Prince's Dolls, Scandals and Splendours of the Hussars* (Barnesley: Pen and Sword, 1997).

Mundy, G., *Standing Orders for the Third, or King's Own Regiment of Dragoons, issued by Lieut. Col. Godfrey Basil Mundy* (Dublin: J. Stewart, 1805).

Neale, A., *Travels Through Some Parts of Germany, Poland, Moldavia and Turkey* (London: Longman, Hurst, Rees, Orme, and Brown, 1818).

Page, J. (ed.), *Intelligence Officer in the Peninsula, letters and diaries of Major the Hon. Edward Charles Cocks* (Staplehurst: Spellmount, 1986).

Pattison F., *Personal Recollections of the Waterloo Campaign* (Glasgow: 1870).

Roberts, D., *The Military Adventures of Johnny Newcome, with an account of his campaign on the Peninsula and in Pall Mall* (London: Methuen, 1904).

Ross-Lewin, H., *With The 32nd in the Peninsula and other Campaigns* (Uckfield: Naval and Military Press, 2001).

Rowlandson, T., *Loyal Volunteers of London and Environs* (London:, Ackermann 1799).

Russell, J., *A series of Experiments of attack and defence made in Hyde Park in 1802, under the sanction of His Royal Highness the Commander in Chief, with Infantry, Cavalry and Artillery; and in the Island of Jersey, in 1805* (London: T. Egerton, 1806).

Sapherson, A., *Figures from Volunteer Regiments of Scotland, England and Wales, 1806.* (Leeds: Raider Books, 1989).

Secretary at War's Office, *A collection of orders, regulations and instructions for the army.* (London: Egerton, 1807).

Sherer, M., *Recollections in the Peninsula* (London: Longman, Hurst, Ress, Orme, Brown and Green, 1824).

Shipp, J., *Memoirs of the extraordinary career of John Shipp* (London: Hurst, Chance and Co, 1829).

Simcoe, J., *Simcoe's military journal* (New York: Bartlett and Welford, 1844).

Simmons G., *A British Rifle Man* (Uckfield: Naval & Military Press, 2007).

St Clair, T., *Recollections of A soldier in the West Indies and America* (London: Bentley, 1834).

Stewart, W., *Regulations for the Rifle Corps, formed at Blatchinton Barracks, under the command of Colonel Manningham* (London: T. Egerton, 1801).

Strachan, H., *British Military Uniforms 1768-1796: the Dress of the British Army from Official Sources* (London: Arms and Armour Press, 1975).

Surtees, W., *Surtees of the 95th (Rifles)* (London: Leonaur 2006).

Thackeray, W., *Sketches and Travels in London* (London: Tauchnitz, 1856).

Thornton, J., *Your most obedient servant, Cook to the Duke of Wellington* (Exeter: Webb and Bower, 1985).

White, A., *The Calvert Papers* (London: J. Murphy & Co, 1889).

Wraxall, N., *Memoirs of his own Time* (London: Richard Bentley, 1836).

Newspapers

Edinburgh Advertiser, 1802.

The Monthly Magazine, or Register, 806.

Morning Herald, 1805.

Index

GENERAL INDEX

INDEX OF REGIMENTS AND CORPS

From Reason to Revolution – Warfare 1721-1815

http://www.helion.co.uk/published-by-helion/reason-to-revolution-1721-1815.html

- From -
Reason
— to —
Revolution
1721-1815

The 'From Reason to Revolution' series covers the period of military history 1721–1815, an era in which fortress-based strategy and linear battles gave way to the nation-in-arms and the beginnings of total war.

This era saw the evolution and growth of light troops of all arms, and of increasingly flexible command systems to cope with the growing armies fielded by nations able to mobilise far greater proportions of their manpower than ever before. Many of these developments were fired by the great political upheavals of the era, with revolutions in America and France bringing about social change which in turn fed back into the military sphere as whole nations readied themselves for war. Only in the closing years of the period, as the reactionary powers began to regain the upper hand, did a military synthesis of the best of the old and the new become possible.

The series will examine the military and naval history of the period in a greater degree of detail than has hitherto been attempted, and has a very wide brief, with the intention of covering all aspects from the battles, campaigns, logistics, and tactics, to the personalities, armies, uniforms, and equipment.

Submissions

The publishers would be pleased to receive submissions for this series. Please contact series editor Andrew Bamford via email (andrewbamford18@gmail.com), or in writing to Helion & Company Limited, Unit 8 Amherst Business Centre, Budbrooke Road, Warwick, CV34 5WE

Titles

No 1   *Lobositz to Leuthen. Horace St Paul and the Campaigns of the Austrian Army in the Seven Years War 1756-57* Translated with additional materials by Neil Cogswell (ISBN 978-1-911096-67-2)

No 2   *Glories to Useless Heroism. The Seven Years War in North America from the French journals of Comte Maurés de Malartic, 1755-1760* William Raffle (ISBN 978-1-1911512-19-6) (paperback)

No 3   *Reminiscences 1808-1815 Under Wellington. The Peninsular and Waterloo Memoirs of William Hay* William Hay, with notes and commentary by Andrew Bamford (ISBN 978-1-1911512-32-5)

No 4   *Far Distant Ships. The Royal Navy and the Blockade of Brest 1793-1815* Quintin Barry (ISBN 978-1-1911512-14-1)

No 5   *Godoy's Army. Spanish Regiments and Uniforms from the Estado Militar of 1800* Charles Esdaile and Alan Perry (ISBN 978-1-911512-65-3) (paperback)

No 6   *On Gladsmuir Shall the Battle Be! The Battle of Prestonpans 1745* Arran Johnston (ISBN 978-1-911512-83-7)

No 7   *The French Army of the Orient 1798-1801. Napoleon's Beloved 'Egyptians'* Yves Martin (ISBN 978-1-911512-71-4)*

No 8   *The Autobiography, or Narrative of a Soldier. The Peninsular War Memoirs of William Brown of the 45th Foot* William Brown, with notes and commentary by Steve Brown (ISBN 978-1-911512-94-3) (paperback)

No 9   *Recollections from the Ranks. Three Russian Soldiers' Autobiographies from the Napoleonic Wars* Translated and annotated by Darrin Boland (ISBN 978-1-912174-18-8) (paperback)

* indicates 'Falconet' format paperbacks, page size 248mm x 180 mm, with high visual content including colour plates; other titles are hardback monographs unless otherwise noted.